D1590992

The Foreign Missionary Enterprise at Home

RELIGION AND AMERICAN CULTURE

Series Editors
David Edwin Harrell Jr.
Wayne Flynt
Edith L. Blumhofer

The Foreign Missionary Enterprise at Home

Explorations in North American Cultural History

EDITED BY DANIEL H. BAYS AND GRANT WACKER

THE UNIVERSITY OF ALABAMA PRESS
Tuscaloosa and London

The paper on which this book is printed meets the minimum requirements of American National
Standard for Information Science-Permanence of Paper for Printed Library Materials, ANSI
Z39.48-1984.

Library of Congress Cataloging-in-Publication Data

The foreign missionary enterprise at home : explorations in North American cultural history / edited
by Daniel H. Bays and Grant Wacker.
       p.   cm.—(Religion and American culture)
              Includes index.
       ISBN 0-8173-1245-5 (cloth : alk. paper)
1. Missions, American—History. 2. United States—Church history. 3. Missions, Canadian—History.
4. Canada—Church history. I. Bays, Daniel H. II. Wacker, Grant, 1945– III. Religion and American
                               culture (Tuscaloosa, Ala.)
                                BV2121.U6 F67 2003
                                  266'.02373—dc21

                                                                                    2002010609

British Library Cataloguing-in-Publication Data available

For Joel Carpenter
Scholar, provost, and friend
Who got us into this

Contents

Acknowledgments

This book originated with a major grant from the Pew Charitable Trusts to the Institute for the Study of American Evangelicals (ISAE) at Wheaton College (Illinois) in 1995. The grant aimed to support scholars studying the social and cultural influence of the foreign missionary enterprise within U.S. history. A nationally advertised competition drew more than 150 applications. The essays published here, plus several commissioned ones, represent some of the most promising of those projects. Several of the papers given at the public conference, "The Missionary Impulse in North America," also funded by Pew and hosted by Wheaton in the summer of 1998, have been published elsewhere.

Many colleagues contributed to the thinking that informs this volume. Some served as advisors, others as commenters at the Wheaton conference, and still others as authors of project-funded papers published or awaiting publication elsewhere. A partial list includes Stephen Alter, Carmin Ballou, Edward Brett, Joel Carpenter, Lorraine Coops, David Daniels, Jennifer Farmer, Susan Fitzpatrick-Behrens, James Gilbert, Lydia Hoyle, William R. Hutchison, Roger Lundin, Richard Madsen, Margaret Ovenden, Richard Pierard, Dana Robert, Wilbert Shenk, John Stackhouse, James Turner, Andrew Walls, R. Stephen Warner, Charles Weber, and Everett Wilson.

The individuals who helped bring the book to completion merit special appreciation. They include copyeditor Anthony Chiffolo, indexer Anne Blue Wills, and proofreaders Laura Stern and Julia Wacker.

Finally, we wish to thank Edith Blumhofer and Larry Eskridge, the director and the associate director of the ISAE, for writing the grant proposal to Pew and for helping to organize the ensuing conference at Wheaton. We also thank Katri Delac,

ISAE resource and research assistant, and Seth Dowland, a doctoral candidate in religion at Duke University, for their conscientious help in smoothing out troublesome details and checking elusive sources. Mark Noll, one of the original editors, left for other projects once this one was well launched. To him we owe our greatest debt.

THE FOREIGN MISSIONARY ENTERPRISE AT HOME

Introduction

The Many Faces of the Missionary Enterprise at Home

Daniel H. Bays and Grant Wacker

"Don't apologize. All Americans are missionaries."
Arnold Rose

History writing, no less than history itself, evinces discernible trends. In his 1968 presidential address to the American Historical Association, China historian John King Fairbank described the overseas missionary as the "invisible man of American history." Happily, that claim is no longer valid. In the last quarter-century the story of the American foreign missionary enterprise has received significant scholarly attention. Indeed, it is now possible to speak of distinct stages and traditions of missionary history, some of it hagiographic, some of it disparaging, but much of it simply very good by anyone's standards.[1]

Even so, in a very real sense, scholars of American foreign missions have told only half the tale. The other half is the social and cultural role of the foreign missionary at home—the reflex story, we might call it. The standard textbooks on U.S. history have virtually ignored the missionary's domestic significance, and the standard textbooks on U.S. religious history have done only slightly better. Though a few important monographs and scholarly articles have addressed the question, they remain a handful compared with the abundance of works focused on U.S. missions abroad.[2] This volume seeks to redress that imbalance.

The foreign missionary has occupied a significant place in American public life from the early nineteenth century to the present. Consider, for example, two high-profile novels of the late 1990s, Barbara Kingsolver's *The Poisonwood Bible* (1998) and John Grisham's *The Testament* (1999). Both provided memorable portraits of missionaries, one negative, the other positive. And both made clear, intentionally or not, that those earnest, controversial, often misunderstood souls continue to haunt the popular imagination. These novels extended a long literary tradition in which overseas missionaries have played a prominent role. Authors who have featured missionaries or missionary themes run from Herman Melville and Mark Twain in the nineteenth century to Finley Peter Dunne, A. J. Cronin, James Michener, and John Hersey in the twentieth.[3]

For another example of missionary influence, consider international public policy. Two important books of the 1990s that examined U.S. involvement in the Middle East and China attributed key parts of contemporary policy dilemmas to Christian missions. In *The Arabists: The Romance of an American Elite* (1993), Robert D. Kaplan wrote that "mission work defines the American Arabist, much as imperialism defines the British Arabist." To understand anything of post–World War II problems, he added, we have to go back to the "American missionary colonies in the Moslem world." And in *China and the American Dream: A Moral Inquiry* (1995), Richard Madsen argued that recognition of the long, deep engagement of U.S. Protestant missions in China was crucial to understanding the moralism and emotional volatility that characterized United States–China relations in the latter part of the twentieth century, including the popular anger with China over human-rights transgressions.[4] In the fall of 2001, part of the drama of the United States–led attack on the Taliban government of Afghanistan derived from the perilous situation and eventual rescue of Western aid workers on trial for propagating Christianity—a charge that was certainly true of the two American women, who clearly considered themselves missionaries.

These examples, drawn from many possibilities, suggest that analysis of the influence of the foreign missionary enterprise at home opens a window into the United States's own past. For one thing, nineteenth-century missionaries' indefatigable writing and speaking efforts constituted most Americans' first significant exposure to non-Western cultures and non-Christian religions. China missionary S. Wells Williams published *The Middle Kingdom* in 1847, and it remained the standard reference on China for Americans for half a century or more.[5] Missionaries helped establish a variety of academic disciplines, including anthropology, linguistics, and comparative religion, as well as area-studies programs.[6] In the mid–nineteenth century, missionaries found themselves on the ground floor in forming the American Oriental Society, and missionary linguists wrote some of the first dictionaries and language primers for the study of non-Western languages. In the twentieth century, distinguished U.S. scholars of Asia who have shaped their academic disciplines included historian Edwin O. Reischauer and political scientist Lucian Pye, born of missionary families in Japan and China. Former missionaries returned to both secular and seminary teaching careers in the United States. In 1896, after more than thirty years' service in China as a teacher and translator, John Fryer became the first holder of the Agassiz Professorship of Oriental Languages and Literature at the University of California, Berkeley.[7] Edward T. Williams, a successor to Fryer in this chair in 1918, was also a former missionary and diplomat. At elite U.S. Ivy League schools, similar patterns prevailed. The first Asia-centered think tank for high-level research in

Sinology, the Harvard-Yenching Institute, was established in the late 1920s at Harvard in close cooperation with Yenching University in Beijing, the foremost of the U.S. missionary colleges in China.[8] In U.S. seminaries, a number of former missionaries proved important to the rise of theological liberalism. One of the most significant of these was Daniel Johnson Fleming, a missionary to India from 1899 to 1911 and professor of missions at Union Theological Seminary in New York.[9]

The influence of the missionary theme in American popular culture during the nineteenth and twentieth centuries ranges far beyond novels and printed texts. In the twentieth century, Hollywood frequently portrayed missionary figures—sometimes positively, sometimes negatively, but almost never neutrally. From the 1930s to the 1960s, top film stars appeared in Hollywood films that featured missionaries as important characters and the American missionary enterprise as part of the film's context. The usual image was of a well-intentioned and commendable, if also innocent or naïve, missionary effort. For China alone, these films included *The Bitter Tea of General Yen* (Barbara Stanwyck, 1933), *The Keys of the Kingdom* (Gregory Peck, 1944), *The Left Hand of God* (Humphrey Bogart, 1955), *The Inn of the Sixth Happiness* (Ingrid Bergman, 1958), *55 Days at Peking* (Charlton Heston, Ava Gardner, David Niven, 1963), and *The Sand Pebbles* (Steve McQueen, Candace Bergen, 1966). As the last essay in this volume shows, more recent films dealing with missionaries hold a dimmer view of the legitimacy of the missionary endeavor.

In the very different realm of diplomacy, missionaries and their children molded both the conceptualization and the implementation of U.S. foreign policy until well into the twentieth century. Especially in the Middle East and the Far East, for most of the first half of the twentieth century, the State Department would have been poorer in personnel but for missionary offspring. Some extended families such as the Luces in China and the Blisses and Dodges in the Middle East influenced U.S. policymakers at a high level for generations. The Presbyterian Henry Winters Luce built Yenching University, and his son Henry R. Luce, born and reared in China, exerted remarkable influence on public opinion and diplomacy through his Time-Life empire from the 1930s to the 1960s.[10] In the Middle East, the tangled skein of missionary ties with foreign policy was even tighter. The descendents of Daniel Bliss, founder of Syrian Protestant College (later the American University of Beirut), and of his close associate, W. E. Dodge, directly influenced Woodrow Wilson's foreign policy during World War I. Cleveland H. Dodge, a third-generation member of the Dodge family (which had been involved in educational missions in Constantinople and Beirut for many years), distinguished himself as Wilson's college classmate, lifelong friend, and trusted advisor on Middle Eastern affairs. Dodge clearly influenced Wilson's views of Turkey and its oppressed Christian minorities, especially the Armenians.[11] At the highest diplomatic posts, Woodrow Wilson tried to appoint missionary statesman John R. Mott as ambassador to China, and Franklin Roosevelt did appoint missionary educator Leighton Stuart of Yenching University to that post in the 1940s.

Attention to the foreign missionary enterprise illumines U.S. religious history with particular clarity. From the early nineteenth to the beginning of the twenty-first century, many aspects of American religion bore, in the words of historian Joel Carpenter, "a missions intensifier." Decade after decade, the overseas endeavor vitalized the tiniest of local churches as well as the largest of national denominations. It prompted the first sustained examination of age-old assumptions about Christian exclusivism, heightened the evangelism versus social gospel tension, aggravated the fundamentalist-modernist controversy, energized church fundraising techniques, sharpened entrepreneurial skills, sustained scores of Bible institutes and seminaries, and helped amplify and reconfigure women's opportunities.[12] Returned missionaries deployed themselves into an extensive network of training schools, retreat centers, and retirement homes. They married one another, and sometimes a pattern of clubby familiarity persisted long after the initial evangelizing impulse had evaporated.[13] Indeed, the outlines of the kinship systems that perpetuated the (China) Corbetts, the (Hawaii) Binghams, and the (India) Thoburns and Fairbanks, among other dynasties such as the Hamlins, Blisses, and Dodges of the Middle East, remained visible for generations. Many were articulate—and had much to say. Biographies, autobiographies, travelogues, news accounts, editorials, and children's literature tumbled from both in-house and trade presses in a profusion of words. They constitute a treasure trove for researchers today. In short, study of the missionary movement's effects at home may tell us as much about religion back home as it tells us about the American evangelists' encounters with non-Christian religions and societies in other countries.

HIGHLIGHTS OF THIS VOLUME

We have drawn the essays in this book from the twenty-three papers presented at the "Missionary Impulse in North America" conference at Wheaton College in 1998 (revised for publication and supplemented by Edith Blumhofer's essay on Pandita Ramabai). In the fifteen studies included here, we have endeavored to analyze the missionary enterprise's effects at home, from the early nineteenth to the late twentieth centuries.

The chapters in part 1 focus on the first two-thirds of the nineteenth century, the period of nation building, or the National Era, as it is commonly called. The first two essays probe the relation between the missionary enterprise and growing African-American self-consciousness. John Saillant's examination of black missionaries and settlers to Liberia in the middle third of the century explores the connection between that endeavor and the emerging image of blacks as free, responsible citizens, architects of their own political destiny. Saillant moves beyond the images of the era, however, to limn the moral failures as well as the moral successes of free blacks in a frontierlike colonial setting. In the same years, African-American emigrants and missionaries to Haiti came to believe that blacks, not whites, played the providential, world-centered roles in that country's long history and political turmoil. This process, explored by Laurie Maffly-Kipp, exemplifies a larger saga in which black Protestants, like white ones generally, discovered their own religious and ethnic identity most clearly when they confronted peoples and places new to themselves.

The remaining chapters of part 1 examine the ramifications of missionary consciousness on important U.S. institutions. In his study of the annual sermons given before the American Board of Commissioners for Foreign Missions, Mark Hanley challenges the widely held assumption that missionary theoreticians unselfconsciously and indiscriminately mixed Christ and (American) civilization. Hanley argues, instead, that these influential pastors proved acutely self-conscious—and often surprisingly self-critical—about the Christ versus civilization tension. In rhetoric, if not always in practice, they sought to erase national boundaries in favor of worldwide spiritual renovation. Jay Riley Case shows, in turn, that the powerful American Baptist Missionary Society served as a model for white support of black colleges in the South. Case demonstrates that the extensive efforts of northern evangelicals after the Civil War to educate southern freedpersons took many of its operating cues from antebellum missionary efforts in South Asia. In the section's final essay, Russell Richey finds that from the outset the Methodist Church, the largest of the nineteenth-century denominations, conceived itself as essentially a missionary endeavor. Early Methodists imagined that every believer was called to serve as a witness to the lost. Over time, however, partisans inexorably institutionalized that concern. By the end of the century, they had transformed—some would say reduced—missions to an interlocking grid of professionalized, bureaucratized, centralized conference structures.

The chapters in part 2 address developments in the High Imperial Era, the decades flanking the turn of the twentieth century that saw vigorous commercial, political, and military expansion. It was also an age marked by a new level of organizational maturity, institutional growth, and, by most lights, muscle-flexing in the missionary enterprise. These trends manifested themselves with conspicuous force in the literary works examined in the section's first two chapters. Anne Blue Wills, focusing on the 1890s, finds (unlike Hanley for the period several decades earlier) a dense knotting of Christianizing and civilizing threads—in this case, in the pages of one of the premier mission periodicals of the era, *The Church at Home and Abroad*. Blue Wills urges that efforts to reclaim African Americans, Roman Catholics, and Latter-day Saints for Protestant Christianity rested on deeply rooted assumptions about the essential otherness of each of these groups. Their sin lay in ignorance, indolence, and unpatriotism, respectively. Though Blue Wills's data involved souls living squarely within the United States's geographic boundaries, *The Church at Home and Abroad* beheld them as foreign as anyone living abroad. Nancy Hardesty examines the nearly threescore textbooks written in the early twentieth century under the sponsorship of the interdenominational Central Committee on the United Study of Foreign Missions. These works undoubtedly predisposed missionaries to see some things and not others when they arrived "over there." More important, for many Americans they also provided a rich source of reasonably objective information about lifeways on the shores beyond. Hardesty's data suggest that thousands of thoughtful women passed many a Sunday morning—and winter evening for that matter—with the imagination lost in the siren call of distant lands.

The essays by Marilyn Färdig Whiteley and Alvyn Austin, focusing on voluntary and educational institutions in Canada, indicate that the foreign missionary enterprise played a role in Canadian society and culture comparable to that in the United States. Whiteley explores the texture of day-to-day life in Methodist women's organizations. She challenges those who dubbed—and dismissed—women's spirituality as "folding wing" piety. Whiteley argues, in contrast, that such organizations functioned as conduits, intensifying and energizing women's participation in Canadian public life in general and church life in particular. At the conference, Whiteley's essay complemented Dana Robert's overview (published elsewhere) of the impact of U.S. women missionaries on American culture generally. Robert showed that the ideal and reality of foreign missionary service helped define women's identity by providing a public role for them both abroad and at home. The network of personal and financial connections that linked independent Bible schools and nondenominational faith missions forms the subject of Alvyn Austin's essay. Concentrating especially on the complex ties between Toronto Bible College and the China Inland Mission, Austin shows how each served as a perennial and reliable feeder of personnel for the other. Such institutions functioned as social worlds unto themselves, even as they drew recruits into cultural worlds scarcely imagined (or imaginable) by the mass of Christians at home.

The remaining chapters in part 2 assess the reflex influence of missions to India and Latin America. In the first, Edith Blumhofer explores the impact of India missionary convert Pandita Ramabai on American "highbrow" and, later, "midbrow" circles. Blumhofer indicates that Ramabai, one of the most gifted intellectuals of any era, moved effortlessly among linked religious subcultures in South Asia, Britain, and the United States. Though Ramabai was always and insistently Indian, her later iconic status in holiness and Pentecostal churches in the United States proved especially revealing of larger patterns of cultural exchange. Finally, William Svelmoe concentrates on the improbable friendship that developed in the 1930s and 1940s

between William Cameron Townsend and Lázaro Cárdenas, the former a fundamentalist U.S. missionary to Mexico, the latter the secular socialist president of
Mexico. Svelmoe marshals persuasive evidence to demonstrate that Townsend favorably influenced American public opinion toward Cárdenas's radical land-reform
programs. The key for both men lay in a shared concern for the plight of impover-
ished and illiterate native peoples. This is a remarkable story of informal missionary
diplomacy at work.

World War II changed the face of the globe in countless ways, and a more contested role for the missionary in American social and cultural life was one of them.
Such complications, or second thoughts, constitute the thrust of this volume's third
and final section. By the eve of World War II, and more clearly afterward, many
thoughtful American Christians had come to believe that the missionary endeavor
exacted too high a price in lives disoriented, families broken, and cultures disrupted.
Missionaries constituted an obsolete manifestation of North American hubris and
cultural arrogance. Grant Wacker traces the bitter second thoughts of returned missionary and famed novelist Pearl S. Buck. He shows that for Buck, at least, the
deconversion process stemmed from multiple factors, including but by no means
limited to disillusionment with the viability of the missionary enterprise. In an illu-
minating study presented at the conference and separately published as part of a
monograph, Edward Brett chronicled the dramatically changing reaction of the U.S.
Roman Catholic press to political turmoil in Central America from the 1940s to the
1960s, based on the reports of U.S. Catholic missionaries on the scene. Brett showed
that these politically charged missionary reports influenced policymakers who had
an eye to their Catholic constituency, accentuating disillusionment with the results
of a hard-line anticommunist foreign policy. Dana Robert's paper similarly recounted the story of how Speaker of the House Tip O'Neill of Massachusetts was
profoundly influenced by information on Central America given him by his aunt, a
Maryknoll nun, and her Maryknoll associates. In this volume, Scott Flipse's analysis
of mainline missionary volunteer agencies in Vietnam follows a similar trajectory of
disillusion followed by heightened self-awareness. Originally supportive of U.S. foreign policy in Southeast Asia, several agencies gradually embraced a principled neutrality, then active opposition to U.S. policy on both pragmatic and humanitarian
grounds. Flipse's evidence, like that of Brett and Robert, intimates that when missionaries or missionary organizations talked, policymakers often listened.

The volume's remaining two chapters focus on the missionary enterprise's relation to the popular media. Kathryn Long's essay charts the virtual apotheosizing of
the five young men widely known as the "Auca martyrs" in the popular press of the
1950s, both secular and religious. Long shows how missionaries both exploited and
were exploited by the media, always eager for marketable tales about the Wholesome
Hero versus the Noble Savage. The Auca martyrs incident offers a sobering case

study of the missionary establishment's power, in tandem with the evangelical and secular press, to create as well as to record the stories of our times. In the book's final essay, Jay Blossom examines four recent Hollywood movies. Blossom explores the cinematic stereotypes the film medium used to portray both the missionaries and the native peoples whom the missionaries served. Not surprisingly, the four films he cites pressed both groups through grids of preconceptions. The result, in these recent depictions, represents a reversal of the optimistic tilt of Hollywood's older portrayals. And though missionaries, like native peoples, seemed almost always to lose in the end, they also continued to serve as powerful icons of the old ambivalence many in the United States felt about extending the benefits of their culture to others, wanted or not.

IMPLICATIONS

The case studies presented in this volume harbor a multitude of themes, three of which seem especially insistent.

Cultural Exchange

First, the home base of the missionary enterprise served as a perennial and fertile site for cultural exchange. Millions of Americans learned everything they knew, or thought they knew, about other lands and peoples through the eyes of the overseas missionary force. One can only guess, for example, at the multiplicity of ways that returned China missionaries filtered American perceptions of that storied land during the Cold War.[14] But there was more. Though some missionaries and their home-base supporters fell into imperialistic ways of seeing and treating the Other, the evidence presented in these essays suggests that often they learned from the Other as much as they taught (or imposed). The missionary culture placed a human face on the alien, making it seem less distant, less foreign. Indeed, more than a few missionaries functioned as critics of the homeland itself, enabling, sometimes forcing, their compatriots to see the United States as outsiders saw it.

Self-awareness

Second, the missionary enterprise spurred the self-definition of important ethnic and demographic groups. Through missionary activities, blacks, for example, came to understand themselves as *African* Americans, with a definable African history and Africa-centered providential destiny. Through missionary activities, women, too, defined themselves not simply as Christians like all other Christians, nor as citizens like all other citizens, but as individuals with a recognizable identity and calling as Christian women. Even so, the missionary culture provided more than a venue for identity politics. It also provided a public face for private people. Oversized heroes like Harriett Newell, Lottie Moon, and Nate Saint enabled ordinary churchgoers to place themselves in a history larger and more meaningful than the history of their own clan or social grouping.

Self-criticism

Finally, the missionary enterprise complicated many of the larger culture's assumptions in unexpected and sometimes quite unsettling ways. For one thing, missionaries and their supporters evinced unpredictable political profiles. With surprising frequency, they refused to endorse certain leaders or policies at home and abroad when, by conventional measures of self-interest, they should have done so. Time after time, their actions seemed prompted less by their own or their nation's economic and security interests than by values drawn from an ancient book. They also showed that it was possible to be ethnocentric without being racist. Though neither label was one that later Christians would be eager to own, the missionary at home helped the average American at least begin to imagine that culture might be separable from race. And if the church in the United States found that it had something to learn from the church overseas, that, too, was a lesson driven home by the missionary force. In sum, missionaries inspired many moments of self-reflection and self-criticism, moments not felt by others unencumbered by loyalties to spiritual kith and kin overseas. Anne Blue Wills makes the point memorably: "We may look back on the history of American Christian missions with embarrassment for its insensitivities. Yet to tell any human story is to remember the complications of insensitivity, ambiguity, mixed motives, good faith, wounds bound, gifts given."

The essays gathered here offer an introduction to this craggy and barely explored terrain. They help tell the American story with deepened awareness of its complications and heightened appreciation of its richness. And just as they reveal foundations laid down in its distant past, they also open vistas to its beckoning future.

I

The National Era: Years of Expansion

                                      ~

In his 1961 inaugural address, President John F. Kennedy promised that the United States would "pay any price, bear any burden, meet any hardship, support any friend, oppose any foe, to ensure the survival and success of liberty." This expansive sense of responsibility for the well-being of the entire world could claim deep roots in U.S. history. Many of those roots originated in the foreign missionary enterprise.

Precisely where the story properly starts is open to debate. The colonial period saw impressive efforts by both Roman Catholics and Protestants to convert Native Americans, and those efforts won significant successes in New England and lower Canada. Still, the idea of taking the gospel message over the waters to other lands and to other peoples remained largely a creation of the decades stretching from the American Revolution to the Civil War. In those years, a potent mix of nationalistic and theological motives fueled the endeavor. If nationalism flowed from insurgent feelings of Manifest Destiny for the young nation, theological enthusiasm surged from a felt need to obey the Great Commission of Matthew 28:18–20 ("Go into all the world and preach the gospel"). And streaming through it all was a growing sense of human agency, working in collaboration with Divine Providence. In the nineteenth century, this was, for the most part, a Protestant story. Until the end of the century, U.S. Catholics would find themselves overwhelmed with the task of mere survival in a new and often hostile land.

The starting point for the foreign-mission enterprise is commonly traced to the founding of the American Board of Commissioners for Foreign Missions (ABCFM) in 1810. The ABCFM commissioned the first men and women for service in India in 1812. Though most of the historic denominations soon organized their own agencies, the ABCFM would for many decades remain the largest, strongest, and by far the best known of the sending agencies. In those years, too, both white and black

Christians pioneered colonization efforts in West Africa. Elsewhere, U.S. endeavors followed European and especially British colonial undertakings (hence the disproportionate presence of U.S. missionaries in India, Egypt, and Palestine). They also followed U.S. commercial ventures (thus the many U.S. missionaries in Hawaii and, especially, China). To be sure, for many decades, foreign missions struggled for pride of place with missions to Native Americans and African Americans. Even so, the National Era would be remembered, with fondness by some and embarrassment by others, as the age when U.S. Protestants first undertook in a serious and systematic way to spread the knowledge of the Lord "as the waters covered the sea."

1 / Missions in Liberia and Race Relations in the United States, 1822–1860

John Saillant

At an 1861 meeting of the New York State Colonization Society, Alexander Crummell, a black Episcopal minister, then a U.S.-born Liberian traveling in the United States, recalled that when he first landed in Monrovia in 1853, his "views and purposes were almost entirely missionary in their character." He had, Crummell attested, nothing "civil or national" around him then. However, in the course of "three days"—here Crummell was surely alluding to the time from the Crucifixion to the Resurrection—he saw in Liberia such "manliness, . . . thrift, energy, and national life" that his "governmental indifference at once vanished." He became a new man as feelings of "citizenship and nationality" swelled within him. He swore an "oath of allegiance" to the Republic of Liberia, becoming for the first time a "citizen." He assured his audience that in Liberia, even "the most casual observer can perceive strength, confidence, self-reliance, development, increase of wealth, manliness, and greater hardiment of character." "The acquisitive principle," up to that point "latent" in black men, was surfacing in Liberia. The "freed black man of America," he argued, possessed "clearer knowledge of free government" and a "nobler fitness for its requirements" than did many white Europeans. Finally, Liberia's "Black Yankees," Crummell argued, would as governors soon advance to their "master aim," "the evangelization and enlightenment of heathen Africa."[1]

Born in New York in 1819, tutored privately in theology, ordained in 1844, and graduated from Queen's College of Cambridge University in 1853, Crummell became a farmer, businessman, schoolmaster, colonizationist spokesman, and Episcopal missionary in Liberia. Perhaps impelled by the Union victory in the Civil War, perhaps weary of Liberia, Crummell returned to the United States for good in 1872, settled in Washington, D.C., and spent the rest of his life working for the uplift of African Americans. He wrote and lectured, as well as leading in the establishment of institutions like St. Luke's Episcopal Church of Washington, D.C., and the American Negro Academy. He died in 1898.[2] Although he spent only nineteen years of a long life in Liberia, he has been remembered invariably as an African missionary and civilizationist.

This chapter situates Crummell's first three days in Africa—when his transfiguration from missionary to citizen took place—in two contexts. First, beginning in 1822, in the context of four decades of missionary, colonizationist, and settler activity in Liberia. Second, in the context of U.S. race relations from the Revolutionary War to the "uplift" decades of the second half of the nineteenth century and beginning of the twentieth. Crummell was prompted to his transfiguration in these contexts. In general, missionary, colonizationist, and settler activity (as reported in periodicals, sermons, missionary tracts, and letters) were the strongest sources of a modern, postslavery understanding of blacks as citizens, an understanding found in virtually no other source in the Atlantic world at the beginning of the nineteenth century. In relation to the missions in Liberia, missionaries had an intermittent insight into the disruption of native life caused by the settlement of that country. Although colonization was initially envisioned as a means of expatriating African Americans, it became a tool of coexistence (though not of true integration) as news of blacks as citizens and missionaries—and, indeed, as Crummell's example shows, as Americo-Liberians themselves—flowed westward across the Atlantic. Together, the missionaries, colonizationists, and settlers provided a convincing model of blacks for the postslavery era.

This model rests on the notion of "manhood." Scholars have noted the ubiquity of this word in discourse about U.S. race relations from the time of Frederick Douglass onward.[3] But the notion of manhood—men as participatory citizens, free-will Christians, individual achievers in commerce, and governors of subordinate people like the indigenes of North America and Africa as well as women, children, and servants—was affixed to Americo-Liberian settlers beginning in the 1820s. This idea of black manhood answered a question about African Americans that arose in the 1770s and that was articulated in its fullest and clearest form in missionary and colonizationist reports about Liberia beginning in the 1820s. U.S. slavery and oppression produced doubts about black manhood; missionary, colonizationist, and settler activity overcame those doubts; black social thought—and, indeed, the liberal tradition in race relations, beginning with Frederick Douglass—grew from that idea of black manhood.

Although Douglass denounced both colonization and Liberia, colonizationists had articulated many of the elements of his thought long before he began writing for the public. Famously, Douglass claimed that his autobiography revealed the way in which a man was made a slave, then a slave a man.[4] Crummell, for his part, interpreted the establishment of Liberia to mean for blacks that "the manhood of our race has been won," since in Liberia was possible "a manly, noble, and complete African nationality" in which black men need not act as "ladies' maids."[5] Not fully aware of the sources of their ideas and values, Douglass and Crummell believed that there was a universal manhood to which neither African Americans (because of U.S. slavery) nor Africans (because of African "barbarism") had advanced. Far from being beguiled ourselves by a notion of universal "manhood," we should understand the cultural and historical specificity of masculinities—in this case, the way colonization and missions in Liberia formed a notion of black manhood.

For the first U.S. proponents of the expatriation of free blacks to West Africa (the West Indies and the North American West were also occasionally mentioned as possible destinations), the paramount question was whether black men could function as citizens of an American nation-state. White colonizationists like Thomas Jefferson, Samuel Hopkins, James Madison, Henry Clay, Leonard Bacon, and Robert Finley reflected the ethnocentrism of their times, but they were not racist in the sense of believing that black men and black women were innately inferior in body, mind, or morals to whites. Rather, they believed that a combination of natural and historical circumstances had so separated whites from blacks that the two races could never live equally and happily in one society. "Distinctions of color" and the obvious cruelties and inequities of the slave trade and of slavery implied to a critical mass of whites of the Revolutionary War generation that blacks and whites could never be co-citizens. The "race problem," as late-eighteenth-century republicans saw it, was essentially civic, not biological.

One important strain in republican thought instructed that if a dissenting part of a society's population were too dangerous to the well-being of the society, it should be either enslaved or banished. French writers like Montesquieu and Brissot were invoked in favor of colonization because they asseverated the injustice of slavery yet emphasized both the necessity of a unifying "spirit" in society and their corollary belief, in Brissot's words, that "there can never exist a sincere union between the whites and the blacks, even on admitting the latter to the rights of freeman."[6] (We may call this strain of Euro-American thought "racist" since it encourages fear and dislike of blacks, but we should recognize that it was antiblack only insofar as it opposed many forms of difference, diversity, and dissent that are accepted, even welcomed, in the early twenty-first century.) Beginning with the endorsement of prominent figures in the 1770s, solidifying with the formation of the American Colonization Society (ACS) in 1817, and reaching momentum with the establishment of Liberia on land gained from local leaders by the ACS in 1822, colonization influenced U.S. race relations. Between 1822 and 1865, only about thirteen thousand African Americans emigrated to Liberia, but the role the settlement played in U.S. culture was in great disproportion to this number, which represented only a small fraction of North American blacks.[7]

White colonizationists expressed in words and in actions some of the ugliness of a dominant group that had long and heavily utilized the productive labor of most members of a subordinate group. Colonizationists proclaimed that free blacks were lazy and vicious, but, in fact, most free African Americans worked at whatever trades were open to them, and many sought the benefits of church and school, as black opponents of colonization like Samuel Cornish noted.[8] Emigration, colonizationists proclaimed, was to be entirely voluntary, when, in fact, leading colonizationists were plotting privately to force free blacks to emigrate. Even traces of genocide appear in colonizationist proposals. In the 1820s, for instance, it became apparent that the mortality of the Americo-Liberian settlers was extraordinarily high (probably the highest ever recorded), yet that caused only little erosion of white support for colonization. Some proposals (such as shipping infants to Africa while their mothers, whose labor was more valuable than that of newborn children, remained on U.S. plantations) seem to be genocidal, made in full knowledge of the fact that "African fever" (malaria) was especially pernicious for those born in the temperate zone as well as for children.[9] The idea of providing a "natural" site for blacks was often the excuse for executing a death sentence.

Yet colonizationists black and white did not believe that the United States was merely casting off a bothersome, dysfunctional class but was, rather, placing black men in a context in which they could thrive as individuals, citizens, and governors of their own society. Indeed, free blacks, once expatriated, were believed to be fine representatives of democracy, Christianity, and civilization. Thus Clay could write with no feeling of inconsistency that, on the one hand, "Of all classes in our population the most vicious is the free colored" and, on the other, "Every emigrant to Africa is a missionary carrying with him credentials in the holy cause of civilization, religion, and free institutions."[10] Without equivocation, Jefferson considered blacks to be natural republicans who would inevitably be free.[11]

This notion of free blacks as degraded and vicious beings yet paragons of civilization, Christianity, and democracy did not jar the United States's sense of consistency.[12] Indeed, the notion appeared everywhere in political culture, from the highest levels of discourse to the homeliest commentaries in the colonizationist effort. As a national political figure, Clay was articulating ideas that an anonymous writer in the *African Repository and Colonial Journal,* the periodical of the ACS, expressed in 1825: the "restoration of thousands of free, though degraded people of colour to their own native land, and there exalting them to the rank, intelligence, and enjoyment of rational beings, is an object which must commend itself to a nation of freemen as worthy of their vigorous support."[13] By the early 1830s, officers of the ACS were confident that Liberia proved that even the most "debased" and "ignorant" blacks could become "intelligent, industrious, and competent, in every point of view, for all the offices of an independent, social, and civil community. . . . The slave, when he leaps a free man upon the shore of his own ancient land, seems to throw off his very nature with his chains."[14]

From the outset, missions were an essential part of the colonization effort. One of the pioneering monographs in African-American history, George W. Williams's *History of the Negro Race in America,* reported the nineteenth-century judgment that Liberia was "a missionary republic."[15] From its first issue, in 1825, the *African Repository and Colonial Journal* noted the convergence of the goals of the missionaries and the colonizationists.[16] A characteristic comment reads: "Whether the population of Africa is to remain under the power of its dark superstitions, or to be enlightened and saved by Christianity, will not be regarded by any religious mind as a question of small importance. We have long hoped, and believed, that the establishment of the African colony, would afford rare facilities for the operations of those noble Institutions which are directly engaged in the holy cause of missions."[17] When a minister from Basel, Switzerland, inquired in 1827 about establishing a mission in Liberia, the ACS agent, Jehudi Ashmun, assured him that "a large portion of our settlers are by profession, the devoted servants of the Redeemer. . . . A deep, lively, and I hope, sincere and lasting interest is felt by many, for the salvation of their pagan African brethren."[18] In 1830, the Young Men's Missionary Society of the Methodist Episcopal Church in New York announced that, "feeling deeply impressed with the solemn importance of the great cause in which the friends of African Colonization are laboring," the Society was planning "the establishment of a mission in Liberia."[19] When Liberia was investigated by the League of Nations and condemned for slave-trade-like practices, the old idea of Liberian missions allowed an ACS spokesman, who conceded the export of unfree laborers, to recall a religious golden age in Liberian history: "Mission work and Liberia have always gone hand in hand." Indeed, he cast the first U.S. missionary to West Africa, Samuel Mills, as "the father of foreign missionary enterprise in America."[20]

Almost immediately arose the question of the effectiveness of black missionaries to Africa. It is possible to name the individual black missionaries—Daniel Coker (African Methodist Episcopal [A.M.E.], Liberia, 1820); Lott Cary and Colin Teague (Baptist, Liberia, 1821); James Temple (Presbyterian, Liberia, 1833); Mr. and Mrs. James Thompson (Episcopal, Liberia, 1836); A. P. Davis (Baptist, Liberia, 1834, appointed missionary 1847).[21] And it is possible to stress that black missionaries were the "natural" evangelists for Africans, as was argued in the early nineteenth century. In 1828, for instance, one commenter on the African Mission School Society argued that "men of colour should be educated and sent forth without delay to this glorious work. These are, doubtless, destined to be the principal agents in communicating the arts of civilization and the ever-blessed Gospel, to the long neglected and degraded tribes of Africa."[22]

We should, however, look beyond the individuals and transcend the belief in "natural" evangelists so that we can examine the function of missionary work in Liberia. The existence of black missionaries in West Africa and African-American governors and citizens in Liberia forced into public discourse the notions of educability and competence of blacks in a way that had never before occurred in the United States. In the 1780s, Jefferson initially thought that blacks might be educated for "agrarian" pursuits in a new colony, while in the 1790s Samuel Hopkins tried to prepare two black men for missionary work in Africa but, in his own view, failed.[23] From such small beginnings grew the idea of black men as governors of a new nation in Liberia.

The keynote was the civic competence of black men. Blacks and whites agreed on this point. An 1828 "Address by the Citizens of Monrovia, to the Free Coloured People of the United States" (probably white-authored and published as an alternative to a black-authored address that had been sent from Monrovia)[24] elaborated on this point. The Americo-Liberian settlers claimed to have migrated voluntarily in search of "liberty, in the sober, simple, but complete sense of the word:—not a licentious liberty—nor a liberty without government. . . . But that liberty of speech, action, and conscience, which distinguished the free, enfranchised citizens of a free state." Lacking liberty, property, suffrage, and other rights in the United States, the settlers emigrated and created their own government and laws and gained their own "community," "commerce," "soil," and "resources" in Liberia. Without the "debasing inferiority, with which our very colour stamped us in America," the settlers reached "moral emancipation— . . . liberation of the mind." Understandably, the address continued, "the white man" can never associate with slaves and freedmen and freedwomen in the United States "on terms of equality." But "which is the white man who would decline such association with one of our number [that is, the settlers], whose intellectual and moral qualities are not an objection? . . . There is no such white man." The "industrious and virtuous" can achieve "independence and plenty and happiness," can rule themselves, and can establish "Christian worship . . . in a land of brooding pagan darkness" if they will remove to Liberia. North and South, such ideas were continually reiterated in U.S. publications.[25] There was little doubt that the civic advances of the settlers were paving the way for a bright future. One traveler, the Reverend William B. Hoyt, wrote that although recently freed blacks were uncivilized, in Liberia "the enjoyment of civil and religious liberty by the parents results in a marked mental improvement in their offspring."[26]

Evidently, the experience of freedom and self-sufficiency spurred some Americo-Liberians to religious conversion and the desire to exhort and preach. James C. Minor, a freed slave from Fredericksburg, Virginia, and editor of the *Liberia Herald,* wrote to his ex-master, John Minor, about freedom and religion. "Africa is a land of freedom," the black Minor argued. "Where else can the man of color enjoy temporal freedom but in Africa?" "Trying to live a Christian's life in this dark and benighted land" is difficult, Minor implied, but a "miraculous scene took place in my heart on the Sabbath day, 29 of January, 1831; Oh, the wonders of redeeming grace! On this subject I could pen nothing but what you are acquainted with. Remember, I beseech thee, that I wish to become one of the blowers of the Gospel trumpet. That I cannot be without such books as are adapted to prepare me."[27]

Probably even the experience of masculinity—the day-to-day awareness of being a man—was different for black men in Liberia from what they knew in the United States. One of Crummell's patrons, Episcopal Bishop John Payne, who had for years worked in African missions, reported that although Crummell was meek in the United States, he was imperious in Liberia.[28] Americo-Liberian Zion (probably Sion) Harris wrote in 1851 with a graphic description of the way masculinity and governance were united in settlers' minds: "I was eighteen years old when I came here. I have grown to be a man; in America I never could have been a man—never would get large enough. . . . I have grown so large that I have had the honor and the pleasure of being a member of the Legislature for five or six years. Did you ever hear of such a thing in America?"[29] An 1852 letter from Americo-Liberian Jasper Bouch reveals that civic masculinity could also be antifemale: "In America the free colored man can never be 'a man.' I believe it true that the free colored women are the great hinderance [sic] to the full tide of emigration which would have, and, indeed, ought to have poured long since into Liberia." Women who resisted emigrating, Bouch continued, were "stupidly blind" and should be abandoned by their husbands.[30]

Minor knew his audience well in pleading with his ex-master to provide books that would lead to ordination, for with the plea he approached his Virginian patron not just as a past owner but as a representative of a white nation in which northern and southern states were not at odds. If slavery and abolition divided the United States, colonization and African missions united it. In 1828, New England minister J. M. Wainwright argued for black missionaries. "To make colonization effectual, it is not sufficient that the arts of civilized society be carried to a new country: the Gospel is also needed," he began. "Now where is Africa, dark, degraded, ignorant Africa; where is it to obtain this blessed gift? How shall they hear without a preacher? . . . But . . . we cannot obtain missionaries." British missionaries, already at work in the field, had written to their U.S. counterparts, Wainwright continued, "stating that they looked anxiously to this country for missionaries, catechists and school-masters—they wished for pious, intelligent, and active men of colour for this pur-pose, and stood prepared to give them an ample support. . . . The call then is loud for African Missionaries throughout the christian world." "Now, to supply this deficiency so universally and so deeply felt, the African Mission School Society has been projected," he concluded. "Its hope is, in the present year, to obtain a few pious and intelligent young men of colour, and to educate them with reference to the propagation of the Gospel in Africa. . . . In addition to this, we would give them a knowledge of the first principles of the useful sciences and arts; viz., botany, mineralogy, surveying, civil and municipal law, and political economy."[31] Presciently, Wainwright argued that the education of black men for missionary work was an essential part of liberal advances in political freedom and thought, as well as of economic progress. This argument bears examination, partly because scholars have usually seen colonization as a conservative thrust aimed at maintaining slavery in the United States and partly because scholars have generally failed to see the way in which liberal ideology was articulated when topics like slavery, freedom, blacks, and African missions were discussed.

Isaiah 11:9 reads in part, "The earth shall be full of the knowledge of the Lord, as the waters cover the sea"—a promising text, it would seem, for a statement favoring missionary endeavors. Wainwright commenced by dismissing "the doctrine of human perfectibility" and "benevolent fantasies" as unrealistic. Scripture, he claimed, promised not "dreams and speculations" but, rather, a "happier and better condition." "Perfection," thus, is an irrelevant goal, but humankind may well come to understand the "sublime principle of political economy, that the happiness and prosperity of each tends to the advantage of the whole." The arc of human improvement, he argued, was gauged not by great accomplishments in the arts and philosophy (or else the classical and medieval worlds would be supreme) but by the erosion of "inequality, and contrasted opulence and wretchedness among men." Today, when "these would not be tolerated," we hold tight to "the rights of man." In the modern, mercantile era, we envision the possibility of "demand" for commodities that "proceeds without any assignable term." "Merchants" are continually acting to better the "balance of the agricultural, the manufacturing, and commercial interests of nations." Wainwright understood Isaiah 11:9 to mean that Christianity and civilization—the latter encompassing the liberal, mercantile spirit sketched above—would cover the nations. Blacks could not be free in modern nations, Wainwright argued, because they "have never been accustomed to provide for themselves." But educated and "useful" black missionaries would create a civilized nation in Liberia, where both Africans and freedmen and freedwomen from the United States could thrive.[32]

This emphasis on black men as instruments of liberal progress led to claims that seem highly improbable today but that were deadly serious for proponents of colonization and African missions. Lott Cary, Baptist missionary to Monrovia, for instance, apparently read Adam Smith's *Wealth of Nations* during his breaks as a hired slave in Richmond tobacco warehouses.[33] The *African Repository* reported with hope the story of a twenty-five-year-old slave, Edward Frazer, educated only at home, who "has made himself master of the first six books of Euclid, has been reading the writings of Locke, and most of the standard divines of the church of England."[34] The settlers came to understand themselves as progressive and liberal in that they wrote themselves into U.S. history by describing the first ship that carried black expatriates to Africa as the *Mayflower* and in that they found parallels with the colonial and early national history of the United States, including the subjugation of natives (Native American or African), the Declaration of Independence, and the ratification of a national constitution—even the mustering of the militia and the Fourth of July.[35] All this suggested that the Americo-Liberians were "pioneers of civilization."[36] Indeed, not only was the national past of Liberia merged into U.S. history, but as one scholar of Crummell notes, he "conceived the future of Africa in terms of American history, applying manifest destiny myths to the great African undertaking."[37]

The British experience of missionary work in West Africa, by contrast to that of the United States, had little to do with expatriating blacks from Great Britain and establishing them as governors in an African settlement. Some of the "black poor" of London had been removed to Sierra Leone in the 1780s, but they sickened with deadly fever or merged into native groups.[38] Much larger issues for the British were instruction and texts in the native languages of people served by missionaries; encounters with "paganisms," "heathenisms," and "superstitions"; and Christian masculinity, not of blacks, but of Europeans who seemed willing to risk disease and death to spread the gospel. U.S. missionary work, to the degree that it submerged Liberian history into U.S. history, was narrowly nationalistic.[39] Indeed, the Americo-Liberian settlers may even have opposed missionaries' efforts to preach in indigenous languages, since the Christianization of the natives would have implied the ascension of rival black groups in the polity.[40]

News of black men in U.S.-sponsored missionary work—pious, devoted, learned men—strengthened the notion of the civic competence of those who would be "educated for self-government [and] independence."[41] Jacob Oson, for example, a martyr to the cause, built on his "early piety, his natural strength of mind, and his prudence and sound judgment" by educating himself, "keeping a school for coloured children," studying for orders, and accepting an appointment as "Missionary to Liberia."[42] Settler James Benson, despite having only one functional arm, reached out to the natives "to impress them with the superiority of our character, arts, morals, and means of happiness," an exercise of his "fidelity to [the] state."[43] A U.S. missionary, Harriette G. Brittan, described an encounter with "one of the first missionaries in Liberia": "He is a colored gentleman, . . . an educated and refined man. . . . He has charge of the school here."[44] She continued with news of the black Monrovian "considered a very efficient and able physician," and of Crummell and his wife, who while in England "mixed in the best society."[45] A Good Friday sermon by a settler minister impressed Brittan as "a most excellent sermon, . . . really a beautiful discourse."[46] Some of the news from Liberia was less inspirational—the white missionaries of the Protestant Episcopal Church seem to have been the most likely to criticize the process of Americo-Liberian settlement—but ironically, it sent the same message of forceful, independent black men back across the Atlantic.

A white female missionary who had been in Liberia, Mrs. E. F. Hening, noted the early involvement of the Episcopal Church in the ACS, but she also noted the conflicts between settlers and natives. Evangelical work among the natives was hindered, she wrote, by their dislike for the settlers. Yet, she continued, the natives believed that the white man's "fash" will ultimately prevail, so that settlers and missions alike will come to dominate the indigenous peoples.[47] Another white female missionary, Anna M. Scott, reported that the settlers had done little to aid the natives spiritually.[48] Missionary George S. Brown reported that Monrovians "mocked me openly to my face, that I should think of civilizing, and much more, christianizing [the] natives."[49] Even one of Lott Cary's hagiographers conceded that there was no evidence that the man sent as a Baptist missionary from Richmond actually evangelized among the natives.[50] Indeed, news from Liberia often reported friction and fighting between the settlers and the natives; it was in one such battle that Cary gained a reputation as a warrior, and it was in preparation for one such battle that he lost his life in an explosion of gunpowder and cartridges.[51] Another early settler, Elijah Johnson, was remembered as "a host in himself."[52]

The settlers themselves well understood their situation in Liberia. Settler Alexander Hance wrote in 1838 that "the natives do not like to be governed by a colored Man."[53] Settlers Peyton Skipwith and Sion Harris wrote to the United States in 1840 with a terrifying account of a battle between natives and Americo-Liberians at "Headington [Heddington], a Missionary establishment [with George S. Brown in residence] about five miles from Millsburg." An attack on the local people by the settlers led to a retaliation by a native force of "about four Hundred men." The settlers, few but well armed, loaded and aimed more muskets than they had men to fire them, then shifted from one gun to another, decimating the more numerous natives. Then, with some loyal natives, the settlers pursued the retreating forces, discovered their leader's body "slightly intomed about twenty miles from the feeld of Battle," and decapitated the corpse. The "ornament" of Goterah's head was presented to the first settler governor, Thomas Buchanan, who was among the most vocal of the opponents of white missions in Liberia.[54] Still, Heddington's missionary sent home reports of "the great courage of Mr. [Sion] Harris," who, indeed, had "administered the handful of slugs which caused his death," then preserved "Goterah's head for the governor."[55]

Missions at Cape Palmas, Maryland County, Liberia, provide a clear view of the way that relations among missionaries, settlers, and natives produced a notion of black men as citizens and governors.[56] The first Americo-Liberian settlers arrived in Cape Palmas in 1834 with the support of the Maryland State Colonization Society (MSCS), the American Board of Commissioners for Foreign Missions (ABCFM), and the Episcopal Domestic and Foreign Missionary Society. The ABCFM established a mission named Fair Hope on six acres of land at Cape Palmas. The Protestant Episcopal Board of Missions established one named Mount Vaughan three miles from the Cape. Later, Methodists, Baptists, and Roman Catholics arrived as missionaries. The initial expectation was that the missionaries and settlers would cooperate in the Christianization of the Glebo, the most numerous local group. But the white missionaries and the black settlers soon came to disagree vehemently over the proper treatment of natives. To white missionaries like Episcopal Bishop John Payne, Glebo society seemed to be naturally the "purest of democracies" because of its decentralized power structure.[57] However, white missionary Anna M. Scott thought that the Glebo shared among one another so much that their "industry and enterprise" were hampered; she also considered the Glebo too fun-loving, relaxed, and promiscuous.[58] The members of the MSCS promoted an unsustainable plan for the development of the Cape Palmas area, suggesting that the colonizationists understood less of the black expatriates than they should have. The center of the plan was agricultural development, with both settlers and the Glebo producing goods for trade to North America. But the settlers, unwilling to cooperate with the MSCS, did not farm or identify themselves as farmers but, rather, essentially as governors who would rule a new state with tribal people as laborers. Farming seemed irrelevant to the settlers when local laborers seemed available. In 1847, John B. Russwurm, governor of the colony, expressed his belief (probably unfounded at that time) in the governing power of the settlers: "Our influence with all the tribes is increasing, and if I desired it I might almost dictate in their palavers, but this would be going to needless trouble and expense; and unless requested, never interfere."[59] In the first few decades of settlement, the settlers, on the one hand, and the Episcopal missionaries and the Glebo, on the other, disputed the nature of governance in Cape Palmas.

The Episcopal missionaries objected to the settlers' mistreatment of the local people. After a protest from a white Episcopal missionary, the MSCS stated its view of the treaties by which the emigrants had settled themselves at Cape Palmas. After the missionary's challenge to settler dominance, the colonizationist spokesman wrote, "You ask me then is there no remnant of sovereignty left in the native tribes, the parties with whom our treaties have been made. I answer no: because the treaties made them one people with the colonists, the power was given to the American government to set all palavers, by which I understand in this connection, to decide all questions—and the reservation of the land which they had under cultivation was but the designation of boundaries, not the reservation of sovereignty." In response to the missionary's challenge to the legitimacy of the original transfer of land and rule from the tribes to the settlers, the colonizationist spokesman wrote, "You ask me—was this the construction of the treaties understood by the natives at the time. From all the information I have received I should answer in the affirmative. The treaty speaks for itself and its language is explicit." In response to the missionary's challenge to the settlers' claim that they were offering the natives a quid pro quo, the colonizationist spokesman wrote, "You have asked me—what was the consideration passing to the natives for this abandonment of their rights and sovereigns. I answer at once—the blessings of civilized government—I would add—the blessings of Christianity—but that you would say this was not appreciated by the natives when they made the treaty, and could not have entered into their minds as a part of the consideration for the contract, which would be very true."[60] Yet the statements and actions of the Glebo suggest that they understood the treaties as "friendship pacts," not contracts involving the permanent alienation of their land.

The Glebo were not the "natural men"—at once primitives and democrats—that Bishop Payne perceived them to be, for they had long traded with Europe and the United States, yet they were probably also not aware of the quality of governance and land ownership desired by the settlers. Objections soon came to the MSCS from the Glebo: "The colonies wants to take away our own ground on which we build our houses by force, but it is not good for force man from his home. We have given all rest of land yet they wants our town. We think you tell them to drive us away by force therefore we wants to know the truth. . . . Send us back a note . . . and send it to our town that we may read it ourself."[61]

White missionaries objected to what they perceived as mistreatment of the natives, and they participated, therefore, in a larger discourse about clashes between "civilized" nations and native people. The missionaries drew a parallel between the treatment of the Glebo and the treatment of the Cherokee in the southeastern United States in the 1830s; missionaries elsewhere in Africa were similarly criticizing the treatment of the Zulu by the Boer. The Cape Palmas missionaries first noted, in 1837, that the settlers were colluding, at least in the slave trade from the Windward Coast—a particularly egregious offense since one reason given in the United States for the establishment of missions and settlements was to halt the trade. Russwurm, in turn, objected to "the interfering of gentlemen who are in no wise connected with the government."[62] In 1838, missionaries began complaining about the settlers' mistreatment of Glebo children who had been placed in settlers' homes as apprentices or "pawns." Pawning was a traditional West African means of providing training to children as well as of retiring debts, but the Americo-Liberians were accused of treating their pawns as slaves. Also in 1838, missionaries and settlers clashed over the use of arms against the natives: Russwurm claimed that all able-bodied men except ministers were obliged to enroll in the militia and defend the settlement, while the missionaries claimed that their mission employees, whether Glebo or Americo-Liberian, were exempt from the requirement. The MSCS threw its weight behind Russwurm in the dispute. In 1839, the comparison to the Jacksonians who pushed the Cherokees from the southeastern United States not lost on him, Russwurm boasted that the Americo-Liberian settlers were treating the Glebo just as Euro-Americans had treated the Native Americans.[63]

Conflicts between the missionaries and the settlers came to a head around 1840, resulting in the withdrawal of the ABCFM from Cape Palmas in 1842. *The Missionary Herald* reported the withdrawal, noting that "the temporal interests of the colonists, as such, necessarily conflict with the objects of the Board in establishing its missionary stations in the colony or its neighborhood, to civilize and Christianize the native inhabitants."[64] Several incidents led to this dramatic move and the condemnation of the settlers. Both ABCFM and Episcopal missionaries sought to evangelize in areas outside settler control. In 1838, the ABCFM missionaries infuriated Russwurm by signing with the Glebo of Fishtown, which was outside territory claimed by the settlers, a treaty that allotted a portion of land to the mission and left the Fishtown inhabitants in control of their traditional possessions, but that allowed the missionaries to decree which foreigners could live there. "Have any individuals or society a right to buy land on our borders from natives without your consent?" Russwurm queried the MSCS.[65] In 1841, the Episcopal missionaries ceased ministering to the settlers and formed a new mission at Taboo, thirty miles east of the Cape, far from the center of settler authority and outside its territorial claims. Russwurm responded by reiterating that mission employees must serve in the colony militia even if the service set one Glebo against another, by passing a law forcing missionaries, who were short on funds, to pay in cash, not goods, for commodities procured from the settlers, and by challenging the missionaries' rights to house freed children who had been sent from the United States by masters who had manumitted them to be educated in mission schools. As missionaries began complaining of the misdeeds of the settlers, U.S. colonizationists like R. R. Gurley and J. B. Latrobe became distressed at the cost to their cause. To the spokesman for the New York Colonization Society in 1843, for instance, it seemed as though the missionaries were turning many whites in the United States away from colonizationism.

By the 1850s, however, missionaries and settlers were cooperating. The missionaries had been rattled by a dispute with the Glebo following an accusation of stealing that one of the former made against one of the latter. Payne, moreover, believed that in the long run the most effective evangelists in Africa would be black men, not white, and he hoped that some ministers would arise from the Americo-Liberians. (He would welcome Crummell in 1853, but the black man would always resent the white cleric's authority in Liberia.) In 1861, for instance, Payne guided a corps of four white missionaries and eight black missionaries at Cape Palmas.[66] Independent in 1854 from the MSCS, Cape Palmas in 1855 joined the Republic of Liberia, then eight years old. In 1856, full-scale war erupted between the settlers and the Glebo. The defeat of the Glebo brought them under the nominal protection of the Liberian state, but it also meant the loss of their traditional lands and the dispersal of many communities. Fifteen dollars a lot was the going price at which settlers could purchase the land from which the natives had been removed. An author writing in the *Maryland Colonization Journal* in 1859 recollected that once he had seen near the Cape "some two or three acres . . . thickly covered with circular thatched houses, running up to a point like hay stacks, containing some ten or twelve hundred souls." But after the war, "not a vestige of it remained, save a few blackened cocoa nut trees, the circular hearths or hard beaten earthen floors of the huts of the departed natives, and masses of broken crockery, which had once constituted their principal wealth."[67] An 1860 missionary account relayed that "in the war . . . between the natives and the colonists, at Cape Palmas, the colonists burnt the natives [*sic*] towns, and made them move across to the other side of the river. They have never liked it there."[68]

A late convert to the colonizationist cause, Martin Delany, recapitulated the main themes of the movement in his writings of the 1850s and 1860s. In 1852, before he had settled on emigration to West Africa as a likely goal for African Americans, Delany lamented that "one part of the American people, though living in near proximity and together, are quite unacquainted with the other" and noted that his object was "to make each acquainted." He initially spurned Liberia because he saw its government as a "dependency" on white organizations.[69] His despair in the 1850s over the possibilities of black progress in the United States (like many people, he objected mightily to the Fugitive Slave Law) led Delany in 1859 to Liberia and other points in West Africa and, perhaps with an irony he did not comprehend, led him toward his earlier object of making U.S. blacks and whites more familiar with one another. Delany echoed Payne's judgment that white missionaries were merely preparing the field for black evangelists in Africa; he furthered Crummell's and Russwurm's judgment of the white missionaries by arguing that they were too tolerant of native culture and too spiritual in orientation. The prescription for West Africa, Delaney declared, was the extirpation of indigenous cultures and the religious and political leadership of "black men." He noted the "deference" the white missionaries received from the "natives"; he evidently expected the same for himself once black leaders supplanted the white missionaries.[70] Liberia gave Delany an opportunity to place himself in the mainstream of U.S. thought.

Like Russwurm, Crummell savored the analogy that set both Euro-Americans and Americo-Liberians over the native peoples they encountered while settling a new land and forming a new state and economy. A few years after the defeat of the Glebo, Crummell was warning of a recombination of native forces "from Gallinas to Palmas [that is, from north to south]": "Here, in Africa, such a league of natives as the Indians once formed against the early colonists of Massachusetts . . . will come down to the sea-board, in sanguinary ferocity and terrible array, to destroy every vestige of religion, every relic of civilization, and sweep us, if possible, into the sea."[71] In this situation, Crummell argued, "force, that is authority, must be used in the exercise of guardianship over heathen tribes. Mere theories of democracy are trivial in this case, and can never nullify this necessity. . . . Hence also the stern necessity of assuming the nonage—the childhood of the natives; and, consequently, our responsibility of guardianship over them."[72] It is almost certainly relevant to Crummell's and Russwurm's comments that missionary efforts aimed at Native Americans living in the United States were generally regarded in the mid–nineteenth century as failures.[73] The establishment of a class of men like Crummell and Russwurm, seemingly of the same race as those to be converted to Christianity, offered to whites another chance at national missionary glory following the failure of the missions to Native Americans.

By the 1850s, a consensus had been achieved among people in the United States and Americo-Liberians about the ability of black men to govern and evangelize effectively. "Colored men" were seen as indispensably the leaders of African missions.[74] Payne, for instance, in arguing for black missionaries, wrote, "It is only *men* who are qualified to be guides and instructors. . . . The Americo-African Colonists . . . are struggling rapidly into *manhood*. . . . Colonists already fill every civil office in Liberia, the higher ones, most ably; why should they not also, in time, fill all in the church?"[75] U.S. missionaries told their compatriots that the "founders" of Liberia were "martyrs for the sacred cause of liberty" and that current Liberian politicians were "gentlemen" of "noble" appearance.[76] Colonizationists argued for the education for missionary labors of "young colored persons of piety, docility, and sterling worth."[77] The Republic of Liberia itself came to exist in 1847 as a black-governed state, not a creature of the ACS; and Maryland in Liberia, including the Cape Palmas settlement, joined the new republic.

Like Crummell, the image of the black man as citizen and governor traveled from Liberia to the United States for good. The notoriety that the ACS and Liberia had among abolitionists, black and white—as elements in a scheme to remove blacks from North America—was undeserved, though it was based on a literal understanding of colonization.[78] By nineteenth-century standards of marine travel, Liberia, at about six weeks' voyage, was not far from the United States. "Small is the stream" that separates the eastern shores of the Atlantic Ocean from the western, announced *The African Repository and Colonial Journal* in 1825.[79] African Americans, as well as white missionaries, traversed the Atlantic, sailing from Monrovia and Cape Palmas to Boston, New York, Philadelphia, Baltimore, Norfolk, and Charleston—and back.[80] News, letters, money, books, trade goods, and charitable donations as well moved between Liberia and the United States. Douglass saw black manhood undercut in the missionary and colonizationist enterprises, but it seems more accurate to say that it was formed and articulated in them. The essential notion of a black man as a modern citizen—a free citizen, capable of education, commerce, governance, religious faith, and rule over dependents—was articulated for the first time any-where in the Atlantic world in Liberia.[81]

After this articulation, the notion flooded the market in a deluge of news and commentaries about Liberia, which was probably, after slavery, the topic relevant to race relations most discussed in the United States between 1822 and 1860. If we understand U.S. race relations between the Revolutionary War years and the "up-lift" era, we can see that the battles between Crummell and Payne (over the dislike of the former to subordination to the latter) and between Delany and Doug-lass (over whether blacks should emigrate from the United States) were really in-house squabbles among men who were enunciating one idea of black citizenship, manhood, and modernity. The nationalist impulse in U.S. missionary work—the post–Revolutionary War push toward a world-historical ideological, economic, and religious role in foreign territories—has often been emphasized. If we see nineteenth-century Liberian missionary work as occurring not merely in foreign territory but in a site economically, ideologically, racially, and religiously an exten-sion of the United States, we can see missions not only in their expressions of na-tionalism but also in their contributions to the construction of a modern nation in the United States.

2 / The Serpentine Trail

Haitian Missions and the Construction of African-American Religious Identity

Laurie F. Maffly-Kipp

In 1878, Amanda Smith received a call to preach overseas. Smith, by then forty-one years old and perhaps the best-known African-American traveling evangelist of the day, had pressed her call to the pulpit with the African Methodist Episcopal (A.M.E.) Church for nearly a decade. But given the overwhelming sentiment against female preaching among her church's bishops, her case repeatedly had been rejected. Nonetheless, she persisted on her own. Supported by sympathetic Methodists along her preaching circuits, Smith made her way from the British Isles through France, Italy, Egypt, India, Burma, and West Africa over a twelve-year period.

It was in 1893 that Smith, like many enterprising and successful itinerants, published her memoirs. Smith's story is unique in its details and singular in its evocative image of a black female preacher evangelizing her way around the world; no other African-American missionaries of the nineteenth century, male or female, commented at such length upon the practices of Roman Catholicism, Hinduism, Buddhism, Anglicanism, Islam, and indigenous African customs in a single volume. Yet the thick work, titled *An Autobiography: The Story of the Lord's Dealings with Mrs. Amanda Smith the Colored Evangelist,* is highly formulaic in other respects. "There has been no attempt to show a dash of rhetoric or intellectual ability," she commented in the final pages, "but just the simple story of God's dealing with a worm."[1]

Despite her attempts at self-effacement, Smith spent hundreds of pages detailing her spiritual trials and triumphs, in an effort to show others the way to salvation, the goal of the Christian life. Yet what is most striking about her descriptions of her overseas travels is the extent to which she, like many other missionaries of the late nineteenth century, came to define that Christian life through a process of negation and elimination. For Smith, as for many U.S. Christians confronting non-Protestant religions for the first time in the postbellum period, Protestantism was most easily and graphically defined by what it was *not:* it was not Roman Catholic "priestcraft," nor the highly ritualized behaviors of "Mohammedans" or "Hindoos," nor the "devil worship" that she encountered in Africa.

Such missionary accounts were only one determining factor in the increasing U.S. fascination with non-Protestant religions—and indeed, with "religion" as a category of individual reflection and scholarly analysis—in the nineteenth century. Dramatic growth in the numbers of Roman Catholic, Jewish, Buddhist, and later Muslim immigrants to the United States; the movement of Christians from rural areas to urban centers where they lived in intimate surroundings with people of other traditions; and the emergence of new intellectual currents that encouraged the classification of various religious systems within a comparative and hierarchical framework all combined with the vastly increased ethnographic knowledge about non-Protestant religions to produce a new interest in comparing religions.[2]

African Americans faced this specter of religious comparison from both sides. Southern blacks were frequently held up as the object of northern Protestant scorn and sympathy in the postbellum decades for their "heathenish" practices and "child-like" religious beliefs. Yet like other evangelical adherents, many African Americans simultaneously served as agents for the spread of an "enlightened" Protestantism, and they, too, confronted the intellectual challenges presented by increasing religious diversity. Smith's volume, like those missionary and travel accounts written by scores of whites over the course of the century, found a ready audience among Protestants, both black and white, eager for knowledge of other cultures.[3] Indeed, because of their long-standing psychic connections with Africa and with enslaved Africans in other parts of the Americas, many African Americans gained an acute consciousness of—and interest in—religious diversity long before most Euro-Americans began to worry about those "benighted pagans" abroad.

This encounter with religious difference, and the attendant discussions about Protestant truth and cultural difference to which it inevitably gave rise, had a particular valence and complexity for African-American Protestants. For many, a consciousness of racial identity emerged in the late eighteenth century alongside a commitment to Christian faith; the awakening to Christ was thus in part constituted by, and dependent on, an awakening to a racialized community.[4] As Christians, they were heirs to a tradition not entirely of their own making; unlike whites, they were not nearly as quick to equate their own racial identities with "true" Protestantism. Moreover, African-American missionary literature emphasized two contradictory yet entwined impulses: first, the need for an increase of enlightened Protestant believers around the globe; and second, the growing obligations of racial loyalty to others of African descent, irrespective of their religious practices. Reconciling these loyalties in the face of the growing interest in and knowledge of other religious systems entailed the creation of a new kind of communal history, one that directly linked the growth of Protestant faith to the fate of the African diaspora. And it was the creation of a communal history, in turn, that aided in the construction of a distinctive Afro-Protestant identity for blacks in the United States by the beginning of the twentieth century.

This chapter explores one of the earliest instances of this intellectual and bodily encounter and aims to reveal some of the dynamics that continued to shape and refine African-American racial and religious identities throughout the nineteenth century. Its focus is not Africa but Haiti, a small Caribbean republic with enormous symbolic importance for nineteenth-century African Americans. In 1804, after thirteen years of bloody battle and political struggle, Haiti became the first European colony to be overthrown by formerly enslaved Africans and to establish itself as an independent black republic. It would be hard to underestimate the enduring effect that this event had on whites and blacks throughout the New World. In its aftermath, slaveholding southerners feared even more intensely the potential for slave insurrection on their own soil; conversely, African Americans, both enslaved and free, took courage in the example set by the some 500,000 former slaves in the Caribbean.[5]

Over the century that followed, and punctuated by emigrationist movements in the 1820s and again in the 1860s, African-American interest in Haiti—and public discourse about its religious and racial significance—continued unabated. Although this discussion has not received nearly the visibility of debates about the meaning of Africa for American blacks, it attracted the interest of a similarly broad cross section of people. Moreover, as with interest in Africa, two connected phenomena sustained continuing knowledge of Haiti: the emigration movement and the missionary movement.

EMIGRATIONISTS AND MISSIONARIES

Throughout the century, black interest in permanent migration out of the United States waxed and waned, depending in part on perceptions of the racial and economic climate for African Americans at home. Blacks in the northern ports of Boston, Newport, and Providence promoted schemes for emigration as early as the 1780s. In doing so, they drew upon a two-pronged argument: first, that blacks would never achieve true equality in the United States; and second, that emigrants, in the process of building a new society elsewhere, could in turn carry "civilization" and education to less advanced peoples in other parts of the world.[6] Africa was the first and most often mentioned site of emigrationist interest. Over the course of the ensuing decades, however, advocates championed a variety of locales, including Mexico, South America, California, and Canada. Emigration fervor reached several peaks of activity: in the 1820s, both Haiti and Africa enjoyed a fair measure of interest; Haitian emigration resurged briefly in 1861–1862; and African emigration resumed with the demise of Reconstruction in the southern states in 1878.

Missionary efforts, while initially linked in the minds of black Protestants with the notion of permanent resettlement, followed a more gradual trajectory and were more intensively focused on Africa. Although interest in missions to Africa stretched back to the late eighteenth century, and a few enterprising black leaders such as Paul Cuffee tried to realize the dream of a Christianized Africa before the Civil War, the financial and political realities of life in the United States rendered such plans difficult to implement. Black churches simply did not have the financial resources to undertake extensive missionary work until the 1880s, and most free blacks remained hostile to the efforts of the American Colonization Society (ACS), established in 1816, which bore the marks of a white southern plot to deport all dark-skinned peoples from the United States. A handful of African-American Christians were sent out under the auspices of white church organizations in the antebellum period. Since many whites already assumed that Africa was a "white man's grave," it seemed to make sense to equip black missionaries for the task of evangelization there.[7]

Haitian missionary activity began largely as a result of the surge of emigration in the 1820s and, thereafter, was supported primarily by the promotional activities of prominent black leaders. Many free blacks who were unwilling to entertain the advances of the ACS did consider emigration to Haiti. Encouraged by the official endorsement of Haitian President Jean Pierre Boyer, who hoped to gain recognition for his government from the United States, the emigration movement received the backing of prominent black church leaders in New York, Philadelphia, Boston, and other eastern cities. As a result of this grassroots support from prominent black churches, a number of Protestant clergy joined the ranks in an effort to tend to the needs of emigrating church members. Benjamin F. Hughes, pastor of Philadelphia's First African Presbyterian Church, emigrated in 1824. The Reverends Peter Williams, a prominent black Episcopal priest in New York City, and Thomas Paul, a Baptist pastor from Boston, took extended tours of Haiti in the mid-1820s to survey its religious conditions and prospects. Even John Allen, the son of Richard Allen, first bishop of the A.M.E. Church, emigrated to Haiti. Although John Allen remained there for many years as a printer, he also saw himself as aiding the Methodist cause in the new republic.[8]

During the second wave of migration beginning in the 1850s, concern for Haiti as a site of Protestant evangelism increased. Black church leaders once again played prominent roles in promoting popular interest. James Theodore Holly, who would later become the first Episcopal bishop of Haiti and founder of the independent Orthodox Apostolic Church, embarked on lecture tours in Connecticut, New York, Ohio, Michigan, and western Canada in the mid-1850s and published information about Haiti in a wide variety of secular and religious periodicals. In the same decade,

William Wells Brown, perhaps the best-known black historian of the nineteenth century, lectured in both the United States and Great Britain on *St. Domingo: Its Revolutions and Its Patriots,* a tract that likened the heroes of Haiti to Protestant luminaries. And during the height of emigration activity in 1861–1862, the Haytien Bureau of Emigration (under the auspices of the Haitian government) published a paper in Boston and New York to encourage U.S. interest in migration. Edited by chief emigration agent James Redpath, *Pine and the Palm* printed dozens of letters from recent and potential migrants that underscored the religious importance of Haiti for African Americans. Some lecturers, such as J. Dennis Harris, a black plasterer from Cleveland who lectured widely in Ohio in the late 1850s and early 1860s, mingled the causes of emigration and antislavery. In the postbellum era, A.M.E. missionary C. W. Mossell undertook speaking tours from Maine to Georgia and even sent a handful of Haitian students back to Wilberforce University for continued education.[9]

These two "seasons" of missionary activity fostered public interest at home in the missions field and heightened awareness of Haiti's cultural, social, and religious circumstances. But they served an ideological purpose as well: they invited African Americans back home into a realizable international story of racial and religious struggle that placed them beyond the bounds of their immediate political and social situation. Unlike the dream of Africa, this one was within travel distance for many free blacks. Moreover, Haitian independence had proven the ability of Africans to overcome their enslavement and build a stable and enduring racial community. As the pages of *Pine and the Palm* advertised, U.S. black emigrants and supporters could enter the development of a Negro nation: "Hayti is the common country of the black race."[10] The symbolic significance of the Haitian revolution, combined with the promotional interests of missionaries and emigrationists, gave rise to a century-long discourse among African Americans that played itself out in published volumes, religious and secular periodicals, and even educational materials for freed blacks and children.

But if Haiti seemed like the perfect answer to dreams of black freedom, for most African Americans one "problem" remained: the country was, at least nominally, Roman Catholic. Worse yet, most black Haitians engaged in local religious practices such as voodoo that were even less comprehensible to African Americans. How could this republic fulfill the dreams of free men and women who were, increasingly, joining Protestant churches and identifying themselves with the heroes of a centuries-long struggle against "heathenism" and "popery"? Reconciling these conflicting goals, the ideals of racial unity and the fulfillment of religious truth, was one of the unspoken themes of much black writing about Haiti in the nineteenth century. Missionaries and emigrationists penned accounts that were not simply nationalist or protonationalist, promoting the virtues of an independent black society; they were also framed with the context of a Protestant story of providential destiny.[11] Through the resulting narratives, African Americans learned and communicated important truths about themselves, their religious and racial awareness, and the sense of community that connected these central concerns.

COUNTERING EURO-AMERICAN ETHNOGRAPHY

Although the primary audience for these accounts was African-American, black writers also kept one eye focused on European and U.S. accounts of Haitian history. White observers gauged the republic's religious difficulties and publicized its short-comings to an international audience. Two of the most widely circulated volumes were written by British observers but published concurrently in the United States. One of the earliest white observers in Haiti was a Wesleyan missionary, M. B. Bird, who served in the field from 1840 to 1867. Bird dedicated his work, a lengthy volume endorsed by the Haitian government and published by the author in the United States in 1869, "to the government and people of Hayti." It presented a sympathetic view of the Haitian struggle for independence, blaming many of its problems on the inherent cruelties of the French colonial system. Bird saw the rise of Haiti as a provi-dential movement, one ultimately meant to banish the "evils" of Roman Catholi-cism and "Vandouism" from the nation. "African superstitions," he noted, "were believed and practiced to an awful extent. In fact, to enter fully into detail on this question, would require a volume of no ordinary size, and would most certainly bring out some awful developments." Vestiges of a repressive French colonial system, in which "religion and knowledge were wielded as mighty powers, to awe the en-slaved masses into the degrading belief, that they were really inferior beings," these religions would soon be vanquished under the divine march of Protestant religion. While Bird argued for the legitimacy of a separate black nation, and consistently linked the fate of Haiti to that of Liberia, his main attentions were turned to the transformational power of evangelical Christianity in an otherwise degraded situa-tion. In effect, the Haitian struggle was subsumed into the grand march of Protes-tant history, as one more instance of the healing powers of true belief.[12]

More negative, however, was the scathing testimony published by Sir Spenser St. John, *Hayti; or the Black Republic,* a work that was first published in 1883. St. John had served as a British minister-resident and consul general in Haiti between 1863 and 1875. While there, he attended the Episcopal church at which James Theodore Holly was the presiding minister, and he considered Holly an "intimate friend." Nonetheless, his subsequent attack on the nation and on blacks in general was re-lentless. He characterized Haiti as "a country in a state of rapid decadence," ready at any moment to sink back into "the state of an African tribe." Linking "van-douism" to cannibalism, debauchery, and, above all, vestigial African practice, St.

John concluded that Haiti was regressing as a nation. Even the Roman Catholics there had not been able to penetrate the veil of ignorance, he noted: "They cannot cope with so vast a mass of brutal ignorance and gross superstition."[13]

While one might be tempted to dismiss the observations of St. John as the ravings of a disgruntled civil servant,[14] it is significant that his book remained the standard interpretive work on Haiti well into the twentieth century. Moreover, in painting his picture of a degraded and uncivilized backwater, he drew on a standard repertoire of ethnographic accounts that enjoyed wide circulation in the latter part of the nineteenth century. Far from being idiosyncratic, St. John's depiction both reflected and set future standards for European and Euro-American depictions of Haiti for many decades.[15]

African Americans confronted these negative images, remaining conscious both of black political and religious aspirations as well as regnant European and U.S. opinions of Haiti as a country desperately in need of white civilization and culture. Black authors countered with narratives that placed Haiti squarely in the center of world history. James Theodore Holly described the nation as "the political prodigy of universal history," referring to the providential significance of a black-led revolution.[16] Many of these accounts and descriptions portrayed Haiti not simply as another example of the progress of Protestantism but as a place where the particular destiny of black peoples providentially intersected with the Christian story. To understand African-American views of Haiti, it is important to explore further the complexity of this historical consciousness.

Some of the earliest African-American observers of Haiti emphasized the virtues of its climate, likening it to a modern-day Eden and playing on the spiritual significance of its beauty and location. Well before the first rush of emigration in the 1820s, Prince Saunders promoted Haiti and asserted its religious importance. Born in Vermont, Saunders had been sent to England as a youth with the support of sympathetic whites. He received his education there and, in the process, met up with antislavery advocates including Thomas Clarkson and William Wilberforce. Later, he emigrated to Haiti and became the minister of education during the reign of Henri Christophe. By 1818, he was in Boston, where he published a U.S. edition of his *Haytian Papers,* a compilation of national history, legal codes, and observations about contemporary Haiti.[17] He also lectured widely in the United States, finally settling in Philadelphia and joining St. Thomas Episcopal Church. Colleagues noted his "great popularity among the people." In his speeches, he placed Haiti within a broader history of God's providential dealings with African peoples and predicted that Haiti would be the scene of future divine workings: "God in the mysterious operation of his providence has seen fit to permit the most astonishing changes to transpire upon that naturally beautiful . . . astonishingly luxuriant island." Haiti was, in Saunders's account, the "paradise" of the New World.[18]

At midcentury, James Holly and J. Dennis Harris, both employed as regional recruiting agents for the Haytien Bureau of Emigration in 1860, presented Haiti in much the same way. Holly consistently referred to the country as a new Eden, and Harris enthused about the providential coincidence of its location. "Central America," wrote Harris, "by common assent, not only realizes in its geographical position the ancient idea of the centre of the world, but is in its physical aspect and configuration of surface an epitome of all the countries and of all climes."[19] Inverting prevailing Euro-American views of the backwardness of the region, Harris transformed Haiti into the geographical standard by which all other regions should be judged.

Several promoters also linked Haiti to an ancient legacy of black achievement. C. W. Mossell, an A.M.E. missionary to Haiti in the 1870s and 1880s, compared the Haitian revolution to the glorious battles of classical civilization. He likened the Europeans to "Romans" and termed the black Haitians "Spartans" in describing their revolutionary effort.[20] Saunders detected the origins of Haitian culture in the civilizations of Egypt and Ethiopia, the founts of early knowledge, rather than those of Greece, Germany, and Gaul.[21] Holly furnished even more extensive similes of Haitian destiny in a seven-part series of articles published in the *Anglo-African Magazine* in 1859. Indeed, he argued that past glories were dwarfed by the recent history of Haiti. "The ancient glory of Ethiopia, Egypt, and Greece, grows pale in comparison with the splendor of this Haytian achievement." The appropriate comparison, he reasoned, seemed to lie much closer to home, with the only other nation in the Western Hemisphere that had shaken off European control in the preceding century: "If the United States can claim to have preceded her in this respect, Hayti can claim the honor of having contributed to the success of American Independence, by the effusion of the blood of her sable sons, who . . . fought side by side with the American heroes."[22]

Toussaint L'Ouverture, the revolutionary hero of the Haitian cause, figured large in nearly every description of Haiti, and many renderings of him make explicit his connection to a racial destiny. Over the course of the century, both white (mostly abolitionist) and black writers celebrated his achievements: Lydia Maria Child, James Redpath, Wendell Phillips, James McCune Smith, and C. W. Mossell all published biographies, and many other observers spoke enthusiastically of his virtues. William Wells Brown delivered and later published a swashbuckling history of Haiti in which L'Ouverture appeared as a hero descended from an African chief, "one of the most wealthy, powerful, and influential monarchs on the west coast of Africa." Brown also emphasized that the revolutionary shared in the "soul" of Africa: "That soul, when once the soul of a man, and no longer that of a slave, can overthrow the Pyramids and the Alps themselves, sooner than again be crushed down into slavery."

Here, too, his choice of allusion echoed the notion that Haitian history eclipsed the glories of past civilizations.[23]

L'Ouverture's symbolic importance for African-American leaders hardly merits explanation, given the political context of black life in antebellum America. Even the allusion to ancient historical precedents, of course, was a trope in common usage among nineteenth-century leaders who were increasingly intrigued by the comparative merits of diverse cultures. But the links to a glorious African past, in particular, ran counter to popular Euro-American theorizing about the hierarchy of civilizations and were certainly intended as a direct attack on the claims increasingly being made by white U.S. scientists about the degradations of the African race. Holly spoke most directly to those theorists when he assured his (black) readers that their historical legacy was secure: "We need not resort to any long drawn arguments to defend negro-Ethnography against the Notts and Gliddons of our day."[24] His words directly addressed—and dismissed the findings of—some of the most influential white racial theorists of the era.

The theme that one might assume would be most dissonant for nineteenth-century African-American readers, in light of the political commitments of most black leaders of the day to U.S. democratic theory (and, indeed, of William Wells Brown's likening of L'Ouverture himself to George Washington, the great anti-royalist), is the valorization of the Haitian monarchy as a positive feature of the nation's culture. James Holly, admittedly an exceedingly "high church" Episcopalian, dedicated a Masonic lodge in Detroit in the 1850s "to the greatness of Haiti and her monarch." References to L'Ouverture's African ancestry, moreover, specifically his relation to an African king or chieftain, invariably marked not only a geographical referent but a position of regal bearing as well.[25] But the valorization of the notion of kingship itself also linked Haiti to African precedents, making still more explicit the historical movement from Ethiopia to Egypt to Haiti. The monarchy might have been explained as a legacy of French colonialism, a vestige to be done away with in the fervor of revolutionary housekeeping. But African Americans tended instead to claim it as a heritage of African origin: Holly termed it "an ancient traditionary predilection of the race derived from Africa. . . . The gorgeous splendor and august prestige of aristrocratic [sic] rank and title, always attendant on this form of government, hold an imperious sway over the minds of this race of men who have such a keen appreciation of the beautiful."[26]

In linking Haiti to an ancient past, and in connecting all dark-skinned peoples to the fate of the Caribbean republic, missionaries and emigrationists assisted in the creation of a racialized history, according to blacks a particularistic providence that linked Africa to Haiti and ultimately to African Americans, in whose hands the fate of Haiti supposedly resided. Publicists thus resolved some of the thornier issues of political consistency within an aesthetically appealing African legacy, monarchy included, that made sense of the Haitian system.

But one must not dismiss too readily the commitment that many African-American leaders felt to a U.S. political and religious legacy, and the continuing dissonances to which this commitment could give rise.[27] Historical precedents from U.S. history, most notably that of the Puritans in New England, figured into descriptions of the movement of African Americans to Haiti as well. The Reverend John Lewis wrote from St. Mark's, Haiti, that he likened his position there to that of the early settlers of the Plymouth colony: "I take, as a precedent, the position of the Pilgrim Fathers of New England." Holly also advocated the settling of the Caribbean nation on the model of early New England, in "well-organized religious communities, headed by an educated ministry, and backed and sustained by learned laymen." The Episcopal minister formed a *Madeira* Compact with his fellow migrants based on New England models and described the group as a "Mayflower expedition of sable pioneers in the cause of civil and religious liberty, which it falls to your lot to Hayti in the name of New England." He continually likened the band to pilgrims and reminded them of the trials undergone by those early Puritans.[28]

The invocation of New England precedents reflected the coexistence of multiple understandings of African-American communal identity. But it highlights once again the extent to which these representations of Haiti reflected African-American selves; these stories took the intellectual tools available to African Americans—from ancient Egypt and Ethiopia to the Puritans—and reshaped them, weaving them in new ways. Like many history writers of the day, black authors were less concerned with the "verification" of facts, and of explaining the precise links between ancient history and the present, than they were with compiling examples in a historical bricolage that narrated in dramatic fashion the development of the African community. In doing so, they informed African-American readers about what it meant to be part of a racial and religious community, one not well defined by Euro-American renderings of the past and present.

One issue remained unresolved by recourse to Africa: Haiti was, at least in name, a Roman Catholic nation. How could a country controlled by the pope secure a future for Protestant African Americans? Moreover, if Haitian blacks represented the pinnacle of a long history of African achievement, why had they not thrown off the shackles of "heathenism" and Roman Catholicism after the Haitian revolution?

THE "PROBLEM" OF ROMAN CATHOLICISM

Black promoters employed several strategies to describe and analyze the religious history and current conditions of Haiti. To some extent, the strategic interests of emigrationists and missions advocates differed on this point. Those committed to selling the wonders of the republic to potential settlers had a great deal to gain by accentuating the positive, by representing Haiti as morally familiar and inviting. Missions supporters, conversely, characteristically sought to raise money for further evangelistic efforts by emphasizing dire religious need. Because the Haitian emigration and missions movements were so entwined with respect to their leadership and constituencies, however, most of the literature reveals a blending of these approaches. The same publicists at different moments spoke of both promise and peril. Most significant, they sought to understand the tension between Haiti's racial glory and its religious ignominy. For purposes of analysis, African-American representations of religion in Haiti can be broken into several categories.

The first kind of response reflected the stock images of Roman Catholicism borrowed from a long history of anti-Catholic rhetoric in Europe and the United States. In this view, Catholicism in Haiti was a sham or a "puppet of the state," a repressive system imposed for selfish reasons by the few and believed by none. Ordinary followers were, thereby, blameless victims, caught in the autocratic grip of power- and money-hungry priests and bishops. At the height of anti-Catholic fever among white Protestants in the United States during the 1830s, the editor of the New York–based *Colored American* voiced an observation passed along by the British and Foreign Bible Society, a Baptist organization. The Haitian people "learn nothing useful or valuable from the priests, who officiate among them," the missionary commented. "Mummery and external show being almost the exclusive character of their miscalled religion."[29] "Poor Hayti," echoed another missionary touring the West Indies in the 1840s. "Religion . . . is the mere puppet of the State, used by those in power, feared by the degraded and superstitious masses, and despised by the intelligent."[30]

At the same time, publicists lauded the "natural" religiosity of the Haitian people, a testament to their innate (racial) morality. "The African character is decidedly religious," asserted Holly. "It is therefore impossible to make him an out and out atheist." Left to the combined influences of French colonialism and Catholic oppression, Holly concluded, the Haitian people had remained mired in "heathen" practices: "On the Sabbath, after participating in the ceremonial observances at the Roman Catholic temples in the forepart of that holy day, they assemble together in the afternoon and evening of the same day, in portable tents, and celebrate by dancing and singing the heathen mysteries of Africa."[31] One of the few female reporters on Haitian life, the missionary wife Mary Ella Mossell, provided an extended description of a "Voudoux" ceremony in the 1880s, expressing both her disgust and her sympathy for the poor practitioners who had been kept from the true knowledge of Christ by the Catholic Church. "There are rites the most abominable and dissipations the most obscene," she wrote. "It was terrible, it was abominable, it was degrading, it could not but strike all right-minded people with horror, filling their souls with sadness and sorrow."[32]

The "natural" religiosity of the Haitian people, and by extension of all blacks, took the form of superstition and vestigial African practices in its lower forms. But many observers of Haiti also seemed to suggest that Haitians were, at their best, what might be termed "crypto-Protestant"—tolerant, individualistic, divinely inspired Bible readers—called by the true God despite the outward formalism of their religious beliefs. One newly arrived Haitian emigrant, the Reverend John W. Lewis, explained in the pages of *Pine and the Palm* that Haitian national heroes had exhibited divine inspiration. "Although theirs was, and mine is, a country full of ceremonies, they need no Te Deum chanted for the repose of their souls, nor a virgin saint to commend them to God or good angels. As master-spirits of their age, they were moved by an inward holy inspiration, which made their deeds heroic."[33]

L'Ouverture himself, although a practicing Catholic, frequently assumed Protestant characteristics at the hands of his U.S. biographers. C. W. Mossell took great pains to demonstrate the Haitian leader's personal piety in a form that looked stereotypically Protestant. During his imprisonment in France, Mossell noted, L'Ouverture had been sustained by his great faith, which had taken the form of private devotions and Bible-reading. "Page after page of the open Bible on the table was devoured. It was light in the darkness." Mossell also cited the great piety of another Haitian leader, Christophe, by describing how he readily distributed copies of the Bible among his subjects.[34] The missionary seemed to suggest, then, that despite a nominal allegiance to Roman Catholicism, these leaders nonetheless remained loyal to a "higher" form of spiritual life. Holly made the same point with his assertion that Emperor Faustin, in power in the 1850s, was quite sympathetic to Protestant missionaries; they apparently enjoyed his support and protection to a greater extent than did the Catholic priests.[35]

Despite the reputedly repressive nature of the Catholic Church, most observers concurred that Haiti was a country of remarkable religious toleration. This message was most often geared at potential Protestant settlers, but many writers suggested that it reflected on the character of the country as well. James Redpath, the white agent of the Haytien Bureau of Emigration, assured readers in the first issue of *Pine and the Palm* that they would have liberty to practice their religion and would never be asked to support the Catholic Church. In his *Guide to Hayti,* published in 1861 and distributed widely in the northern states, Redpath elaborated: the Haitian people are "naturally" tolerant, he explained. And the pope, after all, was white; therefore, black Haitians really felt no particular allegiance to him. Holly, too, asserted that the Haitian people were really seeking a "reformed faith" and would look to settlers and missionaries for help.[36]

While these claims can be seen as a somewhat veiled version of the notion that Haitians were actually Protestants in disguise, or at least potential Protestants, C. W. Mossell seemed to veer closer to a form of religious relativism. An A.M.E. missionary in Haiti for nearly a decade, Mossell was a staunch advocate of black Methodism. He, too, elaborated on the toleration accorded to Protestant missionaries. Yet most Haitian people, he suggested, freely mixed Catholicism and Protestantism: they were buried in the same graveyards, they worshipped together, and they appeared "alike impressed with the sacredness of the service." He cautioned that, of course, the "two great religions" were inherently antagonistic; nevertheless, "it may be discovered in the near or remote future 'when the mist is rolled away,' that each contains an element the other cannot supply and that these double forces are necessary to the wellbeing of society and the progress of civilization."[37]

What sounds like religious relativism, or at least an unusual degree of tolerance, once again tells us less about religion in Haiti than it does about African Americans' understandings of their own domestic situation. Mossell concluded his book on this note of comparison, but in his words one can trace not simply generosity toward Catholicism but condemnation of Protestant churches. If one wants to discuss intolerance, he pointed out, one need look no further than the United States, where "wholesale extermination" of Native Americans and oppression of slaves were facts of life. We criticize the notion that Catholics in our own country owe their allegiance to the pope, he charged; yet why do we find such loyalty more alarming than Protestants' lifting above the Constitution "that which it has pleased them to call by the name of Anglo Saxon civilization and White supremacy?"[38] Commentary on Haiti provided a means for critiquing the political and religious context of black life in the United States, and in turn, these interpretations shaped the ways that African Americans understood their place in a society defined by racial and religious allegiances.

Mossell's uncharacteristic vitriol also reveals an important feature of the vantage from which many African-American Protestants spoke about other religions. Because of an emerging consciousness of racial history, a legacy of African unity and pride, black Protestants had another measure by which to judge and evaluate the course of Protestant history. Just as slaves learned quickly to distinguish between "true" Christianity and the Christianity of the master, Protestant leaders discerned that "true" religion could be judged by standards other than those outlined by historical Protestantism. It was not that most of them failed to *believe* the reformed narrative. But they filtered it through a lens of racial awareness and noted the points, such as the history of Haiti, where it intersected with the equally significant tale of black achievement, enslavement, and freedom. Thus, black domestic observers of Islam and Hinduism, as early as the 1840s, could weigh the various triumphs of world religions on another scale. Commenting on the eradication of slavery in other parts of the world, one writer noted that "Mohammedanism [in Turkey and Tunis] has taken one step in advance of our Christianity. But this honor is not confined to the religion of Mahomet. Hindooism, which we are seeking by our missionaries to extirpate, has also become an example to the Christendom of America."[39]

African-American responses to Haiti and its religious practices are perhaps best viewed as historical and ethnographic accounts that enabled black Protestants to articulate and potentially reconcile the conflicts between racial and religious loyalties. Through these stories, African Americans critiqued the shortcomings of a Protestant tradition that had been complicit in their enslavement without forsaking the religious truths that helped define their understandings of the world. On the other hand, the same stories could link them to a glorious racial past and to other dark-skinned peoples in the present but could also explain the awkward sense of foreignness they felt while encountering other African-based cultures.

Implied in some of these stories, particularly those of James Theodore Holly, was also a future referent. Holly claims to have spent much of his early life dreaming of the glories of Haiti. The son of a shoemaker who was reared Roman Catholic, Holly later wrote that he had been interested in the nation ever since his youth in Washington, D.C., when he met Catholic missionaries who had returned from Haiti. Beginning in the early 1850s, the recent convert to the Episcopal Church wrote and spoke more extensively than almost anyone else about the significance of Haiti, a place he did not visit until 1855. Many of his sermons and speeches aimed at helping African Americans understand the links between their racial destiny and their Christian faith. Holly invited blacks to Haiti as an invitation into a grand history, a narrative of which they could become a part and, ultimately, that they could shape. To black Christians, he phrased this as an obligation: "It becomes then an important question for the negro race in America to well consider the weighty responsibility that the present exigency devolves upon them."[40]

Holly's understanding of Haiti's importance encompassed past and future, the Old World as well as the New. As participants in a history that had moved from Ethiopia and Egypt and later to Haiti, African Americans were now called upon to bring true Christianity to the Caribbean republic so that someday it could be brought back to Africa. "The serpentine trail of civilization and Christianity, like the ancient philosophic symbol of eternity, must coil backward to its fountain head," he asserted. Haiti would be the location where racial greatness and Christianity at last would meet and combine. "If Haytien independence shall cease to exist, the sky of negro-destiny shall be hung in impenetrable blackness; the hope of Princes coming out of Egypt and Ethiopia soon stretching forth her hands unto God, will die out."[41]

A GLORIOUS DESTINY

By the end of the nineteenth century, however, African-American promoters of Haiti were acknowledging their lack of progress in realizing their dream. Both the emigration movement of 1824–1825 and that of 1861–1862 had ended in miserable failure, with hundreds of disillusioned migrants returning to the United States and scores more dying of disease in their new homeland. As a result, some African

Americans mounted anti-emigration campaigns and roundly denounced the movement as ill-conceived.[42] Even Holly, who remained a staunch believer in a Christianized Haiti throughout his life, lost his mother, wife, and young child, along with
many members of his pilgrim band of immigrants, within the first year of settlement. Financial support from the A.M.E. and Episcopal Churches, which had increased significantly in the 1870s and 1880s, declined in the ensuing years as interest
in African missions increased. Many promoters expressed the same poignant combination of images of glory and dampened hopes voiced by Solomon Hood of the
A.M.E. Church in 1890: "As for patriots the world has produced no greater than
Toussaint L'Ouverture and Dessalines, and as for rulers, we are not ashamed of the
stern and mighty Christophe, and the wise and diplomatic President Salomon, but
Hayti needs more than this."[43]

Fleeting as it was, the heyday of African-American public interest in Haiti had
significant and quantifiable results. It has been estimated that approximately eight
thousand migrants left for the republic during the 1820s and another two thousand
set off in 1861–1862. These numbers may seem small in contrast to the total population of some 3.5 million blacks in the United States by the time of the Civil War,
but compared to the movement of perhaps ten thousand African Americans to all
of Africa prior to 1861 (most of them sponsored by the ACS), the less well organized
and chronically underfunded Haitian cause was remarkably popular.[44] The messages
disseminated by promoters spoke directly to the needs and desires of free urban,
northern blacks, people with the education and means to act upon a dream of African diasporic religious unity.[45]

But in retrospect, Haiti endured longest, and still endures, as a mirror for
African-American aspirations, a way of knitting various threads of racial destiny and
religious truth in a single, proximate site. The movement to Haiti, be it a movement
of bodies, religious practices and beliefs, or both, promised to bring together in time
and space a story of African-American life. It was a story that gave history, pride,
and community to black Americans in exchange for religious transformation, with
a reciprocity that pledged to make the serpentine trail of African destiny complete.
If African Americans could impart the blessings of Protestantism to their brothers
and sisters in Haiti, then the small Caribbean republic could in turn link blacks in
the United States to a glorious racial destiny.

3 / Revolution at Home and Abroad

Radical Implications of the Protestant Call to Missions, 1825–1870

Mark Y. Hanley

"No greater calamity . . . could befall our churches," Joel Hawes thundered in 1846, "than the suspension or breaking up of our foreign missions. . . . Our poorest churches and the poorest members in them cannot afford to be thus relieved." To abandon the cause, Hawes explained, would siphon the spirit of God from the local churches, leaving them mere "worldly associations" investing in schemes "to mislead, corrupt and destroy." Redoubling his plea, he insisted that it was no "solecism" to claim that domestic spiritual bankruptcy would be the result of churches that could no longer "afford" missions. "The spirit of missions departing from our churches," he concluded, would leave them "dead, fruitless bodies" no longer invigorated by the "Spirit of God."[1]

Hawes staked his position in the 1846 annual sermon delivered to the American Board of Commissioners for Foreign Missions (ABCFM), the formally independent flagship of mainstream Protestant outreach in nineteenth-century America. Following the first collaboration of Congregational enthusiasts at Williams College and Andover Theological Seminary in 1808, the ABCFM received a Massachusetts charter in 1812 and within a decade boasted outposts in British-controlled portions of India and Ceylon, as well as an independent operation in the Sandwich Islands. Substantial Presbyterian support, especially from the New School side after theological squabbling divided that body in 1838, made the ABCFM an anchor of New England orthodoxy. Presbyterians chose an independent course after sealing their breach in 1870.[2]

At the center of the ABCFM's domestic existence were the annual meetings for planning and mutual encouragement held in cities throughout the northern United States. No small part of these gatherings was the annual sermon delivered by an invited minister called to renew the group's collective vision. The homily typically combined general exhortations affirming God's abiding interest in missions with a more meticulous unraveling of a selected theme.[3] Most important, it predicted that Christianity's triumphant march of conquest across the globe would ultimately establish Christ's millennial reign on earth.

There is, perhaps, no better venue for probing the deeper implications of American Protestant triumphalism than the ABCFM keynote sermons. Aggressive, collective self-confidence flowed freely at ABCFM gatherings, reflecting the prevailing postmillennial core of nineteenth-century evangelical mission theology.[4] At the heart of postmillennialism was the "Great Commission," Christ's final command to "preach the gospel to every creature." Evangelicals expected fulfillment of that charge to yield a thousand years of Christ's spiritual reign on earth before the final judgment opened onto eternity. Consequently, foreign missions represented more than an optional appendage to the sedentary nurturing and home mission programs of the United States's domestic churches. ABCFM sermons made the local congregation's spiritual rectitude contingent upon its commitment to the global scope of the Great Commission. This fundamental understanding of Christ's charge and the means of ripening the millennial fruit kept ABCFM ministers fixed upon a triumphalist path.

Modern investigators have found good reason to plant the evangelical clergy's victory garden amid the larger culture's seeding of "manifest destiny" and its accoutrements—territorial expansion, physical progress, and the march of republicanism.[5] ABCFM ministers bowed generously to the U.S. experiment and claimed that such endowments as democratic government, personal freedom, and material abundance anticipated the radical global renovations that lay ahead. Unfortunately, such trumpeting invites dismissal of the annual sermons as little more than formulaic contributions to a national creed. ABCFM ministers fulfilled their cheerleading responsibilities, but the braggadocio and occasional mingling of causes sacred and secular rested upon a far deeper reservoir of discrete spiritual substance hostile to the cultural boosterism flooding secular arenas.[6]

Helpful here is William Hutchison's insightful rendering of missionary motivation. He has underscored the importance of cultural objectives and "America's special agency" while acknowledging their "second class status" in comparison to religious motivations.[7] In terms of historical significance, however, scholars have generally upgraded secondary incentives, particularly because they speak forcefully to modern concerns about national self-righteousness and cultural meddling. Yet historians' recent calls to "take religion seriously" invite a renewed focus on the radical otherness of the evangelical vision. Rather than empowering missionaries as cultural plenipotentiaries or national representatives, the spiritual and millennial edge of ABCFM sermons cut a swath toward *global* revolution. In their most expansive moments, featured ministers erased national distinctions, predicted comprehensive cultural upheaval, and signaled retreat from their own provincialism.

These yearly exhortations rarely detailed mission field progress. Rather, they concentrated on ultimate spiritual and millennial outcomes thoroughly informed by church history and New Testament scripture. They cautioned against an unwitting embrace of secular strategies and aims that could subvert collective devotion to core principles—universal human depravity, the need for individual salvation, and the hope of heaven. This fundamental message granted no indulgences to Western culture and assumed the supremacy of eternal hope over more immediate millennial rewards. It also represented an essential theological bridge between regular domestic preaching and occasional calls to the mission field.[8]

A strategic defense of foreign missions did not replace tactical assaults on cultural maladies.[9] Robert Abzug is surely correct in having observed that evangelical reformers often assigned "transcendent significance" to their wars against slavery, intemperance, and Sabbath-breaking.[10] Yet the doctrinal and millennial principles guiding ABCFM sermons demonstrate the higher integrity of evangelical purposes and reveal an avenue of transcultural confrontation that pointed beyond narrower domestic assaults. Ministers incorporated domestic listeners into a broader human collective and called for a world that operated on radically different terms. Just as the spiritual regeneration of each believer defied definition as "reform," so too the millennial razing of the social and moral status quo would be realized only as individual revolutions of the heart turned the desires of fallen humanity to an eternity beyond the millennial paradise. A decade before his appointment as ABCFM president in 1857, Williams College President Mark Hopkins stated the case plainly: Christians could expect the gospel to "revolutionize and radically transform society" only as they resisted a worldly dependence on "[removing] directly specific forms of evil" and nurtured a "simple desire to preach Christ and him crucified, and to save men."[11]

From the 1820s to the leading edge of the Gilded Age, the ABCFM's militant language of conquest provided more an alternative than alter ego to the culture's lexicon of national advancement and material progress. Five essential features of this distinctive triumphalist course deserve particular consideration: the elevation of the church as the agent of individual and collective renovation; universal human equality as the governing social principle of Christ's kingdom; physical improvements and an equitable distribution of resources driven by Christian benevolence; a plan of conquest that rejected war, militarism, and nationalism; and, finally, a conception of foreign missions that underscored U.S. Protestant obligation even as it predicted radical *domestic* transformation and assimilation into a larger Christian whole. The anticipated millennium bore the revolutionary promise of racial justice; an end to the abuse of wealth and political power; and a social order in which national, class, and cultural distinctions would be irrelevant. This foundational message set domestic Christianity and the foreign mission field upon a common course. The church is "essentially a missionary organization," New York Presbyterian minister Henry Smith told the ABCFM in 1862, and "the true missionary spirit is the measure of her Christian principle."[12]

THE CHURCH'S PECULIAR MISSION

In assigning evangelistic responsibilities and identifying the earthly agencies of gospel triumph, the annual sermons drilled one theme with rhythmic clarity: Christ appointed the church, not the United States, as the agent of global transformation.[13] Without reference to national identities or covenants, the Great Commission assigned responsibility to a "peculiar people" united by faith. Ministers addressing an "American" missionary board, of course, had ample incentive to cull examples of national advantages. But they explained that the Great Commission fell inescapably upon a worldwide body of believers unified by a common spiritual understanding. Great Commission theology, in other words, melded easily with church responsibility. Reconciling its spiritual logic with exceptional national status required a more substantial overhaul.

Archibald Alexander told the Board in 1829 that the Great Commission necessarily obliterated "all national distinction between Jews and gentiles" and obligated modern missionaries to embrace the corollary: the church expanding in tandem with the number of believers could be neither identified with political entities nor shaped by political priorities. In rebuking British political leaders who linked missionary activity with popular unrest in the empire, he insisted that "principles merely political" ought to have "no weight with Christians." Not that Alexander was incapable of pragmatic maneuvering under fire. It was a "notorious fact," he admitted, that India's population was, if anything, rendered more "tranquil and submissive" by the missionary enterprise.[14]

Alexander's combined defense of a church mission with reassurances to commercial and political antagonists reveals the hazardous cultural terrain that ABCFM ministers were obliged to negotiate. In 1836, for example, Massachusetts pastor John Codman parlayed popular conceits into a charge against domestic chauvinism and complacency. U.S. believers might count their freedom and material prosperity "vastly superior to [those of] any other Christian nation," he conceded, but that fact obligated U.S. Christians to use those "advantages for the propagation of the gospel." To champion missions as an agent of the "country's free institutions" or as "balm" for the "woes of suffering humanity" merely allowed "selfish principle" to prevail.[15] Leonard Bacon told the 1852 gathering that U.S. churches existed as "human arrangement[s]," specifically lacking in universal legitimacy. The church that ultimately mattered had "no parochial or national boundaries [and was] defined by no human regulations or arrangements." Only by placing missions in this context could U.S. believers make claims for a church "universal and immortal." Believers labor rightly, he said, for "the extension of the church considered as the universal commonwealth of the redeemed," and "not in any narrow, local, national, or sectarian sense."[16]

Such pleas still left ministers free to celebrate U.S. opportunity. Early ABCFM sermons, echoing the optimism of the Second Great Awakening, honed this theme with particular zeal. John Rice of Richmond's Union Theological Seminary, for example, insisted that U.S. believers' "peculiarly favorable situation" required also that they make the United States a "blessing among the nations of the earth." While "our opportunities are peculiarly favorable, so our obligations are peculiarly weighty." Yet even this focused challenge heaped the burden upon U.S. *churches,* not the nation, and extolled Christian effort as a global crusade. There could be no alliance with "*force,*" "*authority,*" or other "*carnal weapons,*" he maintained. Missions depended on "*the simple gospel of Christ.*" National revival might enable the churches of the United States to beam a "warmer piety" to the rest of the globe, but it conferred no spiritual sovereignty over the cause. They must fulfill their obligation, Rice cautioned, out of deference to the "universal church of Christ" and the "whole body of the faithful." While nations premised their actions upon "dignity" and "indulgence," the Christian community must recognize that "God made of one blood all nations of men" and must rely upon "humility" and "self-denial."[17] In the millennium beyond missions, there would be no flagship nation.

ABCFM ministers also identified the church's peculiar mission with the New Testament call for a "city upon a hill." Preaching in 1857, M. L. P. Thompson called the New Testament phrase a textbook definition of the church. Presbyterian Joseph Thompson used the same text a decade later to remind listeners that the church's organic unity remained distinct from national or political connections.[18] Domestic hubris could also infect local ministries. As the nation entered a second year of sectional conflict in 1862, New York Presbyterian pastor Henry Smith told his northern audience to calm their patriotic enthusiasm long enough to dismantle "the iron gates of national and ecclesiastical bigotry" that would destroy the church's mission. Even an undue "love of the local church" led to the same destructive ends. It was the missionary's commitment to Christ's "love for universal man" that pronounced the nation an unsuitable vessel for the gospel message. Christianity, he concluded, "puts itself in contrast with the *love of country.*" Smith reassured his audience that he bore no mandate to renounce patriotism or the northern cause. Rather, he sought to preserve a hierarchy of sacred and secular purposes.[19]

While the millennium eluded nineteenth-century evangelicals, their Great Commission theology in some ways anticipated demographic transformations that have obliged twentieth-century believers to reevaluate their global position. As Andrew F.

Walls has recently observed, the adaptive, diffusive nature of Christianity continues to erode older conceptions of "Christian states," leaving a world where "no longer does the word *Christianity* have a territorial connotation."[20]

SPIRITUAL FOUNDATIONS OF UNITY

Defending the church's special obligation and proscribing nationalistic bombast helped blur the distinctions between foreign and domestic outreach and made missions a standing measure of the local church's integrity. This strategy also gave form to a radical millennial design, but rather than launching ABCFM ministers on a spiritual trek from reality, sketching the earthly foreshadowings of final, heavenly victory provided opportunity for serious consideration of cultural inequalities and human suffering. While spiritual change marked the road to renovation, the promised radical transformations shattered the boundaries of patchwork reforms limited by domestic cultural compromise. As a revolution deemed attainable in real time, the ABCFM's millennial speculations represent one of the most forceful and frank agendas for cultural transformation that the nineteenth century produced. The millennium would be "the meridian of its day, not another day," Samuel Hanson Cox, pastor of First Presbyterian Church in Brooklyn, told the ABCFM in 1849, to be superseded only by "eternity and glory in heaven."[21] The details of this evangelical hope deserve closer scrutiny.

First, ABCFM sermons set a standard of human equality that must have given pause to thoughtful listeners culturally conditioned to the language of racism, slavery, and class distinctions. Nathan Beman told the ABCFM in 1840 that God's U.S. contingent must place their domestic hopes within the context of a global population almost "infinitely diversified." The gospel, however, confronted humanity as a single race, "notwithstanding their national peculiarities."[22] The missionary's charge was to "root out, all suffering from the kingdom of Christ," relying on the gospel's "general" capacity to unite all humanity, rather than on "particular" interests "restricted to one country or one age." Even the promises of specific domestic reform movements ultimately foundered on their local character. Only the gospel, as a seamless wrap around domestic and foreign outreach, could reveal Christ's message as giving "no respect to age, station, learning, country, kindred, sex, family, or profession in life." It addressed no "specific class or order of men, but *man* in the large and generic sense," ultimately revealing the "common wants" and "common circumstances" that united global humanity.[23]

New York pastor Isaac Ferris insisted that the missionary cause attested to the "common interest, common duties, common aims" that drove the movement. God simply made "no distinctions" and "[marked] no differences" in the message of salvation to humankind.[24] A year later, Cox told the ABCFM that in the new millennial future, Christians should expect to "feel an interest in the weal of every other member of the species." "Slavery [will] be no more," while skin color will no longer create privileged status. The millennium will transform nations into "commonwealth[s] of Christians," Cox declared, void of "ambition, usurpation, envy, or military coercion." In the world to come, "CHRISTIAN will be all, the brotherhood of human nature will be restored."[25]

New York minister William Adams added even stronger appeals, chiding domestic believers for their parochial smugness and urging them to see the Christian as the only "true Cosmopolite." Whatever the pretensions or purposes of U.S. congregations, he warned, all of their claims to local legitimacy—indeed, their own hopes for salvation—rested on the principle that Christianity applies "equally to all mankind." It addresses human beings "simply as men."[26] Such "citizens of the world" must acknowledge "no national distinction and no territorial boundaries. The nations are many; but the world is one. . . . It is the race of man, the whole race, that have felt the direful visitations of sin. . . . Question this universality in the gospel's own structure and adaptation, and you quench the hopes which brighten your own path; since you are but one of a common race."[27]

Chicago Presbyterian pastor Robert Patterson powerfully seconded this message of unity on the eve of the Civil War. While the ABCFM had historically avoided direct engagement with the slavery issue, Patterson fashioned arguments that not only continued standard spiritual themes but also challenged the racial hierarchies of proslavery apologists. The true element of Christian power, he reasoned, could be developed only by dismantling the cultural and racial barriers that created false distinctions. "The Gospel clothes this doctrine of our *race-unity* with a divine energy," Patterson explained. Believers who "caviled at [the doctrine] of human unity and equality" failed to see that it lay at "the centre of our religion."

Patterson no doubt jolted southern sensibilities with his insistence that "there is no distinction between the Caucasian, the Tartar, the Malay, the Negro, and the Indian. . . . *Every man* is a brother in one great family." His claim that all believers shared a "common brotherhood with all the race of sinners," and a concomitant obligation to fulfill the Great Commission, effectively indicted slavery as an intolerable hindrance to that essential unity and a key domestic obstruction to the church's primary mission. Patterson's plea for foreign missions, in other words, could easily be enlisted in an assault on domestic slavery.[28] Likewise, a mission premised upon human equality and universal brotherhood placed U.S. cultural complicity with racism and slavery in sharp relief.

LIMITATIONS OF SECULAR STRIVING

While ABCFM ministers often riveted audiences by describing the radical physical improvements that would mark Christ's earthly kingdom, they also counseled caution in assigning millennial significance to the West's expanding infrastructure and commercial and industrial growth. Granting spiritual agency to earthly ambitions, however, was certainly not troubling to all. Charles White, president of Wabash College in Indiana, said in 1854 that the material trophies of Western progress could serve as coadjutors for the gospel as long as they were "divinely directed." After comparing a donation to missions to an investment in commerce, scientific development, education, and "universal intelligence," he registered his ultimate claim: "Actually and truly, Great Britain and the United States are to be reproduced, intellectually upon all pagan countries! To have done this, is glory enough!"[29] White exercised some restraint, declaring that human achievements not restrained by faith could produce only "insolent selfishness, monstrous recklessness of human rights, gaunt rapacity, and grinding oppression."

Nevertheless, the ABCFM's Prudential Committee powerfully branded such stridency a spiritual misfire, attesting to a broader ABCFM interest in restraining cultural conceits.[30] Other ministers thus urged expediency in negotiating the spiritual limitations of the secular community. Edward Kirk, for example, claimed that as native contact with missionaries "[created] new ideas, aspirations, and tastes in the savage," the consequent "demands for our merchandise" would confirm "the beneficial workings and reaction of Christian missions." He also defined the audience and purpose for such claims. For "men of the world, walking by sight," he explained, such ancillary benefits fell within the "range of their vision" and could, at the very least, assuage hostility reminiscent of France's Revolutionary struggle.[31] Kirk and his compatriots predictably placed material progress under providential design and control, but their spiritual and millennial commitments usually trumped largess toward the culture.

Others went further. After rejecting the notion that "civilization" must precede "Christianization," Thomas De Witt emphasized that "commerce and science" could never bring light to the "darkness and sin" that engulfed the unsaved soul. Even in "our own favored country," he warned, "the prejudices, interest, and policy of the world rise in opposition." Dewitt placed his hopes not on the nation but on spiritual renewal "appearing in the church."[32] George Bethune's 1856 sermon caricatured the "foolish babbling" of Christians who would abandon the "simple gospel" and align with "the progressive spirits of this steam-driven and electric age."[33] William Adams shared the confidence of Bethune and others who predicted that the "wrath of man" would finally be turned to divine purpose. "All the appliances of modern invention and enterprise," Adams observed, would cease to be the "heralds of mere political and mercantile tidings" and would find their "true dignity and use in diffusing the truth of God."[34] Just as they redefined human equality in millennial terms, ABCFM ministers explained that material progress could neither explain nor sustain the spiritual revolution they expected.

Adams's primary objective, for example, charted a far more visionary course. He affirmed not only God's providential interest in turning the material world toward divine ends but also an economic future that would virtually destroy the controlling influence of the commercial world. Present conditions, he explained, made it too easy for Christian love to become little more than a "frozen compound of obligation and self-interest." Property interests and the marketplace often made benevolence little more than a perfunctory act of "conscience" and "duty." Citizens of the new millennial order, however, would offer freely what is now "extorted reluctantly." "Commerce, and art, and enterprise" would be filtered through the "channels of justice, love and mercy."[35] The missionary enterprise, in other words, might exploit the avenues of commerce, but it would also neutralize the selfish economic forces that had created them.

In the ABCFM's 1832 sermon, William Allen placed similar predictions alongside an equally forceful critique of modern economic dislocations. He rejected placing the hopes of "enslaved humanity" on the promises of "political economy." The plight of Britain's displaced factory and handloom workers, he pointed out, only confirmed that humanity's "history of crime and misery" continued unabated. Hopes of perfection outside faith glistened only as "webs of gossamer." While Britain boasted of its "political economy," he concluded, "let the ten thousands of [its] degraded and starving population . . . who have been poured upon our shores . . . bear witness." The world to come, however, would cast aside the self-interest that fired worldly political and economic ambitions and expose the futility of secular striving. Allen shattered the chimera of linking missions to cultural outreach, arguing instead that domestic obligations rested on "the bonds of our common nature."[36]

Protestant ministers routinely dismissed socialist reformers as misguided materialists, but ironically, ABCFM sermons often elevated cooperation over competition and, indirectly at least, anticipated a revolutionary framework for material exchange well beyond the culturally respectable boundaries of enlightened self-interest.

SPIRITUAL WARFARE

Heralds of both missionary outreach and the nation's commercial and geographic expansion in the mid–nineteenth century warmed to the lexicon of war and conquest.[37] ABCFM ministers, however, resisted entangling rhetorical alliances. They challenged both domestic Christian complacency and prevailing national militancies, conscripting the language of territorial conquest and militarism in the service of church supremacy, equality before God, and humankind's common stake in the gospel. Even as ministers confirmed their republican credentials, their primary message was clear: the people of the United States, just as certainly as the populations on any foreign shore, must brace for extraordinary change.

William McMurray's 1833 sermon illustrates the strategy. He called for a Christian "army" adequate to subdue the "hostile force" opposed to the gospel. The greatest threats stood upon "the territory of nominal Christendom," subtly blending faith with the "inventions of men" and eschewing "open and declared hostility." Roman Catholicism, corrupted Protestantism, and modern infidelity that "exalts the human understanding against the revelation of God" all fit this category. Yet the heart's "*natural, total depravity*" remained the greatest "strong-hold" uniting all opposition. McMurray confidently predicted that even such formidable opposition would ultimately "crumble into ruins under the weapons of the church's warfare," with the missionary movement at the vanguard of a "mighty conquest."[38]

McMurray's plan for "subduing" the world extended his military metaphor to a fuller consideration of means and ends, further limiting opportunities for listeners seeking easy endorsements of secular power. No "carnal" weapons, "military conquests," or "force of human reason" could accomplish the task. Civil governments, "even in their greatest perfection," could achieve only a superficial submission to religion and leave the church "degraded." The millennium, after all, would render government structures largely irrelevant since the universal sovereignty of God would establish a common standard of justice and mercy and become the basis of social peace. The church, focused on the "preaching of Christ," was the only effectual means of conquest. McMurray did exhort listeners to exploit the Protestant heritage and material advantages of "our highly favored country," holding up medieval Roman Catholicism as the antithesis of the world order he expected. Yet rather than elevating U.S. republicanism as the holy alternative, he turned a critical eye homeward, identifying the nation's political system with other "corrupt" institutions, salvageable only as it conformed to higher spiritual principles.[39]

McMurray's denouement gave no broad license to U.S. cultural exports. Rulers in the new millennial order would be guided by principles of "justice, equity, and love." The gospel would reign not because of the "craft or ambition of its professors," seeking to "seize upon, or to guide, the reins of government." Instead, leaders would act from an understanding of their roles as "benefactors, and not the oppressors, of their race." Nations would reject "war and bloodshed, and [substitute] a peaceful policy for the lust of conquest and the glory of military achievement." Most important, McMurray announced, the task was "*no visionary enterprise.*" Christian hopes would be realized in an earthly millennium, and "success [was] certain." By calling for a radical, comprehensive reorganization of human relations in real time, he denied his listeners domestic immunity.[40]

A decade later, New York Presbyterian minister Thomas Skinner called for the "universal empire" of Christ, but he deliberately separated his "imperial" design from "worldly policy and martial power, under the cloak of religion, aiming chiefly at temporal aggrandizement and nominal submission." Since collective selfishness drove worldly policy, he charged, U.S. Christians must either erase artificial distinctions between foreign and domestic outreach or stand guilty of perverting the gospel's message of universal human equality. Lavishing material indulgences on local churches while 80 percent of the world remained ignorant of the gospel "tramples upon the great foundation law of God's empire." Tolerating a cloistered spirituality, Skinner thundered, pressed upon U.S. believers "a guilt which should fill the church with the profoundest grief."[41]

Like McMurray, Skinner conceded that "America, in its prospective greatness and power, rises in our thought above all the rest of the globe," but he purposefully steered listeners toward a church-centered outlook rather than national hubris. U.S. churches may or may not be granted a leading role in the conversion of the world, he concluded, but one thing remained certain: if they identified their cause with "selfish nationality, or pride, or carnal reasoning," they would also obstruct "the plans and counsels of Infinite Love."[42]

Board sermons also called the churches to reject worldly conceptions of power and authority. "We talk of power," David Riddle mused in 1851, "physical or mechanical power, intellectual power, the power of money, of numbers, of nations." But questers after such seeming advantages could only hope to attract "the astonishment and admiration of worms like themselves." "God's Israel" is the church, he explained, and "*through the church*" God will bring global transformation.[43]

George Bethune called upon ABCFM missionaries to allow the "gentle benign character of Christians" to overwhelm the false promises of "worldly force." Only the "transforming power" of the gospel message could elevate "mercy" as the ultimate expression of Christian power and demolish the "fierceness and bitterness and severity" that marked the fanatic. Bethune established a direct correlation between successful foreign missions and the domestic church's humility and sense of its own limitations. True Christian power, he insisted, was inversely proportional to the level of human pride in the church.[44]

New York pastor Richard Storrs, addressing the ABCFM just months after Fort Sumter's surrender to insurgent southerners, certainly had ample cultural encouragements to anoint northern patriotism. Instead, he placed the war in broad historical context and promised ultimate victory through the "things which are not," that is, those spiritual tools largely ignored by worldly strategists but ultimately destined to subject "the forces which are already at work in the world" to divine purpose. Not surprisingly, he predicted northern victory and placed the outbreak of war securely within the framework of God's providential designs. Surging patriotism and northern resolve would help destroy the nation's "unnatural alliance" with slavery. Instead of being a "bulwark of bondage, [shutting] the book of God to a race," he thundered, the nation would now become a legitimate emblem of human freedom.[45]

While Abraham Lincoln remained focused on preserving the Union, Storrs confidently predicted that "slavery is going down." Conquering armies moving south in a crusade of liberation did not figure into his revolutionary scheme. Instead, he recalled early abolitionist voices of moral outrage that "started in so much feeble-ness" and ultimately commanded the nation's attention. This "radical righteousness" of the gospel now stood poised to complete the revolution against slavery. In utter contradiction to the world's conception of power, and in the manner of ancient Christian struggles against Roman despotism, God would use that "which mankind had despised" and make "weakness, as used by Omnipotence," the stuff of victory. Storrs rejected the material schemes of nations and called repeatedly for revolution "in the souls of believers,—rushing with fleet though silent contagion from heart to heart."[46]

Storrs, like other ABCFM ministers, worked from his own cultural framework even as he anticipated radical transcendence. He factored southern defeat, as well as purified commerce, republicanism, and education, into his millennial scheme. But cultural affirmations reveal the lesser part of Storrs's hopes. Listeners who considered the full implications of his message found anything but a simple plea for Union victory and domestic social reconstruction. To achieve the gospel's ultimate goal—"Universal Freedom"—required far more than the abolition of domestic slavery. Storrs recounted the stillborn material schemes of nations from Rome to the U.S. Republic in order to focus on the "unseen and impalpable" spiritual forces that would conform all human striving to providential design and bring "great revolu-tions" on a scale far exceeding the parochial expectations of nations.[47] God's "reduc-tion of the world to allegiance to his Son" would mark the final triumph of "things feeble and obscure."

Even as Storrs burnished his patriotism and cheered the Union, his spiritual and millennial focus reduced conventional victory markers to relative insignificance. Doubtless, few of his listeners pondered fully the implications of a millennial future that made domestic cultural upheaval an inevitable corollary to successful mission-ary outreach. ABCFM sermons, however, gave ministers a unique opportunity to combine foreign and domestic outreach in a revolutionary cause that pointed be-yond cultural restraints. The world they imagined included social equality, economic justice, and, as Storrs put it, an end to "'The Things That Were,'—so ancient, proud and full of might."[48]

PASSION FOR LOST SOULS

When New School and Old School Presbyterians reunited in 1870, they also ended decades of cooperation with Congregationalists on the ABCFM.[49] During their final years of cooperation, ABCFM sermons focused intensively on missionary outreach as both the maker and measure of the domestic churches' *spiritual* power. They also sustained one of the ABCFM's historic guiding principles: radical millennial transformations represented the temporal rewards of missionary work, not the motivating principle behind it. For all their promises of a better world to come, ministers remained essentially committed to converting individual souls and affirming the heavenly destiny of all believers. Holding humanity to a common spiritual standard validated the church's domestic mission even as it required believers to transcend their own parochialism. In a decade marked by the unprecedented clash of modern material forces on the battlefield, these sermons reset the salvific mainspring of the Great Commission.

A few weeks prior to Lincoln's recommitment of the nation at Gettysburg in 1863, Connecticut pastor Elisha Cleaveland called ABCFM members to a similar task. Taking his cue from Luke's gospel, Cleaveland held missionaries to the singular purpose of "[proclaiming] repentance and remission of sins" as the only way to "[give] reality to things unseen and eternal." "Higher than these we cannot rise— beyond them we never can pass," he explained. Cleaveland took God's providential control in wartime for granted. He also separated sectional ambitions from Christian purposes, calling believers to erase distinctions between the global missionary enterprise and domestic Christianity. "Love for the perishing souls of men" led not to a peculiar regional or national mandate but to a universal obligation that assumed the irrelevance of place. This theme of collective duty also placed spiritual community above the pragmatic claims of earthly combinations. Cleaveland called it a "great evil, to regard the spirit of missions as a peculiar kind of Christianity."[50]

Like Cleaveland, Auburn Theological Seminary professor Jonathan Condit lobbied for revival of the "*essential elements of a spiritual, living church*" and a requisite reinvigoration of the "inner life." Christ's sanction of "human instrumentality" in expanding the kingdom carried no endorsement of "human policy" designed to protect theological distinctiveness or "issue edicts against error and sin."[51] Condit granted that God would turn human schemes to providential designs, but he also unhitched his global spiritual vision from the car of war in order to reaffirm a dominant ABCFM theme: the life of the domestic church and the vitality of the missionary enterprise must be sustained by faith's transformative power, not by the reformer's particular crusades. The church as a global extension of U.S. values became all but nonsensical in Condit's vision of a "redeemed multitude" drawn from "all nations, and kindreds, and people and tongues." While humanity's common guilt before God dimmed the narrow beacons of racial, national, or cultural pride, faith lit a brighter path toward "mercy for our lost race." Only this "primary impelling force" could radically alter human relations and lead to a "universal empire" stripped of oppression, greed, and want.[52] Condit issued clear warning to the kingdom's U.S. contingent: those expecting a millennium of U.S. Christianity and republicanism writ large had best prepare for a far more comprehensive revolution.

Lauren Hickok, president of Union College in Schenectady, New York, pressed the revolutionary call to the next level in 1866. Missionary efforts, he warned, must either fix upon the gospel's highest, heavenly character or be fatally diverted to worldly aims. To restore the "Christian idea in all its completeness," Hickok prescribed a radical spiritual reorientation for domestic Christians, one that made missionary outreach essential to sustaining a right hierarchy of Christian purpose. To yearn for the worldly renovations of a millennial future or even to ground missions in the hope of rescuing souls from the misery of hell significantly distorted the Christian cause. Missions must testify to a deeper consciousness of God's divine majesty, Hickok explained. If "preaching the Gospel to every creature" represented the peculiar purpose of all believers, then that work must be prosecuted "*to the glory of God the Father.*" Hickok echoed Jonathan Edwards's insistence that human benevolence attained a truly godly character only as it grew from total obedience to the divine will and not from mere human compassion. Christians labor too much, Hickok explained, out of "considerations of human kindness only."[53] He recited his version of the false catechism: "The prominent evil is human misery. . . . The grand consummation of Christian effort is human relief from human woe. Charity and prayer, the church and the Bible, are for man's happiness only. . . . Humanity is thus put as the ultimate end and measure, and even God and heaven come to be estimated for man's sake. If man may be relieved from suffering in this world and the next, the Christian's prayer is answered and his religion is satisfied."[54]

For Hickok, this adulterated missionary vision compared to the stillborn hopes of secular reformers. Millennial splendors, in other words, had to be subordinated to a restored understanding of divine sovereignty. Human redemption and the coming millennium must not be viewed as the primary goals of Christian effort and obedience. Rather, they must be seen as means to the restoration of "God in his authority and majesty, God in his holiness and purity, so bright that all else pales and fades beneath it."[55]

In narrowing the purpose of outreach, Hickok demanded not simply a changed perspective toward missions but a revolutionary spiritual reorientation of U.S. believers. Standing at the threshold of the Social Gospel movement and in the wake of northern victory, his approach may seem oddly out of place. Yet it betrays a spiritual optimism born of radical disillusionment with human schemes and a desire to check human pride. Hickok hoped a revitalized focus on the majesty of God would temper humanity's natural inclination toward materialism and self-promotion.

GLOBAL SPIRITUAL REVOLUTION

In the middle years of the nineteenth century, ABCFM sermons upheld individual salvation as the foundation of foreign and domestic outreach. The millennium, never an end in itself, would be God's divine blessing of a missionary enterprise ultimately fixed upon higher aims. Believers who limited their hopes to an earthly paradise remained shackled to selfish hopes for material comfort and personal peace. Nevertheless, as ABCFM ministers combined millennial speculations with the defense of foreign missions, they gave Protestant triumphalism a radical turn, one that challenged both the premises of emergent liberal culture and the individualism and parochialism that clouded the domestic church's vision. More than a simplistic celebration of millennial optimism, these sermons targeted the complacent and the culturally contented.

ABCFM sermons, it must also be emphasized, showcased foundational ideas, not realities in the mission field. They provided the means for measuring the distance between principle and practice. Evangelicals of all stripes furnished champions of cultural exclusivity, exceptionalism, and intolerance. ABCFM ministers to a man remained patriots and patrons of U.S. culture. Likewise, beyond the confines of religiously homogeneous and sympathetic audiences, Protestant leaders often retreated to a less threatening position that emphasized reform over spiritual revolution. But Great Commission theology, centered on the basic doctrines of individual sin, salvation, and divine judgment, provided the singular dynamic of ABCFM sermons and enabled ministers to cut forcefully against the cultural grain.

If, as Gordon Wood has suggested, the supplanting of classical republicanism with cultural liberalism depleted the nation's ideological resources for self-criticism, these keynote appeals show how mainstream Protestants preserved an alternative spiritual route to resistance.[56] That doctrinal resources provided a powerful if not always successful defense against complacency and conceit is not surprising. As Christopher Lasch has recently pointed out, self-satisfaction and easy cultural endorsements are not the standard issue of religious communities that retain a vital theological core: "Instead of discouraging moral inquiry, religious prompting can just as easily stimulate it by calling attention to the disjunction between verbal profession and practice . . . and by encouraging believers at every step to question their own motives. It judges those who profess the faith more harshly than it judges unbelievers. . . . For those who take religion seriously, belief is a burden, not a self-righteous claim to some privileged moral status. Self-righteousness, indeed, may well be more prevalent among skeptics than among believers. The spiritual discipline against self-righteousness is the very essence of religion."[57]

ABCFM ministers laid before U.S. churches a millennial blueprint that dissolved established boundaries regarding human equality, race, national status, and economic relations. Their paeans to U.S. advantage were always sincere and occasionally extreme, but doctrinal commitments compelled them to acknowledge a relationship between domestic faith and foreign missions that obligated Christians to embrace a far more radical transformation. Doctrinal principles, not cultural considerations, formed the vital center of this crusade. Universal human corruption and the renovative potential of individual salvation necessarily swept *all* peoples into a common revolutionary tide. ABCFM ministers rejected neat distinctions between domestic and foreign outreach. They often waxed macabre in describing the "darkness" of "heathen" cultures, but they also freely canvassed the inanities of their own.

4 / From the Native Ministry to the Talented Tenth

The Foreign Missionary Origins of White Support for Black Colleges

Jay Riley Case

In May 1867, a white minister from Connecticut named Edward Lathrop traveled to the First Baptist Church of Chicago to meet with 615 other delegates of the American Baptist Missionary Union (ABMU), the foreign missionary agency for northern Baptists. The subject of educating indigenous Christian leaders overseas engrossed the annual meeting. Lathrop's Committee on Missions in India reported that missionary work would be strengthened if the "native preachers" could be given an education that ensured "wise and energetic supervision" of the young churches. In response to a request from five Karen pastors in Burma for more missionaries to teach theology, the executive committee proudly noted that Dr. James Binney would soon leave the United States to revive the theological school that he had established several years earlier. Another report contained statements from missionaries in Burma urging more financial support for the Normal School in Rangoon as a means to prepare the indigenous men and women as "preachers, school-teachers, book-makers, translators, &c., &c." It also proposed the establishment of a female boarding school in Maulmain, believing it would "exert a direct and powerful influence in favor of Christian civilization in Burmah [*sic*]." In response to this report, a special committee approved the requests of the missionaries, noting that "Christianity cannot be expected to remain pure and permanent among an unlettered and ignorant people." Schools must "follow close on the heels of the church," and education in the wake of faith.[1]

Immediately after the ABMU adjourned these meetings, the American Baptist Home Missionary Society (ABHMS) convened its own annual meeting in the same building. As a longtime executive board member of the ABHMS, Lathrop naturally stayed to participate. Among the news from various ABHMS activities Lathrop listened to was the report on the "Education of Colored Preachers." The theological school in Richmond, Virginia, had failed, but its failure had at least freed its principal, James Binney, to return to Burma to train a "native ministry." Nevertheless, the ABHMS vowed to continue administering its existing schools in thirteen southern cities, since "intelligent pastors and evangelists are the great need of these colored churches." Later, Lathrop listened as the education committee commended the society for its efforts in providing education to freedpeople, a matter "vital to the interests of pure Christianity" and "efficient preaching of the gospel." While the ABHMS willingly turned its primary schools over to the American Freedman's Union Commission, the education committee resolved to expand its program of educating black ministers. As the head of a school for ministers in New Orleans declared, blacks everywhere had separated from white churches and yearned for an educated ministry. "They desire to have pastors of their own race. But these pastors are not competent to render efficient service without training." Who were prepared to undertake this task, he asked, other than northern Baptists?[2]

If Lathrop, as he returned by train to Connecticut that spring of 1867, had been asked by a fellow passenger to explain the philosophy behind the northern Baptist missionary work among freedpeople, he undoubtedly would have used language very similar to that used to describe foreign missionary work. Tied in close relationship to the foreign mission agency, the home missionary leaders who established colleges in the South after the Civil War appropriated a concept of indigenous leadership from the foreign-missionary movement in their attempts to assist newly emancipated blacks, commonly referred to as the "native ministry." This foreign-missionary model made educated indigenous preachers and teachers the key to the effective evangelism, moral leadership, and social development of a given people.[3] This missionary model, which evolved into the concept of the Talented Tenth by the 1890s, made possible white evangelical support for black liberal-arts colleges like Spelman and Morehouse.

Despite producing a rich literature on African-American education, historians have not adequately situated black colleges within the religious dynamics of evangelicalism. Yet the formation of black colleges cannot be fully understood apart from the particular features of the foreign missionary movement because white Baptist leaders grounded their educational efforts for blacks in the sacred cause of missions. Never a static or systematic theory, the missionary model of the "native ministry" shifted around concepts of evangelism, autonomy, female education, moral authority, ethnicity, and social uplift. Those shifting terms infused the model with increasingly assimilationist and elitist tendencies as the nineteenth century came to a close. At the same time, however, the model provided the basis for persistent support for black liberal-arts education by white northern Baptists. This support persisted despite pressure to abandon black liberal-arts education for industrial education, a system popular among northern whites who believed blacks ought to be trained for manual labor.

THE FOREIGN MISSIONARY CONTEXT

The roots of the native ministry concept reached back to William Carey and the first English Baptist missionaries in India at the beginning of the nineteenth century. In his decade-long search for an effective mode of evangelism, Carey argued that missionaries needed to cultivate the gifts of indigenous converts since they understood the vernacular and indigenous customs better than the missionaries. By 1805, Carey's agency sought to develop "native preachers" to evangelize India and founded Serampore College in 1818 to train Indian Christians as missionaries.[4] When Baptists in the United States launched their own foreign missionary society in 1814, they drew upon the examples set by English Baptists, from whom they had been receiving reports. Despite a paucity of converts, the first generation of American Baptist missionaries regularly expressed the hope that indigenous Christians would actively evangelize and teach their own people. The annual report of 1835 envisioned a bright future of Burmese evangelism that rested almost exclusively on the shoulders of indigenous Christians. Burmese Christians would produce literature reflecting "the varied and flickering habits and fashions that distinguish each people from their neighbors." Skilled translations would flow from the pens of indigenous Christians steeped in the vernacular, while Burmese preachers and evangelists, trained by Burmese teachers, would spread across the land.[5]

The concept of indigenous evangelization received a further boost with the rapid extension of Christianity among the Karen in Burma. Two decades of effort had produced only a handful of converts among the largely Buddhist Burmese, but hundreds of the preliterate and animist Karen people began to convert to Christianity in the late 1830s. "Native assistants" or "native preachers" carried out the most effective evangelism. In fact, a legal prohibition of any U.S. presence in southern Burma from 1838 to 1852 forced Baptist missionaries to rely more heavily than ever upon the work of indigenous evangelists. The zeal of the Karen preachers who penetrated remote villages reinforced American Baptist confidence in the vital role of the native ministry. "Our main reliance here, as in every highly successful mission, must be upon the native evangelists and pastors God shall raise up and endow," the ABMU Board declared in 1845.[6]

The decentralized nature of the Karen evangelistic movement compelled missionaries to grant more indigenous autonomy than their rhetoric allowed. Fearing that his presence in southern Burma would bring persecution upon Karen Christians, Elisha Abbott established his station in the neighboring British-controlled territory of Arracan in 1840. For the next twelve years, Karen preachers evangelized, organized congregations, and administered Karen churches apart from Abbott's direct supervision, though they periodically crossed the border to receive instruction. Then the native assistants reported that six hundred to one thousand new converts in southern Burma had not been baptized. Although Abbott had baptized more than four hundred Karens who had traveled to Arracan, he realized that most converts could not make the trip. Impressed with the piety, dedication, and evangelistic abilities of the native assistants, troubled by the presence of hundreds of unbaptized converts in southern Burma, and confronted with the reality that Karen evangelists already functioned as pastors in every respect except the administration of the ordinances, Abbott decided to begin ordaining Karen preachers. "If God has called these men to *preach* the gospel, has He not also called them to administer its ordinances?" he asked the Board.[7]

Abbott's ordination of two Karen preachers in 1844 paved the way for further ordinations.[8] It also marked the beginning of systematic efforts to establish theological education for the newly ordained pastors. Before the 1840s, evangelism had so dominated American Baptist missionary efforts that education had been relegated to the role of a helpful but auxiliary function. With the surge in Karen conversions, however, the number of indigenous assistants and converts began to outstrip the educational resources of the U.S. missionaries.[9] One missionary reported that a very successful Karen evangelist, who had been baptized a decade earlier, had recently asked, "Paul, Paul, who was Paul? Was he a Christian?"[10] Troubled by a new vision of poorly educated Karen pastors leading illiterate congregations, the ABMU began to make systematic efforts to establish theological education in Burma. In 1843, it formed a Committee on the Education of Native Teachers and Preachers and decided that for Christianity in Burma to maintain any sort of permanence, missionaries must cultivate literacy, primary education, and an educated ministry. The Board then sent Joseph Binney to Burma in 1844 for the express purpose of establishing the Karen Theological Seminary. The midcentury surge in female missionaries further reinforced educational work as women argued for the importance of educated motherhood, teacher training, and female evangelism.[11]

These new educational programs reconfigured Baptist conceptions of missionary work. A new generation of Baptist missionary leaders argued that the health, vitality, and orthodoxy of indigenous churches depended upon the sound education of their leaders. In 1848, Binney sent a "Plan of Education for Karen Native Preachers" to the Board. In it he argued that the current educational system in Burma did not provide for the thorough education of a class of men who would soon "fill important posts in the church" and "wield controlling influence in their councils." Binney recommended that the school create departments of theology and classical studies to train a small class of the most promising students.[12] When a young missionary later issued the familiar plea for additional missionaries, Binney argued that the Karen did not need U.S. volunteers for evangelism as much as missionaries who could teach theology and prepare Karen leaders to be teachers of their own people. In 1857, the missionary who appealed for support for the Karen Theological Seminary explained that everyone who understood missionary work in Burma did not doubt that the native ministry would be the agency to evangelize the Karen. The ultimate success of that evangelism, though, depended upon a "scripturally enlightened native ministry."[13]

THE NATIVE MINISTRY AND HOME MISSIONS

By the outbreak of the Civil War, then, the native ministry model in Burma formed a distinct conception of missionary work in the minds of white northern Baptist leaders. The Civil War turned the attention of home missionary officials toward the many African-American Baptists in the South, who clearly excelled in evangelizing fellow blacks. When it became apparent that most freedpeople clamored for educational opportunities, including religious and theological education, ABHMS officials could not help but feel that Providence had handed them a task for which they were specially qualified.[14] Just as the ABMU directed its energies toward developing preachers and teachers among the Karen, Burmese, Indians, and Chinese, the ABHMS set itself to the task of training African-American preachers and teachers. Rhetoric supporting the education of black preachers and teachers flooded ABHMS literature from 1863 through the 1880s, reflecting the conviction that the key to evangelism, pure Christianity, and social prosperity among blacks lay in providing them with theological and normal education.[15]

The foreign missionary wing could not help but influence home mission thinking. Much of that influence grew from the close relationship that the ABMU and the ABHMS enjoyed in the mid–nineteenth century. The ABHMS always held its annual meetings immediately after the ABMU's and in the same church, allowing many Baptists to serve as delegates to both organizations. Besides attending both meetings, most of the men who established policy for the home mission society also served in leadership roles in the foreign agency. Nine of the ten ABHMS presidents between 1861 and 1882 spent time on the ABMU Board of Managers, while eight of the twenty-one members on the executive board of the ABHMS in 1867 had also served on the Board of Managers of the ABMU. The most important link, though, resided in the ABHMS's corresponding secretary, who administered day-to-day tasks, initiated policy, handled missionary correspondence, and edited the organization's periodical. Seven of the eight corresponding secretaries of the ABHMS between 1861 and 1893 served on the ABMU's Board, including the man who coined the term "Talented Tenth," Henry Morehouse, for whom Morehouse College was later named.[16]

The relationship between the two agencies involved more than just overlapping leadership, though. The leaders of the ABMU and the ABHMS perceived the evangelical purpose of the two agencies to be essentially the same.[17] Thus, home missionary leaders who looked for examples of work among racially distinct populations instinctively drew upon the long experience of the foreign missionary wing, as the concept of the native ministry seemed to fit the African-American situation. Home mission officials usually spoke of the "colored ministry" or "Freedmen preachers," but the imprimatur of foreign missions clearly stamped their thinking. To describe the "successful prosecution of the Home Mission work in the South," Corresponding Secretary James Simmons explained that "we must have a native ministry trained up as fast as possible."[18] Comparisons of missionary work among blacks to missionary work among Asians continued into the 1880s, usually employing the terminology of uplift by educated indigenous leaders.[19]

Education among African-American women reflected the influence of foreign missions as well.[20] The dominant foreign missionary theory for women in the 1860s and 1870s centered upon a concept called "Woman's Work for Woman." Part of this thinking, present among ABMU missionaries as early as 1853, held that the gender segregation of some Asian societies required women to evangelize segments of society that were beyond the reach of male missionaries. Female missionaries trained Asian "female native assistants" or "Bible women" who could take the gospel into the homes of their families and friends.[21] Drawing upon this model, missionaries of the Woman's American Baptist Home Mission Society (WABHMS) trained black women to evangelize fellow African Americans, originally calling these students "Bible women" before changing the term to "colored assistant" and, finally, "missionary."[22] Sophia Packard, the founder of Spelman College, drew upon well-established arguments for indigenous evangelism when she reported that her students "go among their own people and help Christianize and educate them, doing what white people cannot do, going where white people cannot go, and reaching hearts that white people cannot reach."[23]

African-American leaders did not miss the conceptual link between foreign missions and black education either. Joseph E. Jones, a black Baptist professor at the Richmond Institute, urged delegates at the 1880 ABHMS meeting to continue to educate and Christianize African Americans "as you do the Indian, the Burmese, the Chinese, and the other races of the world." Jones, however, pointedly included an admonition with his plea: "Do not check and modify their efforts to rise higher in the scale of being by telling them they cannot become the equals of white men."[24]

THE SHIFTING TERMS OF THE NATIVE MINISTRY MODEL

Jones understood that the native ministry model could be implemented in different ways. Throughout the nineteenth century, the native ministry model validated the intellectual and moral capabilities of non-Anglo Christians, enabling African-American leaders like Jones to seize upon its implications of equality with whites.[25] But the terms of that equality, as well as issues of autonomy, assimilation, and moral authority, took on new dimensions in the last part of the century. The shifts occurred when white Baptist officials fused theological and normal school training to their original goal of evangelism in the 1850s and 1860s, and then again when they added professional and liberal-arts education in the 1880s and 1890s.

From the very beginning of ABHMS's involvement with freedpeople, the primary educational issue for policymakers did not center on whether or not the highest academic training should be made available to African Americans but, rather, on how best to provide it.[26] This does not mean that all white Baptists understood the native ministry concept to promote social equality, for the ABHMS's supporters ranged from those who objected to any educational work for freedpeople to those who actively tried to combat racism.[27] Despite this varied constituency, the leaders who formulated policy for the ABHMS through the end of the century persistently argued and worked for an educational system that they thought would provide blacks with the same academic opportunities that whites enjoyed.

The ABMU had already established this principle. An 1853 convention of missionaries in Burma recommended that a portion of "native" ministers ought to be "thoroughly educated and enlightened," hoping to make the "talents and acquirements" of these men "equal to those of the missionaries themselves." Postbellum missionaries in Burma did not miss the comparison of their situation to home missions. Upon reading an article in a U.S. paper in 1866 criticizing northern Baptists for trying to teach theology to African-American pastors who had limited reading and spelling skills, a missionary in Burma had to protest. "Every Burman missionary in Burmah [sic] is giving instruction in theology to native preachers who cannot write and spell correctly," he rejoined. Moreover, few of the white pioneer Baptist preachers in New York and Pennsylvania could have "written out and spelled correctly a report of their labors," he continued, yet they converted souls, planted churches, and prepared the way to establish Baptist seminaries like Hamilton, Rochester, and Lewisburg.[28]

Even when race relations deteriorated at the end of the century, the two most influential white leaders of the ABHMS continued to argue for the equal intellectual capabilities of blacks. In 1888, Henry Morehouse declared that the best way to uplift the masses lay in bringing Christian teachers and ministers into contact with high intellectual influences.[29] That speech proved to be only a short step away from his 1896 "Talented Tenth" speech in which Morehouse argued for support for black colleges with the plea that while industrial education might be satisfactory for the nine, the "tenth man ought to have the best opportunities for making the most of himself for humanity and God."[30] Thomas Jefferson Morgan, who served as corresponding secretary of the ABHMS from 1893 to 1902, argued several times that black institutions could do for black men and women what Brown, Rochester, Bucknell, and Vassar had done for whites in the North. "What argument, therefore, avails for educating the white element of our republic, is equally valid for the education of the black element," he declared.[31]

Northern Baptists extended the native ministry assumption of equal intellectual capabilities to women as well. As early as 1822, Ann Judson, the popular first wife of the Baptist missionary patriarch Adoniram Judson, gave a widely published address in which she decried the limited education among Burmese and Indian women. Judson exalted the activities of a Burmese convert, Mahmen-la, as evidence that properly educated Asian women would equal the intellectual attainments of women in the United States.[32] That characteristic carried over to the ABHMS's thinking about black women. The 1881 annual report of the ABHMS stated that it did not have to remind its audience of "the importance of educating the women of a race." The experience of ABHMS schools "has shown both the capacity of colored girls for education and the unspeakable value of their Christian influence among their people."[33]

Because the native ministry model supported the ability of nonwhites to attain equal intellectual achievements, it also implied that nonwhites could administer institutions as well. Just as foreign missionaries supported Karen and Burmese autonomy in local congregations and primary schools, home missionaries validated the authority of African-American pastors and elementary school teachers.[34] The ABHMS voted black pastors onto its executive board in 1867 and 1869 while the fledgling seminaries sought out black teachers and trustees.[35] In 1867, ABHMS officials instructed the principal of the Richmond Institute to aim for autonomy. "The time will soon come when that School must be put upon a permanent basis and properly endowed, when we shall want to work into the Board much of the colored element," explained James Simmons. "Train them for it as fast as you can."[36] Another white missionary in 1873 wrote that these schools "are theirs in the sense they *never can be ours;* theirs to cherish, theirs ultimately to own and manage, either with or without their Northern brethren; and theirs from which to derive untold benefits."[37]

Not everyone agreed that local autonomy and black representation on white-dominated boards served the missionary cause the best. Arguing that a separate black missionary organization would foster black evangelism, independence, and maturity, many northern African-American Baptist leaders merged two regional black bodies to form the Consolidated American Baptist Missionary Convention (CABMC) in 1867. CABMC leaders agreed that African Americans most effectively evangelized and educated fellow African Americans but reconfigured the terms of autonomy by contending that only blacks should work as missionaries in the South.

They proposed that the ABHMS grant the money it raised for southern missionary work to the CABMC.[38] ABHMS officials rejected this idea with a variety of objections. Officials feared a drop in financial giving, balked at a plan that removed whites from southern missionary work at a time when so much education was needed, and disapproved of a structure that gave them no say over money that the ABHMS had raised, an issue that had sparked a battle between ABMU officials and several missionaries in Burma just a decade earlier.[39]

The conflict between the CABMC and the ABHMS gave a racialized twist to the thorniest problem of nineteenth-century Baptist polity, reconciling denominational activity with the congregational principle of autonomy. The missionary agencies constantly wrestled with the issue. When ABMU leaders in the 1850s added theological education to their missionary vision in Burma, they drew opposition, ironically enough, from Francis Wayland, who urged missionaries to scale back their educational efforts and focus on evangelism. President of Brown University and author of an enormously popular textbook on moral philosophy, Wayland can hardly be accused of anti-intellectualism. He did see dangers, however, in systems that created an elite class of leaders upon whom the common people would be dependent. Locating church vitality in a disestablished system in which the tools of the gospel enabled a given people to chart their own course, Wayland championed the well-known "Three-Self" theory of missionary work.[40] Arguing that an extensive system of missionary education made converts dependent on missionaries, Wayland declared that "a foreign people may give the impulse and set the example, but the natives themselves must carry the work forward. If we teach the natives to rely upon us, nothing like a permanent impression can ever be made upon their character."[41] Linking the evangelistic success of the poorly educated Karen evangelists of Burma with the poorly educated American Baptist evangelists of the early republic, Wayland argued that in both the United States and Burma, erudite leaders who only dimly understood their congregations would have stifled church growth and vitality.[42]

The ABMU committed itself to the principle of autonomy, but under different terms than Wayland envisioned. By placing evangelism and church planting at the center of missionary work, Wayland's understanding of the "Three-Self" theory would have required missionaries to pull out of a field once indigenous churches had developed sufficient piety. Convinced, instead, that the health of churches depended upon sound theological education, Wayland's successors made an educated ministry not only the key to successful evangelism but also the measuring stick for autonomy. In 1864, the ABMU suggested that leaders in Burma form a general convention that would transfer much of the organizational authority from the executive committee to the field so that the churches in Burma might soon be able to operate their own convention completely independent of missionaries. "If true to itself, and true to the best interests of the people it would bless, [the missionary agency] will withdraw," the officials declared. The U.S. and Asian leaders responded by forming the Burmah Baptist Missionary Convention in 1865, complete with indigenous majorities among the delegates and the board. The terms of indigenous autonomy were then spelled out in one of the five resolutions that the new body immediately adopted. Before the Christians of Burma could be "rendered even comparatively independent of the guidance of foreign missionaries," it declared, their leaders must receive "an education which shall approach the breadth and thoroughness to that of their present foreign teachers." That goal did not seem to come quickly. In 1873, ABMU leaders figured that effective education would enable missionaries to withdraw after another twenty years.[43]

By this time, the concerns that Wayland had raised about creating elites had been completely forgotten, for even in the 1850s Wayland had been swimming against the tide. Over the course of the nineteenth century, Baptists in the northeastern United States actively reinserted mediating elites into a movement that had received much of its initial energy from opposing just such a religious system.[44] In their zeal to build scores of theological schools and denominational colleges, white northern Baptists invested higher education with a moral authority that made highly trained ministers and pious educators the custodians of a healthy church and society.[45] As a result, the ABHMS's policy in the 1860s and 1870s was to work to provide black congregations and primary schools with black preachers and teachers, but it was assumed that it would take several decades before enough black educators could obtain the theological expertise to act as the sole custodians of "uplift" to their people. Mirroring the native ministry system in Burma, official support for local black autonomy did not translate into immediate autonomy in institutions of higher education.

Ironically, the native ministry argument that black elites could reach the same intellectual standards as white elites simultaneously created additional requirements for withdrawing missionary oversight. Even as the number of black teachers in these seminaries and colleges increased over the next few decades, the terms for black control shifted with changes in higher education. The generation of Baptist leaders of the 1880s and 1890s, represented by Morehouse and Morgan, pushed missionary educational goals beyond theological and normal education. In their transition from seminaries to liberal-arts colleges, ABHMS schools added professional education to their curricula, changing the nature and mission of the schools.[46] With that shift, white officials once again moved the goalposts back. Wayland had based Burmese autonomy on basic pastoral skills; Simmons and the missionary leaders of the 1860s and 1870s had added a thorough theological education. Morehouse and Morgan not only required all of these characteristics but also added the emerging professional emphasis on administrative and financial management skills onto their list of qualifications for Christian custodianship.[47]

This shifting basis for autonomy also reinforced assimilationist thinking among Baptist missionary leaders. Paternalism intensified as the earlier recognition of the importance of cultural distinctions faded from view. The observation by early Baptist missionaries that Asian Christians possessed evangelistic skills that exceeded those of the missionaries led Wayland to argue that Christianity should take on characteristics of the host culture. "Nor ought we to attempt to transform the Oriental into the European character by any process of instruction," Wayland declared. "We should strive to improve and perfect the forms of character now existing rather than making them into our own. . . . We should know the character of the people as it is, and modify our plans by the developments which arise."[48]

But the cultural terms shifted as Baptist missionaries elevated the educated ministry as a requirement for institutional autonomy in the 1860s and 1870s. The conviction that education ensured effective pastoral care overwhelmed the early insight that Asian evangelists understood the indigenous language and character better than the missionaries. The 1873 ABMU report cautioned that while regeneration could be effected as easily by the "unlettered as by the cultivated mind," the masses could advance only through highly educated ministers.[49] The definition of a healthy indigenous church changed from one in which Asian ministers profited from an intimate knowledge of the cultural dynamics of their own people to one in which Asian ministers profited from possessing the same academic knowledge as the missionaries.

These terms molded the ABHMS's conceptions of the black church in the 1860s and 1870s. Home mission officials never doubted African-American piety and skills for evangelism, while Baptist periodicals praised the oratorical and evangelistic abilities of black ministers, regularly noting the number of conversions under the ministry of various black preachers.[50] However, Baptist officials assumed that black preachers' success stemmed from their ability to match the worldview of white missionaries, not from any distinctive cultural or religious understanding. In 1869, the ABHMS pointed out that the most effective home missionary in the previous year had been a black preacher. The writer did not conclude, however, that this preacher understood his own people better than white missionaries did but exclaimed that "the complexion of ministers does not seem to have much influence with Christ, either way!" Meanwhile, white missionaries bemoaned the ignorance, error, "fanaticism," and superstition they perceived among African-American Christians and emphatically insisted that an educated black ministry would both elevate blacks and purify their Christianity.[51]

White Baptist leaders, thus, did not see how a black agency like the CABMC offered any advantages over the ABHMS. Nor did an increasingly color-blind educational policy rooted in respectable Victorian notions of uplift give them an effective means for understanding how the African-American experience pointed to flaws in the system. Indeed, the demise of the CABMC in 1879 may have added fuel to the white Baptist belief that the black community had not yet attained the financial, educational, and moral tools to administer effectively a separate agency or theological school.[52] Meanwhile, many black intellectuals who accepted this model distanced themselves from the mass of African Americans who did not meet the proper standards of respectability. But even as the ABHMS continued to train blacks through their own system, some African-American leaders asserted not only their readiness and right to control black educational institutions but also the need to instill values of race pride within those institutions.[53] These black leaders continued to turn the native ministry concept back on white officials, challenging white leaders to follow through on their promise of ethnic autonomy.

The conflict did not resolve easily. In 1883, Morehouse asserted that the goal of missionary education should be "America in the Negro," a concept that, consciously or unconsciously, he tied to northeastern Anglo culture. He very well may have had Philip Fisher Morris on his mind. In the previous year, Morris, a graduate of Howard University, had asked Morehouse to allow the black Baptist convention in Virginia to name a new building and add more blacks to the board of trustees of Richmond Theological Institute, adding that African Americans had difficulty identifying with the school. Morehouse turned down his request, provoking Morris to attempt to establish a seminary for blacks built totally with African-American support.[54] As Morehouse and Morgan became embroiled in more conflicts with black leaders in the following decades, they hardened their positions against racial pride while simultaneously strengthening their assertions about the color-blind nature of black intellectual capacities. Although they began relinquishing control of the colleges to black leaders after 1900, ABHMS officials in the 1890s built bridges with the cooperationist black Baptists while turning cold shoulders toward the racial-pride wing.[55]

Nevertheless, much of the appeal of the Talented Tenth model for blacks lay in its implicit support of social equality.[56] Although the variety of African-American responses to home mission education lies outside the scope of this study, the black-pride issue suggests that non-Anglos could find in the native ministry model a spur to ethnic or nationalistic identity.[57] The disputes between missionaries and black leaders over indigenous autonomy and cultural identity paralleled the issues raised in foreign missions. Missionary schools in China and India developed indigenous Christian leaders who claimed their intellectual equality, pushed for greater autonomy, and resisted moves to shape their Christianity according to Anglo norms. Ultimately, both movements produced leaders who stripped the educated-leadership concept of its evangelistic purposes for the primary cause of racial or nationalistic identity. Just as Asian leaders found tools from their missionary education to assert nationalistic identity, the Talented Tenth philosophy acted, in the words of Evelyn Brooks Higginbotham, as a "conduit of race pride" for African Americans. In his ethnic reformulation of the Talented Tenth concept, W. E. B. DuBois declared that black leaders "must be made leaders of thought and missionaries of culture among their people."[58]

EVANGELISTIC ZEAL AND BLACK HIGHER EDUCATION

Despite the conflicts, misunderstandings, and differing perceptions of the African-American situation, black and white Baptists still shared a deep evangelical faith. Evangelical concerns dominated the language, goals, and actions of both black and white leaders. For white members of the ABHMS, the missionary impulse led them to engage blacks in a significantly different manner from most whites in U.S. society. White support for black higher education, therefore, cannot be fully understood apart from the dynamics of the foreign missionary movement.

Foreign missionary experience, for instance, prompted evangelical denominations to establish higher education for blacks when other benevolent agencies focused on common-school education. While some colleges for blacks grew from the dogged efforts of financially strapped black denominations, virtually every other black liberal-arts college established in the late nineteenth century came from northern evangelical denominations deeply involved in the foreign missionary movement.[59] The northern Presbyterians, northern Methodists, and Congregationalists divided their organizations into a foreign missionary wing and a home missionary wing, placing their efforts for black education under the latter, just as the northern Baptists did.[60] Each of these denominations actively promoted foreign missionary work before the Civil War, weaving the "Three-Self" theory into their policies. And as with the Baptists, the home missionary wing of these denominations sought to educate black preachers and teachers during Reconstruction, establishing seminaries and normal schools, which evolved into black liberal-arts colleges.[61]

Meanwhile, the American Freedman's Union Commission (AFUC), the primary white ideological competitor to evangelical home missions to blacks, concerned itself wholly with primary-school education. Composed mainly of reformers in the Garrisonian, Rationalist, Universalist, and Unitarian traditions who expressed a civil rather than a religious vision, the AFUC tied its African-American educational philosophy to the expansion of the New England common school. Consistent with its common-school philosophy, the AFUC downplayed distinctive religious doctrines, insisting that a broadly ethical philosophy should underlie black educational work.[62] Active support for that philosophy did not last beyond 1869, however, when the AFUC disbanded with the declaration that it had completed its work.[63] With the demise of free-labor ideology and the collapse of Reconstruction, Republican reformers and some Garrisonians lost interest in freedpeople, leading some historians to conclude that missionary support for black education faded with the rest of the northern reform efforts.[64]

The exact opposite occurred among evangelical missionaries. Financial giving for black education among the four major northern evangelical denominations actually increased after 1877. The missions budget for black education within these denominations doubled from 1870 to 1891 and quadrupled by 1906, a trajectory that paralleled evangelical interest in foreign missions.[65] Up through 1888, the annual expenditures for black education from the ABHMS alone far exceeded the annual income of the highly visible Slater Fund.[66]

With black education effectively lodged under the sacred rubric of missionary work, northern evangelical support for black higher education persisted well into the twentieth century, while other educational programs dissolved during Reconstruction. This growing support cannot be divorced from the religious dynamics of the missionary movement. Baptists consistently viewed home missionary work as an act of compassion and responsibility in response to divine commands. ABHMS Corresponding Secretaries Simmons and Morehouse touched the nerve center of evangelicalism by regularly quoting Nathan Bishop, who donated money to establish Bishop Baptist College in Marshall, Texas. "I have been blamed for giving so many thousand dollars for the benefit of colored men," Bishop told Simmons. "But I expect to stand side by side with these men on the Day of Judgment. Their Lord is my Lord. They and I are brethren; and I am determined to be prepared for that meeting."[67]

With black higher education enshrined as a hallowed cause, Baptist officials looked warily upon new ideological competitors. The ABHMS refused to embrace the assumptions driving an ascending support for industrial education, despite incentives to do so.[68] In their long search for an adequate endowment for black colleges, ABHMS officials could have tapped into a lucrative source of northern philanthropy while simultaneously cultivating the good graces of southern white Baptists, if they had only agreed to jettison classical education for industrial education.[69] However, evangelical missionary leaders remained firm in their emphasis on theological, professional, and liberal-arts education, mirroring foreign missionaries who supported the academic capabilities of non-Westerners with ambitious college-building programs around the world.[70]

These religious dynamics raise questions about the "social control" thesis that some historians use to explain evangelical involvement with black education.[71] While the intersection of religion, class, gender, and race among ABHMS leaders could stand further examination, the notion that home missionaries involved themselves in black education primarily to create and control a docile economic class of black workers seems simplistic, at best. The occasional references to class anxiety do not appear in ABHMS literature until the 1880s and 1890s, after two decades of work in African-American education. Baptist leaders of the 1860s and 1870s expressed a concern that education would enable blacks to vote intelligently, but they rarely revealed any sense that blacks posed a threat to the social order and sometimes argued just the opposite. An 1866 article that asked "What Does the Freedman Want?" presented work, wages, land, education, and churches as the answer. "Surely these are all innocent and reasonable desires," the Baptist writer declared. "Such a people can not be dangerous members of society."[72]

Undoubtedly, by the late 1880s and 1890s, northern Baptist leaders occasionally declared that education would defuse African-American rebellion.[73] Yet they also argued that Baptist education would counteract Roman Catholicism among blacks. And both of these concerns paled in comparison to the frequent and consistent declarations that educated African Americans would prove to be effective missionaries to Africa.[74] If evangelical leaders wanted "to limit both black aspirations and mobility," as one historian has declared, why would Morgan have tried to rally northern white support for black colleges by arguing that these institutions worked for the "development of great preachers, lawyers, physicians, philosophers, scientists and statesmen"?[75]

Like many foreign missionaries, ABHMS officials blended ethnocentric assumptions with an abiding concern for the welfare of those they sought to help. Home mission leaders slipped into paternalistic patterns, failed to see the significance of African-American culture, and only relinquished control of black colleges after painful conflicts. At the same time, they maintained a commitment to and faith in black intellectual achievement at a time when the American educational establishment offered little beyond inattention or the restrictive proscriptions of industrial education. The financially strapped black denominations built what colleges they could. But without the religious zeal of the missionary movement, the remaining black liberal-arts colleges of the late nineteenth century would not have been built.

5 / Organizing for Missions

A Methodist Case Study

Russell E. Richey

Though American Methodism was many years without a distinct missionary organization, it was owing to the fact that its whole organization was essentially a missionary scheme. It was, in fine, the great Home Mission enterprise of the north American continent, and its domestic work demanded all its resources of men and money.

> Abel Stevens, *The Centenary of American Methodism: A Sketch of Its History, Theology, Practical System, and Success*

Abel Stevens, one of the "ablest" nineteenth-century observers of Methodism, saw clearly, perhaps as clearly as any, the importance of the Protestant missionary impulse.[1] Stevens both discerned and effected the centrality of missions on a national level within Methodism. He had a role in the great celebration and capital campaign that gave title to the volume from which the chapter epigraph was taken, *The Centenary of American Methodism: A Sketch of Its History, Theology, Practical System, and Success*. This event might be seen as U.S. Methodism's coming of age (that is, the northern church's, the Methodist Episcopal Church's, coming of age), a campaign hesitantly launched for $2 million that elicited $5 million in pledges and eventually produced $8.7 million in receipts. Much of this the church dedicated to education, specifically theological education, but a portion of the monies raised went to mission work, including the construction of a new missions building.

Stevens had earned the right to comment on the place of missions in Methodist endeavor.[2] Indeed, he served as Methodism's official midcentury spokesperson. Its historian and apologist, he produced in addition to the *Centenary* assessment a four-volume history of U.S. Methodism, a three-volume history of the larger Methodist movement, two single-volume overviews, two books on the introduction of Methodism into the eastern states, defenses of Methodist polity, and a history of Methodist women.[3] And Stevens took these longer views not from the isolation of an academic's study but from amidst the turmoil and conflicts of a church torn asunder by sectionalism and slavery. He held, by the church's election in General Conference assembled, a series of the most vital and important editorships in the denomination, those of *Zion's Herald*, the New England Methodist paper, then of *The National Magazine*, and, finally, of *The Christian Advocate*, northern Episcopal Methodism's national paper. For his day, then, Stevens represented one of the most respected and discerning observers of the Methodist scene. He thought Methodism a missionary movement. Was it? If so, in what sense? And did it maintain its "missionary" aspect once it did create its own distinct missionary organization and when some, if not all, of its missionary impulse was channeled through that structure?

PHASES OF MISSIONARY ORGANIZATION

To test Stevens's judgment, one might focus on the national missionary agencies, male and female, that sent out foreign missionaries.[4] The obvious alternative might seem to be the local congregation. However, in Methodism, the intervening structure, today spoken of in colorless terms as "the middle judicatory," constituted the real engine, the drive wheel, for missions,[5] particularly in the nineteenth century. Methodists term that middle judicatory "conference" and recognize it as the basic body of the church.[6]

The focus on conference permits us to differentiate three phases of Methodist missions in the nineteenth century and to observe, from an instructive angle, how organizing for missions transformed the denomination. On the first, pre-1820, pre-missionary society, phase, we will comment only briefly. In this period, before the Methodist encounter with the Wyandots, Methodism as a whole, the system itself, was indeed missionary in the sense of which Stevens spoke. This "Wesleyan" phase followed the founder's precept in making the people the instrumentalities of their own evangelization. Leaders, including preachers, emerged out of those missionized—poor whites, Germans, African Americans, and occasionally women (white and black). Methodism drew boundaries of class rather than race, language, or ethnicity. Turning the world upside down—denouncing worldliness, gentility, and, especially, slaveholding—Methodists embraced those not privileged by society. Methodists undertook missions in intrinsic, local, face-to-face, and inclusive fashion.

In contrast, Methodist missions became extrinsic, distant, mediated, and exclusive in what we will term the third, post-1872, national, proto-bureaucratic, centrally administered, accountable-to-General-Conference phase. Then the church drew clear boundaries of race, language, gender, and ethnicity. Missions would not be left to those missionized but would be run by quasi-professionals—paid national staff and recruited and trained missionaries. The church embraced the "other" in totally separate, noninterfacing systems, schemes of organization and order that put distance even between people who lived close together. The missionary system and the church-extension system ran on their own tracks, distinct from those of regular conferences. The church designated bishops as "missionary" to distinguish them clearly (in power and prerogative) from regular bishops. Methodist preachers increasingly behaved less like evangelists called from the folk and more like clergy of established churches, "pastors" to a parish.

Much of this chapter will concern the transition to the third phase from a second, 1820–1872, conference-based and conference-administered but centrally funded phase. With respect to the qualifiers—intrinsic-extrinsic, local-distant, face-to-face or mediated, inclusive-exclusive—Methodist missions during this middle period were clearly hybrid, or in transition. If looked at nationally, missions might still seem intrinsic, local, direct, inclusive. If looked at in relation to local Methodism, missions would seem extrinsic, removed, delegated, exclusive. By focusing on the conference, we can observe the transitions through which Methodism was going, transitions having essentially to do with missions but affecting every aspect of Methodist life. Evangelization might be undertaken close at hand or across international borders, but in either case, the new communities would be socially segregated in some fashion from those mounting the mission. The church increasingly respected boundaries of race, language, and ethnicity but on a local level and not always through formal recognition or legislation. Methodism put regular preachers into missions still but on special assignment. It termed them "missionaries." The church still embraced "the other" within society, camp meetings, and quarterly meetings but often in separate classes, in distant or distinct parts of the camp meeting (such as separate camp meetings for Cherokees or for Germans), or through distinguishing treatment. Missions carried Methodism slowly, gradually toward an interesting, world-respecting set of distinctions, transforming in so doing the basic structure of the church, the annual conference.

Hence, when thinking about missions and the church or missions in the church, one appropriately focuses on missions in relation to the annual conference. It was initially the agent of missions. And it remained, and remains to this day, the basic structure of the church. By Stevens's time, however, the role of conference in missions was shifting. It had been both the locus and agent of missions. Then it became the primary collection agency for more distant missions. Eventually, it became the cheerleader for missions at a distance and primarily a conduit for monies raised and allocated locally. By focusing on conference, we can observe (a) the changes through which Methodism went in the effort to conduct missions, (b) how conferences themselves evolved to cope with the increased fiscal responsibility, (c) how perceptions of mission gradually altered as it became less a regular aspect of conference life and more a sponsored and specialized distant operation, and (d) the way Methodism's understanding of itself as missionary altered. Those transitions will be the exploration of this chapter.

CONFERENCES AS MISSIONARY

Stevens rightly termed Methodism "essentially a missionary movement." Its conference-based structure had functioned in missionary fashion from the start. The effective beginnings of Methodism date from the calling of the first conferences, though, to be sure, spontaneous efforts to witness in a Methodist manner and carry on religious life in a Methodist spirit anticipated Wesley's sending of missionaries and their convening a conference. The first conference, bearing the quaint title "Minutes of Some Conversations Between the Preachers in Connection with the Rev. Mr. John Wesley," committed itself to obedience to Wesley and his rules, doctrine, and discipline; adherence to conference minutes (the British at this point); and acceptance of the Methodist pattern of sending or appointing preachers to circuits.[7] Thereafter, U.S. Methodism followed the missionary scheme established by Wesley.

In conference, the assistant—later superintendent, still later bishop—stationed preachers for the following year. Conference and bishop sent out ministers into mission. They returned a year later to conference, only to be sent out again. Missions constituted the business of Methodist ministry. Methodist structure also functioned on missionary behalf and in missionary fashion. In early U.S. Methodism, conferences expanded their circuits to encompass newly settled or unmissionized territory and then divided when growth made further effective strategizing and missionizing difficult. Methodism quite literally conferenced the frontier and conferenced the nation.[8] Ministry was missionary and conference the agency, framework, and resource for mission. That is what Stevens meant when he said, "Though American Methodism was many years without a distinct missionary organization, it was owing to the fact that its whole organization was essentially a missionary scheme. It was, in fine, the great Home Mission enterprise of the north American continent, and its domestic work demanded all its resources of men and money."

By the time Stevens wrote, conferences were less intrinsically the missionary "scheme" that they had been originally. Indeed, from 1819 Methodism recognized

that special situations, as, for instance, the evangelization of the Wyandot Native Americans, did not lend themselves to the standard formulae of conference expansion through enlarged circuits and revolving itinerants;
that some efforts at Christianization would require specialization and sustained commitment;
and that these special missionary settings required financial underwriting quite beyond the capacity of those receiving the evangelistic efforts or even of the sponsoring conference.

So the church founded a Missionary Society to provide "pecuniary aid . . . to enable the Conferences to carry on their missionary labours on a more extended plan" and "to extend the influence of divine truth, by means of those missionaries which may, from time to time, be approved and employed by the Bishops and Conferences for that purpose."[9] Around the same time, Methodist women, led by Mary W. Mason, formed an Auxiliary Society to the Missionary Society of the Methodist Episcopal Church.[10] Conferences created their own auxiliaries, male and female, and encouraged the same at local levels.[11]

NATIONAL SOCIETY—CONFERENCE ACTIVITY

Through such auxiliaries and their collections, through the fees paid for membership in its own ranks ($2.00 annually, $20.00 for a life membership), and through special larger benefactions, the Missionary Society raised funds to support work among the Wyandots, among the French in Louisiana, in the territories, including those on the west coast of North America, in Liberia, and eventually throughout the world. The founding of the society did not remove mission from conferences. Indeed, conferences still carried on all those missions, except those few beyond the bounds of existing conferences and abroad. Initially, the Missionary Society functioned to promote and finance, to raise and distribute funds. The society had no staff, neither selected nor sent missionaries, and did not even authorize its own disbursements. The bishops drew on its funds to support missionaries whom they appointed, as they appointed others within conferences.[12]

Conferences played the major role in supporting missions financially, but given how the monies were disbursed, conferences may well have been tempted to cut out the intermediary and expend their own resources locally. Certainly, the Philadelphia Conference (a focus of the rest of this chapter), initially hesitated to support the Missionary Society. It had good reason for hesitation,

> competing as it did with New York for preeminence in denominational affairs,
> objecting to the way the Missionary Society was originally structured as a combined Bible and Missionary endeavor,
> wanting to retain its and the denomination's affiliation with the American Bible Society,
> and preferring to conduct missions through its own "Mite" society.[13]

The Philadelphia resistance, doubtless unique, underscores, however, the nature of the missionary enterprise. The "national" society was less a denominational agency than a New York–based and –controlled voluntary society. That was the pattern of denominational endeavor. Lacking any central apparatus for oversight, possessing itinerant bishops, gathering in general conference only every four years, Methodism found it necessary—and had from the beginning of the nineteenth century—to assign supervisory responsibility for agencies like the Book Concern and Missions to a specific annual conference. It must have been galling to Philadelphia, where the Book Concern had been originally sited, that New York had now gotten both missions and publications.

Given such competitive and differing conference stake in the ostensibly denominational endeavors, it is not surprising that the conference auxiliary societies functioned variously. And yet, it was their responsibility, as also that of auxiliaries at any level, to raise funds for the national society.

The monies flowed slowly. So, beginning in 1832, the General Conference decreed that annual conferences were to monitor and report the monies raised for these "voluntary" commitments the church had made. Specifically, the General Conference added a mandate in the Methodist manner, namely, by the addition of a question to those inherited from Wesley by which conferences conducted their business and made the annual report. The *Discipline* then directed for the conduct "Of the Annual Conference" in a new *Quest. 6* ("What is the method wherein we usually proceed in the yearly conferences?") the following report and mandate: "What has been contributed for the support of missions, and what for the publication of Bibles, tracts, and Sunday schools books?"[14] Steadily from 1832, the church and, particularly, the Missionary Society sought to achieve greater stability and larger resources and a more effective outreach by drawing in and mandating support from the primary agency of Methodist life, namely, the conferences.[15] We will chart that progress from 1832 to 1872, the point at which focus shifted again to the national scene.

THE PHILADELPHIA CONFERENCE

The Philadelphia Conference well serves our purpose as a test conference. It was, as indicated, initially reluctant in its support of the Missionary Society. As an East Coast and older conference with mostly settled circuits and stations, by the 1830s it no longer functioned in the older Methodist missionary fashion that Stevens outlined. By 1837, it had only six missionaries functioning within its bounds—in Southwark, Susquehannah, Fairchount, Easton, German, and Longneck missions.[16] At that point, it was a huge conference encompassing much of Pennsylvania, all of Delaware, and the eastern shore of Virginia and Maryland.[17] The Philadelphia Conference was typical in generating initially modest support for the Missionary Society. For instance, in the first year after 1832, when the General Conference had mandated the query, "What has been contributed for the support of missions . . . ?" Philadelphia failed to report its contributions. Its receipts then grew gradually, as follows:

1833	no report
1834	$2,129.60
1835	$2,838.13
1836	no report
1837	$2,892.65
1838	$3,417.70
1839	no report [18]
1840	$1,814.31*
1841	$3,000.00*
1842	no report
1843	$4,403.23
1844	$4,399.00
1845	$4,409.33 [19]
1846	$6,062.51
1847	$5,584.97
1848	$6,374.98
1849	$6,050.51
1850	$7,994.73
1851	$9,121.32 [20]
1852	$11,246.71
1853	$14,492.43
1854	$18,371.40
1855	$19,085.58 [21]
1856	$19,438.52
1857	$25,863.62 [22]

By the late 1850s, Philadelphia led the denomination, exceeding all other conferences in the amount given. For 1834, Philadelphia produced $2,129 of the total $35,700 raised nationally; for 1857, $25,863 of a total $268,890; for 1882, $46,500 of a total $751,469. By that point, Philadelphia produced the most for missions of any conference, being followed by New York and New York East, both over $32,000, and then Baltimore at $26,500. The rest of the then ninety-nine conferences obviously trailed.[23] There were, as we shall discover, good reasons for Philadelphia's growing affirmation of missions.

Through the 1830s, the Philadelphia Conference's efforts for missions remained primarily financial. And the money must not have flowed automatically. In 1839, the conference listed as the first of six resolutions, "That it is the duty of every member of this conference to take up the conference collections in every principal congregation in his circuit and station."[24] To underscore that responsibility, the conference restructured its *Minutes* to make the efforts of individual preachers and charges toward that duty highly visible. Beginning with 1839, the conference arrayed its "Statistics of the Philadelphia Annual Conference" by individual charges (circuits and stations), including a line for "Missionary Money." The other lines for that year were Sabbath Scholars, Library Books, Teachers, Superintendents, and Local Preachers.[25] Since by that point the conference was printing the *Minutes,* the whole conference saw what individual preachers and churches did for missions. The display at once individualized or localized duty and registered the corporate or conference performance as an aggregate.

Persuading charges of the importance of such stewardship remained (and remains) one of conference's challenges. In 1842, Philadelphia "Resolved, That we heartily concur in the recommendation of the Missionary Board of New York, that all our members contribute one cent a week, towards the support of our Missions, and that all our ministers be requested to use their best efforts to get this plan into speedy operation."[26]

This effort to regularize benevolences went hand-in-glove with efforts to stabilize the entire financial machinery of the circuits and stations. At the same time, the conference also adopted a fairly intricate "uniform and efficient plan, for the management of the temporal supplies of the preachers." It recommended working out apportionments for support of the ministry of the church and provided for collections *by class* and through *Class Collectors.*[27]

The next innovation in Philadelphia's encouragement of contributions was the establishment throughout the conference of specific times of collections for each of the benevolent projects. So in 1846, the conference "Resolved, That the public collections ordered by this conference be taken at the following periods of the Conference Year, viz: 1, The Bible collection in June; 2, the Sunday School Union in July; 3, the Educational, in October; 4, the Missionary in November, December and January; 5, the Conference and ten cent, in January, February and March."[28]

This became, then, a way of distributing the benevolences over the year, avoiding some competition among the causes, and providing for some regularity of funding. In 1848, for instance, the conference again set "Times of Collections": "1. The Bible collection in June: 2. the Sunday School Union in July, August or September; 3. The Education in October; 4. The Missionary in November or December; 5. The Philadelphia Conference in February and March; 6. The ten cent collection during the year at the discretion of each preacher."[29]

MISSIONS FROM CONFERENCE: SPECIAL APPOINTMENTS

Conferences so encompassed Methodist life and work that the church had no way of visualizing ministry other than in relation to conference, no way of achieving supervision or oversight other than through conferences, no way of assigning persons to outreach other than from conference. In 1839, the Missionary Society had been incorporated in New York as a voluntary society with a self-perpetuating board.[30] However, it remained, in effect, under the New York Conference; its resident corresponding secretary, Nathan Bangs, was under appointment through New York;[31] and its ministerial board members were accountable to the denomination through that or some conference. Missionaries were also under conference appointment—those, obviously, who worked within the bounds of the conference, but also those sent abroad. In 1847, the last item under Snow Hill District appointments in the Philadelphia Conference was "Buenos Ayres, D. D. Lore, Missionary."[32] The *Minutes* also listed, of course, the domestic missions, as, for instance, that year, a North Philadelphia Mission and a South Philadelphia Mission.[33] However, from this point, Philadelphia had a special attachment to the global missionary cause. One of its own was abroad under support from the Missionary Society. Envisioning missions abroad in this fresh way, the conference seemingly saw local efforts afresh as well. The next year, it carried "German Mission" in the *Minutes* in brackets with Union under the South Philadelphia appointments. D. D. Lore continued in Buenos Ayres.[34] By that point, the denomination had a paper dedicated to representation of missions alone, *Missionary Advocate,* by 1848 in its fourth year. The same year, the General Conference adopted and outlined in the *Discipline* a multipoint program to enhance missions, a program that would give much higher visibility to and involvement in missions for conferences.[35]

Dramatically changing Philadelphia's visualization of and investment in missions was an individual who rose to prominence within the conference, then to prominence in missions for the denomination, who put the *Discipline's* new expectations into operation, and who, perhaps more than any other person, transformed missions from a voluntary into a denominational endeavor.[36] This man was John Price Durbin.[37] Durbin served briefly as chaplain of the U.S. Senate and also briefly as editor of the *Christian Advocate* (New York), the paper later edited by Stevens. In 1834, Durbin became principal (later president) of Dickinson College.[38] He transferred to the Philadelphia Conference in 1836 and eight times earned the conference's token of highest respect, election to represent it at the General Conference. Five of those times he led the delegation (being elected first), the highest accolade that conferences then or now accord their own.[39] Philadelphia turned to him at every point. The 1845 conference appointed or elected him to preach the conference sermon (for 1846).

Also, he served as examiner in the Committees for Examination of the second-year exam on the "Bible as to ordinance or Sacraments."[40] Durbin also headed the Visiting Committee to Dickinson College in 1846 (the agency through which the church exercised its oversight of institutions).[41] In 1849, the bishop concurred in the conference's high estimation of J. P. Durbin and made him presiding elder (P.E.) of North Philadelphia.[42]

A year later, in 1850, Durbin succeeded Charles Pitman as secretary of the Missionary Society.[43] The Philadelphia *Minutes* registered that change with yet another special appointment—"Cor. Sec. of Miss. Soc. of M. E. Church"—and carried the new national or denominational role under the North Philadelphia District appointments.[44] Thereafter, Philadelphia had a personal and direct connection to the mission enterprise. Durbin found a way of making missions personal for other conferences as well.

ORGANIZING FOR MISSIONS

Durbin clearly began his new work with a fresh vision of what conferences might be and do in missions and set out immediately to make conferences a more significant instrument in the missionary cause. His efforts, really endeavors to translate the *Discipline*'s mandates into conference operations, came apparently too late to catch the 1850 Philadelphia Conference. They drew responses elsewhere. For instance, the Troy Conference for 1850 passed an eight-point program, one apparently outlined in a communiqué from Durbin. It called for missionary organization at every level, annual missionary meetings, appointment of collectors in "every class or neighborhood," and reports and publication of the amounts collected—all muscled by the presiding elders who were to meet with the preachers and preach on missions.[45]

Other conferences passed similar sets of programs for missions, often with some such introduction as "The Committee to whom was referred the papers from Dr. Durbin, Corresponding Secretary of the Missionary Society of the M. E. Church, presented their report, which was adopted."[46] Each conference seemed to configure the program to suit its own taste. But they typically included the above ingredients, often adding an item that Troy omitted and that must have been part of Durbin's program, namely, promotion within the conference of *The Missionary Advocate*.[47] The following year, Philadelphia got on the program. It adopted a "Report of Committee on Missions," which called for a nine-point program: (1) monthly missionary prayer meetings or lectures in each church, (2) promotion of "our *Missionary Advocate*," (3) annual missionary collections in November or December, (4) appointment of local missionary collectors, (5) publication annually of donors, collectors, and officers, (6) the establishment of a missionary sermon at the conference and the holding of the anniversary during the conference, (7) use of the Sunday schools as "a powerful auxiliary to the Missionary cause," (8) and their formal organization as auxiliaries where feasible, and (9) the creation of the category of life membership in the denominational society, a recommendation that the conference made to "the Parent Society."[48] By then, Philadelphia had further incentive for missionary enthusiasm. In addition to Durbin at the helm, it boasted two missionaries from its ranks: J. Calder, missionary to China, and D. D. Lore, missionary to Buenos Ayres.[49]

In 1852, Durbin and the Missionary Society pushed a revised constitution through the General Conference and the New York legislatures. It provided, among other things, that the board, rather than the New York Conference, would have responsibility for removal or replacement of the corresponding secretary between sessions of the General Conference. It also allowed each annual conference a "vice-president from its own body."[50] By this point, the Missionary Society had also recognized the strategic value of moving its annual meetings out of New York and around the country, Philadelphia already having been the first of the alternative anniversary meeting sites, followed by Boston and Buffalo.[51]

In 1856, Philadelphia passed a resolution of approbation for African colonization, calling for sermons and a collection "on or about the 4th of July." By this point as well, the conference, in establishing what was becoming an increasingly complex committee structure, gave missions unusual prominence by appointing as its members "The Presiding Elders."[52] Complexity, order, priority, regimen, reporting, and numbers had become, by that point, important to Methodists. And conferences displayed their concerns with elaborate statistics and their values with money. By 1859, Philadelphia needed two committees to deal with missions, one with that title, another entitled "Missionary Statistics." And appropriately, the conference projected for itself a "Plan of Statistics for Annual Minutes," a thirteen-item report expected of each charge (church or circuit), including the "Missionary Report for Philadelphia Conference."[53] Thereafter, the *Minutes* showed very clearly just how each charge performed on this and other points of religious vitality.

WAR, RACE, MISSIONS

As Methodism embroiled itself in the Civil War, missions competed for conference attention with matters of loyalty, support for the war effort, supply of chaplains, stands on slavery, and the like. Philadelphia, though continuing its active support of missions, had to worry about its own slave-holding members and the care of its African-American membership, free and slave. In 1861, by official action, it actively supported the war cause but initially not the "New Chapter," the stronger stand against slavery passed in 1860 by the denomination.[54] In 1864, "on motion of G. Quigley, the Presiding Elders were instructed not to employ as supplies, any person who is either disloyal or pro-slavery." That year's "Report on the State of the

Country" reaffirmed previous stands, supported the war, issued a declaration of loy-alty to the government and the U.S. Constitution, urged it as "a religious duty not to speak evil of ministers and magistrates," and denounced slavery as against the law of God and the principles of the Revolution.[55]

This same conference took another action that had to do with its own life and work but that had implications for missions. It passed a resolution calling for the bishops and presiding elders to organize "our colored people into district Circuits . . . with a view of furnishing them with ministerial service by preachers of their own color."[56] The General Conference of that year, indeed, authorized the establishment of mission conferences "for the benefit of our colored members and populations."[57] For "their benefit," Bishop Edmund Janes that year transferred the African Ameri-can ministers, members, and churches of the Philadelphia Conference into a new Delaware Conference.[58] While African Americans also requested this action, the segregation distinguished within the church a large population (black) that had long been the recipient of missions from another large population (white) that thought of itself as the supplier of missions. Some peoples would thereafter be the objects of missions, others the agents of missionary endeavor. And across the boundary between the two only the missionaries would cross. Conferences—white conferences, at least—would need fewer missionaries in their midst because the ob-jects of mission would be given their own ecclesial organization. That had been permitted since 1856 for Germans, and from 1864 it would increasingly characterize Methodist activity with African Americans as well. Missions externalized certain peoples from Methodist society. It did so mostly at a distance. It could do so nearer at hand.

At the same time, perhaps not coincidentally, support for missions took on more of a social character. By 1862, the Philadelphia Conference, still an all-male and clergy-only affair, featured a whole set of "Anniversaries," annual meetings set to coincide with or follow the conference, sometimes evening affairs—the Female Bible Society of the M. E. Church, the Philadelphia City Home Mission, the Young Men's Central Home Mission, the Philadelphia Conference Tract Society, and the Phila-delphia Conference Missionary Society. Including laity as well as clergy, women as well as men, these affairs transacted necessary business, heard annual reports, and featured multiple addresses.[59] Speakers would often be the key denominational play-ers in the cause of the day; for missions, that would be the conference's own John Durbin.

"FIRST PLACE IN OUR AFFECTIONS"

At the end of the war, northern Methodism geared up for larger conquests, a capital campaign among them. Clearly, missions also claimed the church's heart. That was made most visible, perhaps, by the new priority the Conference Missionary Society had in conference affairs. For starters, beginning in 1867, the conference published the *Annual Report of the Missionary Society* as part of its own *Minutes* and numbered it sequentially.[60] The *Minutes* also gave a new prominence to the society, listing its officers second after the stewards among the conference bodies. Two years later, it would stand first. The presiding elders still served as the standing committee on missions.

The 1867 conference, meeting in Harrisburg, took such symbolic gestures seriously. It heard fraternal addresses from other denominations, notably the A.M.E. Zion Church, the Presbyterian Church, and the Lutheran Church, and introduced members of other denominations. It welcomed an invitation to "visit the rooms of the Young Men's Christian Association."[61] It received communiqués from the various denominational agencies and responded appropriately. It invited to sit with it the members of the Senate and House of Representatives then in session and welcomed the reciprocal invitation to hold services in the House. It passed various resolutions, including one dispatched to the U.S. Senate and House.

Missions claimed further ritual gestures. J. B. McCullough, "appointed at the last session to preach the Annual Missionary Sermon before the Conference," did so to "marked attention." That evening, the fifth night of its meeting, the conference celebrated the Missionary Society's anniversary, completely packing "with ladies and gentlemen" the Locust Street M. E. Church (the site for the conference as a whole). After the opening devotions and the treasurer's report, the Reverend S. Pancoast of Upper Iowa spoke. The society then sang "From Greenland's Icy Mountains." Next, the Reverend Dr. De Hass of the Metropolitan Church, Washington, spoke. After a hymn, Dr. Durbin spoke and "sketched the field of missions as it now exists and is occupied by the M. E. Church, in an elaborate and eloquent manner, for which he is so peculiar." The assemblage then nominated and elected the board of managers for the following year and were dismissed.[62]

The next day, "J. P. Durbin addressed the Conference in behalf of the Missionary Cause." Following his speech, the conference resolved "that the Missionary Cause in the future, as in the past, shall hold the first place in our affections, and that we hereby pledge ourselves to do our full part in paying any indebtedness that may be incurred by our Parent Board in maintaining our Missionary work at home and abroad."

The conference then passed a resolution thanking "Bro. McCullough" for his missionary sermon and requesting a copy for publication.[63] Another ritual action turned attention away from leaders and the pulpit to every member. When passing the character of its members—the annual review by and through which the church assessed and guaranteed orthodoxy, effectiveness, integrity, and conformity—the conference did so with a significant formula: "The names of all the effective Elders on this District were called, their collections reported, and their character passed."[64] This action, which connected approval of the individual's standing as a minister to his charge's collections, put into dramatic form what the *Minutes* and *Report* accomplished by table and statistic. It identified the mission of every station and circuit with what it contributed. It made clear that holding "the Missionary Cause . . . first . . . in our affections" meant organizing Methodism around collections. Missions, once the activity of conferences, had become a benevolence.

A NEW CHAPTER

In 1868, Philadelphia recognized the half-century of Durbin's service: a motion "requesting J. P. Durbin, D.D., to preach a semi-centennial sermon at our next session, was adopted by a rising vote."[65] It was a fitting tribute to Durbin. He had made Methodist missions effective by harnessing the main engine of Methodist life, the annual conference, to the missionary cause. By 1872, when Philadelphia elected him again and for the last time to the General Conference, missions stood, indeed, first in conference affections. The *Minutes* registered its centrality with a new title page, *Minutes of the Eighty-Fifth Session of the Philadelphia Annual Conference of the Methodist Episcopal Church, Convened at St. Paul's M. E. Church, Philadelphia, Pa. Together with the Missionary Report.* The sessions brimmed with actions about or statements concerning missions. The conferences had indeed responded to the overtures that Durbin had made in 1850.

At the General Conference that year, Durbin did not stand for reelection to the Missionary Society's helm. He took a timely departure. The same conference passed enabling legislation effectively transforming all its agencies from voluntary societies into denominational agencies. It did so by making their boards, not just the corresponding secretary, elective by and accountable to itself. From this action flowed the eventual nationalization and centralization of denominational enterprise. Though the full development of bureaucracy would take some time, missions, like other denominational endeavors, would increasingly be run from the top. Durbin's career and the Philadelphia Conference, over his nearly fifty-year association with it, illustrate an earlier chapter in the mission saga—one in which the church depended upon annual conferences to do its work.

Methodism had been no less a missionary movement in its initial penetration into U.S. society. Indeed, in some respects in the earliest period, as Stevens intimated, Methodism possessed in its very structure, in its conference form, a missionary character. During the second phase, when Methodism found it necessary to mount missions to evangelize areas or peoples that could not be cared for with existing circuits and appointments, the conferences remained the main agents and context of missions. Durbin presided over yet another development, the harnessing of conference strength to raise funds for these special situations, at home and abroad. He also envisioned and encouraged the changes in conference life that would make such fund-raising possible. When he entered the Philadelphia Conference, it was a relatively informal body that had only recently begun to publish its own minutes. Its major responsibility was assessing the integrity of its members and those who sought to enter it. Durbin led Methodism and the conference into restructuring itself so as to garner resources for the missionary task. In so doing, wittingly or unwittingly, he facilitated and/or nurtured the subtle changes in Methodist life that would make Methodism less a mission than a body having missions. He can scarcely be blamed for the changes in Methodist missions that would make them engines of colonial or imperial conquest, the treating of the evangelized as objects to be converted rather than brothers or sisters to be welcomed into the family. Yet those changes did come.

Throughout these transformations, did the Philadelphia Conference—indeed, did Methodism as a whole—remain "essentially a missionary movement, domestic and foreign"? Perhaps, but only if one concedes that both "missionary" and "movement" were effecting important changes on each other. Organizing for missions changed Methodism. And the missions that Methodism organized changed as well.

II
The High Imperial Era: Years of Maturity

The foreign missionary enterprise came into its own in the post–Civil War era, especially the decades flanking the end of the nineteenth and the beginning of the twentieth centuries. The tone of those decades—commonly called the High Imperial Era—now seems quite different from the tones that both preceded and succeeded them. In those years, U.S. crusaders poured into other countries, first rivaling then decisively eclipsing their European counterparts in numbers, funding, and activist fervor. Though the sum of outright conversions always remained modest (except in Hawaii and Burma), American missionaries exercised an enduring impact on other cultures. With a fervor and efficiency astonishing by almost anyone's standards, they founded schools, hospitals, orphanages, and relief programs. They tried to stop the most baleful of native practices, including foot binding, female circumcision, and suttee (the burning of widows). They also distinguished themselves as translators, linguists, ethnographers, nascent anthropologists, and, surprisingly often, natural scientists (even vulcanologists!).

In the High Imperial Era, the missionary enterprise scored notable successes, even in the eyes of its critics. For one thing, the institutional framework of missions gradually shifted from an interdenominational voluntary model toward a streamlined professional model more attuned to the mandates of the sponsoring denominations. The emergence of women's missionary organizations, which took both interdenominational and denominational forms, proved especially striking. By the eve of World War I, more than three million women had organized themselves into forty separate societies.[1] Other landmark events of the era included the founding in 1886 of the Student Volunteer Movement (SVM) through the influence of the famed evangelist Dwight L. Moody and the founding in 1895 of the World's Student Christian Federation under the direction of the missionary statesman John R. Mott.

In its first forty years, the SVM alone would motivate twenty thousand youth, mostly college age and college trained, to enter missionary service, many of them in YMCAs and YWCAs around the world.[2] Such efforts paid handsome dividends. After a trip around the world in 1914, a Vanderbilt University professor wrote, with telling overstatement, that six powers dominated the globe: "The British empire, the Russian Empire, the Japanese empire, the Chinese Republic, the American Republic, and the Young Men's Christian Association."[3]

In those heady High Imperial years, the theological motivations for missionary service also shifted. They moved from dutiful obedience to God's will toward an exhilarating expectation that missions represented the very vanguard of global history. Some efforts took a postmillennial form—missions aiming to renovate the world in preparation for (or increasingly in place of) the Lord's return. Others took a premillennial form—missions aiming to prepare the world for the Lord's return by winning humankind to Christ, one by one. A kind of roseate expansiveness suffused the entire enterprise. Both postmillennialist and premillennialist missionaries could comfortably embrace the SVM's motto: The Evangelization of the World in this Generation. And both assumed the normativeness of (Western) Christian civilization—"define and conquer," in William R. Hutchison's apt words.[4]

Still, the story reveals surprising turns as well. Though rarely self-critical about their own propensities toward cultural imperialism, missionaries often distinguished themselves by denouncing and sometimes vigorously resisting the most egregious forms of Western military and economic exploitation. The sunlit progressivism of the age nurtured a variety of grand cooperative ventures, such as the Foreign Missions Conference of North America, founded in 1893, and the Ecumenical Foreign Missions Conferences in New York in 1900 and in Edinburgh in 1910. In 1900, U.S. missionaries overseas numbered nearly five thousand, more than a quarter of the world's Protestant missionary force. By 1925, their numbers had nearly tripled, equaling almost half of the world total.

Nonetheless, fault lines dividing mainline from independent (or, in the parlance of the era, board from faith) missions were clearly visible by the early 1900s. Mainline missions refined business procedures for raising and disbursing funds and developed specialized training programs for overseas workers. These trends culminated in a new academic discipline of missiology: the "science" of missions. Independent mission agencies took a different tack. They distinguished themselves by a reliance on the Lord for daily provisions (instead of guaranteed financial support), by the favoring of direct proclamation of individual salvation over social service, by a determined effort to indigenize the gospel message among national peoples, and by a marked willingness to use women, including unmarried ones, to herald the Good News. The age saw the rise of great and powerful missionary agencies, including those established by all the major Protestant denominations and interdenominational boards as well, such as the Woman's Union Missionary Society of America. The most powerful players in the Protestant establishment were the sophisticated entities developed by the Presbyterians, Methodists, Episcopalians, and Southern Baptists. This period also witnessed the rapid growth of tough, resilient nondenominational missionary agencies, such as the China Inland Mission, the Africa Inland Mission, the Christian and Missionary Alliance, and the Sudan Interior Mission. These were all international agencies but were staffed increasingly by North Americans and largely operated on the faith principles of expansion funded by contributions, not by allocations from a denomination. Euphoric times they were, days of expansion, achievement, optimism, and seeming boundless promise. At the same time, though few could see it, they also proved to be days of peril.

6 / Mapping Presbyterian Missionary Identity in *The Church at Home and Abroad*, 1890–1898

Anne Blue Wills

Now there are varieties of gifts, but the same Spirit; and there are varieties of services, but the same Lord; and there are varieties of activities, but it is the same God who activates all of them in everyone.

1 Corinthians 12:4–6

ATTRIBUTES AND "AMERICANNESS"

In much of the literature produced and circulated by missionary societies and their sponsoring denominations, one hears the rumble of the dual engine that powered U.S. missions. U.S. Protestants aimed to win the world for Christ, yes; but the movement saw that Christ through unmistakably "American" eyes. The U.S. Protestant vocabulary for missions fused theological and political terms, which were mutually reinforcing and inseparable to the point of near indistinguishability. Missionaries spoke in both registers at once, ignoring the boundaries between the sacred and the secular that historians prefer to maintain. When we ask, "Were missionaries ruthless imperialists or self-sacrificial servants?" we reveal a desire to keep Christian missions and political missions separated, for fear, perhaps, that any mixture of the political with the religious sullies both elements.

But in the pages of *The Church at Home and Abroad* between 1890 and 1898—years of U.S. political imperialism and fervent Christian missionizing[1]—the home- and foreign missions magazine of the Presbyterian Church in the United States of America (PCUSA) did not separate "political" goals from "Christian" ones. Publication of this Presbyterian monthly began in December of 1886, the result of the Philadelphia-based denomination's consolidation of its home- and foreign mission magazines.[2] Its editorial writers and missionary correspondents traced, for a popular denominational audience,[3] the broad outline of an ideal at once Christian and "American": a "Christian civilization" that would be Bible-reading, individualistic, industrious, democratic, and "colorless."[4] U.S. civilization would follow that outline first and best, serving as the world's beacon to liberty and piety. In *The Church at Home and Abroad,* political interests were not seen as softened because they were carrying Christian freight; neither were Christian concerns seen as compromised because they were framed in political terms as well. The magazine's writers resisted asking either-or questions because they understood the Christian and the "American" as essentially improved by each one partaking of the other.

The vocabulary of Christian civilization showed itself most clearly in the magazine's reports from the mission landscape's more contested sites: those occupied by blacks, Roman Catholics, and Mormons.[5] Mission writers revealed their conceptualizations of Christian civilization—and their self-conceptualizations as Christian citizens—in the assumptions woven through their reports and commentaries on these three groups. Each posed singular challenges to a Christian civilization constructed according to the model set by the United States.

The determinative condition for Presbyterian involvement in missions to each group seems not to have been only their status as "the least of these," those for whom Christ died. Joined to that motive was their status as citizens (or potential citizens) of the Christian civilization. Yet something in each case militated against their being fully accepted as citizens by the missionaries. Presbyterians saw blacks as crippled by an ignorance that impeded their full exercise of U.S. citizenship; they saw Roman Catholics as hindered by a pervasive laziness symptomatic of a misdirected material religiosity; they saw Mormons as seriously misguided in their understanding of what the founders intended these United States to be. In the interest of Christian civilization, these groups' respective edges had to be planed down, these ways made straight. This variety of particularities called forth, at different moments, different aspects of the missionaries' identities.

One might imagine these missionaries as saints, portrayed in *The Church at Home and Abroad* with their "attributes," identifying them as at once Christian and "American." To southern freedpeople, Presbyterians saw themselves acting as Presbyterians, bringing education and decorum in worship to southern freedpeople to make them better citizens. To Roman Catholics, Presbyterians identified themselves as Protestants, carrying the Bible to Catholics around the world to stimulate industry. To the Mormons of the Great West, Presbyterians identified themselves as U.S. citizens, explicating the First Amendment to clarify the nature of true "Americanness," understood as a state of grace.

In reports on their mission progress, Presbyterians writing in *The Church at Home and Abroad* revealed both whom they saw as their mission objects and how they saw themselves. The magazine's writers repeatedly counseled, "Christianize first, civilize afterward,"[6] but their reports on these three communities evidence that the two works proceeded together, inseparably, and that the missionaries themselves—as Presbyterians, Protestants, and Americans—saw their work as at once redemptive and republic-centered. *The Church at Home and Abroad* advocated an "American incarnation" and knew it as Christianity.[7]

PRESBYTERIANS AND CITIZEN FREEDPEOPLE

"What shall we do with the Negro? is a universal question, asked with an increasing degree of alarm."[8] Reports on missions to freedpeople in *The Church at Home and Abroad* tried to undermine readers' fear-driven and deterministic notions about "color" and other traits conceived of as innate or immutable.[9] Indeed, the magazine published a Presbyterian "confession of faith" announcing the denomination's rejection of culturally accepted racial categories.[10] This statement proclaimed the denomination's position overtly. Two other strategies for missions to freedpeople, however, evidenced that Presbyterian identity more subtly: first, they countered the emotionalism they saw in black worship through careful preaching of the Word and emphasis on the Westminster Catechism;[11] second, they battled pervasive ignorance by starting dozens of schools.[12] Using methods and extending traditions they saw as particularly Presbyterian—educating individuals to read and understand the Scriptures—these missionaries felt that they offered a unique curative for freedpeople's ills.[13]

Boisterous worship—evidence of a religion based on "an enthusiasm rather than a principle"[14]—stood as one proof to the missionaries that southern freedpeople were every bit as "heathen" as those superstitious masses of humanity overseas. Blacks were variously described in *The Church at Home and Abroad* as excessively emotional, childlike, primitive, irresponsible, and immoral.[15] The missionaries ascribed the freedpeople's strange ways not to any inherent and unalterable racial shortcoming but to their need for a "plain, simple" gospel clearly preached.[16] In so doing, they attempted both to bypass the complications of race and to normalize mission work with freedpeople by making "heathenness" rather than "blackness" the determinative issue.[17]

Even so, this decomplication and normalization could take place precisely because the missionaries aimed to make blacks "colorless." This "colorlessness" was nothing else but "whiteness": "Let us pray God to help these intelligent leaders among the Negroes . . . to inspire the people with this wise and patient confidence in steady educational growth as their sure way to full possession of equal rights, in all respects, with their *colorless fellow citizens*."[18] The education of freedpeople in the States entailed their assimilation into the U.S. ideal, a white ideal. The argument that had allowed the work with freedpeople to continue contained within it the assumption that converts from among freedpeople would renounce their "heathen" customs.

Observers repeatedly noted, however, that U.S. blacks were not simply "heathen" in need of character or moral reform by way of the gospel. These blacks were "fellow citizens, entitled to all the rights of citizens."[19] "The Negro . . . needs to be developed, not because he is a Negro, but because [he] is a man and a citizen."[20] Indicating, in turn, something of the shape of "Christian citizenship," one writer noted, "These people have American traits. They form strong attachments. They love their native land. They love their kindred. They love their benefactors. They are loyal. They obey the laws."[21] If the danger presented by free but uneducated blacks could only be mitigated, they could be enlisted to fight other dangers to the Republic. "They love the country and the government, and unlike many of the foreigners who are crowding our shores, they are in hearty sympathy with every feature of our government which is Christian. Educated and Christianized, we believe they are destined, under God, to be a mighty bulwark against the infidelity, anarchism and socialism that threaten our land."[22] Fitting blacks in the United States for Christian civilization was, therefore, "a patriotic as well as a Christian work," meant to prepare them for the rights and privileges of citizenship in a participatory democracy, a free society.[23]

The model blacks featured in *The Church at Home and Abroad* evidenced "an earnest, patriotic Christian spirit."[24] Commenting upon the presence of Booker T. Washington at the Cotton States and International Exposition, held in Atlanta in December 1895, an editor recognized in him the very model of what the free black should become: "manly and self-reliant."[25] The work of making freedpeople into citizens—"wise, trusty and governable"—fell to all, "statesmen, philanthropists and Christians," since their ignorance endangered the survival of the nation, not just the stability of its southern regions: "that which threatens the safety of the inheritance for which our fathers fought, bled and died, should interest us, no matter how far it be removed from us."[26]

Educating freed blacks for the intelligent use of their votes stood as a central concern to the writers in *The Church at Home and Abroad*. "In the power of the illiterate, immoral, ungodly voter there is danger, no matter where he be."[27] The details of citizenship's curriculum indicate still more about what Christian civilization and participation in it required. "The spelling book, arithmetic and pen, the sword of the Spirit, and Westminster Catechism, . . . are all cooperating . . . to develop the industrial, moral and religious man, capable of being a good citizen and an honored Christian."[28]

The strategy of Presbyterian missionaries to the freedpeople assumed that blacks' "heathenness" could be redeemed through proper worship and education—things they saw as particularly Presbyterian offerings, correctives with roots in the Reformed tradition that they saw themselves as continuing. Coming out of that tradition, these missionaries understood themselves as uniquely qualified to solve the freedpeople's preoccupying "problems" of boisterousness and ignorance. The Presbyterian missionaries asserted the legitimacy of their work, however, not by justifying it simply as the saving of "heathens" or as the enlarging of the Presbyterian communion. They also saw freedpeople as fellow citizens, in need of restraint and education. Ordered and schooled—made Presbyterian, as the missionaries saw it—freedpeople became, at the same time, true citizens.

This fusion of Presbyterianism and political democracy defied neat dualistic oppositions. Yet that complexity may not have been that unique to Presbyterians. Other northern Protestant denominations—Congregationalists, Baptists, Methodists, white and black—responded to southern freedpeople in very similar ways, in response to comparably understood "problems" of mechanistic superstition and unrestrained worship.[29] What linked all those northern denominations' efforts? Their concern that, the Union preserved through bitter sectional conflict, freedpeople be added to its numbers and come into full possession of their U.S. citizenship, as participants in a democracy.

PROTESTANTS AND "CITIZENS AFTERWARD"

Roman Catholics posed a different kind of challenge to Protestant mission advocates than that posed by freedpeople.[30] Catholics in the United States appeared as the leading edge of a foreign conspiracy against the nation in which Catholics around the world participated, a conspiracy against U.S. sovereignty, culture, intellectual development, and economic prosperity.[31] U.S. Catholics especially stood as an outrage against the seat of Christian civilization, "alien in their ideas of citizenship, Roman in their religion."[32] Papal claims that "there should be 'no free education, no freedom of worship, no freedom of the press'" were condemned in appropriately biblical terms as "an abomination to true American citizens" who stood for all those freedoms.[33] The script of Christian civilization cast U.S. Catholics as villains, or at best pawns, providing Rome its route into the heart and soul of the United States—even into New England, the cradle of U.S. liberty[34]—waging "the Romish campaign of moulding American opinion."[35] Fighting the spread of Catholicism anywhere on the globe became a matter of "local patriotism."[36] Failing to respond to the call for aid would mean "making a sinful mistake, either as a Christian or an American."[37] The notion that national boundaries were irrelevant to "papism" constituted a major source of U.S. Protestant worry.

At the same time that this political indictment was sent down, however, so was a theological one: described as "Romanists" or "papists," Catholics around the world appeared in the pages of *The Church at Home and Abroad* as the sorry vestiges of recalcitrant "Romishness" left over from the Reformation.[38] Such characterizations allowed Presbyterian missionaries to assume the role of Protestant foil wherever they encountered Catholic faithful.[39] Here, then, the missionaries claimed not to be offering potential Catholic converts something uniquely Presbyterian but, rather, stood against "Romanism" shoulder-to-shoulder with other Protestant faithful.

By encouraging the private act of Bible reading, missionaries hoped to encourage defiance of priestly authority and the development of individual initiative allowed by U.S. liberty and allowing for U.S.-style progress. The solution to the religious and political quandary posed by Catholicism was stated simply: "an open Bible is the palladium of civil liberty."[40] "There is a vitality," one correspondent noted, "in the liberty of the Gospel which all the power of the Roman hierarchy cannot repress." The Church of Rome, he continued, had had centuries to improve the lot of its people; its adherents "have learned much about the ceremonies of that Church but nothing about the Bible or the enterprises of Christian civilization."[41]

"Romanism's" aversion to the Bible was a common topic in the magazine's pages. A pastor in New York City catalogued the many ways the Roman Catholic Church there "threaten[ed] American liberty"—by interfering in the schools, by submitting to "foreign domination," by "withholding the Bible from her Communion."[42] One South American missionary told of a local colporteur's run-in with a local vicar: "Under pressure of this threat [to be burned with his books], the colporteur was obliged to submit to the confiscation of his books, and subsequently 47 Bibles, 50 Testaments, and 100 Gospels were saturated with coal oil and set on fire in the market-place."[43] Converts starved for the newfound Word.[44] Catholics, one correspondent wrote from New Mexico, "are strictly prohibited from reading the word of God, and many of these people have only the Bible and perhaps a few tracts, on which to nourish their Christianity." "The zealous devotee of Rome," he continued, "flashes up in a rage at the very idea of mentioning the Bible or Protestantism to him; calls the evangelist a devil and the Bible the devil's book."[45]

One aspect of Christian civilization—industriousness—loomed particularly large in Presbyterian missionary work with Catholics. Catholics in the United States were seen to threaten the nation's economic prosperity; Catholics around the world wasted the economic potential of their respective nations. The disturbing effect of Catholicism, for these missionaries, was its production of indolent adherents.

Missionaries expressed their anxieties about Catholics in the language of enterprise and progress—personal and national, economic and political. "The Roman Catholic Church," a home missions note declared, "has never made a nation great. It has wielded tremendous power, but it has never rebuked oppression nor struck a blow for liberty."[46] One correspondent bewailed the state of Catholic Mexican Americans, whose ancestors had come three hundred years before, "not as pious pilgrims seeking freedom to worship God" but to "spoil the cities and make slaves of the inhabitants." These ambitions had not yet been realized: lacking "patient industry," the conquerors and their descendants "have never caught step with the march of progress" and have been "void of aspiration toward anything useful. . . . Rome is not the mother of progress." Protestantism, however, was: "the forces which have so recently aroused [the community] to life and action were led by the missionaries of the cross."[47] Recounting New Mexico's centuries of thralldom to the pope, one correspondent cited the "priesthood which paralized [sic] industry, forbade free thought and progressive enterprises." The writer continued, "From the time when the Mexicans providentially found access to the Bible and came to know . . . the more perfect accord of Protestantism with [its] teachings, . . . the stimulus which we give to all enterprises, . . . the obstructions [to progress] began to disappear."[48]

The Roman Catholic Church discouraged "enterprise"—a word suggestive of great doings, the engine of progress, driven by liberty on the way to greatness and riches. "Enterprise" formed part of Protestantism's "hope and aim": "We are compelled . . . to attribute that which is great and good in our nation and its institutions to the spirit and enterprise of Protestantism."[49] People caught in the grip of Catholicism's religious "monopoly"—and the word held some significance in the era of the Sherman Anti-Trust Act[50]—sacrificed real material riches in their satiation with spurious material devotions, and in the blind obedience to a pope set against a Protestant United States.[51] Reporting from Mexico, one missionary noted the futility of that country's religiously motivated attempts to ignore the United States as a trading partner, "as natural laws and our own great enterprise give to us a great advantage" and force Mexico's "consent to the incoming of American capital and labor and institutions only under protest."[52]

Report upon report in *The Church at Home and Abroad* claimed that the Bible's introduction into a community could drastically change its financial prospects. The Bible betokened progress—the means of Protestant liberation of Catholics and, in turn, the means for converted Catholics to embolden their sense of independence from the pope, their sense of individuality, their hunger for economic accomplishment—all sensibilities deadened by the Roman religion.

One correspondent reported from Venice, Italy, that local residents "broke the fourth commandment in two ways" by not working during the week on saints' days, then working on Sunday, when the priests would not penalize them. The observer not only noted the detriment such practices had for one's soul but also for one's pocketbook. Those converts who began to keep Sunday "holy" by not working reported to him "that they are gainers in health, and happiness, and purse, and business, by keeping holy the Lord's Day." The missionary added to his report that a certain store manager, ordered by the owner to resign for his support of the Sabbath movement, opened his own shop and "quite a crowd entered to congratulate and to patronize him."[53]

These Protestant missionaries understood Roman Catholicism as a material religion fraught with superstitious idolatry. Yet here, one sees that they preached a very material Protestantism, a Bible-based Christianity that taught the ordered use of material wealth.[54] They hoped to convert Catholic sacramentalism to Protestant industriousness—still material-focused, but sacralized in a different way. One goal of mission work was to "kindle [Catholics'] enthusiasm for material prosperity."[55] Conversion to Protestantism entailed conversion to acquisition and development, away from incarnations of mystery, which the missionaries saw only as "empty form."[56]

"AMERICANS" AND THE "ASIATIC INSTITUTION"

In dealing with upstart Mormons, Presbyterian missionaries evidenced a more overtly political identity. As much as mission advocates feared alleged Catholic designs on the nation's sovereignty, they yet identified themselves as Protestants encouraging regular Bible devotions.[57] Their political and economic dispute with Roman Catholicism played out through Bible and tract distributions. Reporting on their work with the Mormons, however, Presbyterian missionaries called themselves "Americans."[58] The missionaries dreaded the presence of Mormons, that "exceptional population" of the chaotic but potentially wealthy West,[59] and championed republican government in response to an innovative politics that they claimed merely masqueraded as a religion.[60] Denying Mormonism religious status, they went on to indict it as a political system as well. In *The Church at Home and Abroad,* Presbyterian missionaries worried most about the insularity of Mormonism, acted out most vividly in the institution of polygamy. The doctrine of plural marriage posed primarily a political, rather than a moral or theological, problem for the missionaries.[61]

Would Utah, with its Mormon tribes, gain statehood? Before 1896 and the arrival of statehood, this question exercised many correspondents from the western missions.[62] The preservation and extension of Christian civilization within the bounds of the United States depended, according to these voices, on keeping a Mormon Utah out of the Union. For these missionaries, whether Utah won statehood represented a much more important issue: who would serve as definer and model of Christian civilization? Protestant mainliners in the East? Or Mormons, who possessed a great part of the Great West and were, it was claimed, ready to fill the country with their offspring?

Mormons, it seemed, stood ready to propagate their own version of Christian civilization, and this threatened Protestant missionaries because the soul of Christian civilization was "American," understood as eastern and evangelical. Freedpeople could not mount a similar challenge because, despite the missionaries' claims that they could be made model citizens, race prejudice prevented many whites from following a freedperson's lead. Roman Catholics found themselves similarly excluded from mounting an alternative Christian civilization, as they were understood as "really" Roman. But these Latter-day Saints, as "Americans"—"Many of them . . . from New England and descendants of Pilgrim fathers"[63]—might well have overtaken and overthrown the Protestant model of Christian civilization, and therein lay their threat.[64]

Mormons presented an alternative politics taking root in U.S. soil, in which "the church and the priesthood" would "control the thinking and acting of the people"[65]—a "Catholic" result without the mitigating familiarity of the Protestant-Catholic conflict. Readers of *The Church at Home and Abroad* learned that Mormons saw themselves in the role of chosen people, taming North America, the chosen land.[66] Mormons, although physically far removed from the U.S. East, hit close to home with their vision for the country.

Polygamy stood as a major stumbling block to Utah's entry into the Union.[67] It was morally objectionable, offensive to nineteenth-century sensibilities that cherished virtuous mothers as the spiritual guardians of individually nurtured future citizens. "A state is but the aggregate of its families. The citizens are the products of the homes and home influences in which they have been reared."[68] Yet immorality was not the aspect of polygamy that most galled missionaries; the practice served to set Mormons apart, to underpin and perpetuate their separateness from the Republic. "Whatever may have led to [polygamy's] adoption this is the great service which it has rendered and which it was intended to render. They sought every means of separation from the rest of the world but failed in every attempt even in their removal to Utah, until polygamy was proclaimed and established. This was successful."[69]

The fact that polygamy's political implications—separateness from the United States—held at least as large a place in the minds of missionaries as its moral ones showed how severely the Mormons tested the missionaries' understanding of and loyalty to the "fundamental principle of . . . the liberty of conscience in worship."[70] "The Mormons," one editor opined, "are not yet reconciled to the American idea of religious toleration."[71] Another writer affirmed the Latter-day Saints' legal right "to worship whom or what they please, so long as they so order their worship as not to interfere with constitutional rights." They did not meet this stipulation, however, since "the government which they established has been opposed in theory and in operation, to the government of the United States." The trouble with Mormons, this writer continued, was that "the Mormon people erected not only an ecclesiastical but a civil government as well—a government whose antagonism to the constitution of the United States existed both in form and intent." Comparing the Mormon polity to the bygone southern Confederacy, the writer held that at least the Confederacy was a republic, not a hierarchy or monarchy, as the Mormon system was.[72]

Just as conversion had particular implications for freedpeople as citizens, and implications for Roman Catholics as participants in economic progress, it had particular, and political, implications for Mormons. Missionaries saw favorable signs in Mormon alignments with "American" political parties. The solid Mormon front gave way in "an overthrow of priestly rule"[73] as some became Democrats, others became Republicans.[74] A similar developing diversity had excited missionaries among Catholics; yet while that diversity was "denominationalism in full bloom,"[75] meaningful diversity among Mormons was political. It was ultimately the presence of that diversity that would announce Utah's readiness for statehood. Political diversity would prove that the ideals of the Union flowed through Utah freely, that it was part of the U.S. political body, not cut off from it by "foreign" institutions like polygamy. That political diversity was understood as a gift of grace: "The division on party lines has come to stay. . . . The political pot has boiled and boiled. It has been a blessing to Utah."[76]

The thoroughness of political conversion brought about by missionaries to the Mormons played out in significant ways. One missionary wrote that the streets in his district had been renamed as part of an effort to "wipe out" Mormon "landmarks." Yet the streets' new names were not Matthew, Mark, Luke, Calvin, or Knox. "Where once they were called Young and Smith, they are now called Washington, Adams, Jefferson, etc. 'The name of the wicked shall rot.'"[77] "American" virtues were, of course, encouraged: missionaries celebrated the growth in Mormon areas of "freedom of thought, of speech and of action," which all Christians should support.[78] Yet even the presence of "American" vices, as opposed to Mormon ones, seemed a beneficial substitution: "The Mormons are enough like other people to let their love of money modify their religious zeal, and in this case, at least, covetousness may be preferable to [Mormon] religious zeal, and serve a higher purpose. It is better for them to worship American money than the Mormon god."[79]

Utah's salvation looked quite earthly: "Utah is to be redeemed and purified, and will yet take her place in the sisterhood of states, a star of the first magnitude."[80] The first alternative to Mormonism was not Presbyterianism but "Americanness"—but an Americanness spread and supported by Christianity. Not the presence of Presbyterians, or even Christians, but the presence of "the loyal American element" made so by Christian missionaries, qualified the Mormon territories for statehood. The missionaries labored to redeem their Mormon targets from a political heresy to "civilization and righteousness."[81]

"VARIETIES OF ACTIVITIES"

The pages of *The Church at Home and Abroad* show the difficulty of fixing stable missionary identities and motives. These missionaries were at once Presbyterians and citizens, Protestants and entrepreneurs, Americans and advocates of a certain kind of religious liberty. Different mission contexts called forth different aspects of missionary identity. In a sense, workers in these fields did "go native"; they responded to what they understood as the local population's particular need.

One might continue to insist that the missionaries went to southern freedpeople to do political work under religious pretenses, or to Roman Catholics in the Southwest and cities in the same spirit. Yet the examples cited here make the point that such a description would fail to appreciate not only the authentic religious commitments of teachers and preachers but also the no less authentic religious investments the missionaries held in their political ends. The ideal of a "Christian civilization" disallowed any clear separation of theology or doctrine and politics.

Perhaps this inseparability appeared most clearly vis-à-vis the Mormons—missions to whom could be described as political work driven by the missionaries' religious conviction that Mormonism was not itself a religion. The missionaries certainly did not dismiss their own Christian beliefs in their work with Mormons or proceed to crusade against them on a purely legal or governmental level. They did use the law and the muscle of the government—they acted as Americans—but they continued to understand their "American" identity as a "blessing," as God's grace for them.

The fact that all of this work proceeded under the flag of a Christian civilization stamped "American"—democratic, capitalistic, Protestant, white—means, of course, that we cannot dispense with all questions about imperialism or ideology. We may look back on the history of U.S. Christian missions with embarrassment for its insensitivities. Yet to tell any human story is to remember the complications of insensitivity, ambiguity, mixed motives, good faith, wounds bound, and gifts given.

Indeed, my ultimate point here has been to understand how seriously these missionaries took the familiar words of the apostle Paul: "Now there are varieties of gifts, but the same Spirit; and there are varieties of services, but the same Lord; and there are varieties of activities, but it is the same God who activates all of them in everyone."[82] These missionaries felt liberated, within the context of their civilizing task, to respond to the variety they encountered in the field. For them, Paul's words blessed the fluidity of missionary identity.

7 / The Scientific Study of Missions

Textbooks of the Central Committee on the United Study of Foreign Missions

Nancy A. Hardesty

At a dinner party one night in Washington, D.C., a foreign diplomat was seated next to Abby Gunn Baker. Impressed with the depth of her knowledge of various foreign countries, the man asked, "Is your husband a diplomat?"

"No," she replied. "I have studied the textbooks of the Central Committee on the United Study of Foreign Missions."

Then, according to Helen Barrett Montgomery in *The Preaching Value of World Missions,* she told the amazed young man that "all the women of the Protestant world" participated in a joint study of mission fields around the world, that since 1900 they had used a joint textbook each year, and that hundreds of thousands of these books had been published. She noted that she had her own shelf of these textbooks at home, and whenever she read anything about a foreign country in the newspapers, she turned to her CCUSFM textbooks.[1]

Between 1901 and 1938, the Central Committee on the United Study of Missions (CCUSM, which sometime between 1912 and 1915 became the Central Committee on the United Study of Foreign Missions, or the CCUSFM) published annual textbooks for adults (see appendix A), a number of study books for young people and children (see appendix B), as well as various study guides, posters, charts, maps, and assorted pamphlets to encourage interest in and support for the foreign mission efforts of the women's boards of seven major northern Protestant denominations.

These inexpensive volumes—often paperback with striking if not exquisite covers—unveiled the world to women and children across the North American continent. This chapter explores the origins of the Central Committee, the role of its textbooks, and the textbooks' and the committee's demise.

FROM MITE TO MIGHTY SOCIETIES

Women supported foreign missions from their inception around 1800, but initially, mission institutions were male enterprises. Women's efforts were auxiliary. Women raised the money; men spent it. Women volunteered for missionary service but were told to get married and serve as model Christian wives and mothers for the "heathen." Women found a multitude of ways to minister but were given little credit and no authority.

In 1861, a group of women in New York City, under the leadership of Sarah Platt Doremus (1802–1877), formed the Woman's Union Missionary Society in order to send out single women missionaries. The organization of women's missionary societies by individual denominations rapidly followed: Methodists and Congregationalists (1869), Presbyterians (1870), Episcopalians and American Baptists (1871). These five denominations formed the basis of the CCUSM in 1900. They were later joined by representatives of the Dutch Reformed Church (whose women's missionary society formed in 1875) and the Lutheran Church (formed in 1879).

The major rationale for the CCUSM/CCUSFM's (hereafter CCUSFM) work lay in the slogan "Women's work for women and children." Victorian women were told that the home was the spiritual center of society and mothers teaching the faith to their children was the hope of the future, yet male missionaries in foreign lands, especially those working among Hindus and Muslims, were not permitted to meet or teach married women. Only women missionaries could gain access to the sacred precincts of the home. Women were also convinced that just as education and health were essential to their own progress in the United States, so teachers and doctors were essential to the uplift of women in foreign lands. And again, in many cultures, only women could treat and teach other women and their children.

In the late nineteenth century, more and more young women were attending high school and even college. Some received professional training in education, medicine, and law. Women's organizations proliferated: the Woman's Christian Temperance Union (WCTU), women's civic and social clubs, suffrage associations, mission societies. Every organization published its own journal. All women's organizations sought to conduct themselves in keeping with the best business practices. The WCTU talked about scientific alcohol and drug education. Religious and nonreligious movements alike moved in the direction of the progressive, the modern, the scientific. The CCUSFM reflected these trends.

In the 1870s, the International Sunday School Conventions established the International Uniform Lesson curriculum. Sunday schools became a part of foreign missions, and uniform study became a part of women's missions activity. The Methodists began such a program in 1879 with lessons printed in *Heathen Woman's Friend.*

Mrs. J. T. Gracey began to prepare the topics and readings for the Uniform Readings Course in 1887. In 1894, *The Study*, as it was known by then, became a separate publication.[2]

In 1888, at the World's Missionary Conference in London, the women founded their own World's Missionary Committee of Christian Women chaired by Abbie B. Child, who had been the only woman on the committee planning the London "Centenary" conference.[3] Home secretary of the Congregationalist Woman's Board of Missions and editor of *Life and Light for Heathen Women*, Child would also serve on the committee to plan the Ecumenical Missionary Conference in New York City in May 1900. It appears to have been her idea to launch a series of textbooks, the first outlining the history of missions in general and then six more, each focusing on the history and current situation of missions in a particular country. Men of the Student Volunteer Movement, which already published its own study books, told her that nobody wanted to study history, but women embraced the project.[4]

By the fall of 1900, the Central Committee had issued a leaflet study and engaged an author (Methodist Louise Manning Hodgkins) and a publisher (Macmillan) for *Via Christi*, published in 1901. It sold fifty thousand copies in the first year. Volumes on India (*Lux Christi*, by Caroline Atwater Mason), China (*Rex Christus*, by Arthur H. Smith), Japan (*Dux Christi*, by William Elliot Griffis), Africa (*Christus Liberator*, by Ellen Parsons), and the islands of the Pacific (*Christus Redemptor*, by Helen Barrett Montgomery) rapidly followed. The 1907 volume was *Gloria Christi: Mission and Social Progress* by Anna Robertson Lindsay. Volumes in 1908 and 1909 covered the Near East (*The Nearer and Farther East*, by Samuel Zwemer and Arthur Judson Brown) and Latin America (*The Gospel in Latin Lands*, by Francis and Harriet Clark).

Although Child died suddenly in 1902, the committee came under the very able leadership of American Baptist Lucy Waterbury (Mrs. Norman Mather Waterbury; Mrs. Henry W. Peabody). A member of the committee since its inception, she would chair it for twenty-eight years and then continue as honorary chair for several more (see appendix C, a chart of committee membership).

The textbooks represented one of the last expressions of the ecumenical hegemony of nineteenth-century evangelical Protestantism. Mason, noting that she had consulted works from many different denominations and missionary agencies in writing *Lux Christi*, declared, "They have furthermore offered convincing evidence of the insignificance of the divisive differences between Christians, of the greatness of the underlying unity." She went on to say, "Too long have we confined ourselves to the detailed study of our own limited fields, missing the sweep and the thrill which come with the wider knowledge of the work of the Church Universal."[5]

CELEBRATING JUBILEE

The undisputed high point of the movement and the textbook series was the publication in 1910 of *Western Women in Eastern Lands,* written by American Baptist leader Montgomery. This volume launched a jubilee celebration of fifty years of women's missions. Montgomery and Peabody formed a formidable team.[6] They issued a challenge to the Protestant women of the United States to raise $1 million for women's colleges in Asia. Montgomery wrote a pageant to dramatize the need. The jubilee began on October 12, 1910, in Oakland, California, and climaxed in New York City in April 1911. The traveling road show, starring Montgomery and Peabody along with various missionaries, put on 48 two-day "great Jubilees" in major cities and many one-day events in smaller towns.[7] Local committees with as many as four hundred members were involved. With the help of a challenge grant from philanthropist Abbie Rockefeller, the effort eventually raised $1.03 million.[8] *Western Women in Eastern Lands* sold fifty thousand copies in its first six weeks, more than one hundred thousand copies during the year, and it continued to sell.

Montgomery authored more of the CCUSFM textbooks than anyone else. In addition to *Christus Redemptor* (1906) and *Western Women in Eastern Lands* (1910), she wrote *The King's Highway: A Study of Present Conditions on the Foreign Field* (1915), which sold more than 160,000 copies, plus *The Bible and Missions* (1920) and *Prayer and Missions* (1925).[9] Her last book, *From Jerusalem to Jerusalem* (1929), reported on the 1928 International Missionary Council in Jerusalem.[10]

In addition to the textbook series, another major accomplishment of the CCUSFM was a summer-school program to prepare teachers. Summer schools, institutes, conferences, and the like were a rage of the age. As R. Pierce Beaver put it, the committee knew that publishing textbooks would not miraculously produce "study," so they proposed to the January 12, 1904, meeting of the Interdenominational Conference of Women's Boards of Foreign Missions that a subcommittee be formed to plan summer schools. The first took place July 12–19, 1904, at D. L. Moody's Northfield site; 235 women attended. The program included corporate worship, Bible study, prayer, discussions of problems of the mission fields, and tips on how to cultivate study in local churches. In 1905, summer schools were held in Northfield; Chautauqua, New York; and Winona Lake, Indiana. Then summer schools proliferated: by 1917 a total of twenty-five schools enrolled 11,693 women and girls.[11] Patricia Hill has noted that the 1915 Northfield school had 916 registrants, while the Minnesota school, in its ninth year, drew 1,300! The 1915 School of Missions in Oklahoma, in its fourth year, enrolled 404. On the West Coast, the schools included those of Mount Hermon and San Francisco. The week often concluded with an emotional consecration service during which young women pledged themselves to mission service.

The CCUSFM was also responsible for the origin of World Day of Prayer, inspired by the jubilee and still celebrated by many people today. In 1912, the Interdenominational Conference of Woman's Boards of Foreign Missions, the parent body of the CCUSFM, recommended a specific day of united intercessory prayer for foreign missions (various groups had kept various days over the past century). By 1924, twelve hundred *local interdenominational* groups were promoting missions. In 1918, the Woman's Council of *Home* Missions reiterated the proposal to the same body (now called the Federation of Woman's Boards of Foreign Missions)[12] that a joint committee be formed to promote a unified mission and Bible-study program, along with a single annual day of united prayer. A Committee on Women's Church and Mission Federations was formed,[13] and it developed the concept of a World Day of Prayer into what it is at present, under the auspices of Church Women United.

The CCUSFM also supported local publications in numerous languages for women and children around the world. An Interdenominational Committee on Christian Literature for Oriental Women, chaired by Alice M. Kyle, eventually became the Committee on Christian Literature for Women and Children in Mission Fields. Initially, the CCUSFM's study textbooks were intended to be international (the 1902 introduction to *Lux Christi* says that the idea had "been taken up with great and unexpected enthusiasm in nearly all of the forty women's foreign missionary societies in the United States and Canada, and in some societies in Great Britain"),[14] but they remained essentially a North American enterprise while the CCUSFM used profits from the textbooks to support other publications around the world.

For example, Peabody, out of her own pocket, published in the United States a magazine called *Everyland* and a series of booklets for small children. They were often advertised on the flyleaves of the CCUSFM textbooks. The committee's first international project was the publication in 1909 of a children's monthly magazine initially called *Chinese Everyland*, which eventually became *Happy Childhood*. The committee also contributed to the founding of the *Women's Messenger* in China and underwrote similar magazines in India, Japan, Africa, and elsewhere. Offerings from the World Day of Prayer also went to this cause. Peabody left a bequest to it in her will. The effort, under the Committee on Christian Literature for Women and Children, survived the demise of the CCUSFM and persisted as a separate entity until 1989, when it became the Standing Committee for Women and Children within the Intermedia Committee of the National Council of Churches.[15] Its story is told in *More Than Paper and Ink* by Sue Weddell.[16]

By 1915, more than three million women were involved in the women's missionary societies of some forty denominations. The ecumenical mission program represented by the CCUSFM was the largest women's movement in America, much larger than the combined efforts of predominantly male movements such as the Student Volunteer Movement and the Laymen's Missionary Movement.[17] Together, the women supported more than nine thousand missionaries, nearly ten times more missionaries than were serving in 1890.[18]

THE SCIENTIFIC STUDY OF MISSIONS

The chief focus of the Central Committee was the annual textbook. During the initial decade, the books were styled in a very academic way. Each chapter began with a timeline. The fact-filled body of the chapter was followed by relevant short selections from other sources, "themes for study and discussion," and a bibliography for further reference. A sizable portion of the book surveyed the country in question: its history, geography, ethnic populations, major religions, and so forth. A history of Christian missions to the country followed, and a history of women's mission work there completed the book. Most volumes included at least one map; some of them were multicolored and folded out. Later volumes (after 1910) had pictures—of missionaries, national Christians, and cute children.

The individual textbooks were intended to be supplemented in their use in local churches with materials specific to one's own denomination's mission work. Mission periodicals published factual articles about the history of their own work, biographies of their own missionaries, descriptions of specific institutions, and engaging personal-interest stories. Both the CCUSFM and individual boards published study helps such as maps.

Over the course of the thirty-eight years of publication, four volumes each were devoted to China and Africa, one per decade: *Rex Christus: An Outline Study of China* (1903), *China's New Day* (1912), *Ming-Kwong* (1924), and *Lady Fourth Daughter of China* (1932); and *Christus Liberator: An Outline Study of Africa* (1905), *An African Trail* (1917), *Friends of Africa* (1928), and *Congo Crosses* (1936). Three volumes were devoted to Japan: *Dux Christus: An Outline Study of Japan* (1904), *The Woman and the Leaven in Japan* (1923), and *Japanese Women Speak* (1934). India was the subject of at least two books: *Lux Christi: An Outline Study of India* (1902) and *Lighted to Lighten the Hope of India* (1922). Samuel Zwemer coauthored two books on the Middle East: *The Nearer and Farther East* (1908) and *Moslem Women* (1926). Latin America was explored in *Gospel in Latin Lands* (1909) and *Women under the Southern Cross* (1935). *Christus Redemptor* (1906) was subtitled *An Outline Study of the Island World of the Pacific.*

A number of books treated women's missions in a general way: the very first book, *Via Christi: An Outline Study of Missions* (1901), and *Western Women in Eastern Lands: An Outline Study of Fifty Years of Woman's Work in Foreign Lands* (1910), as well as *The King's Highway: A Study of Present Conditions on the Foreign Field* (1915), *Women Workers of the Orient* (1918), *From Jerusalem to Jerusalem* (1929), and *Eastern Women Today and Tomorrow* (1933).

Others covered more specific mission-related topics: *The Light of the World: A Brief Comparative Study of Christianity and Non-Christian Religions* (1911), *World Missions and World Peace* (1916), *A Crusade of Compassion for the Healing of the Nations* (on medical missions, 1919), *The Bible and Missions* (1920), *Prayer and Missions* (1925), and *Christ Comes to the Village: A Study of Rural Life in Non-Christian Lands* (1931).

Nine male authors contributed to the series; six volumes were authored entirely by men. During the first decade, The Macmillan Company of New York published the volumes. Starting in 1911 with *The Light of the World,* the books were printed in Boston and published by the Central Committee itself, headquartered in West Medford, Massachusetts.

For the most part, their tone was objective, academic, and rather dry. Some authors managed to describe other religions with measured respect. For example, William Griffis in *Dux Christus* declared that in Japan, "[s]hamanism, the worship of spirits or invisible beings; fetichism, the worship of inanimate objects; phallicism, the worship of the reproductive powers of nature; tree and serpent worship—were and are still, widely prevalent."[19] That was probably, as Griffis said, because "there was nothing shocking in the religious rites of Japanese paganism, as in India, for example (though some of the obscene orgies and emblems displayed in temple processions were at times incredibly vile)."[20]

On the other hand, Mason, writing of India, was much less generous toward Hinduism. She declared, "The curse of India is, that its gods are the base productions of the polluted imaginations of its people." She spoke of Hindus as "grossly idolatrous" and their religion as "a filthy abomination."[21] She described the Vedas as filled with "tedious sensuality, fantastic and monstrous beyond belief." She argued that while Hebrew Scriptures display "moral elevation" and "sustained poetic grandeur," the Vedas "abound . . . in puerile ideas," and its "hymns are childish in the extreme."[22]

While Griffis described the Japanese as "islanders, unconquered, sovereign, proud-spirited, intensely patriotic, and loving their own land and chief ruler even to religious devotions,"[23] Mason was much more critical, even racist. She insisted on drawing odious comparisons between the Hebrew people and the early Indo-Aryans. She asked, "Why should the Jewish people have advanced in civilizations, intellectual force, and in spiritual attainment so far beyond the Hindu?" Her answers were geographic and religious. "The enervating tropical climate has produced in the course of centuries a dreamy and brooding mental habit in place of the early creative and aggressive energy. Palestine, lying well to the north, bred a hardier and more stubborn type of men." The Jews had a "lofty, original Jehovistic faith," while "the religion of the Indo-Aryans . . . while starting with a comparatively pure nature-worship . . . rapidly degenerated into ritualistic and mythological Brahmanism with its monstrous misconceptions and puerile superstitions. With the degeneration of its religion has come the degeneration of the people."[24] *Lux Christi* was one of the few books that had a section on "Racial Characteristics."

Zwemer's description of Islam in *The Nearer and Farther East,* with very little mention of women at all, engaged the mind, focusing on the historical and statistical. His sources were all male, mostly British, with some German or Dutch. His book contained no personal stories.

Other CCUSFM books engaged the heart. In particular, those of Montgomery combined her vast knowledge of women's missionary work around the world with her eye and ear for telling detail and touching vignette. For example, she began a tribute to "Missionary Wives" by noting their sacrifices. Seven men and five wives were the first missionaries to arrive in Sierra Leone; none of the wives survived; in fact, none lived more than six months. But then she immediately cited Jane Williams, who served in New Zealand for sixty-eight years; a Mrs. Baker, who spent seventy-two years in Travancore, twenty-two as a widow; and a Mrs. Thomas of Tinnevelli, who died in 1899 after sixty-one years there, twenty-nine as a widow.[25] Concerning the legendary Isabella Thoburn, Montgomery noted two things. First, she described the year-round flowers that surrounded the home Thoburn purchased for her school in India. Then she quoted from a letter written just after Thoburn's death by her Indian assistant, Lilavati Singh, who had traveled with her in the United States: "Saturday morning she did a little gardening and made cookies for us."[26]

As one might expect from a series of books written by various authors, the volumes are difficult to compare. After the first series, the format varied widely. The 1924 volume, *Ming-Kwong: "City of the Morning Light,"* was a fictionalized account. It incorporated all of the major events in the history of women's missionary work in China but within a narrative about a fictional group of missionaries in a hypothetical city.

Even though the 1925 volume focused on the more abstract topic of *Prayer and Missions,* Montgomery wove her theological insights into the early chapters on the Bible and prayer, then used her vast knowledge of women's missions to illustrate later chapters on the formation of mission organizations, the lives of missionaries, and the spiritual journeys of national Christians. Pictures of prayer warriors illumined the text. Mary Schauffler Platt contributed two books focused on children: *A Child in the Midst* (1914) and *A Straight Way toward Tomorrow* (1927), which was also translated into Spanish and Japanese as well as the languages of India and China. She described the plight of children around the world and detailed missionary efforts to improve their health and education. Her hope was that international cooperation could create a peaceful world that would nurture all children.

The Central Committee tried a variety of approaches to make the textbooks informative and appealing, both factual and emotionally gripping.

The CCUSFM textbooks were only one part of a much wider publishing program. Other organizations published study books; denominational groups publicized their missions; religious publishers found that mission books sold. Popular authors contributed books to several series. For example, the British and Foreign Bible Society published *Bible-Women in Eastern Lands* in 1904. It was the eleventh in a series of "Centenary Pamphlets."[27] Howard B. Grose produced *The Incoming Millions* in 1906 for the "Home Mission Study Course."

The Young People's Missionary Movement published the "Forward Mission Study Courses." Arthur J. Brown's *The Why and How of Foreign Missions* (1908) was part of that series. The Missionary Education Movement published such works as Robert E. Speer's *Servants of the King* (1909) and Ethel Daniel Hubbard's *Under Marching Orders: A Study of Mary Porter Gamewell* (1911).

Fleming H. Revell regularly published missionary books, such as *Our Moslem Sisters,* by Annie Van Sommer and Samuel Zwemer (1907); *The Education of Women in China* (1911) and *The Education of Women in Japan* (1914), both by Margaret E. Burton; and *Chinese Heart-Throbs,* by Jennie V. Hughes (1920).

By the turn of the century, various women's missionary boards were beginning to celebrate anniversaries. In 1904, Sarah Frances Butler published *History of Woman's Foreign Missionary Society, Methodist Episcopal Church, South.* In 1913, Clotilda McDowell chronicled *Our Work for the World,* published by the Methodist Episcopal Church. In 1917, Congregationalists celebrated with Frances J. Dyer's *Looking Backward over Fifty Years: Historical Sketches of the Woman's Board of Missions* and Kate G. Lamson's *Study of Our Work Abroad: Contrasts of Fifty Years.* In 1925, Mrs. W. I. Chamberlain produced *Fifty Years in Foreign Fields: China, Japan, Arabia: A History of Five Decades of the Woman's Board of Foreign Missions, Reformed Church in America.* The list could go on.

In 1914, a Committee of Twenty-Eight was formed to coordinate publishing efforts, choosing annual themes for home- and foreign-missions study. The committee was composed of seven members each from the Federation of Woman's Boards of Foreign Missions, the Woman's Council of Home Missions, the Home Missions Council of North America, and the Foreign Missions Council.[28]

The Central Committee began cooperating in book publication with the Missionary Education Movement (MEM) in the 1920s. For example, the CCUSFM book for 1922 was *Lighted to Lighten the Hope of India.* The junior book was *A Child's*

Garden in India. The MEM book was Daniel Fleming's *Building with India.* In 1923, the CCUSFM book was Charlotte B. DeForest's *The Woman and the Leaven in Japan,* while the MEM volume was Galen Fisher's *Creative Forces in Japan.*

DECLINE AND DEMISE

Why did the women's foreign missionary enterprise decline and virtually disappear from mainline Protestant denominations by World War II?

One might think the question tangential to this discussion except that Hill, in her influential study *The World Their Household,* has seemed to blame the CCUSFM and its textbooks. Hill has charged, "The introduction of systematic mission study did have a definite impact on the character of local auxiliaries that can be linked to the decay of support for the woman's foreign missionary movement at home."[29] The reason seemed clear: "the introduction of textbooks was a dilution of their religious, prayer-meeting atmosphere."[30] Hill has also blamed the "professionalization" of the mission enterprise and the mission boards' emphasis on being scientific, businesslike, and efficient.

Dana Robert, in a more balanced analysis containing far more material from representative textbooks, has suggested that the CCUSFM did reflect a change in missions strategy but was not responsible for it. Prior to World War I, the women's (and men's) missionary movement did emphasize evangelism and the salvation of individual "heathen" souls. Montgomery in her 1910 *Western Women in Eastern Lands* lauded women missionary evangelists and noted, "In everything but name they are preachers." They were often accompanied by a trained national, a "Bible woman," who, said Montgomery, "is first of all an evangelist."[31]

However, times where changing. Missionaries themselves were becoming more specialized and professionalized in the age of the Social Gospel. To legitimate their own enterprise, women's foreign mission boards emphasized female missionaries' unique opportunities to minister to the secular as well as the spiritual needs of women and children. In keeping with the rhetoric of the day and playing on themes of home and motherhood, as well as social uplift, women's work for women and children was seen as not only saving souls but transforming cultures from the inside out. Certainly, women were not alone in viewing the mission enterprise as sharing not only the "truth" of Christianity but also the blessings of capitalism and Western culture. Progress reigned; the millennium was at hand. The whole world could be made homelike. "Scientific" textbooks, female missionary doctors, the celebration of jubilee, and a million dollars for Asian women's colleges were all part of the grand Christianizing and civilizing enterprise.

As Robert has noted, some saw disaster coming; the Central Committee's 1916 book was *World Missions and World Peace* by Mason. The book for juniors was Charles Jefferson's *Soldiers of the Prince*—the Prince of Peace. But it was too late. The world was engulfed in war—not the "heathen" nations but the "Christian" ones.

Chastened by World War I, women (and men) mission executives began to speak more of "World Friendship," to see themselves as partners with national Christians, and to consider working themselves out of a job.[32] One could argue that they succeeded. The goal of supporting women's education and publications in foreign lands was to help women and their children gain the tools of self-sufficiency. As missionaries educated teachers and nurses, they empowered women to become leaders and role models within their own countries. They helped to "plant" and "grow" national churches. Veteran Methodist missionary Mary Ninde Gamewell in *Ming-Kwong,* for example, described the 1922 National Christian Conference in China that gave birth to the National Christian Council and the Church of Christ in China, making Christianity "indigenous." She said, "The missionary would have the joy of seeing the rapid fulfillment of his long cherished hope in the increase of Chinese leadership, and the consequent decrease of his own."[33]

After World War I, women became occupied with both opportunities and pressing issues at home in the United States. They had won the vote with the passage of the Nineteenth Amendment in 1920 and were now more concerned about national politics. They concentrated more on their own education and careers. Within some churches, they began to fight for or exercise lay rights for the first time. With the Great Depression of the 1930s, many struggled for survival, and money to support missions was scarce. Thus, the rapidly changing context of the first three decades of the twentieth century provides several reasons for the loss of momentum.

Robert has offered yet another reason for the decline and demise of women's missions: stated bluntly, men killed them. Men had opposed women's involvement in missions from the inception of the American Board of Commissioners of Foreign Missions (ABCFM) in 1810. Men had refused to let women be full-fledged missionaries, and they carped about the founding of the Woman's Union Missionary Society. Men were not thrilled with the formation of the women's boards. Only for a brief moment in the 1890s did men laud women's work for women because it gave churchwomen something to do.

When women's missionary boards and groups such as the Central Committee succeeded in building powerful organizations and raising substantial sums of money, churchmen began systematically to destroy them. In the 1920s and 1930s, male-dominated boards swallowed up many of the denominational women's mission boards.[34] A reorganization of the Protestant Episcopal Church in 1919 diluted women's power. In 1923, the male Board of Missions subsumed Presbyterian women's missions. And the Congregational women's boards were merged into the ABCFM in 1927. In 1932, the Federation of Woman's Boards of Foreign Missions combined with the Foreign Missions Conference of North America (FMCNA), a goal the latter had been pursuing since 1910. The FMCNA became part of the National Council of Churches at its inception in 1950, eventually becoming its Division of Overseas Ministries (DOM).[35] American Baptist women and Methodist Episcopal women managed to maintain independent institutions much longer, but they had to struggle.

Northern Protestant churchmen were also playing out their own internal equivalent of World War I—the fundamentalist-modernist controversy. As Margaret Bendroth has noted, the conflict was primarily between men. Within the Presbyterian Church of the United States of America, Bendroth has read this clash in part as a defense of orthodox Calvinism against the "feminine" heart religion of the nineteenth century. Male denominational leaders specifically attacked women mission leaders as an "ecclesiastical feminarchy" that threatened the survival of "masculine Calvinistic doctrines."[36] In 1906, a group of laymen founded the Presbyterian Brotherhood of America in order to promote a "strong clear masculine line."[37] In 1920, Presbyterian women celebrated the jubilee of their own foreign mission efforts by raising $608,014.77 for National Jubilee Projects (another scholar estimates that between 1870 and 1920 Presbyterian women gave more than $17 million to foreign missions).[38] In 1923, the Presbyterian General Assembly (with no female delegates yet elected) summarily disbanded the semi-independent women's missionary boards and incorporated them into the Board of Foreign Missions and Board of National Missions. Ironically, delegates then commissioned a study of "the Causes of Unrest Among the Women of the Church." The report led to overtures from local presbyteries that would have opened the offices of ruling elder, evangelist, and ordained minister to women. In 1930, the presbyteries accepted female ruling elders but rejected evangelists and teaching elders.[39]

In effect, women were told they could no longer be trusted; women who had been seen as allies in the missionary enterprise were now seen as adversaries. Women who had been seen as keepers of the true flame were now accused of playing with strange fire. In the ordination debate, for example, fundamentalist leader Clarence Macartney warned that to allow women's ordination would "increase the spread of heresy, schism, error, and fanaticism." Another minister argued that the Presbyterian pulpit needed "real men" with "more manhood and more masculine power."[40] One might suggest that in the face of such an onslaught, rank-and-file laywomen understandably might have lost interest in raising money for missions in particular and in church participation in general.

Another reason for a slowdown in the momentum of women's missions may have been theological. The fundamentalist-modernist controversy split denominational missionary boards and fractured ecumenical relationships among missionaries in foreign fields. More conservative, evangelism-oriented missionaries and their lay supporters put their energies into faith missions.[41] And faith missions were less likely to be supported by the kinds of well-organized women's societies that had financed much of the old mainline denominations' mission work.

Yet another explanation for the fate of these organizations might be that the women's foreign missionary effort simply ran its course. Christians believe in immortality and sometimes expect it of their institutions. Christianity lacks a theology of change, a religious conceptualization of birth, growth, and death as a natural and holy cycle.

THE WORK OF A LIFETIME

A remarkable group of nineteenth-century women poured their energies into missions organizations (see appendix C). Their working lives defined the lifespan of numerous other organizations as well. For example, Jennie Fowler Willing (1834–1916) was instrumental in founding both the Woman's Foreign Missionary Society and the Woman's Home Missionary Society for the Methodist Episcopal Church. We have spoken of the work of American Baptists Lucy Waterbury Peabody (1861–1949) and Helen Barrett Montgomery (1861–1934) on behalf of the CCUSFM. Its subsidiary, the Committee on Christian Literature for Women and Children in Mission Fields, was led by Alice Kyle from 1912 to 1928; Montgomery, 1928–1930; and Clementina Butler, 1930–1945. Butler was secretary-treasurer of the original CCUSFM committee from 1900 to 1908. Olivia Lawrence, also a member of the CCUSFM from 1910 to 1935, was secretary of the Committee on Christian Literature from 1918 to 1934. Miss A. V. Pohlman served on the Central Committee from 1910 to 1927; Gertrude Schultz from 1923 to 1935; Mrs. Frederick G. Platt from 1924 to 1935. Margaret G. Applegarth, who wrote at least four of the CCUSFM junior textbooks, chaired the World Day of Prayer Committee for a decade beginning in 1937.[42] Women gave decades of their adult lives to this work. Succeeding generations of women had other things to do. Thus, one might conclude that the Central Committee, along with its leaders, merely died a natural death.

In 1938, the Central Committee published its final book, *Women and the Way: Christ and the World's Womanhood*, with essays by leading Christian women from around the world, including Madame Chiang Kai-shek of China and Michi Kawai, a Japanese educator.[43] The American women's foreign missionary movement had raised up a generation of Christian women leaders worldwide. They had accomplished their task. They could already see World War II looming. Since their parent group, the Federation of Woman's Boards of Foreign Missions, had merged into the Foreign Missions Conference of North America in 1932, the Central Committee simply voted to dissolve itself into the MEM, a subsidiary of the FMCNA.[44]

As a final observation on the historical place of the CCUSFM, we might note that the Central Committee rode the crest of a technological wave when it began publishing its textbooks—hardback version for 75 cents; paperback, 50 cents. In the last half of the nineteenth century, periodicals flourished. In the early twentieth century, inexpensive paperback books flooded the market. Later, Christian organizations would use radio, films, television, and the World Wide Web to publicize their work. The Central Committee also appealed to the public's desire at the time for education and for information that was objective and "scientific." In providing this through textbooks, they also documented the evolving roles of mainline denominational missions, from evangelizing the "heathen," to caring for women and children through the establishment of educational and medical institutions, to cooperative work with women leaders in national churches. Many of the dynamics and currents of U.S. Protestant life in the first four decades of the twentieth century, and the role of women in that life, are visible in the life and death of the CCUSFM.

Appendix A

Central Committee on the United Study of Foreign Missions Annual Textbooks

1901 *Via Christi: An Outline Study of Missions.* By Louise Manning Hodgkins.

1902 *Lux Christi: An Outline Study of India.* By Caroline Atwater Mason.

1903 *Rex Christus: An Outline Study of China.* By Arthur H. Smith.

1904 *Dux Christus: An Outline Study of Japan.* By William Elliot Griffis.

1905 *Christus Liberator: An Outline Study of Africa.* By Ellen Parsons.

1906 *Christus Redemptor: An Outline Study of the Island World of the Pacific.* By Helen Barrett Montgomery.

1907 *Gloria Christi: Mission and Social Progress.* By Anna Robertson Lindsay.

1908 *The Nearer and Farther East.* By Samuel Zwemer and Arthur Judson Brown.

1909 *The Gospel in Latin Lands.* By Francis E. and Harriet Clark.

1910 *Western Women in Eastern Lands: An Outline Study of Fifty Years of Woman's Work in Foreign Lands.* By Helen Barrett Montgomery.

1911 *The Light of the World: A Brief Comparative Study of Christianity and Non-Christian Religions.* By Robert E. Speer.

1912 *China's New Day.* By Isaac T. Headland.

1913 *The King's Business.* By Mrs. Maud Mary [Wotring] Raymond.

1914 *The Child in the Midst.* By Mary Schauffler Laboree [Platt].

1915 *The King's Highway: A Study of Present Conditions on the Foreign Field.* By Helen Barrett Montgomery.

1916 *World Missions and World Peace.* By Caroline Atwater Mason.

1917 *An African Trail.* By Jean Kenyon Mackenzie.

1918 *Women Workers of the Orient.* By Margaret E. Burton.

1919   *A Crusade of Compassion for the Healing of the Nations.* By Belle Allen; edited by Caroline Atwater Mason.

1920   *The Bible and Missions.* By Helen Barrett Montgomery.

1921   *The Kingdom and the Nations.* By Eric M. North.

1922   *Lighted to Lighten the Hope of India.* By Alice Boucher Van Doren. *Building with India.* By Daniel Johnson Fleming. MEM but carries CCUSFM imprint.

1923   *The Woman and the Leaven in Japan.* By Charlotte B. DeForest. *Creative Forces in Japan.* By Galen M. Fisher. MEM but carries CCUSFM imprint.

1924   *Ming-Kwong: City of the Morning Light.* By Mary Ninde Gamewell.

1925   *Prayer and Missions.* By Helen Barrett Montgomery.

1926   *Moslem Women.* By A. E. and Samuel M. Zwemer.

1927   *A Straight Way toward Tomorrow.* By Mary Schauffler Platt.

1928   *Friends of Africa.* By Jean Kenyon Mackenzie.

1929   *From Jerusalem to Jerusalem.* By Helen Barrett Montgomery.

1930   *A Cloud of Witnesses.* By Elsie Singmaster.

1931   *Christ Comes to the Village: A Study of Rural Life in Non-Christian Lands.* By Eleanor T. Calverley, M.D., Mabel Ruth Nowlin, Alice B. Van Doren, and E. Stanley Jones; edited by Mary Schauffler Platt.

1932   *Lady Fourth Daughter of China: Sharer of Life.* By Mary Brewster Hollister.

1933   *Eastern Women Today and Tomorrow.* By Ruth Frances Woodsmall.

1934   *Japanese Women Speak: A Message from the Christian Women of Japan to the Christian Women of America.* By Michi Kawai and Ochimi Kubushira.

1935   *Women under the Southern Cross.* By Margaret Ross Miller.

1936   *Congo Crosses: A Study of Congo Womanhood.* By Julia Lake Kellersberger.

1937   no title

1938   *Women and the Way: Christ and the World's Womanhood.* By Madame Chiang Kai-shek, Michi Kawai, et al. This is the final book.

Appendix B

Central Committee on the United Study of Foreign Missions Junior Textbooks

1912   *The Young China Hunters.* By Isaac Taylor Headland.

1913   no title

1914   no title

1915 *Around the World with Jack and Janet.* By Norma B. Waterbury [Thomas].

1916 *Soldiers of the Prince.* By Charles E. Jefferson.

1917 *African Adventurers.* By Jean Kenyon Mackenzie.

1918 *Jack and Janet in the Philippines.* By Norma Waterbury Thomas.

1919 *Mook, A True Tale.* By Evelyn Worthley Sites (ca. 1918).

1920 *Lamp-Lighters across the Sea.* By Margaret Applegarth.

1921 no title

1922 no title

1923 *Honorable Japanese Fan.* By Margaret Applegarth.

1924 *Ming-Kwong: City of the Morning Light.* By Mary Ninde Gamewell. Same book as for adults.

1925 *Brave Adventurers* [about prayer]. By Mrs. E. C. [Katharine Scherer] Cronk.

1926 *Two Young Arabs.* By Samuel Zwemer.

1927 *Please Stand By.* By Margaret Applegarth.

1928 *Camp Fires in the Congo.* Mrs. John M. Springer.

1929 *Going to Jerusalem.* By Margaret Applegarth.

1930 no title

1931 *Open Windows.* By Mary Entwistle. Joint publication with MEM.

1932 *Chinese Lanterns.* By [?] Meyer.

1933 no title

1934 no title

1935 no title

1936 no title

1937 *Doorways.* By Mary Entwistle. Joint publication with MEM.

n.d. *The Treasure Hunt.* By [?] Seebach.

Appendix C

Women Who Served on the Central Committee

Miss Abbie Child, Congregationalist, founder and first chair, 1900–1902, the year of her death.

Mrs. Norman Mather Waterbury / Mrs. Henry W. Peabody / Lucy Peabody, American Baptist, Tremont Temple, Boston, served on committee from the beginning, as chair for twenty-eight years, and for a few years thereafter as honorary chair.

Bailey, Miss A. G., treasurer, 1934–1935.

Butler, Miss Clementina, Methodist, Newton Centre, Mass., secretary-treasurer, 1901–1908.

Clark, Mrs. N. Walling, 1924–1929.

Colburn, Miss Grace T., 1910–1920; secretary, 1915–1920.

Cook, Mrs. Frank Gaylord, treasurer, 1923, 1926–1933.

Goodwin, Deaconess Henrietta, 1920.

Gracey, Annie Ryder (Mrs. J. T.), Methodist, Rochester, N.Y., 1901–1908.

Kyle, Miss Alice M., 1918–1923.

Lawrence, Miss Olivia H., 1910–1935.

Lentz, Mrs. Edwin, 1932–1935.

Lodge, Miss Susan C., 1932–1935.

Lowrie, Miss Rachel, 1911–1912.

Marston, Miss Margaret I., 1932–1935.

North, Mrs. Frank Mason, 1912–1923.

Northup, Miss Elizabeth C., 1910–1911.

Parsons, Miss Ellen C., Presbyterian, New York City, 1901–1908.

Platt, Mrs. Frederick G., 1924–1935.

Pohlman, Miss A. V., 1910–1927.

Sawyer, Mrs. Decatur, New York City, 1908–1917.

Schultz, Miss Gertrude, Presbyterian, 1923–1935; secretary, 1923–1929; chair, 1932–1935.

Scudder, Mrs. Harriet L., Reformed Church, New York City, 1903–1904.

Stanwood, Miss E. Harriet, Congregational, Boston, 1908–1917.

Swain, Mrs. Leslie E., 1932–1935.

Thorpe, Mrs. Charles N., 1910.

Tillotson, Miss Emily, 1923–1928.

Webb, Mrs. James A., Jr., 1915–1920.

Wiles, Mrs. Charles C., 1928–1935; secretary, 1932–1935.

Note: This list represents what I can document from the volumes I have. Those listed as serving until 1935 may well have served until the committee's demise in 1937.

8 / Open-Winged Piety

Reflex Influence and the Woman's Missionary Society of the Methodist Church in Canada

Marilyn Färdig Whiteley

"The heathen are saving the church." This statement by one Bishop Lawrence was quoted in 1908 in the Woman's Missionary Society column in the *Christian Guardian,* the weekly newspaper of the Canadian Methodist Church.[1] It is one of many indications of how supporters of foreign missions assumed that work for missions exerted a "reflex influence" on the church at home: in some way the home churches and the people within them benefited from work for missions. Women in missionary societies frequently used this argument, for in attempting to justify their work, they carried a double burden. First, they faced the criticism leveled against foreign mission work in general, that it diverted both human and financial resources from much needed work at home; second, that the general boards of missions already supported missions, and there was no need for separate women's societies. Indeed, some church members said that such groups would divert funds from the general societies. Although the women did not usually refute these charges in terms as strong as those of Bishop Lawrence, they maintained that, both financially and in other ways, their work for missions did not hinder but, rather, aided the church.

The Woman's Missionary Society (WMS) of the Canadian Methodist Church ranked among the many groups that claimed a reflex influence for their work. Organized in 1881,[2] the WMS grew steadily so that in 1925, when the Methodist Church entered into church union, the WMS had more than 61,000 members and financial assets approaching $700,000. It was a major force within the Methodist Church, which during this period was one of the three largest Protestant denominations in Canada. The Methodist Church saw itself as the most Canadian of denominations, with a special role to play in building the nation.[3] Thus, any reflex action of the women's work influenced other women, men, and children in their denomination and their society.

This discussion of the Canadian Methodist WMS, from its beginning in 1881 until its merger in 1925 into the WMS of the United Church of Canada, looks first at what the women saw as benefits of mission work, weighing the evidence regarding the achievement of those benefits. There is, however, an additional task. In her book *The World Their Household,* Patricia Hill has stated that "the primary reflex influence of the massive mobilization of Christian womanhood might not be spiritual at all," and she has given attention to what she has seen as the "nonspiritual reflex influence of mission work."[4] Thus, this discussion goes on to examine "influences" beyond what these women themselves anticipated.

THE PERSONAL BENEFIT

The idea of a reflex influence was not restricted to public apologetics. In gatherings at all levels, WMS members were encouraged to testify regarding "the personal benefit derived from this work." At an 1890 meeting held in Belleville, Ontario, for example, women attested "that it had proved a sure safeguard against selfishness, and had encouraged timid ones to be bold in the Master's name and cause; and while the work of our Woman's Missionary Society had been blessed by the winning of souls abroad and at home, its influence had been felt and seen in the deepening of the interest of the women of our Church in all lines of earnest Christian work."[5]

The most systematic statement, however, appeared in the account of an address given by Annie Robinson McMechan of London, Ontario. McMechan appeared before the London Conference of the Methodist Church as a representative of the WMS. She spoke of "the benefit to the home churches of these Woman's Missionary Societies."[6] The first benefit was education, and she stressed the production and distribution of missionary literature that could "be had almost for the asking." Second was the spiritual benefit. She described the transformation of "the busy mother . . . who has never even uttered a prayer in the presence of others, [who] becomes the head of an efficient and enthusiastic society." The third benefit was financial. Countering fears that the WMS diverted funds from the General Missionary Society of the church, she presented figures to demonstrate that "far from interfering, the existence of an auxiliary helps the General Missionary Society." McMechan's outline suggests a starting point for examining the impact of the WMS on the women within the organization and on their church.

When she said that "zeal is according to knowledge," McMechan articulated a basic assumption of her sisters in the WMS. From its early days, members actively spread information about missions and the need for missions. At first, letters written by missionaries to those at home were copied and circulated, but the women soon replaced that system with the publication of a series of leaflets. They also disseminated information through the *Christian Guardian* and the *Wesleyan,* published in

Halifax, and over the years the women's work filled a significant portion of the denomination's missionary monthly paper, the *Missionary Outlook,* under the supervision of an editor chosen by the WMS from among its ranks.

WMS leaders made an abundance of missionary literature available, and local records indicate that it was extensively used in the homes and church parlors when the Canadian Methodist women met. A small number of groups gathered only to turn in their money and elect officers, deciding "that in future we meet but once in every three months, as there seems to be no business to call us together oftener."[7] In most auxiliaries, however, members shared missionary letters and articles and were encouraged to prepare original essays for presentation at subsequent gatherings. Groups that listened to this original work and found it helpful sometimes recommended that it be submitted to the *Outlook* for publication. This program material was not the product of professionals but of consecrated women whose zeal for missions made them willing to exercise their talents for that cause.

To involve women as broadly as possible in gathering missionary information, the national society encouraged auxiliaries to institute the "Watch Tower." Members were appointed as "Heralds" to make reports of no more than three minutes each on their assigned mission fields. The instructions were clear: "On no account shall a Watchman read her report. If a group of friends should say, 'Madame H., how are your children?' Madame would not read a written statement of their health, nor would she talk about all the children in the neighborhood before answering inquiries for her own."[8] It is obvious from the minute books that reports were frequently read, however, and sometimes they were not given at all. The secretary for the Cataraqui, Ontario, auxiliary was more direct than most. In 1909, she stated, "The Watch Tower Heralds were conspicuous by their silence."[9]

Yet the exercise was a common one and frequently must have filled its function. In 1912, Ada Magrath, corresponding secretary of the Alberta Branch, wrote to the president of a newly formed auxiliary. A few years earlier, Magrath had moved to Edmonton from Belleville, Ontario, and she wrote of her experience "in the East." She attributed her own interest in missions to her Watch Tower assignments. First, she was given China, and as a result, she said, "I was interested in China more than any of our mission fields. After this they gave me Japan and I became equally interested in that field." Still, she was skeptical that she would ever feel enthusiasm for the French work in Montreal when that was assigned to her. After she visited the missions, however, she "became more interested in the French work than either of the other Fields."[10]

When women like Magrath became interested in the work, their enthusiasm impelled them to reach out beyond their auxiliaries. They organized younger boys and girls into mission bands and older girls into mission circles. They saw the groups as sources of future missionaries for both the General Board of Missions and their own society, and they viewed the girls and young women as future members of their auxiliaries. Although they appreciated the funds passed on to the WMS by the children's groups, they insisted that the primary aim of these organizations was educational, not financial. Both young children and their mothers were targets of another section of the work, the cradle roll, and it was assumed that WMS members with children at home were active in the mission education of their offspring.

The women also attempted to pass on missionary information and enthusiasm to Sunday school children, to members of Epworth Leagues, and, in later years, to the girls in the Canadian Girls in Training. Although this work sometimes gave rise to jurisdictional questions, especially regarding money collected for mission work, the women successfully spread missionary education among the young.

Their educational work, however, was not limited to children. The auxiliaries sponsored events that sometimes added entertainment to information, attempting to attract new members, in the case of events for women, and to increase missionary interest, in the case of those open to women and men. They often encouraged their ministers to hold missionary prayer meetings, and a few articulate and well-informed women of the WMS took leadership roles in the missionary meetings that most congregations held yearly to raise interest and money for the General Board of Missions. McMechan spoke at several such services, and a writer reporting on the missionary meetings at Newbury, Ontario, stated, "Mrs. McMechan will do credit to any missionary platform in Methodism."[11]

Many remarked on the spiritual benefits of women's work for missions, claiming that the work had been instrumental in "enlarging our sympathies, increasing our interest in high and noble things, deepening our own spiritual life, and multiplying our joys."[12] Most often, women within the societies made such claims, but sometimes observers outside the group noticed the effect on women's spiritual lives made by their participation in the missionary movement. In her WMS presidential address of 1888, Sarah Gibbs Gooderham stated: "From the testimony of some of our most thoughtful, experienced, and successful class-leaders and Sabbath-school teachers, I am free to say that no scheme of the Church has been more useful than this Society has been in leading the women in to a larger experience of the efficacy of prayer and the faithfulness of God, bringing their lives into more harmony with the divine will, and in sympathy with the compassionate Jesus."[13] More than a century later, we can only note, not test, these perceptions of the spiritual effects of work for missions.

The auxiliaries' records do document, however, what the women did and what they valued. One striking feature of the reports is a continuing emphasis on prayer. While editorials in the denominational press lamented the waning of prayer in the life of church members, women of the WMS felt an obligation to support their missionaries with their prayers as well as their funds. As McMechan asked the London Conference, "Dare we be so derelict as to let their hands hang down for want of our prayer?"[14] The women prayed for the success of the missionaries' work, they prayed that candidates might offer themselves for the mission field, and they prayed for their organization's leadership.

Auxiliary meetings regularly included one or two "seasons of prayer." In many, though not all, Methodist congregations, women had been welcome to pray aloud in prayer meetings, and the records suggest that in some auxiliaries this was a natural activity. Several times when the women of the small auxiliary in Gorrie, Ontario, found themselves with little or no business to transact, they held a short prayer meeting.[15] Elsewhere, leaders sometimes encouraged their members: "The President . . . addressed the meeting and spoke very earnestly to the ladies on the necessity of more and short prayers at our monthly meetings which would not only be a great source of help to her but also a benefit to the ladies themselves."[16] Another president took more direct action, making "an affectionate appeal that at our next monthly meeting on March 11th the members would respond promptly with brief sentence prayers, & on some (6) agreeing to do this, others were kindly urged to bring texts, & 14 promised to do so."[17] Yet if the leaders were sometimes disappointed in the members' failure to enter into prayer as freely as they might, at other times they were gratified by the women's participation. At the 1913 meeting of the Alberta Branch, the secretary wrote about the devotional exercises, "Sentence Prayers of what we most need formed part of this exercise—Almost every woman present sent up a brief petition and in that quiet early hour we felt the presence of the master in our midst as at no other time during our meeting."[18] Records testify not only to the women's faithful inclusion of prayer in the time they spent together but also to the encouragement that leaders gave to women who lacked the confidence to lead in prayer.

Early in its history, the WMS began to publish lists of monthly subjects for prayer, and in 1892 it offered a birthday calendar that contained not only subjects for prayer and study but also the birthdays of missionaries, so that the prayers of the members might focus more specifically on the work of the society.[19] Women were especially called upon to set apart the hour between five and six on Sunday evening to pray for the mission work of the WMS. By 1892, women in Toronto were coming together late on Friday mornings for a missionary prayer meeting. This meeting persisted over the years, and similar meetings were instituted in other cities. In addition, the WMS observed its own day of prayer and participated in an interdenominational one as well.

In the early years of Canadian Methodism, the weeknight prayer meeting had been an important conduit of grace. By the 1880s it had declined in vitality, but for women of the WMS it offered an additional opportunity for both prayer and mission education. From the very early days of the organization, auxiliaries asked their ministers to use one of the prayer meetings each month or quarter as a missionary prayer meeting.[20] Frequently, the women themselves had charge of this meeting. Although the structured, educational component of the service made the meetings far different from those of early Methodism, through these gatherings the women of the WMS encouraged others outside the organization to engage actively in prayer.

According to McMechan, the third result of the reflex influence was financial, and she marshaled figures to demonstrate that the funds of the general society did not suffer but actually increased following the organization of the WMS. Other women used this argument, one suggesting that the WMS might be "the little tug behind the General Fund, pushing it forward."[21] Sometimes, men of the General Board of Missions did so, too, as they acknowledged the good work of the WMS.[22] There was envy in the men's admiration, for the women insisted on raising the money before they spent it, something that the General Board was unable to accomplish.

Owing to the detailed records published by the General Board of Missions and the Woman's Missionary Society, it is possible to look systematically at the contributions that formed the basis of these claims. From the list of societies organized during the first six years of the WMS, fifty-nine were associated with congregations for which continual data are available from 1879 through 1891 for their contributions to the General Missionary Fund.[23] Within this group of fifty-nine, seventeen (30 percent) of the congregations showed sustained increases in their contributions to the General Fund, with the increased giving starting within the first two years that a local WMS auxiliary was organized. Thirty-eight (64 percent) of the congregations showed a steady pattern of missionary giving, and only in four congregations (6 percent) did the contributions to the General Board show a sustained decrease, starting within the two years following the WMS's formation. This pattern of overall growth strongly suggests a generally beneficial effect of WMS activity on giving to the General Board, but some of the credit for robust giving may be attributable to an unrelated event, the Methodist union of 1884.[24] Although results from the representative group of congregations are thus less clear-cut and less dramatic than the examples publicized in support of the WMS, the data confirm that the overall effect was positive.

Another aspect of the financial reflex influence has been overlooked. Early in the history of the WMS, the women adopted the principle of either proportionate or systematic giving. Sometimes the emphasis fell on proportionate giving, with the benefits of tithing extolled, while at other times stress was given to contributing systematically, "rather than on special occasions influenced by emotion."[25] Systematic giving was encouraged as early as 1886, and two years later the WMS printed two thousand leaflets on the subject.[26] In 1896, the London Branch passed this motion: "That the delegates request their pastors to preach a sermon on systematic giving."[27] At about that time, the WMS instituted the position of superintendent of systematic giving as one of the offices to be filled in each group. Over the next years, information on the subject was circulated to the auxiliaries, and many groups and individual members committed themselves to making their missionary contributions according to this principle, frequently adopting the use of envelopes. The subject was kept before the membership through frequent papers and reports, especially after a Herald for systematic giving became part of the Watch Tower.

This principle applied to more than missions. Christians should "carefully set apart, of [their] means, systematically and proportionately, for 'charitable and religious purposes,' which would include the missionary cause, of course, but many other things besides."[28] Furthermore, the women saw it as a subject about which they should educate others. Some groups paid for circulars to be distributed among members of their congregations, while others encouraged their ministers to preach on the subject.[29] The women in New Westminster, British Columbia, conducted an exercise on proportionate giving in one of the church prayer meetings for which they were responsible, recommending that other groups do the same.[30] In Victoria, the women of the Centennial Methodist WMS even took the matter outside their congregation. This group joined the local Council of Women and, in 1895, sent a resolution to the council, encouraging systematic giving. Later, the council representative reported "the case of a lady who had decided to give a tenth of her income to the Lord as the result of the Resolution on this subject sent by our Aux'y to the Women's Council two years ago."[31]

In his article on the institutionalization of Christian stewardship in the Methodist Church in Canada, John Thomas's attention to the Association of Christian Stewards and to the church's Department of Finance suggests that a change in the method of giving was dictated from above.[32] To develop a fuller picture of the stewardship movement, however, we also need to take into account the local commitment and educational work of the women of the WMS, who took it upon themselves to educate others in their societies and their congregations, and even other women in their network of associations.

A BROADER CULTURE

In 1895, the *Guardian* printed a brief report of another address given by McMechan. In it, she spoke of the rewards of mission work, but this time she did not use the systematic categories of educational, spiritual, and financial results. Instead, she referred to "Our reward—A broader culture, a wider experience, an overflowing heart."[33] The report gives no examples, but the minute books record activities McMechan likely approved.

Methodists saw the connectional nature of their work as one of the assets of their denomination. The meetings of the districts, conferences, and General Conference

forged strong bonds of community among the ministers and also among the ministers and those laymen and—late in the period—those few laywomen who were selected to participate in the meetings. Until the development of the WMS, however,
nothing promoted the development of comparable connections among women.
Only the WMS gave women an opportunity for active participation in the national
denomination, thereby broadening their vision of the larger group.

The success of the WMS was attributed to the women's organizational and financial skills and gained them great respect. The WMS came to be a model for women's
work in the church, and there were a few attempts to engage women in other church
work along similar patterns. Women in many churches had formed Ladies' Aids to
support the needs of their local congregations, and beginning in 1913, these groups
also began to band together in unions similar to the district structures of the WMS.
In 1902, the General Conference of the Methodist Church considered whether to
give women's groups representation on Quarterly Official Boards. Delegates saw no
difficulty in giving the presidents of WMS auxiliaries such ex officio status but
tabled the clause regarding Ladies' Aids "until such time as the General Conference
officially recognizes the Ladies' Aid Societies."[34] Formally, the difficulty was that the
Ladies' Aid Societies lacked an official, standard constitution.[35] But they also lacked
the status of the WMS, with its conspicuous administrative skill and financial
acumen.

Work for missions also joined women of the various denominational societies.
Methodist Church conferences commonly welcomed representatives of other denominations who brought greetings, and anniversary meetings of local congregations regularly included other ministers from the town, but the WMS went further.
The Methodist women frequently accepted invitations to the meetings of other societies or extended such invitations themselves. Each society maintained its separate
work, but women who were working for women through missionary activity recognized their kinship with sisters laboring for the same end.

Hill has identified one particular "nonspiritual reflex influence of mission work,"
namely, the personal and organizational skills gained by workers in women's missionary societies. Although the women of the WMS would not have considered this
"the primary reflex influence," as Hill does, they valued the development of their
members' talent, "talent that would have remained latent forever but for the quick-
ening impulse of this great cause."[36] They developed program material with a view
to "the desirability of making persons accustomed to the sound of their own voices
in a public meeting" and "more accustomed to think and speak 'on their feet.'"[37]
Although this cultivation of women's talents was not the goal for which WMS
women organized, they saw it as a benefit of their work, and they chose methods
that would facilitate it.

Another aspect of this broader culture is, at first, more surprising: the experience
of working for missions in the WMS moved many of the women toward involve-

ment in the agenda of social Christianity. This development is particularly evident in the Canadian West from the early years of the twentieth century until the Methodist Church became part of the United Church of Canada in 1925, but it was not restricted to that time or place.[38]

WMS women first sought to change society by encouraging temperance. They shared "sentence prayers on behalf of the Temperance cause; this being the day when the Referendum vote was being taken."[39] Like systematic giving, temperance became one of the subjects of the Watch Tower, reported on regularly by WMS members to their sisters.

Sometimes, the resulting action took the women into less familiar territory, especially after women obtained the franchise. Thus, at a WMS meeting, one group was exhorted "not to be timid" about using the ballot in the fight against liquor, and another was asked for "volunteers to canvass the women of the city & see that they register in order to vote in the coming referendum."[40] This reform activity was not a movement to affect personal conduct through education and persuasion. It was an attempt to change Canadian society, and women in the WMS joined in the work even though it was not central to the mandate of a missionary society.

In 1904, the WMS became involved with work among non-English-speaking immigrants of European background who came to both the cities and rural areas of Canada, and reports of subsequent years included descriptions of the "Galician" and "Ruthenian" work supported by the WMS.[41] Working only in rural areas at first, the society later opened a Ruthenian Home for Girls in Edmonton and a settlement house in Regina. The educational system of the WMS proved well adapted to informing its members about these new activities, and soon Watch Tower Heralds were appointed for this work.

Some of the women on the prairies involved themselves personally with nearby mission efforts. Winnipeg women took their turn in providing lunches for the mothers' meetings there.[42] In 1910, one of the missionaries asked the Norwood auxiliary, near Edmonton, for assistance, and two members volunteered. Then in 1915, "Miss Code gave a talk on the Reuthenian [sic] work in Norwood and asked help on Monday and Wednesdays to teach the girls sewing and other things," and it was arranged that two of the women would attend each session.[43] The women at McDougall Church, Edmonton, also provided items needed at the Ruthenian Home for Girls, and both groups occasionally met there, increasing their knowledge and their sense of connection with the project.[44]

The minutes of Wesley Church in Regina give an indication of the activities of the four auxiliaries in this Saskatchewan city. In 1915, a deaconess working with the Bureau of Public Welfare told the Wesley women about social conditions in the city and of her work, and "several of the members volunteered to help in this social service work." The following year, the women of the Regina auxiliaries presented a memorial to their branch meeting, "asking for a resident & trained worker for the foreign born people who are coming in such numbers to our city." The request was approved, and women of the societies prepared for the arrival of the worker and assisted in establishing—and financing—a settlement house. In later years, the Wesley WMS, and presumably the others in the city, sent visitors to the home one day a week.[45]

Although women in smaller centers worked less formally, they showed similar concern for social conditions in their communities and for the immigrants who had settled among them. In Dominion City, Manitoba, in 1911, women who heard of WMS work among the "Austrians" of Alberta began visiting "the foreign element" in their own town.[46] In attempting to learn about their community, these women engaged in something far different from the traditional work of women's missionary societies. Other auxiliaries also moved away from a narrow interpretation of their role. The women at Wolseley, Saskatchewan, secured a teacher for the Chinese workers of their town, and those in Dauphin, Manitoba, arranged for a teacher of the Galician girls there.[47]

In their opinions as well as in their activities, the women showed an interest in reshaping society. At McDougall Church, Edmonton, in 1917, a Mrs. Perry told her WMS group "that it is not only our duty to help people when in trouble but to do our share to help conditions so a great deal of trouble may be prevented."[48] This comment anticipated the statements of reformers and legislators Nellie McClung and Louise McKinney, both of whom were made honorary vice presidents of the Alberta branch of the WMS in 1921, and both of whom addressed that group's conventions upon several occasions. At the 1923 meeting, McKinney encouraged the delegates, saying, "*Things are not what they seem but what under God we make them.* . . . The big thing in life is to establish the Kingdom of God."[49] In a subsequent session, McClung urged the women not to shirk their "responsibility in bringing in the New Age."[50]

When respected leaders encouraged women of the WMS to "establish the Kingdom of God," they did not issue a call to an unfamiliar type of action. Instead, they encouraged women in work that many were already doing in various parts of Canada. The members' interest in girls and women on foreign shores made them sensitive to the possibility of mission work among immigrants in Canada. Women of the WMS saw no great divide between evangelism and social reform but regarded it all as the proper concern of missionary-minded women.

CONCLUSION

The testimony of WMS women details only part of the benefit gained through participation in the missionary endeavor. Educational work gave the women experience and broadened their horizons, but their educational activities reached out to enlarge the missionary knowledge of children and men as well. The women's attention to prayer stood as an example within their church communities, and in their commitment to systematic giving they not only gave proportionately themselves but also attempted to convince others that this was the proper method of giving for all religious purposes. Work for foreign missions also enlarged their vision, establishing a place for them within their own denomination and leading them to cooperation with women of other denominations. The greatest evidence of the "broader culture" and "wider experience" of WMS women is their involvement in the agenda of social Christianity as shown in their work with immigrants to Canada and in their concern for Canadian social conditions.

Members of the WMS offered their own analysis. In 1889, a Toronto correspondent reported, "We rejoice because our members are more deeply interested, and their enthusiasm is so awakened that they have a mind to work, showing it by their willingness to take part in our meetings. Some of us used to have too much of what one calls 'folding-wing' piety, but the Lord is helping us to open out our wings to do some flying for him, for the King's business requires swift-winged messengers."[51] The women of the Methodist WMS had, indeed, no "folding-wing" piety. On open wings they soared, and not only the "heathen" to whom they took the gospel, but their sisters and brothers and children at home, benefited from their flight.

9 / "Hotbed of Missions"

The China Inland Mission, Toronto Bible College, and the Faith Missions–Bible School Connection

Alvyn Austin

One of the morning newspapers of Toronto, in referring to the large number of our students who have recently gone out to labor in foreign fields, calls the [Toronto Bible Training] School "a Hotbed of Missions." This is not a name we would ourselves have chosen; we should prefer to call it "a Handmaid and Helper of Missions." But understanding by the word "Hotbed," a place which promotes rapid growth or heated activity, we can desire nothing better for the Toronto Bible Training School than that it should continue to manifest this condition and spirit in relation to all missionary service, whether at home or abroad.

Toronto Bible Training School Recorder,
December 1904

DRAWING TOGETHER

One evening in May 1894, a biblical twelve men gathered at Betheden, the "garden of peace," in Toronto to found a Bible school. The Reverend Elmore Harris, at whose home the meeting took place, spoke first. A wealthy Baptist minister (a member of the Massey-Harris farm implement company), he was an evangelical dynamo in "Toronto the Good," one of the great evangelical cities of the world. Church historian Ronald Sawatsky called Harris "Canadian Baptist Extraordinaire." Harris had already built and paid for two churches, including Walmer Road, the largest Baptist edifice in Canada, which he planted in the empty but soon-to-be-filled streets of the Annex, an 1890s suburb. Now he revealed his "Great Design" for a school to train "consecrated men and women as Sunday School Workers, as Pastors' Assistants, and as City, Home and Foreign Missionaries." There was a need for such a school because many people, called but not chosen, were prevented by "age or other reasons" (too old, too young, too poor, too isolated, female, subject to family objections) from going to college for four years and two more for seminary ordination. Theologically, the school would be strictly interdenominational, with at least one board member and teacher from each denomination. Finally, he offered to pay the initial expenses and donate Walmer Road's Sunday school rooms for the school.[1]

Henry Frost spoke next. He was director of the China Inland Mission (CIM), which had its head North American office in Toronto. Of five hundred applications in the previous five years, he said, the CIM had been forced to refuse many "because of want of proper training." The records of the CIM, with comments in candidates' files like "needs training," "scripturally unsound," and "unsuited in every way," bear him out. Some were godly men and women who had no experience in "personal work." Others in the first flush of conversion had little knowledge of the Bible. Still others had studied the Bible alone with such intensity that they became ensnared in prophetic speculation. They would never survive in China.[2]

The other men at the meeting—leading clergymen, captains of industry, and independent evangelists—were all connected with the CIM, most of them on the Toronto Council. They were unanimous, and Toronto Bible Training School (TBTS) opened with eight students in September 1894. Most were transfers from Chicago Bible Institute. TBTS grew into the internationally known Toronto Bible College (TBC) in 1912, which amalgamated with London Bible Institute to become Ontario Bible College and Ontario Theological Seminary in 1970. In 1998, the school changed its name to Tyndale College and Seminary.

Such organizational meetings were repeated many times across North America in the intervening century, as groups of men and women came together to found Bible schools. In a partial listing, Virginia Leeson Brereton enumerates sixty schools, institutes, or colleges in the United States and Canada founded between 1882 and 1930, and a further fifty in the next fifteen years from the Depression to the end of World War II. Beyond these were perhaps hundreds of peripatetic and transient schools whose enthusiasm outran their finances.[3] Inevitably, among first-generation schools, those founded before 1900, a key player at the creation was the CIM (now the Overseas Missionary Fellowship), the first and foremost faith mission.[4]

This chapter examines one case of the symbiotic alliance between the faith mission and Bible school movements that exemplifies the theme of this volume: how foreign missions, and what was happening "over there," shaped the religious life of North America. If evangelicalism is a dense thicket of ideas and practices, "a luxuriant undergrowth of weeds that requires only opportunity to flourish,"[5] the faith missions and Bible schools were vines that linked the regional trees, foreign and domestic entwined. Perhaps most entangled were the CIM, the "father of faith missions," and TBC, the self-styled "handmaid of missions."

A school and a mission are different kinds of institutions, though they share the same constituency. A school is a funnel, which in a short time shapes a wide variety of students into a corporate mold and sends them out into the world, into a wide variety of careers. It needs a broad base to provide a never-ending stream of students, to raise funds, and to spread publicity. At the top, it needs many agencies to employ its graduates, denominational and interdenominational. The conundrum is, who "owns" the school: the president, donors, board, faculty, students, alumni? Or are schools the handmaids of their constituent agencies, the employers? Who can change the theological stance of a school—make it give up or adopt dispensationalism or "faith principles," or go "liberal," for example? These were important questions in the first decades of the twentieth century, as conservative evangelicals began to separate from the historic churches and close ranks.

A mission can pick and choose, for it is inviting "candidates" to become "probationers" and join a family. A denominational mission can replenish its workers through connectional channels, the Sunday schools, academies, colleges, and seminaries that bring volunteers up the ranks. This gives a homogeneous cast to its overseas work. An interdenominational faith mission like the CIM, drawing from many churches—indeed, from many countries—while attached to none, has to cast its nets widely and needs links with many schools in England, Sweden, Germany, Australia, as well as the United States and Canada. The mission, in turn, acts as a feeder to the school, an inspiration to its students, an endless source of deputation speakers, a home away from home for missionary-minded students, an employer of its graduates, the most active alumni association, and the parents of the next generation of Bible-school students: a perfect circle.

Many schools enjoyed a special relationship with one faith mission. A. B. Simpson, founder of the Christian and Missionary Alliance (CMA), established in 1882 the first American Bible school, the Missionary Training School (later Nyack College), in New York City, to train hundreds of missionaries for the Evangelical Missionary Alliance, which eventually became part of the CMA. A. J. Gordon started Boston Bible and Missionary Training School (1889) to recruit for the English-based missions founded by Grattan Guinness to open "darkest Africa," the sub-Saharan Sudan and the Congo. Philadelphia Bible College provided most of the Africa Inland Mission (AIM) recruits, and by the 1920s, the Philadelphia School of the Bible (1913) had interlocking directorships with the AIM, the CIM, the Inland South America Missionary Union, and the Central American Mission. Moody Bible Institute (MBI), "the West Point of Christian Service," sent out tendrils in all directions, attaching itself to many missions.[6]

"Without a doubt," Joel Carpenter has written, Bible schools were "the most important terminals in the fundamentalist network,"[7] where the old-time religion was codified and passed on to the next generation. He has further suggested that in the isolationist 1930s, as mainline missions began to retract, evangelicals became more internationalist, more aware of the developing world and its "problems" than the average person in the street. If so, it was because the faith missions infused the

Bible schools with "a foreign missionary culture" that went out to permeate the churches.[8]

Through missionary study groups, conferences, museums, and "colored slides of the leper colonies," in evangelical and fundamentalist circles the missionary vocation was often held as the highest ideal of Christian devotion. The foreign often eclipsed the domestic; the exotic overshadowed the mundane. What could better represent "separation from the world" than "stepping out on the promises," leaving everything behind and going to live in some Chinese village? At Prairie Bible Institute, the students "ate, drank, studied, slept, and sang missions morning, noon, and night."[9] On graduation, prevented by class, gender, theology, education, and ordination from entering denominational missions, Bible-school graduates staffed the inter-denominational faith missions.

The bare statistics are astounding: between 1932 and 1942, "at least five hundred MBI alumni became missionaries, which brought the school's total missionary production since its founding to 2416." During the same period, the Bible Institute of Los Angeles (BIOLA) graduated 426.[10] TBC, a medium-sized school, could claim a total of 500, one-quarter of its alumni, in foreign fields. Of those, 30 percent (150) had gone under denominational boards, while 350 went with various interdenominational mission societies, about 90 in the CIM and the same in the Sudan Interior Mission (SIM).[11]

The rest, about one-third of TBC's graduates, went out among thirty different faith missions, from large British groups like Regions Beyond Missionary Union or American operations like HCJB, the Voice of the Andes radio station, to small one-family independent efforts. This diversity indicates that the dispensational correspondence between school and agency, while tight, was not exclusive. Most of these missionaries were women. Like the Salvation Army, the faith missions stressed the equality of women, both unmarried and married, thus emphasizing their need for the same education as men. This peculiarity, which grew out of social conditions in mid-nineteenth-century England, became part of the mandate of North American Bible schools a generation later. Faith missions offered a wider ministry to women, who regularly made up two-thirds or more of the foreign force. The corollary was that they usually had to agree to remain unmarried until they passed a two-year probation and language test in the field. This ensured that prospective Bible-school candidates, men and women, were uniformly young, single, and mobile, ready to go anywhere and do anything for the Lord. (On the other hand, denominational missions sent out very few unmarried men, and no more than a handful remained lifelong bachelors: obviously, the thinking went, a man needed a wife, while women could work together.)[12]

China, India, Africa, and South America were not static places in the upheavals of the twentieth century, and the messages the missionaries brought home changed through time. In the 1890s, they spoke of Hermit Kingdoms and Forbidden Cities, of never-never lands where no white person had trod. By the 1920s, it was revolution and the horrors of mass nationalism. Thirty years on, missionaries could graphically describe, from firsthand experience, concentration camps and communist brainwashing. This gave aspiring students the sense of "getting the news in advance."

TBC offers a useful case study, for it—and its daughter, Vancouver Bible Training School, another CIM creation (1917)—ranked among the few Bible schools that did not go "fundamentalist." "We declined to be drawn into the Fundamentalist Controversy," said John McNicol, the principal for forty years (1911–1954). This policy, which made enemies among more radical evangelicals, meant that once the dust settled, he was at ease with separatist Associated Gospel and Fellowship Baptists on the one hand and mainline United Church and Convention Baptists on the other. As his successor, J. B. Rhodes (a second-generation CIM missionary), noted, "That is why he has maintained friendship with some to whom certain of his brethren scorn to show any kindness, scarce extending common courtesy to them."[13] Because of McNicol's long tenure and his personal magnetism, he and TBC helped keep the old evangelical coalition alive in Toronto long after it had collapsed in Britain and the United States. In fact, TBC was so pivotal in Toronto's evangelicalism (which meant on a national scale) that perhaps it kept Canada from "going fundamentalist."

The ups and downs of the relationship between the CIM and TBC illumine the larger evangelical networks in North America and overseas. The CIM was broader than America or fundamentalism: it was one of the few organizations that could reach outside the tent. By the 1920s, the Toronto Council of the CIM was virtually identical to the boards of TBC and the SIM, the other multinational faith mission headquartered in Toronto. Yet the CIM and the SIM were endorsed by the *Sunday School Times* as nondenominational missions worthy of fundamentalists' support, while TBC, because it refused to teach premillennial dispensationalism, was not.

THE MISSION

The Reverend Dr. James Hudson Taylor, one of the great visionaries of nineteenth-century England, founded the CIM in 1865. His vision was to convert China, all 400 million "heathen," from the bottom up, one soul at a time. To do this, he required armies of men and women who would wander through the Chinese Empire, scattering gospels and living like the peasants. The CIM was to be a "special agency" for less qualified, spirit-filled lay workers, men and women. Therefore, he wrote, "persons of moderate ability and limited attainments are not precluded from engaging in the work."[14] Thus, he opened missions to working-class "yeoman types" and artisans, bookkeepers, and milliners who would have been rejected by conventional missions, which insisted on educated clergy or medical doctors. There was something experimental, almost casual, about his recruitment of single women. "The younger they were the sooner they would be fluent in Chinese," he said.[15] Twenty years on, the CIM had so many single women (and as many married ones) that it set aside "women's districts" where they worked under Chinese pastors, and male missionaries were prohibited.

Dressed in a Chinese gown with a pigtail hanging down his back, Taylor became an exotic on the British missions circuit. The center of a large network, he inspired dozens of smaller faith missions and shaped the evangelistic side of British missions. As the CIM grew, he helped establish the prototype Bible schools to train the candidates in practical work. It was these British models that he helped transplant to North America a generation later. By 1888, the CIM had three hundred missionaries located at sixty-four stations throughout China, in some of the most inaccessible places in the world. There seemed "no limit to the number who could be sent to China, and provided for."[16]

The CIM drew most of its British candidates from Mildmay Park, a Church of England complex for deaconesses and nurses, and Grattan Guinness's East London Institute for Home and Foreign Missions, the first interdenominational school to train both men and women—in separate facilities. Between 1873, the year David Livingstone died, and 1900, the institute sent fifteen hundred missionaries to foreign fields, under thirty different societies. Guinness himself and his illustrious family founded several faith missions, including the Regions Beyond Missionary Union and the Sudan United Mission. Guinness located the East London Institute in the slums of East London, where Jack the Ripper prowled, on the assumption that "letting students loose on the Mile End Waste would either make them or break them." The regimen was intensive, classes in the morning and in the afternoon, work at "a trade or craft, mechanics, building, carpentry, basic medicine, cookery, botany and reading the compass and sundial." In the evening, they were out preaching on the streets "to counter the deadening influence of study on their souls."[17]

A group of Anglophile Americans connected with Moody and the Niagara prophetic movement copied the urban British model—a combination of study, manual labor, and evangelism. Among those who made the obligatory pilgrimage to sit at the feet of George Muller, the legendary "grandfather of faith missions," were A. B. Simpson, A. J. Gordon, A. T. Pierson, and D. L. Moody himself, who became an international celebrity as a result of his British campaigns. When he returned stateside, Moody was always talking about England, so when he started his own schools in Northfield and Chicago, he sent Emma Dreyer, his colleague and the real founder of MBI, to study Mildmay and the East London Institute, which were, to him, "ideal."[18]

A further catalyst for the North American Bible-school movement was Hudson Taylor's visit to North America in 1888. Taylor's modus operandi was to whirl into a place, hold a few meetings for the spiritual life, send off sparks in all directions, recruit some missionaries, set up a committee, and then go off to China. At Northfield, he helped found the Student Volunteer Movement, which went off on its own trajectory. At the Niagara Conference, the center of the prophetic movement, he established the North American branch of the CIM, to be based in Toronto. In Chicago, he helped Moody recruit the first students for his Bible Institute, and T. C. Horton in Minneapolis for the first Northwestern Bible Institute. In Kansas and Iowa, he connected with the Swedish-American revivals sparked by Fredrik Franson, the firebrand he had met in Sweden. Eventually, Franson sent so many missionaries overseas, through the CIM, the Scandinavian Alliance Mission, and the International Missionary Alliance, that they became known as "Franson's floods."[19]

The CIM was one of a cluster of British interdenominational associations, like the YMCA and the Salvation Army, that established colonial branches in Toronto, where they could become "Americanized" (that is, Canadianized) and used as beachheads for expansion into the United States. Toronto was a British city on North American soil, connected by strong transatlantic cables to currents in the Old Country and by a spidery network of railways, publishing houses, and national denominations to the rest of Canada, and beyond, with U.S. evangelicals.

When Taylor left Toronto in September 1888 with "the first North American party" of the CIM (twelve Canadians and two Americans), he left behind a temporary North American council under Alfred Sandham, an eccentric YMCA secretary and numismatist, and Henry Frost, a well-to-do engineer who was living in Attica, New York. Sandham ran the Christian Institute, a wholehearted downtown rescue mission, and in February 1889, he helped found the Dominion Alliance, the Canadian branch of the Christian Alliance. The Christian Alliance, founded by the expatriate Canadian A. B. Simpson, was too enthusiastic for most Torontonians, for it preached the controversial doctrine of "divine health," which promised that believers could expect the Holy Spirit to "strengthen their bodies and to keep them physically well. He described this as a higher reality than divine healing, something that one should comprehend while physically well."[20]

By the time Frost moved to Toronto, Sandham wanted to turn the Christian Institute into the flagship of the Alliance, a training school that would "thoroughly equip our would-be-missionaries" and whose teaching would include divine healing. Several CIM recruits were Alliance workers, notably Maggie Smith, first vice president of the Dominion Alliance. Healed by Dr. Cullis of Boston, she became an itinerant healer in rural Ontario at the age of nineteen, went to China in 1889, fell ill within a year, and came home to die. Her sister Christina lived another year, then died in China. Frost, an orthodox premillennial Presbyterian, realized that the CIM could not succeed in a churchy city like Toronto as long as it was associated with sectarians like the faith healers. Moreover, he felt that the CIM's home should not be for "*training*," that is, for Bible study and missionary methods, but for "*testing*," that is, living on faith and praying for money.[21]

Frost quickly took the CIM out of the Christian Institute and gradually built an alliance of local churches in Toronto, primarily among Presbyterians, Baptists, and Anglicans. All the major denominations had their national offices in Toronto, and five seminaries supplied ministers for the nation. Frost's relations with the seminaries were cordial but distant since the CIM, a lay organization, did not normally recruit ordained clergymen. Besides, they suspected its interdenominational appeal would draw people and money away from denominational channels.

Meanwhile, Sandham turned the Christian Institute into the Toronto Missionary Training Institute (TMTI), an Alliance school that funneled its graduates to Nyack.[22] Nevertheless, behind the scenes, the CIM continued to attract graduates of TMTI and Simpson's school. There was, for example, periodic resistance to vaccinations, which the CIM did not make compulsory until 1906. This tension between public leaders and the heterogeneous evangelicalism of its members, which had as much to do with class as theology, was a feature of each country where the CIM had an office: England, the United States, Australia, and China.

Once it left the Christian Institute, the CIM's first years were hardscrabble times of testing. It was receiving a hundred applications a year from all over the continent, primarily from Toronto and places Taylor had visited. Serious candidates were invited to Toronto to stay in the mission home for six weeks or more so that Frost and the council could assess their piety, flexibility, scriptural knowledge, and theological beliefs (that is, premillennialism and holiness) and judge whether they would fit into the family. Often, a dozen candidates and Frost's growing family would sit down to table, without a scrap of food in the house. Miraculously, someone would appear with a brace of partridges, a basket of groceries, a ton of coal—whatever was needed to get them through the week. "We lived from hand to mouth," Frost recalled, "but it was God's hand and our mouth; and this is a distinction which makes a great difference. . . . Our episodes of scarcity were intended to be new revelings of God's love and power, if only we could be attentive to the inner meaning of things."[23]

In 1893, Frost launched the North American CIM on "a new beginning." One goal was to reform the international structure of the mission, which had become increasingly autocratic around Taylor's person and family. Another was to launch a North American edition of *China's Millions,* the mission monthly, larger and more up-to-date than the stodgy British edition, filled with reports from North American missionaries. Most strategic was Frost's decision to ally the CIM with the nascent Bible-school movement.

"We could not do better than take the equipment provided by a Canadian or

American Bible Institute as a standard of preparation," he declared, even though he added parenthetically, "Seminary-bred men were much to be desired. . . . We were convinced that we should seek for the friendship, not of doctrinally and spiritually loose Christians, but of those who were sound in the faith, prayerful in spirit, devoted in service, evangelistic in purpose and, generally but not exclusively pre-millennial in attitude. We felt that one person of this quality would be worth to the Mission and China a hundred persons of another sort, and we were ready, as far as needed, to throw our lot in with the socially humble and financially poor, if only we could maintain scriptural and spiritual integrity."[24]

The effect was immediate. When Taylor visited Chicago Bible Institute a few months later, the CIM received fifty applications. Altogether, 1894 proved a bumper year, with the largest number of applicants in its history: 117 people. Two things were notable: the high proportion of U.S. citizens, eighty-eight, to thirty-four Canadians; and the unusual ratio of seventy-one men and forty-six women. Of these, twelve men and thirteen women were accepted and went to China.

By 1895, the CIM was confident enough to print a list of "approved Bible schools" in Chicago, Brooklyn, Boston, Philadelphia, Kansas City, and Toronto. This list pointedly omitted Simpson's Missionary Training School, an indication of the CIM's old mistrust of the CMA. This oversight was corrected the next year when the CIM approved four additional schools. Behind the scenes, the CIM and the CMA had reached a rapprochement. In China, the Scandinavian Alliance based in Chicago was an associate mission, CIM in all but name, and in the United States, the CMA was reaching out to conservative evangelicals. (A similar softening occurred between TBTS and the Dominion CMA.)

THE SCHOOL

These events formed the background to Frost's plea for TBTS, the transatlantic vision. There were other, more local connections that knitted TBTS into the city. By 1894, after a decade of farewell parties for departing missionaries, Toronto was bursting at the seams with missionary enthusiasm. Like the CIM, TBTS tried to fit in. It never challenged the seminaries, preferring to call itself their "handmaid" and "feeder school." Its teachers were professors from the big-brother seminaries—Knox Presbyterian, McMaster Baptist, and Wycliffe Anglican—who all happened to sit on the council of the CIM. Nevertheless, the churches must have felt threatened that TBTS would draw away its women, for the Methodists, Presbyterians, and Anglicans started deaconess schools to educate prospective missionaries in a denominational atmosphere.

TBTS grew like other schools, from small beginnings. It was housed in Walmer Road Church for four years, an arrangement that imparted a Baptist tone to the school, until it built a pretty, Gothic structure at 110 College Street, paid for by President Elmore Harris. It was near the University of Toronto and McMaster University, the Baptist college that the Harris clan ran like a personal fief, and around the corner from the CIM. This location attracted a higher quality of students, and it grew continually until by World War I it boasted 90 full-time students and 250 in evening classes. It was graduating twenty to thirty a year.

TBTS benefited from its association with the CIM. In fact, the CIM gave it an international clientele, for the Canadian and U.S. candidates who lived in the Toronto home attended classes in remedial English Bible.[25] Missionaries on furlough added an older, wiser voice, an inside sense of what it was like in the field. TBTS grew lopsided, however, for despite its emphasis on foreign missions, its graduates had few outlets. Denominational missions, even the Baptists in Bolivia, took no more than a handful of women. Some graduates drifted off to the United States, others to Winnipeg. TBTS had to be its own employment agency. It created a cluster of rescue missions, missions to the blind, shut-ins, and Jews. It reached out to the smaller, often ethnic, churches that were demanding a more educated ministry, like the Mennonite Brethren among the Germans of Kitchener.

In 1899, TBTS and the CIM helped Roland V. Bingham found the Sudan Interior Mission (SIM), and these three organizations eventually became the triumvirate of Toronto evangelical institutions. Bingham, a Salvation Army captain turned Alliance evangelist, had gone to Nigeria in 1893 with two companions who, in the aftermath of the Benin War, both died because they did not take antimalarial pills. Heartbroken, Bingham returned to Toronto, where he married, studied at MBI, and started his own society. By this time, like Simpson, he had retreated from strict healing teachings.

When, in 1899, Bingham was ready to start the African Industrial Mission—forerunner of the SIM—he asked Frost for advice on how to avoid "jealousy" when starting a faith mission. Frost explained the meaning of comity and then gave him the list of CIM supporters, adding with a quip that the SIM would "not get one dollar for the Sudan that God wants us to have for China." The first missionaries came from TBTS, two men who were invalided home within six months. The second party, four TBTS couples, was also a failure, surviving only three weeks, and of the third (1902), none survived three years. From such unpromising beginnings, the SIM grew steadily, reaching a respectable forty-five missionaries in the field by the end of World War I. The SIM always looked upon the CIM as an elder brother, adopting its statement of faith and its rulebook, the *Principles and Practice*. So, Frost wrote, the SIM grew "up alongside of our own work, interlocking with us in principle, plan, and practice."[26]

The SIM opened branches in England and the United States and became more "thoroughly internationalized" than the CIM.[27] Nevertheless, a majority of its missionaries came from Toronto, where Bingham was a powerhouse, running three of the key evangelical institutions. He took over a defunct paper, the *Evangelical Christian and Missionary Witness* (1904), and made it the only transdenominational evangelical magazine in Canada. To print it, he started Evangelical Publishers (1912), and to bring everyone together, he started Canadian Keswick (1924), the summer conference that brought Holiness teachers from England and mission speakers from the United States.

To return to the TBTS story: in 1901, Frost transferred the North American headquarters of the CIM to Philadelphia. He was missed as teacher and board member, but his leaving had a decisive effect not immediately apparent. Toronto remained the dominant office of the CIM at least until World War I, in fact if not in name, for most U.S. candidates continued to undergo testing and training there. The CIM had always relied on TBTS and MBI to train its candidates. When all else failed, there was always a TBTS student who could leave on three weeks' notice to fill an emergency placement. Inevitably, as Philadelphia took over the U.S. work, TBTS diminished. It lost its international wing and became more regional, more Canadian. Nevertheless, it was the only permanent Canadian school until one of Griffith Thomas's Anglicans and the local CIM secretary, Charles Thompson, established Vancouver Bible Training School (VBTS) (1917). Prairie Bible Institute, a more radical school that eventually became the largest in Canada, opened in 1922.

Beyond the statistics of a school—where the students came from and where they went—lay a doctrinal statement. The founders of TBTS—Harris, Frost, H. M. Parsons, and others—were "warhorses of premillennialism" and regulars at the Niagara Conference. Yet they seldom preached on the subject, and there is little indication of premillennial teachings in the curriculum. TBTS was not founded as an "antimodernist" institution. "A defense of the orthodox position is not even mentioned as a secondary aspect of TBC's purpose. . . . TBC originated in a time when modernism was not a major issue."[28]

Frost, by moving to Philadelphia, became more aware of U.S. currents and attached the U.S. branch of the CIM to the hard-liners who came to call themselves fundamentalists: Cyrus I. Scofield, compiler of the interpretive Bible and founder of Philadelphia School of the Bible (1911), and Charles Trumbull of the *Sunday School Times*. As early as 1894, Frost tried to convince Taylor to expel the "modernists," and when Taylor retired he continued to agitate with his successor, D. E. Hoste. There were only one or two liberals—most CIMers preferred not to speak of whatever disagreements they might have had—and by 1904, the liberals were forced to resign. When the Pentecostal excitements of 1906 and after, with their emphasis on speaking in tongues, caused dissension in China, the CIM eventually moved to expel Pentecostals and faith healers. Thus "cleansed," the CIM led the charge against modernism in foreign missions. In the 1920s, it was instrumental in establishing the Bible Union of China, which distributed millions of copies of *The Fundamentals*.

As Frost grew more conservative, he tried to bring his Toronto friends along. *China's Millions* had regular essays by Scofield, R. A. Torrey, and other dispensationalists. The Second Coming, which had seldom been mentioned, was featured prominently in mission publications. Through Frost's influence, Harris, Parsons, and Griffith Thomas contributed articles to *The Fundamentals*. Frost's article (vol. 12) threw down a gauntlet: "What Missionary Motives Should Prevail?"

By 1908, modernism was an issue at TBTS. Harris could remain silent no longer, and he coordinated a campaign against modernist teachings in churches and seminaries. Jonathan Goforth, founder of the Presbyterian mission in North Henan, flush from stirring revivals in China, called upon the General Assembly of the Presbyterian Church to confess their sins. Sam Blake, an Anglican activist, fought higher critics in the University of Toronto. Harris prowled the halls of McMaster University and shouted in the senate chamber, demanding that the school fire two modernist professors. The "Matthews controversy" was a milestone in Canadian Baptist history, a two-year prelude to twenty years of turmoil.

From the perspective of the secularizing university, Harris was trying to impose an outworn creed on the search for intellectual "freedom, for progress, for investigation . . . [for] truth from whatever quarter."[29] From the perspective of TBTS, he was creating a new interdenominational coalition as the old one was crumbling. However, as George Rawlyk wrote, the "growing obsession" of those around Harris "with preserving theological purity would be matched by a remarkable degree of 'violence in thought and language.' These people would find it far easier to be judgmental than forgiving, destructive rather than constructive, and confrontational rather than accommodating."[30]

Then Harris died suddenly in 1911 while in India on a world tour of Canadian Baptist missions. The news reached Toronto on Christmas Eve 1911. His death, soon followed by those of Parsons and other founders, left a large hole at TBTS. Among the last things Harris had done was to change the school's name and status to Toronto Bible College (TBC). The board retired the title of president, as a mark of respect. Their first choice for principal was Scofield, but he was too busy at Philadelphia School of the Bible. Instead, they chose one of their own, John B. McNicol, a young Presbyterian clergyman from Ottawa who had taught there since 1906. McNicol was the most irenic of men, a "pleasing personality," handsome and nonconfrontational, and his wife, Louise Burpe, was respected by many. Mother McNicol kept an active correspondence with five hundred graduates and called herself simply "the shuttle in the sewing machine."

McNicol made the decision to step back from Harris's brink. Try as he would—

and he did study dispensationalism, going so far as to write an article for *The Fundamentals*—he remained an amillennialist who refused to preach any eschatology. His course of study, which he called *Thinking Through the Bible,* was idiosyncratic, personal, and not tied to any school. He would begin, "In the beginning . . . " and proceed verse by verse, book by book, until three years later he ended with the "Amen" of Revelation. This method, McNicol wrote, "takes the Bible in the form which we have it—the form in which it has come down through the Church and made its impact on the world. It allows the Bible to stand on its own feet, to speak for itself, and wherever possible, to be its own interpreter."[31]

McNicol, who had once applied to the CIM, tried to inculcate its sacrificial piety in the school. His great contribution to Canadian evangelicalism was the spirituality he called "the corporate leadership of the Holy Spirit." This meant that all members of the school—the board, teachers, student council, and alumni association—had to agree before any decision was undertaken. This ineffably impossible dream was actually the policy for more than twenty years. In a school where everyone had to see eye to eye, controversial doctrines like dispensationalism and tongues found no place.

McNicol's policy was not to embroil the school in the "internal deliberations" of the churches, even when they were tearing themselves apart. When the formation of the United Church of Canada in 1925 split the historic Presbyterian Church, not a word appeared that would "allow the blighting breath of controversy to invade the atmosphere of the College."[32] When T. T. Shields of Jarvis Street Baptist took up Harris's cudgel and fragmented the Baptist Convention not once but twice, McNicol said sadly, "In the midst of these depressing conflicts the very meaning of Christianity seems in danger of being lost."

Behind the scenes, the church wars split the school. McNicol himself became a Continuing Presbyterian at Knox Church, its most fundamentalist (self-proclaimed) congregation. Under Parsons, Knox had been intimately connected to TBC, and an annual lecture series was funded in his memory. Parsons's successor, A. B. Winchester, a well-known prophetic teacher, was a member of TBTS and the CIM. Another board member, T. B. Hyde, a former Congregationalist, went into the United Church. W. Griffith Thomas, an English Keswick teacher at Wycliffe College, left to found Dallas Theological Seminary. The fiercest fights were among the Baptists. Dixon Burns, professor of missions, remained in the Baptist Convention and was denounced by Shields and "the Jarvis Street crowd," who included some of Burns's best students.

McNicol's decision not to say anything about the antimodernist wars was strategic for TBC. It grew rapidly after World War I, doubling in 1919–1920, the year the soldiers came home, and redoubling again. By 1927, evicted by the University of

Toronto, it moved uptown to 16 Spadina Road, a large building around the corner from Walmer Road Church where it had started. It was also around the corner from the CIM and the SIM, which both moved to St. George Street. By the 1930s, TBC had three hundred full-time students, with eighty or ninety graduates annually. Its graduation ceremonies, which outgrew the biggest auditorium in the city and had to be held in a hockey arena, were reportedly the largest gatherings of evangelicals in Canada into the 1950s, with up to six thousand in attendance.

To attract that many students from a small constituency, TBC had to broaden its base to appeal to both mainline churches and the new separatist denominations. The board and faculty were still strictly interdenominational, with at least one minister from each church. The student body was broadly evangelical, from United Church and Anglicans to Pentecostals. It was top-heavy, however, with Presbyterians and Baptists, both Convention and Fellowship, who normally were the bitterest of enemies. A leaven of Amish women from Lancaster, Pennsylvania, with their distinctive bonnets and quiet reserve, sent by the CIM in Philadelphia, set the tone. By the 1920s, TBC could reach out in both directions, offering the denominations a cadre of educated women with nursing and teacher training, and providing the CMA, the Associated Gospel, and Fellowship Baptists with an orthodox seminary whose graduates had no taint of modernist teachings.

TBC's broad appeal did not mean the absence of opposition. In 1924, in TBC's own neighborhood, one of its graduates, the firebrand Oswald J. Smith, opened the Canadian Bible Institute, a CMA school. Despite local success, the New York head office closed it in 1929 as part of a policy of retrenchment in the United States. Shields started Toronto Baptist Seminary in opposition to McMaster and TBC, and it has lasted, small and militant, attached to Jarvis Street Church. These schools were forerunners. During the Great Depression, thirty Bible schools opened across Canada, mostly in Alberta and the prairies, but a sprinkling through southern Ontario. Perhaps twice that number have come and gone. The Pentecostal Assemblies of Canada alone launched or relocated a dozen schools between 1924 and 1950, including a short-lived effort in Toronto. But TBC was so influential in Toronto that it could shut out the opposition, which in the 1930s as in the 1890s meant the radicals, not the conciliators.

McNicol of TBC (1912–1954), Bingham of the SIM (1899–1942), and E. A. Brownlee, Canadian director of the CIM (1918–1947), formed a triumvirate of Toronto evangelicalism. They sat on so many interlocking directorships that they would drive each other from one meeting to the next. Each had unusually long tenure, which helped ensure that the turn-of-the-century coalition would remain solid until the end of World War II. Nevertheless, they had their differences. Brownlee might suspect Dixon Burns, but he trusted that McNicol allowed no modernist teaching. And both looked askance at Bingham's brasher "Americanized" style, particularly his policy of "full information, but no solicitation," practically asking for money, a contradiction of pure faith principles of "no solicitation."[33]

McNicol, Brownlee, and Bingham shared the "common Christianity" that was a hallmark of Toronto church life. "In things essential, unity; in non-essentials, liberty; in all things, Christian love." Nonessentials included eschatology, for none professed what one might call straight-arrow, pre-mill, pre-trib dispensationalism. Brownlee was post-trib, McNicol an amillennialist, and Bingham "was always willing to listen to varying points of view and to give space and a fair hearing to the pros and cons."[34]

In 1949, after forty years of silence, on the eve of his retirement, McNicol published a pamphlet called "The Perils of Fundamentalism," which became a rallying cry for the new evangelicals after the war. "During the past generation the greatest peril to the cause of Christ in the Universal Church came from Modernism. In the present generation it comes from Ultra-Fundamentalism," he wrote. The peril of fundamentalism was that it preached "a gospel without love, and developing a carnally minded kind of Christianity—a Christianity that is self-centered and complacent, not the New Testament kind that is pervaded by brotherly love and the fragrance of the presence of Christ."[35]

Even an irenic Canadian could deliver a sharp rebuke.

DRAWING APART

Meanwhile, the U.S. branch of the CIM was on its way to becoming the favorite mission of fundamentalism. While emphasizing sacrificial spirituality and faith principles, it grew, ironically, into a large, rich, influential multinational association much like any other, whose only distinction was the way it raised money. While TBC was broadening its constituency theologically, the CIM, at least in the United States, was narrowing theologically and expanding geographically. It was repeating the process it had pioneered in China, of concentration and diffusion, of regional centers surrounded by clusters of study groups. Just as it had helped establish the prototype Bible schools, it was present at the creation of the second generation of schools. It was no longer the dominant player, however, but one of many that had to line up and await its turn at chapel.

After World War I, the CIM set up regional offices in Vancouver (1916), Chicago (1924), and Los Angeles (1926), each the center of a large network. Vancouver, the jumping-off point for China, became crucial during the war, as dozens of English missionaries were stranded there when they tried to take the safer route via the Canadian Pacific Railway. Charles Thompson, the local CIM secretary, started a transit home, which in usual fashion inaugurated the Vancouver Evangelistic Campaign, which gave birth to VBTS. As a result, between 1919 and 1929, the Pacific Northwest sent twenty-eight CIM recruits. Of all the schools, VBTS was most intimately connected to the CIM, and after the fall of China to the communists in 1949, when the CIM closed its Vancouver home, the school closed shortly thereafter.[36]

In Los Angeles, the stranded missionary was a Scots Canadian, Alexander R. Saunders, one of the legendary pioneers of the CIM. He had worked with Goforth in the student and soldier campaigns, baptizing battalions of soldiers with fire hoses. Blind and crippled by his Boxer injuries in 1900, he was invalided to Los Angeles, where he lived in the BIOLA hotel. He found "wide and effectual doors constantly swung open" and was appointed head of the new missions department at BIOLA. In 1917, despite the embargo, he led twelve BIOLA students to Shanghai, the largest single party since Taylor's memorable group in 1888. "Not with stories of missionary romance did we seek to arouse interest," he wrote, "but with the sterner facts of missionary suffering, blended with incidents showing the power of the Gospel and triumphs of God's grace."[37]

Chicago, which grew into an important center, was linked with Wheaton College, which provided a leaven of well-educated graduates, and MBI, where CIM missionary William H. Hockman was director of missions and editor of the *Moody Monthly's* "Missions Department." The resident secretary, Isaac Page, a "jolly, loveable" Canadian who loved to tell stories, opened the home as a "ministry of hospitality" for MBI students, who became a sort of "China clique." He watched them carefully, conducting "an informal orientation and screening process," but as one said, "he was so nice about it that no one resented it."[38]

All this—the theological tensions, the geographical distance—meant a diminished role for TBC within the CIM. Even within Canada the CIM was as likely to accept students from Shields's seminary or Prairie Bible Institute. Nevertheless, the special relationship continued cordially under Brownlee and his successor William W. Tyler (1947–1975), a second-generation CIMer and TBC alumnus. As a boy at the CIM Chefoo School in China, Tyler had played cricket with John Rhodes, McNicol's successor as TBC principal (a prime example of an old boys' club). Rhodes was often sick and died in office. Principal McNicol came out of retirement until 1954, by which time he had served almost fifty years at the school.

In 1929, the CIM made its most audacious forward movement in forty years, with an appeal for "the Two Hundred" new missionaries in the next two years. The 1920s had been tumultuous in China, years of anti-Christian riots, Bolshevik propaganda, and corrupt warlords. At the height of civil war in 1927, all foreigners, including some six thousand missionaries, were forced to evacuate from their inland stations. For the CIM, which had twelve hundred adults scattered across the outback of China, the gathering of displaced persons in Shanghai was the opportunity of a lifetime. Making an assessment of the whole field, they resolved to pray for 199 recruits—"113 men and 86 women," if it please God—to undertake a new genera-tion of pioneer work in "the regions beyond," among the Muslims of Central Asia and the mountain tribes of Guizhou, and in "the walled cities and other strategic points." The appeal went over the top when 203 men and women sailed before the last day of 1931.

The Two Hundred proved a pivotal event in missions history, paving the way for the dramatic rise of evangelical American missions. The hoped-for balance of men and women was reversed, with 119 women (all but four of whom were single) and 84 men. This ensured that women would continue to dominate the future move-ments, as they had the old ones. Like other conservative organizations, the CIM was trying to restrict the "free and easy life" of women in the field and turn them into regular teachers and nurses. "By the 1920s and 1930s, as a defensive, pessimistic, embattled spirit permeated the movement, fundamentalist leaders began to stress once again the traditional boundaries limiting female leadership."[39] The place of women in the faith missions and Bible schools was so entrenched that the campaign was bound to fail. Indeed, the heavy enrollment of women in Bible schools and faith missions continued throughout the 1930s.

The Two Hundred showed the CIM at the dawn of a new era. As a sign of its Americanization, their outfits and passages were entirely paid by a large legacy in Philadelphia, about $500,000. Almost one-half, or ninety-two, of the Two Hundred came from North America: seventy-two from the United States (fifty-four women and eighteen men) and twenty from Canada (twelve women and eight men). Geo-graphically, the largest contingents came from the West, Washington and California, British Columbia and Alberta. A further seventy-two came from Great Britain (thirty-seven women and thirty-five men), and thirty-eight from Australia (sixteen women and twenty-two men).

They were better educated than the nineteenth-century yeoman types: six doc-tors and nineteen nurses; at least forty with college degrees, bachelors and a sprin-kling of master's and professional degrees from Britain and North America. A dozen were ordained clergymen. Of the sixty-nine North Americans who reported their educational background, eighteen had attended college (six at Wheaton College) and fifty-five had Bible-school training. TBC ranked behind MBI (eighteen), BIOLA (thirteen), and Prairie (twelve). Other North American schools included Simpson Bible Institute in Seattle, St. Paul Bible School in Minnesota, Moose Jaw Bible Institute, and Toronto Baptist Seminary.[40]

In the end, the CIM probably exerted more influence on TBC than vice versa. It infused the school with a spirituality and a vision of fields afar. And it set the stan-dards. In the Cold War 1950s, after the expulsion from China, the CIM and other evangelical missions deployed their troops in a ring of containment around the Bam-boo Curtain. Robert Hall Glover, the CIM's North American director, announced that missions represented "another conflict on a world-wide scale." The CIM, which always had a reputation for pushing into "the regions beyond" in China, opened work among headhunters in Borneo and Roman Catholics in Mindanao. A new generation of faith missions, such as Wycliffe Bible Translators, the New Tribes Mission, and Aviation Missionary Fellowship, demanded specialized, sophisticated (and often "secular") skills—and so TBC added lessons in linguistics and radio transmission. This, in turn, led to a more sophisticated ministry at home, which resulted in the move to turn TBC into Ontario Bible College and then Ontario Theological College.

Within the CIM, TBC remained a distinctive Canadian voice in the international chorus: McNicol's men and women. Michael Griffiths, sixth general director (1969–1980), explained that the "U.S. section was more 'fundamentalist' than the rest of us even as late as the fifties, sixties and seventies: Americans were premill, creationist, anti-ecumenical, antisocialist and later anti-charismatic. The mainland Europeans were at the opposite pole, with the Brits somewhat intermediate as usual—mainly amill, not indisposed to the Creator using evolution, sympathetic to evangelicals within the WCC (many were Anglicans after all); delighted with the post-war social reforms that gave us the welfare state and unpolarized over the charismatic movement."[41] Canadians, "the hyphen in the Anglo-American alliance," would explain each to the other.

10 / "From India's Coral Strand"

Pandita Ramabai and U.S. Support for Foreign Missions

Edith L. Blumhofer

The usual dignitaries filled the platform at the fourteenth annual Woman's Christian Temperance Union (WCTU) convention in Nashville in November 1887. The "who's who" roster of U.S. Protestant womanhood—Frances Willard, Kate Bushnell, Hannah Whitall Smith, Anna Gordon—drew enthusiastic response to their pleas for "God, home and native land." But the crowd reserved its warmest welcome for a slight woman wrapped in a sari whom Willard introduced as "our sister from abroad whose name and character have become dear to each, Pundita Ramabai."[1]

Ramabai had arrived in the United States only the year before, but already she had tasted the vast popularity that would follow her until her death in India in 1922. Her Indian ways, her winsome personality, and her daring vision to uplift the women of India won the hearts of English-speaking Protestants. Those who worked hardest on her behalf composed a liberal Protestant elite—people like Rachel Bodley, president of the Women's Medical College in Philadelphia; Boston pastor and author Edward Everett Hale; Phillips Brooks, rector of Boston's Trinity Church and author of "O Little Town of Bethlehem"; George A. Gordon, pastor of Boston's Old South Street Church; *Outlook* editor Lyman Abbott; lecturers and temperance advocates Frances Willard, Mary Livermore, and Mary Hemenway—women and men of national repute.

Ramabai's popularity arose, in part, from the timeliness of her visit. She arrived in 1887 when a steady stream of news reports sustained curiosity about life in India. Women's missionary societies had come into their own, faith missions were emerging, and grassroots enthusiasm for humanitarian efforts abounded. Perhaps the first high-caste Hindu widow to travel to North America, Ramabai found a responsive audience already attuned to the desperate plight of Indian women. As a representative of a "heathen" land much in the current news, Ramabai made India vivid. It was as if someone had stepped off the pages of one of the new illustrated missionary magazines. She had experienced what women's missionary societies studied; she wore the clothing the study guides pictured; she limited her diet to the vegetables, fruits, and cereals Brahmins ate in India. More important, she spoke in fluent English about Indian religious and social customs. A recent convert to Christianity, she manifested unfailing sympathy toward Hinduism. She seemed what most considered an anomaly if not an oxymoron—a Hindu Christian. She fascinated Americans as she had the British precisely because her life "[drew] away the veil behind which so much that is really of the deepest interest to us is hidden in the East."[2] Her fortunes in the United States and her shifting U.S. support base offer an intriguing glimpse into U.S. Protestantism at the end of the nineteenth century.

BEGINNINGS

The daughter of a high-caste Brahmin scholar and his much younger second wife, Ramabai was born on April 23, 1858.[3] Her father had retreated to a remote site after deciding to defy custom and teach his then nine-year-old wife to read. The youngest of the couple's three children, Ramabai learned to read and write, devoting herself to Hindu writings. Awed contemporaries claimed she could recite in Sanskrit some twenty thousand sacred Hindu texts. She gained fluency in several native languages, but her mastery of Sanskrit and its sacred texts would win her the greatest prestige.

Ramabai spent her childhood in trudging about India with her parents and brother, walking thousands of miles, stopping at one sacred shrine or another. The family performed the expected rituals, prostrating themselves before statues, walking hundreds of times around shrines, fasting, presenting offerings, bathing in sacred waters. They endured tremendous hardships and knew the pangs of hunger and poverty. In the summer of 1874, Ramabai's parents died, leaving her and her brother destitute. They traveled on, earning meager support by reciting Sanskrit texts. Ramabai began insisting publicly that the sacred writings did not support women's slavery to their husbands, mandate their lack of learning, or enjoin marriages arranged in a girl's infancy. Such matches, often unconsummated, frequently left the child a widow and forced her into virtual slavery to her deceased husband's family. (Ramabai's father had neglected to contract a marriage for her, another breach of custom on his part.)

Ramabai and her brother made their way to Calcutta, and there in 1878 she won fame. "Ramabai was the news of the hour," an admirer exuded. "Papers all over India published her with doubtings, trumpetings and amazement. She was unimagined—a woman of purest Brahman birth, twenty years old and unmarried, beautiful and impossibly learned. She dazzled India."[4] After examination by the University of Calcutta faculty (pandits), she was awarded two titles: "pundita" (or "pandita") and "sarasvati," meaning "learned one." From 1878, she was always called "Pandita." The first Indian woman to be so designated, Ramabai now found myriad opportunities to address influential audiences and argue for women's rights. In 1879 and 1880, Ramabai and her brother traveled in Assam and Bengal. Her brother died in 1881. No longer an observant Hindu, Ramabai became attracted to the theism of the Brahmo Samaj, a reformist sect influenced by Western (especially American Unitarian) views.[5] She did not join, but she applauded this sect's forward-looking social program and was more closely associated with it than with any other religious society.

Before Ramabai reached the age of twenty, then, compatriots regarded her as a social leader who surpassed other women in learning and eloquence. As such—and because her interest in women's issues coincided with their own—she had the trust of the British governing cadre as well. A brief, happy marriage in Assam to Bipin Behari Medhavi, a lawyer of a lower caste (and a member of the Brahmo Samaj), gave her the opportunity to model an egalitarian marriage. Her prospects were cut short on February 4, 1882, when Medhavi died of cholera, leaving her with an infant daughter, Manoramabai (Heart's Joy).[6] He also left her with a curiosity about Christianity and an intention to visit England, an adventure they had begun planning together.

In March 1882, Ramabai's eagerness to learn English brought her to the Government Female Training School in Poona, where she and the wife of the Indian chief justice together received instruction from a Miss Hurford. Though not a missionary, Hurford made Bible instruction a condition for private English lessons. Ramabai had first received a Sanskrit Bible from missionaries in Calcutta. A Bengali Gospel of Luke found among her husband's books had whetted her interest in Christianity. A Christian on the street passed her a tract; a Baptist missionary occasionally visited her husband. Ramabai had no thought of converting, but she willingly read the Bible. Through Hurford, Ramabai made her way to the mission school run by the Sisters of St. Mary the Virgin in Poona. Anglo-Catholic in their religious faith, the sisters took Ramabai under their wing. She coped tactfully with their manifest interest in her soul as well as in her mind and graciously accepted their introduction to a prominent Indian convert, Father Goreh. Sister Geraldine, a British missionary, soon came to stand for Ramabai in the stead of a Christian mother.

Ramabai's testimony on behalf of Indian women before a British Commission in February 1883 gained her immediate acclaim in Britain as well as in India. In May 1882, she established in Poona the Aryamahila Samaj, a society dedicated to promoting female education. In November, she founded a Bombay branch with the same intent. She lectured widely and enjoyed the support of prominent local Hindu scholars and community leaders. These endeavors meant that the English press introduced her to their readers before her dream of studying in England materialized. It was reported that Queen Victoria herself read Ramabai's remarks, and the English implemented some of her suggestions.[7] News of Ramabai also reached the United States and eventually made its way into the religious press. The *Presbyterian* noted late in 1883, "One of the most interesting characters in India just now is Ramabai, a gifted and highly educated young Brahmin widow, who has undertaken the difficult task of creating a public sentiment against the social customs which bind down Indian women. She has already achieved a great deal. Her lectures in Bombay have created a wide interest, not only from the novelty of a woman assuming such a position, but from her scholarly and forcible manner of placing her views before the public. She is spoken of as on the 'border line of Christianity,' and her influence in certain directions can scarcely be overrated."[8]

CHRISTIAN PILGRIM

The Sisters of St. Mary the Virgin entered wholeheartedly into Ramabai's plans for studying in England. Sister Geraldine's health forced her to return to the order's motherhouse in Wantage, England. She agreed to be Ramabai's sponsor and mentor during her stay there. Ramabai hoped to study medicine so that she could open a practice dedicated to the well-being of Indian women. She funded her trip by writing a small book in the Marathi language, *Stri-dharma-niti,* outlining the duties of women. The government purchased rights to the book, giving Ramabai her fare. (A later book published in Bombay, *My Voyage to England,* maintained her visibility in her homeland and provided a modest income.)

Prominent people warmly welcomed Ramabai to England, where she arrived on May 17, 1883. She enchanted the venerable Max Müller—foremost Indologist of his day, member of numerous scholarly societies, Oxford University professor, and part of a committee pledged to press the government to reform the marriage laws in India.[9] He exerted his considerable influence on her behalf and generously promoted her as a "representative of Indian progress."[10] Thanks to him and others, Ramabai moved among the educated and socially prominent. The Sisters of St. Mary, eager to circumscribe Ramabai's exposure to England, initiated her into the regulated life of their motherhouse. Conforming to their strict rules, Ramabai found herself exposed to the Church of England in its most Catholic expressions. Her interest in Christianity grew beyond mere curiosity. Sister Geraldine could not satisfy the quick intellect of this woman deeply versed in ancient Eastern philosophies. Ramabai addressed her profoundest spiritual doubts to Father Goreh, perhaps the most influential figure in her life. By the fall of 1883, she declared herself ready for Christian baptism.[11]

On Michaelmas Day, September 29, 1883, a strange procession wended its way to the Wantage parish church. An Indian woman and child in traditional clothing, accompanied by a sister in her severe black habit, found their way to the baptismal font where they stood before Canon Butler. The latter, the Anglo-Catholic founder of the Society of St. John the Evangelist as well as of the Sisters of St. Mary the Virgin, baptized twenty-five-year-old Ramabai and her daughter, Manoramabai. Ramabai took the Christian name Mary Rama.

Although Ramabai affirmed her faith with only Sister Geraldine as sponsor, the news of her conversion soon made headlines in India, where it caused considerable public turmoil. Ramabai had become a public figure of significant stature. Her private choices were public events.[12]

While creeds, ritual, and submission to the church, its bishops, and her order regulated Sister Geraldine's life, Ramabai seemed a free spirit, and friction developed in the women's relationship. Accustomed to thinking, reasoning, and disputing, Ramabai found the constraints of the motherhouse stifling.[13]

In September 1884, she found a larger world at one of England's premier institutions for women's education, Cheltenham Ladies' College.[14] Dorothea Beale, a forceful women's advocate, presided over the college with unfailing aplomb.[15] Beale's Broad Church sympathies allowed Ramabai to question without jeopardizing her soul, and Ramabai welcomed Beale's biblical and religious instruction as well as the educational advantages her new setting offered. Beale's appeal to Prime Minister William Gladstone resulted in funds for Ramabai from the Queen's Scholarship, helping to ease the burden on her sponsors at Wantage.

Within a few months, Ramabai became a teacher as well as a pupil, developing a course in Sanskrit. She suffered increasingly from impaired hearing, and English doctors told her that she could never have a medical career. With the example of Dorothea Beale before her, Ramabai changed her course and determined to devote her life to education. Just as education had been the vehicle of her own emancipation, she believed, it would free India's widows to be productive partners in the emergence of a new India.

With this objective, Ramabai decided early in 1886 to accept an invitation from Anandibai Joshee, a distant cousin who was about to graduate from the Women's Medical College in Philadelphia. Believed by her contemporaries to be the first Hindu woman in the world to receive an M.D., Joshee had left India for the United States at about the same time Ramabai had journeyed to England. The Indian press closely followed her progress and celebrated her appointment to the Albert Edward Hospital in Kolhapur, India. Joshee had kept caste in the United States and had remained a Hindu.[16] Ramabai appreciated the significance for Indian women of Joshee's accomplishments and arrived to celebrate them in Philadelphia on March 6, 1886.[17] She intended to stay long enough to study U.S. education, especially the newly popular adaptations on Froebel's concept of the kindergarten.

THE UNITED STATES AND MISSION: THE EARLY YEARS

Ramabai's reputation preceded her, and curious U.S. Protestants warmly welcomed her. Rachel Bodley, president of the Women's Medical College, took over the roles of Sister Geraldine and Dorothea Beale as mentor and example. A distinguished chemist, socially prominent and well connected, Bodley was ideally situated to help Ramabai find her way in the United States.

A tea for eighty prominent Philadelphia women introduced her to society. Ramabai lost no time in sharing her developing dream to open a home where high-caste widows could keep caste. They would receive no religious instruction, and she would oversee their education and practical training. Convinced that success demanded a religiously neutral facility, Ramabai found support especially among friends who knew India best—like Max Müller. The Sisters of St. Mary the Virgin as well as missions advocates disagreed with her plan to work with a local board of reform-minded Hindus (among them some members of the Brahmo Samaj) and to enlist financial support and administrative oversight from a U.S. committee.

Convinced that the plight of Indian women adversely affected all of society, Ramabai argued simply that mothers deprived of fresh air and sunlight, intellectual stimulation and emotional fulfillment, became "selfish slaves to petty interests," indifferent to the welfare of the nation. Depressed mothers nurtured embittered children. A thousand years of complete submission had destroyed female self-reliance and produced sons as well as daughters who depended on other nations instead of tapping their own resources. In Ramabai's experience, women's ignorance blocked the paths of liberal-minded and progressive men. This ignorance extended from formal learning to common hygiene. Ramabai identified self-reliance, education, and native women teachers as the chief needs of Indian women. Providing these shaped her mission. She buttressed its rationale with figures from the 1881 census: 99.7 million women and girls lived under British rule in India; 99.5 percent could neither read nor write. The vast majority of the remaining females learned the rudiments of reading and writing between the ages of seven and nine and then left their homes for marriage with no hope for further exposure to books or learning. She proposed homes, to be supervised by Hindu men and women, for young high-caste widows. She hoped to recruit U.S. and English women as teachers, thus offering students the advantages of both East and West. Her vision included libraries and guest lectures. In sum, she proposed "a gospel of society's well-being through the elevation of women." She would "prepare the way for the spread of the gospel by throwing open the locked doors of the Indian zenanas" and would prepare women "to bear the dazzling light of the outer world and the perilous blasts of social persecution" that would surely follow.[18]

To enlist support, in 1888, she published *The High-Caste Hindu Woman*. Rachel Bodley provided an introduction, and the book sold well. The task Ramabai had set for herself seemed so vast as to be hopeless, however. She could hardly undertake alone the responsibility for forming and coordinating "circles" of potential partners, yet her preferences denied her the usual approach of turning to institutions for support. She abhorred denominations partly because they made her feel bounded and confined. As one who affirmed the Apostles' Creed and loved Christ, she insisted she had a basis for unity with all Christians.

Early in 1887, Ramabai met Frances Willard, the famous president of the WCTU. The two had already corresponded on the recommendation of Dr. and Mrs. Joseph Cook of Boston. Cook, an internationally acclaimed lecturer and author, found in Ramabai a match for his own social concerns. Cook's was an auspicious recommendation, and Willard had responded with a bundle of WCTU materials. Ramabai promptly joined Willard's White Ribbon Army. In time, Willard made Ramabai a vice president of the India WCTU, superintendent of native work for India, and a World's WCTU lecturer. Their ties of friendship ran deeper than the work of the WCTU. For the rest of her life, Willard kept a picture of Ramabai on her desk. She offered an eloquent description of this "young woman of medium height and ninety-eight pounds weight":

> She is delightful to have about; content if she has books, pen and ink, and peace. She seems a sort of human-like gazelle; incarnate gentleness, combined with such celerity of apprehension, such swiftness of mental pace, adroitness of logic and equipoise of intention as to make her a delightful mental problem. She is impervious to praise, and can be captured only by affection. . . . The Pundita is a woman-lover, not as the antithesis of a man-hater, for she is too great-natured not to love all humanity with equal mother-heartedness, but because women need special help, her zeal for them is like quenchless fire. . . . I cannot help cherishing the earnest hope that, under Pundita Ramabai's Christian sway, women never yet reached by the usual missionary appliances of the church may be . . . led from their darkness into the marvelous light of the gospel that elevates women, and with her lifts the world toward heaven.[19]

Ramabai looked to the WCTU, Willard told the members, as "the largest-hearted band of women on earth."[20] Its members did not disappoint. They embraced Ramabai and devised a strategy that enabled the realization of her ambition. The WCTU created "Ramabai Circles" within local WCTU unions. Members of Ramabai Circles pledged one dollar per year for Ramabai's work.[21] The plan was refined with the appointment of Mary Livermore as national superintendent for Ramabai Circles. Livermore, one of the WCTU's most gifted promoters, the wife of a Universalist minister, a prominent social reformer, a feminist, an editor, and a national lecturer sometimes known as the Queen of the Platform, threw her considerable skills into the task. Ramabai could have had no more efficient assistance.[22] Thanks to Willard, then, Ramabai's funding seemed secure. WCTU conventions sold her book. Willard hoped aloud that two White Ribbon missionaries would accompany Ramabai to India.[23]

Ramabai traveled widely within the WCTU network, addressing state and local conventions. In Boston, Joseph Cook introduced her to his lecture audience in spacious Tremont Temple and gave a reception for her at his home, "opening the way into the hearts of the people" beyond the purview of the WCTU.[24] In Maine, she "captured" her audience. They demanded an encore, and she spoke again and then the audience took up a spontaneous collection.[25] In Rhode Island, First Baptist Church of Newport was completely filled, with scores standing and many turned away.[26] In Bridgeport, Connecticut, she won the hearts of another union.[27]

College audiences participated, too. In Ithaca, students and faculty at Cornell University formed a Circle for the Elevation of Women in India.[28] At the Women's College Chapel at Northwestern University on a winter Sunday afternoon, Ramabai, billed as "the most learned woman of her nation," enlisted one hundred names for a Ramabai Circle.[29] She had, Willard rejoiced, "captured the hearts of the westerners as she did those at the east."[30]

Ramabai's identification with the WCTU offered her access to some of the best-known U.S. citizens of her day. In March 1888, for example, Ramabai appeared in Washington, D.C., on the program of the International Council of Women. Advertised as "the most representative body of women ever convened," the program featured Ramabai's WCTU friends Willard and Livermore but also included Lucy Stone, Julia Ward Howe, Clara Barton, Antoinette Brown Blackwell, Anna Shaw, Elizabeth Cady Stanton, Susan Anthony, and Frederick Douglass, among others from around the world.

Ramabai sought a means outside the WCTU to mobilize other friends. She also wanted a U.S. board to oversee her work. While she had many friends in England, she enjoyed the freedom of the United States where nondenominational Christian enterprises could readily flourish. In England, friends pressured her toward Anglo-Catholicism, which did not suit her tastes. As Willard described her, Ramabai was a devout Christian, "but so broad, that while she earnestly holds to the Apostles' Creed, she cannot subscribe to the Thirty-Nine Articles." Yet she "lives in God beyond almost any one whom I have ever known, and has an ardor of devotion to Christ that is in keeping with her Oriental nature."[31] It was the opportunity for accountability to prominent Christians untroubled by what seemed Ramabai's broadmindedness that drew Ramabai toward U.S. partners for her work.

In Boston's Channing Hall on Tuesday, December 13, 1887, Ramabai realized this hope. Her friends crowded the hall to give tangible evidence to their professed interest. While the crowd was mostly female, a goodly number of prominent men came, too. Edward Everett Hale, the moderate Unitarian pastor of South Congregational Church, chaired the meeting, which moved to create a Ramabai Association and to adopt a constitution calling for establishing in Bombay a nonsectarian home under Ramabai's supervision. Trinity Church pastor Phillips Brooks, a veteran India traveler, assured the crowd that "anything we do for India will reflect its good back upon us. Any good will be good to ourselves."[32] George A. Gordon, pastor of the Old South Church, stressed the rich opportunity to reach out to the world. One Dr. Courtney of St. Paul's challenged the women present to raise the $25,000 Ramabai wanted for the purchase of a house. "The intellectual women of Boston ought to do it even without their husbands' help," he opined.

Elections followed, and Hale was chosen president. Hale had looked beyond the pastorate throughout his professional life, using social reform and his pen as vehicles for religiously informed social change. He seemed the ideal head for the new agency.[33] The venerable Brooks, Gordon, Bodley, Willard, and the Unitarian Boston philanthropist and education reformer Mary Hemenway were chosen vice presidents. (Lyman Abbott would later join this group and succeed Hale as president.)[34] A board of trustees and an executive committee completed the organization. The officers agreed to serve for ten years. The board would hold all property. A second board of advisers would be constituted on-site and would include the Hindus Ramabai chose. Eighteen Ramabai Circles beyond those in the WCTU had awaited the organizing of an association. Now their number grew.

Mid-April 1888 found Ramabai back in Boston for the annual observance of Fast Day. She addressed Gordon's congregation at Old South Church on "Hindoo Society," giving an educational address in which she "claimed for her nation a character better than that which has been allotted to it"—except, of course, in its treatment of women.[35] By the spring of 1888, Ramabai was eager to begin her work in India. In July, she made her way by train to San Francisco, where the National Educational Association was holding its annual convention. Newspapers announced her arrival, and crowds awaited when her train rolled into the station.[36] Local representatives of the WCTU escorted her to a reception at the Occidental Hotel. On Sunday morning, she addressed a Bible class at First Congregational Church, one of the city's historic congregations. In the afternoon, the auditorium of First Presbyterian Church was filled for a 1 P.M. address by "the noted Hindoo woman." A reception followed. The next week, the city's Teachers Mutual Aid Society honored her with another public reception.[37] At the WCTU reception, hundreds, including the wife of the Japanese consul, called to pay respects.[38]

In the fall of 1888, Ramabai sailed from San Francisco for India, via Japan and China, secure in the knowledge that some of the United States's best-known Protestants and forward-thinking people had pledged their help in her new endeavor. Her willingness to work with Hindus to address an enormous social evil elicited Unitarian enthusiasm, but her U.S. board included Congregationalists, Episcopalians, and the staunch Methodist Willard as well. The hundreds of circles, of course, incorporated people of many Protestant affiliations, but Ramabai's overarching goal bore the stamp of liberal Protestantism's hopefulness about education and progress. To be sure, all who signed on did not fully concur. Even so firm an ally as Willard wished publicly that Ramabai would launch a forthrightly Christian endeavor. The Rev. N. G. Clark, foreign secretary of the American Board of Commissioners for Foreign Missions, objected for those who thought Hinduism itself a greater problem than women's degradation: "She has not yet learned that the gospel alone . . . can accomplish the work she has at heart. . . . The whole scheme drops down into a purely humanitarian enterprise, which at the best would only mitigate, without removing, the evils she deplores. The Hindu system, as such, is not to be touched; partial relief only is to be secured for a few whom it now crushes to the earth. The Pundita may learn, through disappointed hopes . . . that the moral and social renovation of woman in India can only be effected by the gospel."[39]

Ramabai had long been incensed by the charge that she proposed to divert "the energies of Christian women and funds" that should properly have gone to missions. As she saw it, even if no widow embraced Christianity, Christians would "have the comfort of having done our duty" by providing the means by which Hindu widows could become productive members of society.[40] Whatever the reservations of some people in the United States—and despite the prominent men who lent their names to the cause—Ramabai's U.S. associates were overwhelmingly Protestant women who saw themselves as women working on behalf of women. Ramabai's winsome presence and powerful intellect fueled the growing awareness of the treatment of women around the world and offered ordinary people a way to do something about it. Under the umbrella of the Ramabai Association mingled tens of thousands who felt passionately about how Christian humanitarian impulses should be at work in non-Christian societies.

RELIGIOUS RESTLESSNESS AND THE "MISSION QUESTION"

"The Pandita Ramabai has met with a kind reception from all parties in Bombay," the *Indian Witness* reported upon Ramabai's arrival in March 1889. "As to opposers, she has none." The paper marveled at the acclaim and money she had found in the United States. It exceeded, the editor ventured, anything ever accorded anyone else.[41] On March 11, 1889, Ramabai opened the long-anticipated home for widows. Hindu reformers warmly welcomed her, accepting her assurances that she would respect their religious scruples. Non-Christians (and non-Westerners) presided at the school's opening and predominated on its local advisory board. Some local Christian press reacted with the criticism Ramabai had anticipated.[42] She called the school Sharada Sadan (Home of Learning). Generous and impulsive, Ramabai spent much of her personal allowance to assist young women who did not fall under the school's mandate. In 1890, she moved the Sharada Sadan from Bombay to the healthier and more economical city of Poona some 140 miles away. Situated on a broad plateau and known for its moderate climate, Poona had a population of some 150,000 and was a stronghold of Brahmanism.[43]

In July 1891, U.S. donations enabled the purchase of two acres of land and the acquisition of a commodious residence for the Sharada Sadan. Some forty widows were in residence, and prospects seemed bright. So far, Ramabai had kept her promise of religious neutrality, although she had taken a first step toward making Christianity a viable option for child widows. She had established a chapter of the King's Daughters, an association started by the U.S. Episcopalian Margaret Bottome and promoted in India especially by the Methodist Women's Missionary Society. It had the dual objectives of benevolence and evangelism. With the motto "In His Name," its members pledged to help the needy.[44]

Soonderbai Powar, a high-caste Indian Christian teacher and reformer, worked closely with Ramabai. The first and best known of a long and changing list of associates, Powar brought a background in education.[45] Everything about their joint endeavor was Indian: food, furnishings, schedule. And Ramabai resisted the missionary tendency to picture India as "vile" or "heathen" (specifically as in the missionary hymn "From Greenland's Icy Mountains" by Reginald Heber, Anglican bishop of Calcutta). "My father was a Brahmin," she once told Willard. "I don't like to hear that every man is vile when I know that my father was so true and so good that he had me taught to read, and to read such books."[46] Ramabai frequently violated Christian norms by speaking in Hindu temples on behalf of women without bearing a Christian witness. In December 1889, she became the first woman to address the Indian National Congress. Hindus watched warily, worried that she might be too Christian; Christians thought her not Christian enough.

Members of the U.S. Ramabai Association as well as Christian leaders in India with whom she had no direct ties began visiting this famous woman. Drawn at first by curiosity, some returned because their hearts were captured by her transparent simplicity. The "Hindu Minerva" proved equally at home in scholarly disputation or in humble Christian services. Missionary periodicals in the United States reported Ramabai's remarkable efforts. James Thoburn, Methodist bishop for India, became a devoted admirer and often stopped at Ramabai's home when traveling his circuit.[47] U.S. women's missionary periodicals carried news of Ramabai's hopes and efforts, as did some reports from denominational boards.[48] Such coverage was a departure, but Ramabai seemed uniquely to "belong" to all.

In 1891, Ramabai came across *From Death Into Life,* a book by William Haslam, an eccentric Anglican evangelist whose atypical ministry had sparked renewal in parishes across England. The book offered anecdotes from Haslam's ministry interspersed with theological insights.[49] Reading Haslam's argument that Christian life was essentially a daily experience of the presence and power of the risen Christ, Ramabai impulsively concluded that she was not truly a Christian. Her intellect had been engaged, but the Christian faith had not warmed her heart.[50]

Haslam described encounters with hundreds of people whose Christianity seemed to resemble her own. They were baptized and affirmed the Creed, but nothing had *happened* to them to transform their lives. Ramabai agonized over this until she came to a moment of repentance and a sense of forgiveness. She had taken another step away from the Anglo-Catholicism Sister Geraldine still pressed upon her in frequent correspondence. In so doing, she moved closer to a segment of the missionary community that understood the Christian life as the moment-by-moment experience of "not I, but Christ."

Ramabai's discovery of Christian circles where people urged one another to "press on" and to "know Jesus better" assuaged her doubts but provoked spiritual restlessness. In the fall of 1892, U.S. Presbyterian evangelist George F. Pentecost, in the midst of a two-year visit to India, arrived in Poona. Open only to "educated Brahmans," his campaign elicited an outpouring of local financial support if not a spate of conversions. The Indian Christian press confirmed "appreciative audiences of educated Hindus" elsewhere, too.[51] Ramabai attended every service during the six weeks Pentecost preached in a Poona theater. Under his tutelage, she concluded that she had known Christ as Savior only "in the general sense of the word." She now confessed him as "her Redeemer."[52] She also began leaving her door open when she, Manoramabai, and a few other girls Ramabai supported with her own funds did their daily 5 A.M. Bible reading. By 1893, half of the sixty widows attended early morning prayers, and Ramabai formed a Christian Endeavor Society.[53]

Max Müller once remarked that Ramabai's intentional religious neutrality ultimately yielded to the force of her own goodness.[54] Her pupils proved naturally curious about why she cared about them when no one else did. To be sure, she had cared before becoming a Christian, but now a newly vivid Christian faith structured her response and provoked a storm of opposition in India and the United States. Families withdrew a third of the widows. "Very fiercely has native society turned upon her," a missionary of the Free Church of Scotland wrote, "and very severely has she been handled as 'a wolf in sheep's clothing' by the native papers."[55] Max Müller admitted: "Accounts that reach us from India are very discouraging. . . . The law did not protect her. . . . She had to give up girls on demand of families. A woman in India always belongs to someone else. She cannot exist by herself."[56] On her part, Ramabai insisted she did not violate her pledge of neutrality: girls came for instruction of their own free will. She continued to respect Hindu caste and customs, but she announced her intention to instruct the curious in the Christian faith. Her Hindu advisory board resigned, Unitarians resigned en masse from the U.S. Ramabai Association, and Ramabai had to rebuild her work.

Meanwhile, her spiritual restlessness persisted. A Hindu pilgrim had become a Christian pilgrim, always aware of the journey, and always looking for more. Her next step was the discovery of the Keswick Convention. Organized in 1875, Keswick Conventions for the deepening of Christian life convened each summer in England's Lake District. The 1886 convention began featuring missions, and in the 1890s the convention authorized representatives to conduct winter preaching tours for missionaries and national workers. Among the first to visit India was a Baptist preacher, J. Gelson Gregson, whose zealous preaching was reportedly attended by "much blessing."[57] Over the next few years, Ramabai listened attentively to such Keswick regulars as Gregson, Haslam, F. B. Meyer, and Henry Varley with increasing empathy for their teaching on present holiness, constant fellowship with God, and knowledge of the specific will of God. General response to these India missioners was such that twelve annual Indian conventions for the deepening of spiritual life resulted from their visits.[58]

Early in the 1890s, William Osborne, Methodist founder of the city of Ocean Grove, New Jersey, visited India, "looking out for some new line of work to glorify Christ." He chose the camp meeting and established a campground between Bombay and Poona. There, in April 1894, under Gelson's preaching, Ramabai concluded that she needed to be filled with the Holy Spirit and professed to "enter on a new experience of God's power to save, bless and use."[59]

Each step into such networks intent on "deeper" or "higher" religious experience brought Ramabai contacts with potential new supporters and different missionaries. Her connections expanded as she attended camp meetings, heard visiting evangelists, and read the books and periodicals produced by the Keswick, higher life, and holiness movements. In India, then, she first examined interrelated expressions of British and U.S. evangelicalism she had not particularly noticed during her stay in the West. Her support base in the United States, while continuing to include many who had first embraced her, expanded toward those who shared her restless longing for "more of God."

In 1897, natural disaster in the form of severe drought abruptly turned Ramabai's energies to practical matters. In the spring, plague and famine gripped the nation. The number of dying was estimated at 37 million, while another 44 million lacked sufficient food.[60] As a small child, Ramabai's family had survived one famine. Her parents had succumbed to another. Now she felt compelled to go to India's devastated Central Provinces to rescue as many starving widows as she could. She had neither shelter nor funds to offer, but the conviction that God wanted her to rescue at least three hundred girls proved irresistible.[61]

The Sharada Sadan could house no more than sixty-five. Ramabai sent small groups of widows from the most devastated areas until she had gathered sixty. She then returned to Poona to plead for help in rescuing women from the moral degradation of the relief camps and poorhouses that were the starving widows' only other alternatives.[62]

An outbreak of plague in Poona cut short her next foray north. She rented tents and sent all her girls out into open country some twenty miles away. In 1893, she had acquired a farm and some land about thirty-six miles from Poona. She obtained permission from her U.S. board to move the famine victims to this property at Kedgaon. This choice opened another chapter in Ramabai's life.

Ramabai's new settlement at Kedgaon, unlike her ongoing Sharada Sadan in Poona, was unapologetically Christian from the start, although Hindus were welcome and assisted in keeping caste. She named the settlement Mukti, meaning "Salvation." By the end of 1897, Ramabai had assembled the three hundred famine widows she had set out to find. She now began to develop plans to make Mukti a place for education, vocational training, and the equipping of Indian female village evangelists. The famine widows constituted the nucleus for this experiment.

THE UNITED STATES AND MISSION: LATER YEARS

In the midst of this expansion, the Ramabai Association's ten-year agreement with Ramabai came to an end early in 1898, necessitating for her a trip to the United States. Ramabai left her work in India in the care of an energetic U.S. associate, Minnie Abrams, who had first come to India under the auspices of the Methodist Women's Missionary Society.[63] After eight years supervising a girls' boarding school in Bombay, Abrams had spent 1897 as a Methodist Conference evangelist, traveling with other women by ox cart throughout the vicinity Ramabai called home.[64] A capable organizer, Abrams brought strengths that nicely complemented Ramabai's. Like Ramabai, she had long been a "White Ribbon lady," serving in 1897 as national superintendent of a department for the prevention of cruelty to children.[65]

Once again, Manoramabai accompanied her mother abroad, this time to enroll in the A. M. Chesbrough Academy in North Chili, New York. Several of Ramabai's girls were already there. Manoramabai's class of 1900 included four who listed Poona, India, as their home address: Manoramabai and Tungabai in the Classical Course; Chumpabai and Nermuddabai in Elective Studies.[66]

In 1898, North Chili was a small town just outside Rochester. Wesleyan Methodist founder B. T. Roberts had established Chesbrough Seminary (later Roberts

Wesleyan College) and named it for a follower who left the school a substantial donation. By 1898, B. T. Roberts was dead, but his widow carried his work forward with the help of their son. Given to impressions, "leadings," and much prayer, Ellen Roberts persisted in the radical holiness views that had occasioned her husband's break with Methodism. Several Chesbrough alumnae served in India and recommended the seminary as an ideal place to settle during furloughs. The attraction this place now held for Ramabai revealed her shifting religious sensibilities.

Manoramabai found herself surrounded by one species of holiness piety. Experiential and separatist though it was, it did not lack appeal. Her mother quickly discovered kindred spirits—those who shared her yearning for "all that God had for them"—among them Albert and Mary Norton, one-time missionaries to India. She met the five Duncan sisters, the daughters of a one-time Methodist minister, James Duncan, and his wife, Mary Burke Duncan. The sisters ran a gospel mission "on faith lines" in downtown Rochester. They also operated a faith home and had sent a young follower, a Miss Edmonds, to North India. Ramabai spoke in their mission, and soon the oldest sister, Elizabeth Baker, sensed a call to India. Ramabai's decision to expand her contacts among the devout on the fringes of the established churches proved significant not only for her daughter's education but also for the future of her work in India.

These new friends did not displace older associations. Ramabai's visit to Rochester included an address at Rochester Theological Seminary, where seminary president Augustus Strong hailed her as "one of the greatest, if not the greatest heroine of the century."[67]

With Manoramabai settled in upstate New York, Ramabai made her way to Boston to deal with her board. The association decided to dissolve and deeded the property in India to Ramabai. Brooks, Willard, Hemenway, and Ramabai's first promoter, Bodley, had died, leaving the association without Ramabai's most ardent early admirers and supporters. But she did not need them now: she had used them well and moved beyond them. Her embrace of conversionist Christianity and affinity for aspects of the higher life and holiness movements had brought her into the flow of growing streams of popular Protestantism in the United States. D. L. Moody and his many networks promoted her as ever in their publications, collecting and forwarding funds. Still hailed for her learning, she now put more confidence in her heart than in her intellect. She had come around to the conviction that only the gospel could accomplish what she had set out to do.

Ramabai's reorganized association was in the hands of evangelicals prominent in many causes of the day, run by people who bridged the old missions boards, women's missionary societies, and faith missions. She could count on kind words from people who had not known what to make of her a decade earlier. She clearly retained the goodwill of vast numbers of people in the United States and enjoyed the endorsement of the networks around Moody; the influential *Missionary Review of the World,* edited by the elder statesman of missions, Arthur Tappan Pierson, and his son, Delavan; and the growing circle around Christian and Missionary Alliance leader A. B. Simpson. She became intrigued by divine healing and premillennialism and, like many U.S. and English evangelicals, she came under the spell of George Müller's teaching about living by faith.[68] (Müller, a German transplanted to England, had established large orphanages without visible means of support. He recounted a steady stream of needs supplied in answer to prayer, and he urged his contemporaries to explore the possibilities of childlike trust in God for every need.) These themes did not predominate in Ramabai's publicity or her presentations, but visitors to India reported on her fascination for such popular evangelical teachings. While retaining the support of many who had pledged their prayers and money in the 1880s, then, she added other circles of friends who made up in fervor what they may have lacked in fame. The *Missionary Review of the World* noted the transition: "Pundita Ramabai . . . intends to give herself more distinctly to religious work. . . . Full of enthusiasm, gifted intellectually and spiritually for such work, she will be able to make as great a success of Gospel work as she has of teaching and organizing."[69]

During a brief stop in England, Ramabai neglected to visit Wantage and Sister Geraldine but found time to participate briefly in the Keswick Convention, where she made an eloquent plea for "1,000 Holy Ghost missionaries" for India's 140 million women, more than 8.5 million of whom were child wives under the age of fourteen.[70] This request she had already urged on her U.S. supporters through Moody's *Northfield Echoes.*

Severe famine in 1899 and 1900 brought another surge of growth to Mukti. Some 1,350 more destitute girls were taken in. Ramabai's friend from Rochester, Baker, arrived to help and arranged for her friend, Edmonds, to oversee a new facility for prostitutes rescued from the famine. Ramabai abandoned her exclusive focus on high-caste widows and welcomed young widows and orphans of any caste.

By 1899, people in the United States could read descriptions of Mukti as "a hive of industry" run by the threefold law of "education for the mind, salvation for the soul, and occupation for the body."[71] Residents learned to weave, cook, farm, and mill, as well as acquiring carpentry and building skills. Abrams adapted the Student Volunteer Movement for Ramabai's widows, and seventy promptly volunteered to train for Christian work. Within a year, some joined the ranks of village evangelists.[72] Ramabai taught her women to use their tithes to support evangelism abroad, and money flowed from Mukti to Korea and China.

The U.S. press, Protestant and secular, followed Ramabai's expanding efforts. A typical observation proclaimed, "There is nothing in all Christian Missions more remarkable than the history of Ramabai, her life and work."[73] "Do not think that

Ramabai has carried away only 1,700 girls whom the nation did not want much; she has laid the foundation of 1,700 new Christian families," noted a Hindu paper.[74] During 1901 alone, visiting pastors baptized twelve hundred women who had been converted at the Mukti church.

At Ramabai's urging, in 1902–1903, Manoramabai and Abrams spent nearly a year in Australia and New Zealand, working to establish Ramabai Circles. Reports of revival in Australia, Korea, and elsewhere had begun reaching India, and Ramabai's spiritual restlessness resumed. When Abrams and Manoramabai returned, Ramabai organized prayer bands. Five hundred widows volunteered to pray for revival. In June 1905, with reports of the Welsh revival circulating widely, hundreds of Ramabai's two thousand girls manifested unusual concern about sin, crying and praying for forgiveness. The noise of hundreds praying aloud individually and simultaneously permeated the compound day and night. "It was wonderful," the impressionable Abrams exulted. "Such a wave of repentance. . . . The people were taken with repentance on their seats and were smitten down that they could not get out of the place where they were sitting."[75] Manoramabai, devoted as she increasingly was to the Anglo-Catholicism of her childhood, nonetheless agreed: "It is manifestly God Himself working."[76]

In 1907, revival fires burned with renewed intensity. A prominent U.S. journalist, William Ellis, heard astonishing revival reports while traveling in India and detoured to Kedgaon to write a story for the U.S. press. At Mukti, he walked in on a scene he called "utterly without parallel in all my wide experience." Thirty or forty of the seven hundred girls had "come into the blessing." They met twice daily, he learned. Contortions, tears, ecstatic speech, and trances marked their behavior.

Other revivals had broken out at about the same time in other parts of India. Writing of them collectively, Ellis observed the absence of missionary domination, the precedence of prayer over preaching, and the prominence of "timid untutored Hindoo maidens, reared to believe in the complete subjection of women."[77]

Some of Ramabai's U.S. friends read this story with particular interest, for similar experiences had been spreading among them since 1901, with a surge after 1906. Controversial teachings about speaking in tongues and being baptized with the Holy Spirit agitated both missionaries and native Christians in India. This idea arrived from the United States and Europe, brought by indomitable participants in a Los Angeles revival who felt impelled to tell the world that an end-times awakening had begun. Ramabai never embraced the speaking in tongues that accompanied this revival. Abrams accepted it but seldom experienced it, though both women dreaded "missing" God.[78] Nonetheless, over the next few months hundreds of the widows apparently spoke in tongues (sometimes English, it was claimed), and Ramabai did not discourage them.[79]

Mukti, meanwhile, kept growing. Revival intensity waned, but steady growth in numbers and programs characterized the next decade. Then apparent tragedy struck. After a brief illness, Manoramabai died unexpectedly on July 24, 1921. On April 5, 1922, her grieving mother died at Kedgaon. Their work continued, altered in many ways by their absence.

As word of Ramabai's death reached the world, Indians, Britons, and Americans eulogized her as a scholar, saint, linguist, patriot, and reformer. One Indian observer put it as follows: "Ramabai was the first Indian to be in charge of an institution in which foreign women worked, a phenomenon unknown in those days when India was under British rule. Every aspect of this Mukti Mission Ashram was Indian: the Indian method of worship in the church; the Indian food served to both Indians and foreigners alike seated on low wooden stools in the dining hall; the Indian dress made of lowly cotton woven mostly on the handlooms worked by the women inmates of Mukti."[80]

Ramabai's spiritual pilgrimage took her from Anglo-Catholicism through middle-class moderate Protestantism to participation in radical expressions of holiness and faith. Her support base—the people in the United States who "claimed" her—moved accordingly. She was variously the darling of Unitarian Boston Brahmins, Methodist bishops, faith missioners, holiness advocates, Pentecostals, and fundamentalists. The impressions she made on the public during her short U.S. sojourn from 1886 to 1889 lasted until her death in 1922, carefully nurtured by the press and by popular biographies in Sunday-school libraries.

The general public remained intrigued, but in a different way. Whereas in the 1880s the plight of Indian women incensed those in the United States intent on redeeming human social relationships, by World War I the country had different, apparently more immediate, foreign-policy concerns. The women's movement was in transition as its leadership and agendas changed. Commitment to traditional foreign missions, too, underwent a shift after the Ecumenical Missions Conference in New York in 1900. As older Protestant churches readjusted their vision, however, newer movements rose to own Ramabai's vision. Her personal experience paralleled theirs in important ways, and so she remained relevant in popular U.S. Protestantism. The character and social location of what was "popular" had changed, and tracing Ramabai's religious experiences and U.S. relationships offers a lens through which to view those changes.

Five years before the World's Parliament of Religions gave Eastern religions visibility in the United States on their own terms, this woman who won the highest accolades from her compatriots also won the United States's heart. Revered as a founder of modern India and acknowledged by feminists for her pioneering work on behalf of Indian women, Ramabai summoned U.S. Protestants to simple faith, moral vision, and humanitarian action. She challenged and prodded them by word and example to recognize and act upon the fundamental unity that overarched their divisions. They responded with prayer, personnel, and funds to one who followed an Anglo-American spiritual trajectory but refused to be co-opted by a Western agenda.

11 / The General and the Gringo

W. Cameron Townsend as Lázaro Cárdenas's "Man in America"

William L. Svelmoe

On a hot July day in 1939, dozens of newly washed and waxed Fords and Chevys wound their way from cities in southern California to the Mexican border town of Agua Caliente. There, in the parking lot of an old casino, they disgorged more than two hundred sharply dressed fundamentalist Protestant pastors, businessmen, doctors, schoolteachers, farmers, and their assorted family members. While the men pulled heavy picnic baskets from the trunks, their wives, clutching tickets to a "Good Neighbors Picnic sponsored by the Summer Institute of Linguistics [SIL]," haltingly garnered directions to the patio. In what W. Cameron Townsend modestly billed as "one of the most unusual picnics . . . in the history of the world," they spent the afternoon dining and conversing with Mexican President Lázaro Cárdenas—widely assumed in the United States to be a socialist (if not a communist)—three members of his cabinet, and other high officials of the Mexican revolutionary government. After dinner and an exchange of impassioned speeches, President Cárdenas shook hands and signed autographs, while Townsend mused that "keen observers . . . realized another Lincoln was in their midst."[1]

What brought these unlikely lunch partners—the religious and social conservatives from the United States and the politically liberal Mexican leaders—to a closed-down casino on July 7, 1939? The answer lay in the fertile mind of Townsend, the founder of the SIL, and in his symbiotic relationship with President Cárdenas.[2] It is the story of a friendship developed around a mutual commitment to the welfare of Mexico's large Indian population. It was a friendship that reconciled opposites. Townsend was a Protestant missionary committed to bringing the Bible to indigenous groups still lacking the Scripture in their language. After almost fifteen years in Guatemala with the Central American Mission, he had solid fundamentalist credentials and a passion for working with Indians, whom he felt had been neglected by both governments and missionaries.[3] Cárdenas, reared in the fires of the Mexican Revolution, espoused a socialist program of education that sought to stamp out the influence of religion on the masses. During his presidency, Mexico turned further left than at any point in its history. Yet Cárdenas permitted Townsend to bring as many SIL workers into Mexico as he could recruit, providing an ideal location for the incubation of what has become the world's largest, and in many ways most influential, independent Protestant mission. Townsend, in turn, vigorously championed Mexico's interests throughout the United States to as broad an audience as he could reach, from his own constituency to the halls of Congress and the White House. The Townsend-Cárdenas story provides an intriguing example of how one U.S. missionary attempted to influence directly both public opinion and political decision-making about Mexico. It also suggests that the common stereotype of missionaries as "behind-the-times" at home and dull purveyors of Western imperialism on the field needs continued revision.

MEXICO IN THE U.S. IMAGINATION

When Townsend first entered Mexico in 1933, U.S. citizens were divided in their opinion of Mexico. Since the beginning of the Mexican Revolution in 1910, the United States had maintained a decidedly uneasy relationship with its southern neighbor. U.S. meddling, both direct and indirect, added to Mexico's instability as one faction after another dominated Mexican politics.[4] U.S. oil companies, distressed by the revolutionary Constitution of 1917, which directly challenged standard interpretations of property rights, intrigued constantly in Mexico and funded a barrage of negative press in the United States. The Roman Catholic Church may well have been Mexico's most bitter critic. The Constitution of 1917 outlawed religious education, regulated religious worship, and prohibited priests from criticizing the government. During the administration of Plutarco Elías Calles (1924–1928), the bitterness between the government and church erupted into the bloody Cristero wars. The Roman Catholic press in the United States vilified Mexico, and books such as *No God Next Door* reinforced the belief that Mexico was merely a "laboratory" for Moscow and its "relentless war against God and Christian civilization."[5] Roman Catholics were not alone in this view. The U.S. State Department was generally convinced that Mexico was going to become a staging ground for Marxist-Leninism in the Western Hemisphere. (Ambassador Josephus Daniels proved an exception to this rule.)[6] As John Britton noted, conversations about Mexico in the 1920s and 1930s probably centered on the widely publicized hostility of the revolution to Catholicism and the "grossly exaggerated perception of international Communism in Mexico."[7]

By the 1930s, Mexico was undergoing a renaissance among certain segments of the public. Mexico's revolutionary project fascinated the U.S. Left, and a small colony of writers, artists, traveling professors, communists, and bohemians made for a moderate Greenwich Village atmosphere in Mexico City. Their rejection of "bourgeois values" and their fascination with all things Indian made them acceptable, even useful, to Mexican politicians and intellectuals.[8] By the 1930s, their views of Mexico were just beginning to have an impact on the popular U.S. media.

Columbia University professor Frank Tannenbaum, who in 1933 would be instrumental in securing Townsend's access to Mexico, typified this group. His publications about Mexico earned him the high regard of Mexico's intellectuals and political leaders—his closeness to Cárdenas was legendary—and the suspicion of the U.S. State Department, which considered him part of the "red" cohort. When he met Townsend in 1933, Tannenbaum had just published his influential study of Mexico, *Peace by Revolution,* and had become the "first major foreign interpreter of the [Mexican] Revolution."[9]

Conservative Protestants were probably more typical of the population at large. They were relieved over Mexico's anti-Catholicism, which seemed to present an opportunity for Protestant missionaries (although no Protestant missionaries who were not already residents were currently gaining access to the country), but concerned over its purported Bolshevist leanings.[10] Elvira, Townsend's first wife, expressed fundamentalism's opinion of Mexico when she wrote to a friend while her husband was trying to gain entrance to the country, "I am afraid that Mexico is not far from going Communistic and in that case we can hope for very little at this time."[11]

TOWNSEND'S INITIAL FORAY INTO MEXICO

Townsend had Tannenbaum partially to thank for his introduction into the good graces of Mexican officialdom. Granted permission to cross the border on November 11, 1933, so long as he did not preach or study Indian languages, Townsend spent hours in the waiting rooms of government offices, trying to find someone to listen to him. After a chance meeting with Tannenbaum, the professor gave Townsend a note of introduction to Rafael Ramírez, the director of rural education. Ramírez, initially hostile, changed his mind upon seeing the recommendation from Tannenbaum. While not permitting Bible translation or "any religious propaganda," he took the other restrictions off Townsend's passport and gave him permission to travel the country freely and study the system of rural education.[12]

Townsend knew full well as he set out on his travels that he had a small window of opportunity in which to win the confidence of the Mexican officials if his overall project was to have any hope of success.[13] The articles he wrote about Mexico after his initial trip must be read in that light. Townsend was a pragmatist, willing to shed preconceived notions and ideologies in pursuit of his central vision of Bible translation and the salvation of the "lost." Indeed, those who judge Townsend superficially see him as the "great American huckster," a swindler willing to say and do anything in order to get his Protestant missionaries access to remote communities. Certainly, there was something of the salesman about Townsend. His powers of persuasion were legendary, and his vision of the truth accented the positive. But to leave Townsend there is only to begin to understand him. For Townsend, what began in pragmatism usually ended in passion. As he traveled the back roads of Mexico alone, a passion for the country and its revolutionary idealists was kindled, a passion that exploded into flame two years later when he met Cárdenas.

For the next two months, Townsend traveled almost five thousand miles through rural Mexico, visiting schools and surveying local languages. Because he was armed with introductions from Ramírez, education officials welcomed and aided him at every turn. "You would think that I were a big gun for sure," he crowed to Elvira and went on to tell her how struck he was with the "spirit of sacrifice" manifested by the rural schoolteachers. He was genuinely impressed by the educational accomplishments of the revolutionary government.[14]

February and March found Townsend back in the United States to tend to his sick wife and write articles about Mexico. Ramírez kept him supplied with Department of Education publications to provide background and answer questions. Although Townsend felt "lost" in trying to write "secular articles," he managed to place three with the *Dallas News* and another with the education journal *School and Society*. While it is hard to judge their effect in the United States, in Mexico they passed from Ramírez to Narciso Bassols, the Marxist secretary of education, and Townsend was on his way to being a well-recognized "fellow traveler."[15]

Over the next year and a half, Townsend continued to travel in and write about Mexico. He was genuinely impressed, even before meeting Cárdenas, with the *ideals* of the leaders of the Revolution. For Townsend, the self-sacrificing commitment of the rural schoolteachers, the devotion by many in the Department of Education to Indians and the rural poor, and the attempts at moral reform were all Christlike activities. This idealism, which he shared, let him see past the rhetoric and the violence (both of which frightened many in the United States) to a common ground that he felt true Christians shared with Mexico's idealistic revolutionaries. Although Townsend honestly laid out the reality of land redistribution and other socialist measures, much of his language (exploitation by capital, class privilege, human betterment, cooperatives, public control of private business) would have been recognizable to an older generation steeped in populist politics. Populist ideas, as well as Mexico's puritanical streak—several Mexican states enforced total prohibition and attempted to enforce other moral-reform measures—might well have appealed to older conservative Protestants who could still remember the evangelical crusades for moral reform and the days when evangelicals embraced many populist ideals. Townsend, with his solid conservative credentials, had a ready, if somewhat grudging, audience.

In two 1934 articles, Townsend described in detail the war in Mexico between church and state. After disclosing some of the harsh measures taken against organized religion, Townsend wrote, "Such an indictment of all religions seems incredible and one wonders if the men who make it are not of a disreputable type . . . are not frightful red demons with pronged forks ready to catch up all Mexico and throw it into hell." To this point, Townsend could be almost any fundamentalist railing against the forces of Satan. But the next few sentences turned in an astonishing direction. After acknowledging that he initially carried with him to Mexico such prejudiced attitudes, he declared, "When I came to know them I found that most of them are sincere, zealous men aflame with a desire to uplift their Fatherland. They feel that religion has played the traitor and like Moctezuma has let down the bars before the invasion of avarice, exploitation, political injustices, foreign imperialism, ignorance, superstition and even immorality. You look almost in vain over the annals of Mexican history for material with which to refute their accusations and then are forced to admit that they are not as unreasonable as you had supposed."

Townsend did not place the blame solely at the feet of the Roman Catholic Church. The evangelical missions, although of more recent advent and in a favored position with Mexican liberals, squandered their opportunity by squabbling "among themselves over matters of dogma and discipline when they should have thrown themselves unitedly [with the revolutionaries] into the campaign for social betterment." The problem for Mexico's leaders, as Townsend saw it, was to find a way to foster personal Christian piety and morality, much needed in a society based on collective living, while combating "ecclesiasticism." After all, Townsend argued, the Christ who called the religious leaders of his day a "generation of vipers" and who blessed the poor while ordering the rich to sell all they had was clearly an ally, not an enemy, of the Revolution.

The solution to Mexico's problem was to find a way to get the Bible to the people unencumbered by self-interested interpreters. With Bible reading would come honesty, a hunger for knowledge, a diminishment of class prejudice, and a "keener sense of the public weal." Townsend concluded, "If the educators find this transformation going on in its early stages before it has been cristalized [sic] in ecclesiastical molds they can guide it so as to greatly aid them in their program of social uplift." Townsend, in reaffirming the possibility of governmental reform combining with religious endeavor to create a truly Christian nation, was applying a uniquely U.S. vision to the Mexican context. He was also, of course, suggesting how his proposed organization of Bible translators might propagate Christianity in a way compatible with the goals of the Revolution.[16]

Although Townsend did not reach as wide an audience with these early articles as he would after befriending Cárdenas, the themes he developed—the positive outlook on Mexico's socialist agenda, the Christlike ideals of some facets of the revolution, and the duty of the United States, particularly U.S. Christians, to find a compatible way both to evangelize and be of assistance to Mexico—would recur again and again in Townsend's public life in the ensuing years. After meeting Cárdenas, Townsend would add to his agenda personal devotion to an extraordinary leader and a noninterventionist (except where invited) model for U.S. foreign policy in Latin America.

CAMERON TOWNSEND AND LÁZARO CÁRDENAS

In the fall of 1935, an old Buick pulling a small house trailer parked in the dusty square in the small Indian village of Tetelcingo, sixty miles (but two hours by car) south of Mexico City. Government officials had finally granted permission for Townsend to study an Indian language. He deliberately picked Tetelcingo, knowing its reputation for being the most primitive ("backward" was the word more often used) "Aztec" settlement in the state of Morelos. There, he could be certain of hearing the indigenous language, as only the mayor spoke Spanish. And there he could demonstrate to Mexican officials that true religion would aid, not hinder, the Revolution's attempt to better the lives of Indians. "It's a miserable little town," he told a friend, "but we hope, by God's grace, to change it."[17]

Before long, Townsend had put together a literacy primer in the local language, and the Department of Education printed five thousand copies to be used throughout the state. An avid amateur farmer (his journals and letters were filled with horticultural notes), Townsend planted a vegetable garden and began to introduce the villagers to lettuce, radishes, celery, and beets. Soon, flowers decorated the village square, and fruit trees, donated by Ramírez, shaded a makeshift park. By the end of the year, word had reached President Cárdenas about the "backward" village in Morelos where a gringo, with the help of several of his own officials, had launched precisely the kind of "make over" envisioned by the Department of Education.[18]

"Yesterday [January 21, 1936] we had a surprise," began Elvira's report to Moody Church in Chicago. "None other than the President of Mexico himself . . . came here to our humble, little makeshift home. We had a delightful visit with President Cárdenas, a most pleasant man to know. He was so interested in what we were doing for the betterment of the town."[19] Cárdenas spent an hour looking over the Townsends' work, and each man came away thoroughly impressed by the other. A lifelong friendship formed immediately.

Townsend was thrilled to have as a benefactor the "peasant president," widely known for his genuine commitment to the welfare of those in Mexico who had been exploited for so long, primarily Indians. On his legendary travels through Mexico's backcountry, Cárdenas, unprotected by bodyguards, patiently listened for hours at each stop to the needs of the people. They returned his affection, as the title of a recent book about Cárdenas, *As If Jesus Walked on Earth,* accurately reflects. Cárdenas's integrity, his commitment to the poor, his refusal to profit personally from his political position, and his opposition to the liquor trade and gambling houses (Cárdenas had shut down the casino mentioned in this chapter's introduction) all had immense appeal for a conservative Protestant. Townsend wrote, "I don't know whether [Cárdenas] is a Christian or not but I do wish that my life were as Christlike."[20] Townsend's admiration for the man heightened his passion for Mexico and the ideals of the Revolution. A few days after their meeting in Tetelcingo, Townsend wrote to Cárdenas, "If before having the pleasure of knowing you, I loved and admired the revolutionary work of Mexico, now, upon knowing its highest representative personally I feel more intimately identified with her and more resolved and determined in service."[21]

As for Cárdenas, he found in Townsend a hands-on ally in his program for Indians, someone actually willing to live in a remote village and oversee a program of "social betterment." In the years ahead, Cárdenas would apply to Townsend a word often used of himself, a word that seemed to resonate in the idealistic circle of Mexican politics. The word was "desinteresado," or "disinterested," as in "the disinterested efforts that the Townsend family is developing in behalf of the town."[22] The word seemed to have much the same meaning for Mexicans of the Revolutionary generation as it did for the leaders of the American Revolution. It implied a certain noblesse oblige, the giving of oneself to public service with no intention of self-aggrandizement, and no better word could be applied to anyone in Mexico during the presidency of Cárdenas. At any rate, a responsible and experienced on-site overseer was simply too good to pass up. Cárdenas seems to have decided on the spot to make Tetelcingo a model community. He ordered two hundred more fruit trees for immediate delivery and virtually gave Townsend a blank check with several government agencies to rebuild the town. As Elvira wonderingly reported to Moody Church, "He . . . promise[d] . . . everything needed to make this backward village an example for others."[23]

What was more, Townsend wanted to recruit other Americans for the same work. Upon assurances from Townsend that any others he might bring would engage in the same type of social service, Cárdenas gave him free reign to bring in as many workers as he could recruit, pledging his administration to give them "every aid which might be necessary."[24] Cárdenas himself oversaw the placement of some of the recruits. He took a personal interest in their work, providing throughout his administration a small stipend for the majority of them, who were "rural school teachers" in the Department of Education. At times, the incoming recruits were feted at the presidential palace before departing to their assigned villages.[25]

It is also quite possible that Cárdenas was genuinely interested in SIL's religious work. Townsend probably convinced him at some point that the Bible held a positive moral power. In addition, Townsend presented his work as both scientific and socialistic. As Marjorie Becker has shown, eventually the Cardenistas had to come to terms with the religiosity of Mexico's "peasants," who were simply not willing to part with their syncretic Catholicism. Cárdenas may have been persuaded by Townsend's argument that the Bible would provide a "religious" antidote to the "peasants'" perceived obscurantism and superstition. Anything that distanced them from the Roman Catholic Church was seen as a positive influence by the Cardenistas. Cárdenas could relax the anticlericalism of Calles—a popular move internationally—while still encouraging a counter to what was seen as the backward fanaticism of the Catholic Church.[26]

The Cárdenas-Townsend friendship continued to grow over the years. Cárdenas frequently invited Townsend to join his traveling party. (Townsend came to know Tannenbaum, another frequent Cárdenas invitee, quite well on these trips.) Cárdenas's wife, Amalia, befriended Elvira, and on several occasions the couples vacationed together. Always concerned about the Townsends' health, Cárdenas frequently offered one of his homes as a vacation spot, insisting they get away from the pressures of Tetelcingo.[27] After Elvira's death, Cárdenas served as the best man at Townsend's second marriage.

MEXICO'S "MAN IN AMERICA"

Bound for the States for the first time since meeting the president, Townsend wrote Cárdenas that he was going to tour eight southern states, "speaking in some Universities and informing the newspapers about the vast program that you are developing in favor of the masses." He requested literature and photographs taken on Cárdenas's most recent tours, which were immediately provided. This request established a pattern. Whenever Townsend traveled in the United States, he combined recruitment for SIL with advocacy for Cárdenas and Mexico. On this particular trip, he contributed a long editorial to the *Tulsa Daily World*, responding to accusations that ex-president Calles had recently made during a trip to that city. The editorial, titled "Commoner, Not Communist, Is Cardenas [sic]," stressed the themes that Townsend enunciated wherever he went—how Cárdenas's personal qualities of honesty, fairness, and compassion had turned Mexico into a more democratic society. Cárdenas was not a communist, simply a man doing everything possible to right the wrongs that the centuries had exacted of Mexico's indigenous population. He was a man of the people, traveling and meeting them incessantly, without ostentation, hard-working, the "Lincoln of Mexico."[28]

During the summer of 1937, Elvira was the one on the road, recruiting for SIL and speaking about Mexico. She concentrated on SIL's natural evangelical constituency, speaking in churches, at schools, and over the radio. Townsend's strategy was to focus on Cárdenas's "personal qualities and humanitarian goals," ideals much admired by evangelicals. He reported that everywhere his wife went "[h]er favorite topic was . . . THE PRESIDENT OF MEXICO," and the reaction she received was "very favorable."[29] The Townsends had the potential to reach an untapped audience for Mexico. Only the U.S. Left used rhetoric such as the Townsends' in the 1930s. Cárdenas knew he would need more than the Left on his side in the difficult days ahead.

SCENES FROM A REVOLUTION

On a Saturday late in February 1938, Cárdenas and Townsend relaxed on folding chairs in the shade behind the Townsends' trailer in Tetelcingo. They had just finished lunch with Cárdenas and his wife, and now, remembered Townsend, the president seemed to want to talk. (Cárdenas had sent an aide the day before to request that Townsend do Cárdenas "the favor [as the aide put it] of inviting him to dine with you tomorrow.") He explained at length the trouble he had been having with the U.S. and British oil companies, who refused to come to terms with the Mexican labor unions, even defying a Supreme Court–mandated wage increase.[30] He seemed to suggest to Townsend that if the oil companies did not comply, drastic action would be taken. He clearly hinted that while he had confidence in the people of the United States, he needed help in reaching them with the facts of the case. Before leaving that evening, the reflective president told Townsend how much his friendship had meant to him and that he hoped it would continue when he was out of office. Cárdenas then gave Townsend the ceremonial fountain pen with which he had signed all his documents and decrees since becoming president. He told Townsend that the pen had given away more land to the poor than any other pen in Mexican history.[31]

A few weeks later, Townsend was in the National Palace overlooking the Plaza de la Constitución, where hour after hour thousands of Mexicans in a patriotic frenzy marched beneath the balcony where Cárdenas stood. The previous Friday, March 18, Cárdenas had electrified the nation by nationalizing the foreign oil companies, igniting patriotic fervor in Mexico and the most serious crisis with its northern neighbor since the early days of the Mexican Revolution.[32] Townsend was busy in a room off the balcony, writing an article. In the United States, articles were also being written. In the months and years ahead, the Mexican situation would be described and rehashed in U.S. papers. The oil companies poured a great deal of money into a propaganda offensive, arguing that Uncle Sam should compel the return of their property, to "teach the Greasers 'Thou Shalt Not Steal.'" Standard Oil published and distributed a free paper called "The Lamp," which tried to inflame public opinion against Mexico and "degenerated to . . . abuse of all things Mexican." The *Atlantic Monthly* devoted an entire issue in July to "Trouble Below the Border," an issue that Ambassador Daniels recalled was "devoted to misrepresentation and slander and hate," and in which "[e]very page smelled of oil."[33]

Moisés Sáenz, known in U.S. intellectual circles for his work in developing the rural school system in Mexico, warned Cárdenas that "the situation require[d] neutralization abroad, especially in the United States." He offered to go immediately to the United States and begin a two-pronged offensive. The first would "attack the question head-on . . . not avoiding polemic if the situation call[ed] for it." The second would "present Mexico in non-controversial aspects (tourism, education) to promote good will toward the country."[34]

Given this climate, Cárdenas readily accepted Townsend's offer to travel to the United States on a similar mission. Armed with funds from Cárdenas to purchase a new car (Elvira was a heart patient, and Cárdenas did not want her riding trains) and a letter from Ambassador Daniels to President Franklin D. Roosevelt's appointment secretary, the Townsends set off. While Townsend worked the East, Elvira and a friend (another heart patient) worked the Midwest.[35]

Elvira made up a one-page flyer complete with Mexican flag and newspaper headlines as talking points. With Mrs. Cárdenas keeping her occasionally supplied with new material, Elvira spoke up to five times a week at places like John Brown University in Arkansas, Christian conferences, women's clubs, and churches throughout the Midwest. Combining her missionary experiences in Mexico with personal stories about the Cárdenases, she undoubtedly presented a compelling case for midwestern Protestants to support Mexico in its current troubles. She reported that most people took a "sympathetic stand" once they understood the true facts. Members of SIL traveling in other parts of the country reported similar sentiments.[36]

Townsend had a more discouraging trip. Unable to see Roosevelt, he had to settle for writing the president and Secretary of State Cordell Hull long letters complaining of the United States's treatment of Mexico and beseeching the government to turn a deaf ear to the "monied interests" and their "hog-it-all-or-cut-your-throat" tactics. He managed to gain an audience with a Standard Oil executive, who listened politely, then responded that Standard Oil intended to continue fighting to get its property back.[37]

Townsend also spoke to evangelical audiences wherever he could. By the end of the summer, he figured that he and Elvira had spoken more than eighty times to religious audiences. Handwritten notes help us reconstruct some of what Townsend may have said. His notes begin, "Christian travelers and missionaries often find it necessary to correct false reports published by unscrupulous newspaper correspon-

dents concerning foreign lands where they journey or live. In fact, it is hard to see
how they could call themselves Christian if they did not, for to remain silent when
one hears his neighbor falsely spoken of is hardly loving others as one's self." Citing
the *Atlantic Monthly* issue devoted to an attack on Mexico, he went on to complain
of the hypocrisy of pretending a "Good Neighbor" policy in the midst of such un-
friendly activity. Mexico, he said, has been patient, "realizing that selfish trusts were
behind it all," and that when the U.S. public learned the facts, they would "react in
a friendly way." He then challenged his audience, saying it was time for evangelicals
in the United States to demonstrate Christlike friendship to Mexico, where "for
centuries selfish exploitation both in religion and economics" had left such friendship in short supply. He closed with personal reminiscences about Cárdenas. Townsend's message was a brilliant mix of populist sentiment, devotion to fair play and
the underdog, and appeal to Christian and missionary idealism.[38]

Townsend continued to write articles, although, as he wearily reported to the
secretary of the American Bible Society in Mexico, "some [have] been published but
most . . . have been rejected due to the fact that the editors feel that I simply cannot
be right in view of the tremendous amount of literature they read from other sources
which tells another story." Frustrated, Townsend wrote to Cárdenas that he felt that
80 percent of the people in the United States would agree that Mexico was in the
right if he could just get the information to them. "But how can one inform them
of the truth," he complained, "when the press is capitalistic and twists the news?"
Townsend's solution was to suggest publishing a magazine to send to members of
Congress, university presidents, libraries, and prominent individuals. Townsend's
"magazine" turned into an eighty-five-page booklet, *The Truth about Mexico's Oil.*
Friends helped him publish one thousand copies, and every person in Congress received one. The booklet was a remarkably thorough airing of the history of the
entire conflict, the expressed purpose being to "tell the American people [Cárdenas's]
side of the story." Raising the echoes of "Teapot Dome," Townsend's theme was that
the "history of the oil industry in the United States is full of pages stained black."
He sought to convince his readers that Mexico's quarrel was with the unscrupulous
oil companies, not with the people of the United States.[39]

One ally Townsend recruited on this trip was Dr. Howard Kelly, the renowned
Johns Hopkins surgeon and gynecologist. He was well known both for his pioneering medical techniques and his old-school fundamentalism. Kelly's pursuit of H. L.
Mencken for the kingdom became somewhat legendary (Mencken called him the
"most implacable Christian I ever knew . . . among educated men"), resulting in
Mencken's famous line that on three separate occasions during one train trip at
Kelly's side Mencken "was on the point of jumping out of the train-window." Kelly
had supported Townsend's work since 1921, and Townsend recognized that his would
be an influential voice. Townsend kept Kelly informed about events and urged him

to use his good name to influence U.S. lawmakers. Kelly, for his part, offered to fund the printing in pamphlet form of an article on Mexico that Townsend had published in the fundamentalist journal *The King's Business*. Later, after Cárdenas retired from office, Kelly offered to put up money to bring the Cárdenases and Townsends to the United States on a goodwill trip. While the trip never came about, and the outcome of the pamphlet plan is unclear, that Townsend was able to bring a man of Kelly's stature to his point of view on Mexico is an indication both of Townsend's powers of persuasion and of the success, at least among evangelicals, of his efforts on Cárdenas's behalf.[40]

LÁZARO CÁRDENAS: MEXICAN DEMOCRAT

Perhaps Townsend's most long-lasting effort on Mexico's behalf was his biography of Cárdenas published in 1952, still the only full-length biography in English. Townsend's experience during the oil crisis convinced him to refocus his efforts on the biography he had first conceived, and suggested to Cárdenas, at SIL's "state dinner" with the president in 1936. His initial vision was to highlight Cárdenas's work on behalf of Mexico's indigenous peoples. As he told Cárdenas's secretary, "The sincere, self-denying and powerful friends of the poor are so scarce that it is imperative to make them well known to the world." Townsend spent months on the work (aided by stacks of information, newspaper clippings, and copies of Cárdenas's speeches sent to him by Subsecretary of Foreign Relations Ramón Beteta). He considered the biography essentially complete when, in 1938, the oil crisis necessitated additional chapters and a whole new dimension for the work. Townsend plugged away at the biography during the 1940s, but as SIL grew and his work expanded into Peru and other Latin American countries, he never seemed to have time to see to its completion.[41]

Finally, in 1948, having been reviewed for accuracy by both Beteta, now secretary of the treasury, and the retired Daniels, the biography was ready for publication. Harold Bentley, head of the publishing department at Columbia and a friend of Townsend, managed to interest Harpers in the book, but that company eventually declined to publish it because it "sounded too much like propaganda."[42]

At this point, the Cárdenas biography had become too important to Townsend, Cárdenas, and the Mexican government to let it wither on the vine. Despite having been out of office for a decade, Cárdenas was still a prominent figure and was again being accused of communist tendencies, a disturbing charge in the postwar world. Although Cárdenas never responded publicly, his friends in the Mexican government spoke up for him. They clearly saw Townsend's biography as one way of supporting Cárdenas. With Beteta offering to provide 25,000 pesos to expedite the book's publication, Townsend turned to a small press in Ann Arbor, Michigan.

Eventually, with an additional $2,000 from the Mexican government, funneled through the national oil company, Petróleos Mexicanos (PEMEX), the biography (with a foreword by Tannenbaum) was published in 1952 by Wahr. With the help of Arnold Kruckman of the Kruckman News Service in Washington, D.C., Townsend managed to get the book favorably reviewed by several major newspapers, including *The New York Times, Christian Science Monitor, Chicago Tribune,* and *The Washington Post.* Kruckman also got a copy of the book to Walter Lippman and other significant journalists, including members of the organization Overseas Writers who had a particular interest in Mexico.[43]

Townsend sent the book to every member of Congress in Washington, D.C., and every state governor, albeit with the help once again of the Mexican government through PEMEX. University presidents and public libraries throughout the Southwest received copies as well.[44] While many in Congress replied via form letter, those with a particular interest in Mexico or Latin America seemed genuinely thankful and eager to read the book. A congressman from a Texas district that bordered Mexico indicated he had heard of the book and had "been wanting a copy." Several years later, Townsend's biography of Cárdenas could still be found in Washington, D.C. While Townsend was visiting then-Senator John F. Kennedy to lobby for increased U.S. aid to Latin America, the senator mentioned that he had his book.[45]

THE NETWORK

While the Cárdenas biography may have exerted some influence in secular and official circles, the consistent advocacy by Townsend and other SIL members for Mexico through "prayer letters," personal letters, and public appeals undoubtedly had its greatest impact among his natural constituency, American fundamentalists and evangelicals. Townsend's immediate constituency numbered in the thousands. By 1952, SIL had more than three hundred members, and their supporters numbered more than twenty thousand.

Although it is impossible now to measure the impact of Townsend's advocacy, a few historical "snapshots" can provide some insight. Eight young people, recruited by Townsend and paid by Cárdenas, worked in community development in Mexico for an Inter-American Service Brigade.[46] In California, an old man—the beginning (and the end as it turned out) of another Townsend dream called the International Association of Friends of Mexico—traveled with his box of letterhead, beating the drum for inter-American good will.[47] The governor of Arkansas agreed at Townsend's insistence to sponsor an official reception for a Mexican government official.[48] Townsend's sister published an article in the *Enid Morning News,* celebrating the "work of the Mexican Revolution."[49] An evangelical pastor in Texas promised to give Cárdenas land he owned in Mexico for distribution among the peasants and offered to visit schools and clubs in the United States, "showing movies of the work that Mexico is carrying out, fomenting in this way not only tourism but better understanding between the two people."[50]

One final "snapshot" returns us to the "Good Neighbors Picnic" referred to in the introduction. At the height of the oil crisis, Townsend convinced more than two hundred friendly Protestants to meet with Cárdenas. After the meal, some who had previously thought Townsend too enthusiastic in his portrait of Cárdenas expressed glowing praise. One lady told Townsend, "Cameron, you did not tell us half." Two images linger: Beteta, then subsecretary of foreign relations, passionately exhorting his audience, "You Christians at least should be able to understand our burning desire to help the masses who have suffered for so long"; and Cárdenas, encouraged with how the day had gone, exclaiming, "Townsend, you will see how when I go out of office I am going to work together with you in matters of the spirit."[51]

And yet, to leave the analysis of Townsend's impact with such glimpses still sells it short. As Joel Carpenter has recently shown us, by 1950 fundamentalists had built up a tremendous network of agencies through which they kept in contact and disseminated their message.[52] The list of Townsend confidants reads like a roll call of leading fundamentalist power-brokers of the era. We can be confident all of them felt at one time or another the force of Townsend's personality on Mexico's behalf, and more than likely, most influenced some members of their own constituencies.

Elvira Townsend's home church was the Moody Church in Chicago, called by Carpenter a "pocket-sized denomination." She exchanged "newsy" letters and collected foreign stamps for Pastor Harry Ironside, whom Carpenter has called "perhaps the preeminent dispensationalist spokesman of his day." Ironside hoped to see the Townsends and Cárdenases together on his platform and vowed to show the president "a little courtesy around the Moody Church." He promised to display a Mexican flag on the platform and to "drape a number of chairs with the Mexican colors."[53] Townsend's home church was the Church of the Open Door in Los Angeles (another of Carpenter's "pocket-sized denominations"), and his pastor, Louis T. Talbot, visited the SIL work in Mexico at Townsend's invitation. Dawson Trotman, founder of The Navigators, served on SIL's board and visited Townsend in Mexico. Charles Fuller, founder of the Old Fashioned Revival Hour, served briefly on the board and voiced the introduction for SIL's first promotional film. Townsend communicated regularly with Oswald J. Smith, pastor of The Peoples Church in Toronto, keeping him informed of his activities with Cárdenas. Smith also visited the work in Mexico. R. G. LeTourneau, millionaire fundamentalist businessman, agreed to assist Cárdenas in the giant Tepalcatepec River Basin project.[54] Clarence Jones, founder of HCJB radio station, distributed Elvira's book on Latin American courtesy over the air. Townsend also had close ties with Torrey Johnson and Jack Wyrtzen of Youth for Christ; Dr. Edman at Wheaton; Henry Crowell at Moody Bible Institute; Clarence Erickson, successor to Paul Rader as pastor of the Chicago Gospel Tabernacle; Robert McQuilkin, president of Columbia Bible College; and Louis Sperry Chafer at Dallas Theological Seminary. Through these men and others like them, Townsend's impressions of Cárdenas and Mexico had at least the potential of reaching a vast audience.

CONCLUSION

Next to Townsend's grave on the campus of SIL's aviation arm, the Jungle Aviation and Radio Service (JAARS) center in Waxhaw, North Carolina, stands the Mexico-Cárdenas Museum, constructed by Townsend during the final decade of his life. It was a fitting tribute to a lifelong friendship that united two very different men in the idealistic pursuit of a better life for Mexico's indigenous people. Townsend was able to find enough common ground between two divergent ideologies, evangelical Christian and secular socialist, to make them, however briefly, allies in the program of Mexico's most highly regarded revolutionary. Motivated by gospel imperatives and immersed in contexts forcing the reevaluation of ideologies learned at home, perhaps a missionary was the only one who could have pulled off the reconciliation of such incongruities.

Townsend never forgot the lessons he learned from Cárdenas. He vigorously promoted Latin American causes throughout his life. Within a year of moving to Peru, he lobbied the U.S. ambassador, complaining that it was "disgraceful and dangerous for a wealthy and powerful nation to pose as a 'good neighbor' while doing little or nothing to help its less fortunate sister nations." When President Dwight D. Eisenhower raised tariffs on Peruvian lead and zinc, Townsend lobbied the administration, arguing that any discomfort caused U.S. miners was outweighed by the United States's duty to be "good neighbors" to Peru. When Guatemala was accused of "going communist," Townsend sent an article to *Reader's Digest,* hoping to demonstrate to its readers that those accusations were wrong. But even if a country did embrace communism, Townsend never countenanced U.S. intervention, particularly to rescue U.S. business interests. He opposed Kennedy's Cuba policy on those grounds.[55] And when a young SIL advance man, frustrated in his attempts to work out a contract with the Venezuelan government, suggested entering as scientists under the aegis of U.S. oil companies, Townsend's chief administrator in Latin America replied in words that undoubtedly echoed his boss's mind: "[W]e should not link ourselves up with any large American corporation, for the type of power they wield has been the traditional reason that Latin Americans have accused the United States government of imperialism. Such association of ours with powerful groups should be the furthest from our thoughts since our mission is to serve and not to command."[56] SIL never entered Venezuela.

It is important to note, however, that Townsend did not become a leftist or socialist because of his friendship with Cárdenas, just as Cárdenas did not become a Protestant. The enduring political lesson Townsend took from this experience was that Latin America should be left free to choose its own path. The United States should intervene only to aid and only when requested. One of the reasons he never publicly criticized a Latin American government was that he felt it was not a North American's place to do so.

Townsend's story suggests that missionaries may have been leaders at home more often than followers. Operating on the "frontiers" of religious and cultural interaction, missionaries were placed in ideal positions to reanalyze, reinterpret, and perhaps even discard facets of their worldview in favor of startling new paradigms. The ease with which Townsend moved through disparate political worlds illustrates this fact. SIL members frequently found themselves caught between the realities of their "frontier" experience and the need to relate to a constituency often oblivious to such conditions. In the process of resolving that tension, many at home found their own outlook inadequate.

Even as missionaries acted as primary interpreters of foreign affairs to their constituencies at home, they also at times offered a critique of American culture itself. Richard Pierard and others have noted that "fortified by the national mood . . . many evangelicals uncritically aligned their efforts with civil religion and capitalism."[57] Missionaries were often the first to recognize the fallacies of this alignment. Living in underdeveloped countries and working intimately with nationals from all social strata, missionaries observed the United States through foreign eyes and, consequently, recognized the ambiguities of U.S. political and economic involvement abroad. That evangelical leaders at home thought critically about such issues may be in some measure owing to their contact with missionaries such as Townsend.

III

After World War II: Years
of Complication

⤮

For the better part of two centuries, in many quarters of American Christianity, no hero ranked higher than the foreign missionary. In the popular Christian imagination, the missionary emerged as a kind of warrior for Christ, slogging through jungle swamps amidst drenching humidity and deadly vipers to carry the gospel to the benighted heathen. That the heathen usually stood poised, spear in hand, ready to slay the intrepid ambassador only made the image more appealing. Caricature for sure, in the same way, perhaps, that the hard-eyed, straight-talking Dick Tracy perennially served as a caricature of law-enforcement agents everywhere. But caricatures persist, partly because they contain a measure of truth, and partly because they meet deep-seated and often hard-to-articulate cultural needs. So one suspects that even if missionaries had never existed, Americans would have invented them in some fictional medium in order to express their sense of themselves as giving, caring, expansively minded folk, a model for the rest of the world.

Still, things never proved so simple in real life. Differences of method and outlook between denominational and independent missions, barely intimated before World War I, broke into deep fissures after that conflict and became virtually unbridgeable chasms after World War II. The mainline Protestant missionary force experienced growing doubts about the very legitimacy of the missionary enterprise. The main factors were spiraling nationalism abroad and theological liberalism at home. The former often expressed itself in intense dislike of all missionaries, who seemed part and parcel of an imperialist onslaught. Theological liberalism at home, which suggested the common origins and evolutionary development of all religions, undercut the notion of the uniqueness of Christian revelation. Many of those doubts culminated in *Re-Thinking Missions*, a 1932 report funded by John D. Rockefeller and written by the Harvard philosopher William Ernest Hocking. A work of extraordinary (and surely unexpected) notoriety, *Re-Thinking Missions* argued that missionaries should seek to nurture the highest impulses within non-Christian religions rather than supplant them with Christianity.[1] These doubts also resulted in the long-term dwindling of resources in mainline traditions once heavily committed to missionary service. By the end of the 1970s, less than 15 percent of the money and fewer than 10 percent of the personnel for foreign missions came from denominational bodies affiliated with the mainline National Council of Churches.[2]

In the meantime, however, the evangelical missionary endeavor, increasingly associated with independent or faith agencies, flourished. Evangelicals' focus on individual conversions rather than broad social renovation enabled them to feel less tainted, or at least less worried, about the perils of cultural imperialism. And their freedom from—or perhaps avoidance of—the challenges of biblical higher criticism liberated them from crippling reservations about the uniqueness of Christian revelation. Thus armed, evangelicals surged ahead, confident that Christianity alone offered a truly saving message. They organized themselves in freestanding associations like the Interdenominational Foreign Missions Association in 1917 and the Evangelical Foreign Missions Association in 1945. In time, even these loose associations proved too confining for many. By the 1980s, entirely unaffiliated groups, such as the missionary arm of the Southern Baptist Convention, Youth with a Mission, Wycliffe Bible Translators, and New Tribes Mission, dominated the American foreign mission ranks, accounting for three-fifths of the personnel and more than one-half of the funds.[3]

Though Protestants monopolized much of the American foreign missions story, they never owned it entirely. Until 1908, Rome designated the Catholic Church in the United States as a mission itself. But U.S. Catholic missions grew rapidly in the twentieth century, especially after the formation of the Catholic Foreign Mission Society of America (Maryknoll) in 1911. Asia and Latin America were the main areas of endeavor for U.S. Catholics.[4] Mormons had also committed themselves to missions, especially in Britain and Scandinavia, from the mid–nineteenth century onward. By the end of the twentieth century, Mormons' missionary numbers had swollen to thirty thousand, and their reach was global, most volunteers being youthful, short-term ambassadors of their faith.

These events, persons, and institutions formed the stuff of legends—in all senses of the word. At the beginning of the new millennium, questions of strategy had for many Americans given way to more fundamental questions of morality: did anyone have the right to displace another person's faith at all? At the same time, did not Christians bear an obligation to speak the truth as they saw it? In an age of cultural conflict manifested in wars from the Balkans to Afghanistan, was there still a role for the North American foreign missionary? For all but the most committed partisans and foes of the foreign missions enterprise, the answers seemed tentative if not elusive. In evaluating missions' role in the present and future, the record of the past, into which the essays in this volume have delved, may make a modest contribution. As we have seen, the historical record of American foreign missions from the nineteenth century until today provides a full spectrum of examples: missionaries as among the most earnest, courageous, and inspiring, yet at the same time as among the most stubborn, blinkered, and exasperating figures in the nation's history. Their legacy and influence are with us still. And their story, which unfolded at home as well as abroad, merits a careful hearing.

12 / The Waning of the Missionary Impulse

The Case of Pearl S. Buck

Grant Wacker

He had come to the Far East with a message that he was on fire to give, but in the process of transmission the East had spoken its message to him. He had gone out to change the East and was returning, himself a changed man.
    Earl H. Cressy, "Converting the Missionary," *Asia*, June 1919

Figuring out exactly when the American missionary impulse started to wane is not an easy task. Some would say that the first nail in the coffin was Hannah Adams's 1784 *Alphabetical Compendium of the Various Sects,* purportedly an "impartial and comprehensive survey" of world religions. Others, looking at the millions of dollars that evangelical Protestants and Roman Catholics continued to pour into the missionary effort at the end of the twentieth century, might well ask, incredulously, "What coffin?"[1]

However one graphs the fortunes of the missionary impulse in the general culture, there can be little doubt that the year 1932 marked a transition within the Protestant establishment itself. On an Indian summer afternoon of that year, two thousand Presbyterian women crowded into New York City's Hotel Astor to hear the most celebrated missionary of the time address the question, "Is There a Case for Foreign Missions?" By all accounts, Pearl Sydenstricker Buck cut a striking figure at the podium that day. Just forty years old, Buck bore her Scottish father's high cheekbones, soft voice, and precise diction. But her fame did not depend on good looks or the kind of evangelistic credentials that China missionaries usually presented in their Sunday night lantern shows. Rather, the locals flocked to hear Buck primarily because her second novel, *The Good Earth,* had just won the Pulitzer Prize for literature. Though she proceeded to answer her own question—"Is There a Case for Foreign Missions?"—with a yes, by the time she came to the end, the yes seemed so muffled by qualifiers that the audience seemed confused and speechless. At first, no one clapped or moved to congratulate her. After a few painful moments, she later recalled, a storm of applause arose, but by then her publisher was abruptly escorting her from the room.[2]

Words may have failed Buck's listeners that day, but they did not long fail the secular and religious press. The John Day Company rushed the talk into print in booklet form before the year was out, *Harper's* published it in January 1933, and way off in China the *Shanghai Evening Post* saw fit to reproduce it in full. Newspapers as far away as Paris and Rio de Janeiro commented. Many portrayed Buck as a prophet. The *Christian Century,* liberal Protestantism's journal of record, ranked Buck with missionary greats Albert Schweitzer, Gilbert Reid, and E. Stanley Jones. The question she courageously raised, asserted the *Century,* was whether the missionary enterprise should remain forever bound by an "authoritative, unchangeable, and exactly phrased body of doctrine," or whether it should be free to adjust to the needs of the time. The mission board's secretary for China praised Buck's ideas as "fine and sound." The *Hartford Courant* and the *Seattle Times* toasted her.[3]

Not everyone agreed. The Jesuit *America* cited Buck as an example of the "sentimentalities and emotionalism . . . loose allegiances and free attachments" not found in the Roman Catholic Church. One Presbyterian clergyman excoriated her views as "etherealized animalism." Another dismissed them as "ruthless, heartless, insane, bigoted, intelligentsiacal cynicism." Still another, Clarence Macartney, the renowned pastor of Pittsburgh's First Presbyterian Church, warned that if the church listened to people like Buck, it would soon lose itself in the "screaming hurricane of the time." Macartney attracted diverse allies. Charles R. Erdman, president of the Presbyterian Board of Foreign Missions and a Princeton Seminary professor respected for good sense and theological moderation, privately hoped that Buck would just resign and quietly go away. She had become a "great liability," he grumbled, and a source of "much unrest throughout the Church." Even the *China Weekly Review,* a secular newsmagazine published in Shanghai, dismissed Buck's criticisms of missionaries as "far-fetched." The novelist undoubtedly possessed a good grasp of China, the *Review* allowed, but "we frankly doubt whether she knows very much about missionaries, or the real missionary problem."[4]

The furor grew. In April 1933, Westminster Seminary professor J. Gresham Machen formally demanded that the mission board fire Buck and disassociate itself from her views. At that point, Robert E. Speer, the missions board's distinguished general secretary, was drawn into the controversy. Publicly, Speer urged his colleagues to handle the situation with Christian charity. Privately, he groused that Buck's case was a "very troublesome one" that stemmed from "psychologic" if not "psychopathic" sources. Before the month was out, Buck decided to save everyone the embarrassment of an ugly heresy trial and quietly submitted her resignation. Buck soon sailed back to her husband, children, teaching post, and writing career in China. *The Nation,* amused by the ruckus, wryly noted that "probably she feels that a place where the 'heathen rage' is preferable to one where the theologians rant."[5]

Though Buck retreated, in her typically lilting words, to the "old winding cobbled streets of Nanking," she remained an imposing fixture of the American imagination until her death four decades later. In all, Buck would write eighty books and countless articles, scripts, and speeches. Sixty-five of her books soared into the best-seller ranks, and fifteen became Book-of-the-Month Club selections. *The Good Earth* alone sold at least four million copies. Besides winning the Pulitzer Prize, the book was translated into thirty languages, inspired a Broadway play and a Hollywood film, and earned Buck more than a million dollars. In 1938, Buck became the first U.S. woman to win a Nobel Prize for literature, primarily for her biographies of her father and mother, published separately as *Fighting Angel* and *The Exile*, and together as *The Spirit and the Flesh*. She was the first and, except for Toni Morrison, remains the only U.S. woman to receive both the Pulitzer and Nobel Prizes for literature.[6]

After World War II, Buck's star dipped but never disappeared. For the average U.S. citizen, she seemed too blind to the cruelties of the Maoist Revolution. For literary critics, she seemed too sugary, too obvious, and too oriented to the tastes of middle-class housewives. Her civil-rights activities provoked J. Edgar Hoover's glare and the dubious honor of an FBI file. Even so, a 1966 Gallup Poll placed Buck among the Ten Most Admired Women in the United States. Eventually, Buck's works appeared in 145 languages and dialects, making her the most widely translated author in U.S. history. At a 1992 symposium commemorating the centennial of Buck's birth, James Thomson, a leading scholar of U.S.-Asian relations, judged that she had influenced more people on the subject of China than any non-Chinese writer since Marco Polo in the thirteenth century. In 1996, Peter Conn, Buck's scholarly biographer, simply stated: "For two generations of Americans, Buck invented China."[7]

If Buck functioned as a popular authority on China for the better part of four decades, she also served as a popular authority on the truthfulness of Christianity and the validity of the Christian missionary enterprise in China. Predictably, what Buck had to say about all three of these topics—China, Christianity, and Christian missions—changed over time. I see three phases. The first, extending through the 1910s, revealed fundamentalist convictions. The second, roughly occupying the 1920s and 1930s, displayed increasingly liberal attitudes. The last, stretching from the 1940s to the end of her life, reflected post-Christian if not anti-Christian feelings.

This chapter holds two purposes. The first is simply to tell a story, a narrative of one thoughtful person's struggle—never entirely successful—to free herself from the grip of a childhood faith. The second is to illustrate the process by which millions of men and women came to doubt the morality of exporting Christianity to a non-Christian culture. It is well recognized that the evangelistic enterprise suffered losses as well as gains on the foreign field. It is less well recognized that the enterprise suffered losses as well as gains at home. This study seeks to correct that oversight by remembering that the battle for the soul of the "heathen" produced casualties as well as trophies on both sides of the seas.

PHASES OF A LIFE

1910S

Born in 1892, Buck spent most of the first forty-two years of her life in China. Her parents, Absalom and Carolyn Sydenstricker, and her first husband, J. Lossing Buck, all served as Presbyterian missionaries in China. Though important differences distinguished them, her parents and her husband displayed a fairly traditional evangelical understanding of their calling. What is pertinent in the present context is that through the 1910s, Buck shared their perspective.

Buck's earliest adult writings disparaged Chinese society. It is possible, of course, that she tailored her words to fit her readers' expectations. Most people do. Yet Buck's image of China proved remarkably consistent in letter after letter to family and friends back in the United States. The most wearing part of missionary work, she wrote to her in-laws in 1918, was the "constant contact with the terrible degradation and wickedness of a heathen people." The Chinese valued human life almost as nothing. Vice, too horrible to be described, made itself "unspeakably prevalent." In the young evangelist's mind, the material deprivation of missionary life seemed minor compared with the constant necessity of dealing with "all kinds of horrible sin."[8]

Other communiqués detailed the spectrum of Chinese failings, ranging from the merely irksome to the morally egregious. They cared little for gardens, she complained, "not [being] a very beauty-loving people." Venality and corruption abounded. "Chinese are all thieves, especially the servant class," charged one letter. Another indicted the "absolute corruption of the official class." Family life, riddled with opium addiction and drunkenness, fostered numerous cruelties. "Their mother in laws [sic] are dreadful, the daughter in law [sic] being only a slave in the family." Foot-binding flourished, "although to read newspapers, etc one might think there was not a bound foot in China." Still worse was the persistence of female infanticide. "Even a merely animal maternal instinct is often lacking," Buck lamented. "Knowing these people as I do makes me thoroughly angry to have China considered as even a semi-civilized country. . . . She is a country given to the devil." The following year, Buck would tell family members that there was "no limit to the ignorance and superstition of these people."[9]

For the youthful missionary, Christianity offered the answer, or at least a large part of it. In a lengthy letter sent to an American friend just after her marriage, she described her evangelistic method and the orthodox theology that undergirded it. Each afternoon, she and a Chinese co-worker would follow a visitation circuit through the villages, warning the local women that they were "worshipping the wrong gods." Buck explained, "I try to tell them as simply as possible of the One who took their sins upon Himself." New believers were supposed to win others: "I am trying to get them imbued with the idea that they must bring others to Christ." Yet the young bride worried about the vastness of the task. "I get oppressed, sometimes, with a realization of how awfully much there is to be done," she wrote to a college friend. "I have *sole* charge of the evangelistic work for the women in a district of about two million people! It is absurd, of course, but it weighs on me terribly at times."[10]

1920s–1930s

As traditional as the foregoing comments seem, other traces dating from the late 1910s suggest that Buck was beginning to experience turmoil about her missionary vocation. Evangelists focused too much on saving souls and too little on saving bodies, she confided to her brother in 1918. "Humanly speaking, missions in China have not been a success because we have gone to work at the wrong end. Too often we have tried to preach the gospel to people who were starving and cold and homeless, instead of first ministering to their physical needs."[11] The qualifier "humanly speaking" proved significant, for stipulations of that sort gradually evaporated from Buck's prose. Christians have given the Chinese science and dogma, she dryly observed in the *International Review of Missions* in 1924, and "being canny creatures, they have applied the science to the dogmas." Soon, she predicted, these same Christians would see "some cherished dogmas and denominations cast aside." Buck did not specify exactly what would have to go, but any perceptive reader would have discerned the very human Jesus of Protestant liberalism elbowing aside the supernatural Christ of Protestant orthodoxy. This updated Savior symbolized the "rare figure of a Man, liberated from the trappings we have put upon Him, which were not of His choosing." Buck remained traditional enough to capitalize all of the sacred nouns and pronouns, yet modern enough to suspect that only a doctrinally streamlined Jesus was preachable in the dusty villages of North China.[12]

In the late 1920s, Buck said little—in public at least—about any of these matters. The inherent worth of Chinese culture, the truth of Christianity, and the right of Christian missionaries to evangelize seemed to recede from her range of concerns. These were troubled years in Buck's personal life, and she may have been too preoccupied to think much about larger questions. But not for long.

By the early 1930s, a butterfly—or a wasp, according to one's point of view—had started to break free from the cocoon. In this later stage of Buck's thinking, Chinese culture seemed perfectly fine just as it was. That vast and ancient land did not need Christianity any more than the West needed Confucianism. The latter religion did not especially commend itself to Buck either, but that was beside the point. In her view, the great majority of ordinary Chinese cared little or nothing about formal religion of any kind. Hardy, passionate, easily angered, most of them worked just enough to feed their families, gambled and drank when the opportunity presented itself, and took a frankly naturalistic and unceremonious delight in sex. Above all, they lived without morbid worries about their souls or sin or feelings of personal unworthiness.[13] Growing respect for freedom, equality, happiness, recreation, education, and economic security marked Chinese culture. Buck's increasingly roseate view of her adopted land contrasted with her increasingly censorious view of her own. She now described the United States as the home of "permanently adolescent spirits," a nation of well-meaning imperialists unable to imagine how they had fostered so much oppression in Asia.[14]

Buck's deepening quarrel with assumptions of Western superiority betokened other, more fundamental doubts as well. By the 1930s, she had grown profoundly skeptical of the truthfulness of evangelical Christianity. In a fast-flowing stream of speeches and magazine articles intended for a mass audience, she outlined what was wrong with the old version of the religion of the West and sketched her ideas for a more viable substitute.

The main problem with the received tradition, Buck charged, was supernaturalism. She took it as simply self-evident that modernity had rendered all forms of supernaturalism obsolete. Buck dismissed Christian rituals that capitalized on mystery as a "narrow and superstitious form of religion." The form of supernaturalism she found most unforgivable was the idea of hell, especially when Christians applied it to non-Christians. With the bravado that had become her trademark, she brushed aside the generations of missionaries who had worried about hell, insisting that they were either superstitious or hypocritical or both.[15]

Buck might have said all this and raised only a few eyebrows if she had avoided attacking the central affirmation of the faith, the deity of Jesus Christ. But in the Hotel Astor speech, and again in a breezy Easter message published the following spring in *Cosmopolitan,* she confronted that question directly. In her portrait, the old notion of Jesus as a semidivine person roaming the hills of Palestine was, well, magic. Maybe an actual historical person named Jesus never existed. That did not matter. Indeed, whether or not a personal God existed, separate from the collective spirit of humans, did not matter very much either. What did matter was the character and spirit—in a word, the "figure"—of Jesus Christ. That figure, that ideal, symbolized "men's dreams of simplest and most beautiful goodness," the highest values of the universal human imagination. If to traditional Christians Buck's Christ figure represented a pastiche of watered-down Buddhism, Transcendentalism, and Positive Thinking, to Buck the Christ figure served as a great purifying, unifying wave overwhelming all the discordant eddies of daily life. It betokened inner serenity, harmony with the environment, and concern for the suffering of others.[16]

Not surprisingly, Buck's growing doubts about the truth of historic Christianity dictated deep reservations about spreading such a dubious message in China. "Missionary, missions!" she exploded before one U.S. audience. "[It is a] name that I for one have come to hate." Though the writer claimed that she regularly gave to a local church, she insisted that none of her money landed in the "missionary pot." Her complaints about organized missions never found systematic expression, but lumped together they fell into three broad categories: incompetence, intolerance, and ineffectiveness.[17]

Incompetence, defined as a simple inability to do the job, loomed in Buck's mind as the least excusable of the missionaries' faults. Sometimes she depicted them as mediocre to start with, zealots who went into professional proselytizing because that was the only work they could find. Other times she allowed that they may have been a bit more talented than most church folk, but given the caliber of the latter, that was not saying much. Incompetence stemmed, in part, from a lack of native ability, but also from poor preparation. The evangelists knew next to nothing about the history and culture of China when they arrived, and many bumbled around in the language for years thereafter. "You send a missionary young and untrained into an immense foreign country like China," she snapped, "with a completely new language to learn, new conditions of living, a vast history, a different culture, and you give him two years. . . . Two years in which to learn about four thousand years!"[18]

Intolerance constituted the missionaries' second pervasive deficiency. This charge probably recurred more often and with more venom than any other. In China, Buck asserted, the evangelists' natural prejudices turned into rigid blinders that prevented them from even trying to see the world from the Asian point of view. They could not even begin to imagine how their message was heard, shielded, as they were, by "contempt and lack of any understanding of the Chinese, not only of the individual Chinese but of Chinese movements and thought." The problem was not that the missionaries chose to be narrow-minded about this or that particular thing. Rather, they were intrinsically intolerant. They attacked one another over minuscule differences of doctrine as vehemently as they assailed the religions of the Chinese. "Almost did I come to hate Christianity because of the narrow, bitter missionaries among whom my life was cast," Buck declared with more than a little bitterness of her own. "Never have I [seen] such criticism . . . of those who did not see eye to eye with them on every point of theology."[19]

Intolerance bred other distortions. What Buck most clearly remembered about the missionary community in which she had grown up was a certain meanness of spirit. The evangelists struck her as—take your pick—quarrelsome, petty, hypocritical, arrogant, lazy, materialistic, selfish, juvenile. Their Christian beliefs worked like a magnifying glass in the sun, intensifying minor personality defects until they exploded into major character flaws. The worst of those flaws was pride. "It seems humanly impossible to be humble and professionally religious at the same time," she lamented. "There may be humble Christians, but there never were humble mission-aries or priests. It is a contradiction in terms."[20]

Incompetence and intolerance spawned ineffectiveness, and that trait formed the third major problem with the missionary enterprise. Buck took it as simply self-evident that centuries of evangelistic efforts had fallen on barren soil. Missionaries mouthed formulas they had learned in school without making any real effort to imagine how the Chinese actually heard their words. Wang Lung, the protagonist of *The Good Earth,* illustrates the preachers' ludicrous ineptness. In the novel, Wang Lung lives his entire life in turn-of-the-century China with no awareness of the evangelists' existence, let alone their purpose. At one point in the narrative, a tall foreigner gives Wang Lung a tract with a drawing of a white-skinned man hanging on a crosspiece of wood. The man looks dead. Chinese characters caption the draw-ing, but, of course, they mean nothing to the illiterate villager. Wang Lung assumes that the white-skinned man must have been very evil. Why was he hung this way? Growing fearful of the tract, Wang Lung wonders why the foreigner has given it to him. Eventually, his wife takes it and sews it into the sole of a shoe. If Buck's Wang Lung lacked subtlety, he did not lack impact. Christianity had come to China "as words seen and not understood." The missionaries had failed, both among peasants and among elites—no first-rate Chinese mind had ever accepted the message, she asserted—and they had no one to blame except themselves.[21]

Incompetence, intolerance, and ineffectiveness. It is hard to imagine a more un-forgiving indictment of the Christian missionary enterprise in China. Buck admit-ted that conversions had occurred from time to time but doubted their genuineness. Most adherents were socially marginal to begin with, she countered. Many blithely added the Christian God to the pantheon of gods they already worshiped, not re-motely understanding that Christianity was supposed to be an exclusive religion. Some bartered their natal religion in order to win education or money or legal privi-leges from the foreigners. Others switched only in name, striving to be polite to the white emissaries, whom they perceived as honored (albeit hated) guests. Still others cast their lot with the new religion because they believed that the missionaries needed converts in order to save their own souls. The tale would have been laughable if it had not been so tragic. If all the evangelists plying their trade along the back roads of China packed up and left at once, she surmised, their long years of labor would prove as negligible as the "old Nestorian church, a windblown, obliterated tablet upon a desert land."[22]

Yet Buck proved strangely, perhaps predictably, unable to jettison her past en-tirely. Through these middle years of her life, the novelist continued to cling to the ghost of the ideal. If Western Christians took their faith at all seriously, she judged, they needed to share it. The message would have to be redefined, of course. New-breed missionaries would not try to change anyone's religion. In place of the old emphasis on miracles and hellfire, updated evangelists would bring practical skills—talents in medicine, agriculture, education, engineering, and the like—seeking only to feed the hungry and to bind up the wounded. To those who worried about what would happen if no one preached about salvation from sin through faith in Jesus Christ, Buck offered a ready response: "And who shall say that by the word we must mean nothing but talk? What people ever understood what the word meant until it was made flesh and dwelt among them?" Christianity equaled the amelioration of physical suffering and social injustice, nothing more, nothing less. Wherever Christianity was truly believed and consistently practiced, outsiders would see a difference. Women would be treated more humanely, beggars fed more often, orphans cared for more tenderly. And the source of that spiritual strength? The perennial power of the Christ figure—not Christ, but the Christ figure—to stir the loftiest aspirations of the human race.[23]

1940s On

By the late 1930s, Buck had largely said all that she had to say about the moral dilemmas of missions. She lived nearly another four decades and wrote literally scores of books, yet she rarely revisited the subject. Though Buck left China in 1934, never to return, over the years she grew increasingly defensive about Chinese traditions. Practices such as foot-binding and infanticide, which she once denounced as evil, she later interpreted to Western audiences as intelligible parts of the culture. Buck favorably contrasted China's indulgent child-rearing habits with Westerners' emotional distance and disregard for family values.[24]

In the 1940s, Buck's identification with Christianity of any sort—liberal, radical, or otherwise—seemed to evaporate. When war swept China in the late 1930s, she initially supported the New York–based China Famine Relief. But hearing that the group held religious connections, she soon withdrew, stating, "I make it a policy never to associate myself with religious organizations." The ex-missionary now saw the institutional church as an organization that perpetuated itself for the organization's sake. Though she eschewed the label atheist, she would insist, "I feel no need for any other faith than my faith in human beings." It is true that in a second autobiography, published in 1961, Buck affirmed the likelihood of life after death. But that possibility had nothing to do with Christianity or even conventional theism. She argued that science, spurred by the speculations of saints, would someday demonstrate through purely technological means the "continuing individual existence, which we call the immortality of the soul." Near the end of her life, she waved aside a question about the afterlife, saying that she was too busy with the present to worry about the "complexities of what is to come hereafter." Then, quoting Eleanor Roosevelt, she added: "Whatever it is I daresay I shall be able to cope with it."[25]

The mature Buck said little about foreign missions. By this point in her life, the subject probably had grown too preposterous, or perhaps too painful to merit serious refutation. In her first autobiography, published in 1954, she claimed—in the face of clear evidence to the contrary—that she had abandoned the very idea of conversionary missions as soon as she graduated from college, having seen "enough of that dangerous business in years gone by." Though admitting that her missionary upbringing had shaped her, Buck now boasted, "I have never been an evangelical missionary, and indeed abhor the general notion." The mature writer discounted all openly Christian work overseas, medical and educational as well as evangelistic, as a cloak for imperialism. "The [e]ffrontery of all this still makes my soul shrink," she judged.[26]

Buck obviously knew better when she shaded the truth of her own past, but she probably did not grasp how profoundly the original missionary impulse continued to govern her outlook and behavior. Having amassed great wealth, she earmarked much of it for charitable endeavors such as an international adoption agency and a program for the children U.S. servicemen had fathered and abandoned overseas. Much like her contemporary Reinhold Niebuhr, Buck became something of a professional critic of U.S. domestic and foreign policies, perennially upbraiding her compatriots for racism at home and chauvinism abroad.[27]

INTERPRETATIONS OF A LIFE

Why did Buck change as she did? Presuming to divine anyone's mind is risky at best. "Between the motion / And the act / Falls the shadow," the poet T. S. Eliot reminds us. Yet Buck left enough clues to allow at least some informed guesses.[28]

At the broadest level, it is crucial to remember that Buck resembled countless late-Victorian Christians who surrendered the dogmas of their adolescent faith in the face of modern thought. For some, that surrender proved a painful loss; for others, a joyful liberation; but for all, a moment of truth. The radical conclusions of the Rockefeller-funded Laymen's Commission of Inquiry, summarized by Harvard philosopher William Ernest Hocking in Re-Thinking Missions (published two weeks after the Hotel Astor speech), confirmed that Buck was marching in strong company. By then, thousands of Christians on both sides of the Pacific had come to view conversionary missions as culturally imperialistic at best, and morally indefensible at worst.[29]

But here the plot thickens. Many of the so-called board missionaries—the men and women of solid education and middle-class means sent by the mainline denominations—had been changing for several decades, and changing exactly as Buck desired. For them, Re-Thinking Missions was not so much a call for reform as a summary of significant transformations already in place.[30] By the 1920s, fresh theological ideas in the West and turbid political changes inside China had combined to dictate more accommodating evangelistic strategies. Hell had nearly disappeared from the missionaries' doctrinal vocabulary, not to mention their weekly preaching. Missionary leaders had determined to separate the kernel of the Christian gospel from the husk of Christian civilization. Some had even suggested that the central task of the evangelist was not to preach at all but, in one historian's words, to introduce a "spirit of regeneration and Christian conscience." In the respectable churches back home, missionary talks that had once emphasized the cruel and strange customs of the Chinese people had given way to calls for better medicine, education, and treatment of women. By the 1920s, in short, leaders had not solved all of the problems of cultural imperialism, but they were working at it, and working harder than Buck remotely acknowledged. If she had desired to work for progressive changes from within the Protestant missionary establishment, there was plenty of room for doing so.[31]

These developments suggest that deeply personal motivations as well as intellectual doubts drove Buck's pilgrimage away from faith. This is not to say that the onetime missionary dissimulated when she said that Christian doctrines were untrue and that Christian missions produced undesirable results. But it is to say that the truth about herself was more complex than she recognized. In a word, her self-professed reasons should be seen as one strand in a rope of many.[32]

One of those strands was Buck's ambivalence about her national identity. Which was home, China or the United States? Her first language was Chinese, and except for a brief childhood visit to her grandparents' farm in West Virginia, she had known only China until she left for Randolph-Macon Woman's College. But she was an "American" through and through. "I grew up in China," she wrote in her autobiography, "in one world and not of it, and belonging to another world and yet not of it." Near the end of her long life, a visiting journalist would conclude that she "never really got used to America, still does not feel completely at home here." The emotional fallout from this dual citizenship was almost predictable. A sizable body of clinical research begun in the 1930s has shown that missionary children experience more than their fair share of adolescent stresses. One specialist calls them "third culture" children. Typically reared in non-Western settings, yet educated following grammar school in Europe or North America, they feel disoriented. Leaving the mission field produces a pain best described as grief. For the rest of their lives, often enough, they yearn for the irretrievable. Though many "mishkids" choose to live outside the United States, they rarely develop true affection or deep empathy for the non-Western cultures in which they were reared. Citizens, then, of an interstitial culture, they end up as citizens of no culture they can securely call their own.[33]

Buck left other, more intimate clues about the way that daily life on the mission field gnawed at the vitals of her faith. Resentment toward the real or perceived financial deprivation of the evangelist's life never went away, and that indignation lingered long after she had grown very wealthy from the sale of millions of books. Marital discord constituted still another hint of the forces shaping her outlook. Buck admitted that her eighteen-year marriage to the agriculture missionary Lossing Buck, which ended in divorce in 1935, had been an unhappy one. More important, she resented the misogyny she experienced in her father's home and in her husband's home and increasingly regarded it as endemic to Christianity itself. Thinking of the way that her mother had been diminished by Christianity, Buck wrote, "I have hated Saint Paul with all my heart and so must all true women hate him, I think, because of what he has done [to] proud, free-born women, yet damned by their very womanhood." While it is hard to know how to interpret, let alone rank, these various factors, there can be little doubt that the acids of envy, incompatibility, and resentment eroded her ties to the missionary community and its purposes.[34]

The tragedy of Carol, Buck's only biological child, further troubled her life. Carol had been born severely mentally handicapped. For years, Buck tried to deny the obvious, but she finally admitted that Carol would have to be placed in permanent residential care back in the United States. "[M]y heart is wrenched in two at the thought," she told a friend at the time. When Carol turned nine in the fall of 1929, Buck settled her in a facility in New Jersey. The separation, Buck told another friend shortly afterward, "rend[ed] flesh from flesh." The emotional bleeding never stopped. Twenty years later, Buck wrote as if the event had taken place the day before, calling it the "sorrow that could not be ended." Buck never directly attributed her loss of faith to Carol's condition but confessed that deep inside the "rebellion burned." The child's departure turned life into an endurance test. "There was no more joy left in anything," she later remembered. "All human relationships became meaningless. Everything became meaningless. I took no more pleasure in the things I had enjoyed before; landscapes, flowers, music were empty." Buck gave up playing the piano and quit praying in the Union Church in the missionary compound. What was the point? No one was listening, she told her husband. In time, Buck would return to music, but not to hymns. Musical entreaties to an unseen God now seemed "infinitely pathetic." Neither Christianity nor Christians offered solace. The disposition to be merciful, she theorized with considerable bitterness, grew from suffering, not from faith. If individual Christians responded to others' distress with kindness or sympathy, it would be "an accident," not a product of their Christian belief.[35]

And finally, there was Andrew, the Lincolnesque protagonist of Buck's most powerful and haunting book, *Fighting Angel*. Andrew was, of course, a barely fictionalized rendering of her own father, Absalom Sydenstricker. With only a bit of reading between the lines, it is evident that he personified everything that she publicly loathed—and privately admired—about the Christian missionary enterprise.[36]

In the novel, as in real life, Andrew—Absalom—spends a half-century trekking the roads of rural China but seems never really to touch the ground. Oblivious to mundane detail, he lives not in time but in eternity, ceaselessly driven by an "awful sense of duty." A single purpose consumes his life: to preach the gospel to the Chinese, whatever hardship that grim duty might entail for himself or his family. It would be a mistake, however, to think that the creed of the Southern Presbyterian Church fires Andrew's zeal. To the contrary, Andrew's character preceded his religion. "Whatever he did he would have done with that swordlike singleness of heart," Buck declared. "He chose the greatest god he knew, and set forth into the universe to make men acknowledge his god to be the one true God, before whom all must bow. It was a magnificent imperialism of the spirit, incredible and not to be understood except by those who have been reared in it and have grown beyond it."[37]

Given Buck's antagonism toward narrow-minded, creed-driven ideologues, we might assume that she would have recoiled from her father. But she did not. She loved him dearly and said so often. She told friends that her critique of the missionary cadre in China did not apply to her father. And with good reason. He took the life of the mind seriously, earning degrees from Washington and Lee University and from Virginia's Union Theological Seminary before sailing, and receiving an honorary doctorate from his alma mater in 1909. In China, Absalom soon distinguished himself by his control of Mandarin, both oral and written, and by his dogged determination to master both the colloquial pronunciation and idiomatic uses of the language. He imposed exacting standards on himself in his own (still important) biblical translation work. Flying in the face of the missionary establishment, Absalom pressed Chinese churches to become self-supporting and self-perpetuating in order to free themselves of foreign domination.[38]

Above all, the veteran missionary won his daughter's affection by his steady compassion for the Chinese. Though he suffered much persecution and sometimes outright violence, especially among rural "peasants," he felt they could do no wrong. He preferred their company to the company of whites, whom he did not trust. The word "heathen" never fouled the air of the Sydenstricker household. Indeed, Absalom refused to sing any hymn that employed that term—or any other term he considered disparaging to the Chinese. Though he found it hard to take Confucianism or Buddhism seriously as religions, he deemed them worthy of serious study and struggled to find continuities between those religions and Christianity. Of course, he believed that Chinese men and women who refused the gospel ultimately would perish. Yet Buck depicted that conviction more as a burden to be shouldered than as a prejudice to be flaunted.[39]

More important for our purposes, Andrew emerges from Buck's pages as a truly superior breed of human. Though the real-life Absalom lived with Pearl and her family the entire last decade of his life (dying only a year before the Hotel Astor speech), she never discussed her unconventional religious views with him. Nor did she permit anyone else to discredit Christian doctrine or missions in his presence. In a response to a condolence letter sent at the time of Absalom's death, Buck proudly asserted that her father had been a "most extraordinary person—so simple and so good. I think I never knew those qualities more complete in anyone."[40]

Remarkably, Buck expressed similar views about many of the other missionaries of his generation as well. They were, she wrote, "born warriors and very great men, for in those days religion was still a banner under which to fight." A unique generation of Anglo-American spiritual imperialists, those willful conquerors proved "proud and quarrelsome and brave and intolerant and passionate," "none the less good and innocent because they were blind." In contrast, she wrote, contemporary missionaries seem weak and despicable, "shot through with doubt and distrust of themselves and their message. They talk of tolerance and mutual esteem, of liberalizing education and of friendly relations and all such gentle feeble things. They see good in all religions. . . . There is no taste in them."[41]

"No taste in them"? How should we interpret this statement by a woman who supposedly despised missionary ideologues?

The plain truth is that Buck was her father's daughter to an extent she never consciously grasped. She followed in his footsteps in obvious ways. For one thing, she replicated his love of books and foreign languages, energized, as he was, by the life of the mind. She echoed his contempt for laziness and shoddiness, as well as his singleness of purpose. Buck never paid attention to literary critics in the United States or to nationalist pundits in China or to theological sharpshooters anywhere: "I have long made it a practice to read no reviews or comments on my work," she bragged to a friend in 1938. One year earlier she had declared, "And I wouldn't be my father's daughter, anyway, as I am—if I cared what people say."[42]

Buck followed in her father's footsteps in ways not so obvious, as well. The impulse constantly to critique public policies, to agitate for reforms, to turn out twenty-five hundred words a day on whatever topic came to her mind—in brief, the determination to press her views on anyone who would listen—flamed brightly to the end. So did the assumption that she enjoyed the *right* to speak, especially for the Chinese. For Buck, the Occident was immersed in the stream of history, but not the Orient. The hardy Chinese stock who people the pages of *The Good Earth* emerge in her rolling cadences as a race fixed outside time and space, changeless and imperturbable. "Life ran very deep and still in this hidden corner of the world," Buck had mused as a young woman. The missionaries, the merchants, the gunboats, all came and went, but nothing ever really changed, for that vast land invariably "enveloped, assimilated" its conquerors. A quarter century later, Buck's views about China's historylessness remained unchanged. For 85 percent of its people, she confidently averred, the "ancient ways still hold. It cannot be otherwise, for people do not change in a day or a night from what they have been for centuries." In Buck's reckoning, then, China could not be Christianized because China's peasants were incapable of transformation. If Absalom patronized the Chinese by presuming to change them, Pearl patronized them even more by presuming that they stood beyond the reach of the changes he sought to introduce.[43]

Buck proved herself a missionary strikingly like her father in one additional respect. Truth mattered. Honesty demanded a straight vote, up or down. "To me," she wrote, "truth is so much dearer than any comforting falsehood, so much kinder in its clean-cutting edge than fencing and evasion." From this perspective, it is easy to understand her tribute to J. Gresham Machen following his untimely death in 1937. Machen, it will be recalled, was the purist who had forced Buck out of the Presbyterian foreign mission cadre in 1933. But Buck found him admirable precisely for that reason. He outweighed a hundred modern princes of the church "who occupy easy places and play their church politics and trim their sails to every wind." Machen, in contrast, "never gave in one inch to anyone. He never bowed his head. It was not in him to trim or compromise, to accept any peace that was less than triumph." In the ex-missionary's mind, Machen was the kind of "honest dogmatist" that an "honest skeptic" like herself could sit down and do business with.[44]

Still, tough-mindedness proved easier to muster when the sun shone. Days before her death, Buck spoke of the essential sadness of life. "We are poised here for a little while, and we can enjoy this through our minds and our senses, but we don't know anything, really." The supreme irony, as she saw it, was that humans recognized that they did not know where they came from or where they were going. And that fact constituted "utmost cruelty." Though Buck felt that the warrant for missions had evaporated in the face of modern science and anthropology, she knew that the loss of faith exacted its own melancholy price.[45]

For Buck's contemporaries, the missionary impulse presented itself as an affair of extraordinary complexity. Sometimes it seemed buoyed by great currents of expansionist hope, like breakers rolling and crashing on a windy shore. Just as often, however, it appeared to be eroded by back currents of regret, like rivulets washing away the sand beneath the feet. If Pearl Buck's journey represented the disillusion felt by many, so did the journey's twists and turns, which made it a pilgrimage of the heart as much as of the mind.

13 / To Save "Free Vietnam" and Lose Our Souls

The Missionary Impulse, Voluntary Agencies, and Protestant Dissent against the War, 1965–1971

Scott Flipse

On a warm October day in the nation's capital, Willard Krabill got out of his cab and hurried up the stairs of the Old Executive Office Building. He was nervous. It was his first time representing the Mennonite Central Committee, and he was to meet with Vice President Hubert Humphrey, no less. When he reached Humphrey's office, the vice president immediately put him at ease, greeting the young doctor and inviting him in for "a visit."[1] Krabill joined others invited to the meeting in a small semicircle around Humphrey's desk. He glanced at the others in the room—Bernard Confer of Lutheran World Relief, Hugh Farley of Church World Services, CARE's Judge Robert Hansen, and Monsignor John McCarthy of Catholic Relief Services. These men represented most of the major religious denominations working in humanitarian services overseas. Krabill noticed how comfortable the other delegates were with the vice president. He watched as they amiably consoled Humphrey about the Minnesota Twins's loss to the Dodgers in the 1965 World Series—a point to which Monsignor McCarthy quipped, "At least Sandy Koufax is a Democrat." They all looked confident in the corridors of power.[2] The meeting with Humphrey culminated a two-day briefing tour for delegates of the major voluntary agencies working in South Vietnam. President Lyndon Johnson had commissioned them to visit Vietnam and report back about that nation's humanitarian needs. In April 1965, Johnson ordered the first massive aerial bombings of North Vietnam. Later that summer, he sent the first U.S. combat troops to Da Nang and Pleiku. The increased fighting displaced an estimated one million people.

Humphrey briefed the delegates on U.S. policy and goals. He stressed "how important" the voluntary agencies would be in carrying out the United States's commitment to Vietnam.[3] The vice president commended the delegates on "the tremendous job" they were already doing but told them that the president "wanted private agencies to initiate immediate expanded programs . . . to meet the problems of refugees."[4] No one in the room questioned this request or thought it inappropriate. The vice president did not ask them to venture into unfamiliar territory. Religiously motivated humanitarian agencies had played a large role in rebuilding postwar Europe, and Vietnam was another episode in the "alliance" existing between church and state abroad.[5]

The humanitarian mission in Vietnam was clear, but left unspoken were the partisan expectations of the task. The Johnson Administration planned a large influx of private U.S. citizens and economic aid to impress skeptics of the benevolent and nonlethal intent of U.S. policy. As conceived by Johnson's political and military planners, the war would be fought on two different fronts—the "main force war" fought by land and air forces, and the "other war" fought by civilians and economic aid. The strategy for the "other war," according to legendary superspy Edward Landsdale, was to "win the hearts and minds" of the Vietnamese people.[6] The critical ammunition was improvements in agriculture, education, health care, housing, and community development—the type of social services the voluntary agencies had decades' worth of experience at providing.[7]

The relationship between the military commitment and religious organizations raised vexing questions in the minds of Krabill and some of his fellow delegates. Krabill, Confer, and Farley expressed private reservations about "the danger posed by close identification with the war effort."[8] "It was clear," said Krabill later about his fact-finding trip to South Vietnam, "that we were not given the entire story . . . [the military and Agency for International Development (AID) representatives] showed us a fraction of the problem."[9] The delegation's final report illustrated these tensions. The delegates were careful to stake out different motivations and spheres of influence among humanitarian, religious, and security concerns—on the one hand stating the need to be independent from military planning, and on the other hand expressing interest "in serving refugees in North Vietnam."[10]

It was not intended, however, that such mild declarations of independence signaled an unwillingness to support a "necessary increase" in their programs. The final report promised to expand voluntary agency presence to "assist displaced persons . . . fleeing from the terrorism of the Viet Cong and the steadily increasing scale of military action."[11] The close relationship between church and state abroad was too well developed and mutually satisfying to turn down direct appeals from the president and vice president. U.S. voluntary agencies shared long-standing common interests and values about their nation's role in the world. In the end, they did not question that U.S. self-interest required a prompt response both to contain communism and "to feed the hungry, care for the sick, and clothe the naked." Voluntary agencies put aside their reservations and decided to pitch in. The final report concluded, "The motivations of the voluntary agencies are humanitarian, often religious, and seldom political. . . . It is a tribute to both parties, however, to find them working in collaboration in Vietnam in such an effective way to meet human need, with respect on each side for the other's integrity."[12]

The mutual respect and collaboration that existed in 1965 dramatically deteriorated by 1971. As the war widened, the worst fears of the delegates came to fruition. Their religious and humanitarian purposes could no longer be separated from an increasingly unpopular war. The very act of assisting war victims was seen as a partisan act—by agency volunteers, by radical critics of the war, by many Vietnamese, and by the military and political leaders who expected support for their security objectives. The ongoing war forced every religious organization working in Vietnam to choose whether to support or oppose the war—a choice that went straight to the heart of their missionary impulse—whether to continue substantial commitments to South Vietnam or walk away in protest, whether to continue trying to "save a free Vietnam" from communism, paganism, and poverty or save the United States from the moral dilemmas and social dislocations posed by the war.

The war split voluntary agency staff in the same way it split the larger public. Not all private organizations and missionary agencies actively opposed the war. That story is beyond the scope of this chapter, however. This essay will track the concerns of those religiously motivated individuals and organizations that took an active stance against the war from within Vietnam. Opposition came from the volunteers and administrators associated with ecumenical Protestantism and the historical peace churches. The Mennonite Central Committee, Church World Service, Lutheran World Relief (which joined together in 1966 to form Vietnam Christian Services), and International Voluntary Services (an ecumenical organization of technical assistance started by the Church of the Brethren) formed the largest and longest-tenured agencies that opposed the war from within Vietnam. By challenging the moral underpinnings of the "other war," voluntary agencies helped influence domestic public opinion against the war, limited government options in conducting the war, and permanently changed the way voluntary agencies interacted with U.S. foreign policy.

A WORKABLE PARTNERSHIP: CHURCH AND STATE ABROAD AFTER WORLD WAR II

The relationship between church and state abroad tapped deep historical roots. In the decades between 1890 and 1930, missionaries acted as diplomats, journalists, business operatives, and experts on foreign cultures for a nation slowly awakening to a role beyond its shores. The devastation of World War II and the onset of the Cold War served as a catalyst for more formal coordination between church groups and government agencies internationally. Surveying the world's prospects near the end of World War II, President Franklin Roosevelt told aides he thought that refugees and humanitarian relief problems should be solved "on a broad religious basis."[13] In the late 1940s and early 1950s, public figures accepted, and even courted, a prominent role for the United States's "three faith coalition," incorporating previously "outsider" religious groups, such as Roman Catholics, evangelical Protestants, and Jews, into the national conversation about U.S. foreign-policy goals.[14] In the early years of the Eisenhower Administration, Secretary of State John Foster Dulles challenged Protestant church leaders to create a world vision that included distribution of foodstuffs and technical-assistance funds. He promised to earmark federal money for religious agencies.[15]

Religiously based humanitarian agencies helped shoulder the enormous task of feeding, clothing, resettling, repatriating, and caring for the millions of homeless and unwanted people affected by world war. In the decades after World War II, this international humanitarian partnership was a popular zone of cooperation between church and state—and it also worked well. For their part, religious agencies needed government funds, foodstuffs, transportation, and protection to carry out their missions on a scale that met postwar needs. Pax Americana found wide support among religious people because religious leaders shared the goals and values of U.S. foreign-policy leaders and because it helped many thousands of U.S. citizens meet the obligations of religiously motivated service abroad.

SAVING "FREE VIETNAM"

The church-state relationship in Vietnam must be seen in the broader context of similar partnerships abroad. With the collapse of French rule in 1954, officials of the United States Operating Mission (USOM), the administrative umbrella for the various economic aid programs for South Vietnam, invited humanitarian organizations to establish refugee and relief projects in that war-torn country. Voluntary agency executives found both U.S. and South Vietnamese government officials eager for their help.[16] After a June 1954 visit, William Snyder, executive secretary of the Mennonite Central Committee and a founding trustee of International Voluntary Services, reported that USOM "definitely wanted voluntary agency help." Snyder later reported to the State Department's Joan Kain that one Vietnamese official said it was important for voluntary agencies to be active in his country "since Vietnam needs visible signs of foreign interest and concern."[17] On July 21, 1954, the day the Geneva Agreement was signed dividing Vietnam into two states, USOM issued a statement saying voluntary agencies "would be welcomed and needed in free Vietnam."[18] They expected a large influx of refugees from North Vietnam (the majority of whom were Roman Catholic) and wanted agency help in stabilizing a politically shaky and war-ravaged country. Without much publicity, religious voluntary agencies played a ma-

jor part in resettling nearly one million people, the largest refugee flow then recorded. By 1958, Catholic Relief Services, Church World Service, International
Voluntary Services, and the Mennonite Central Committee all administered a growing list of projects and personnel.

Religiously motivated voluntary agencies played no small role in helping to stabilize a "free Vietnam." Private agencies and U.S. government sources poured almost
$7 billion into South Vietnam during the Eisenhower Administration. Given South
Vietnam's uncertain beginnings in 1954, this money appeared to be well spent. The
nation was hailed as a "miracle" of stable Asian nationalism by the end of the decade.[19] Missionaries and aid workers did much to create a favorable public perception of South Vietnam. It appeared on maps in Sunday and parochial schools long
before it appeared on the mental maps of most people in the United States.[20] U.S.
Catholic and Protestant news sources consistently sent home enthusiastic reports
from the region. They prepared millions of Christians in the United States to accept
South Vietnam as an ally whose survival depended upon continued U.S. assistance.
A certain amount of paternalistic hubris, however, survived in the notion that a
church-state partnership could effect lasting social and political change in South
Vietnam, especially given the mounting evidence that most Vietnamese disliked the
U.S. presence. Yet, looking at South Vietnam in the light of other countries divided
along ideological lines—Germany, Korea, China—it seemed a model of success, a
"free" nation holding the line against communism's advance in Southeast Asia. Voluntary agencies and U.S. policymakers had reasons to feel optimistic about that
nation's future and their own role in it.

The expansion of a bloody civil war and increased political unrest dashed these
hopes. South Vietnam became a dangerous place to live and work. Assassinations,
demonstrations, kidnappings, and threats hampered the work of voluntary agencies.[21] They could no longer move freely or safely to large areas of the country. Their
projects and personnel eventually concentrated on militarily secure regions among
peoples often the most loyal to the South Vietnamese government.

THINGS FALL APART

After 1963, the U.S. military began committing troops and a massive array of technology to a small guerrilla war. Watching the situation escalate from the Oval Office, President Johnson repeatedly expressed his hatred for its military side. He
wanted to encourage a "social revolution . . . determined not only to achieve victory
over aggression but to win victory over hunger, disease, and despair."[22] Johnson
eagerly looked for opportunities to expand the Great Society abroad. He wanted
to "leave the footprints of America [in Vietnam] . . . schools and hospitals, and
dams."[23] At Johnson's urging, USOM officials again encouraged a rapid expansion

of voluntary agencies' programs. Government officials coordinating U.S. economic aid expected the cooperation of voluntary agencies. From the early stages of the Vietnam War, voluntary agencies were expected to adopt a partisan position in carrying out their humanitarian missions.

Questions of purpose and relations with the U.S. military presence went to the heart of Vietnam Christian Services (VNCS). VNCS was a joint project of Lutheran World Relief, Mennonite Central Committee (MCC), and Church World Service (CWS). MCC was chosen to carry the agency's administrative burden because Mennonite missionaries and aid workers already had extensive experience there.[24] From its inception, VNCS walked a tightrope between conscience and cooperation. The new agency, warned Frank Hutchison, director of CWS Southeast Asian Programs, would be inherently "political." It would be asked to "win the hearts and minds of the Vietnamese people."[25] On the other hand, Harold Row, a founding trustee of International Voluntary Services (IVS) and a Church of the Brethren clergyman long interested in Vietnam, argued that U.S. churches "must place their own presence permanently in Vietnam." This would serve as "a counter Christian image" and a source of information about the situation in Vietnam that existed outside official channels. Row's greatest fear was that if the religious agencies withdrew, the Vietnamese would be left with an image of the United States shaped solely by the military occupation.[26]

The creation of a large U.S. religious presence in Vietnam posed some vexing problems. What role would VNCS play in the larger economic assistance programs? VNCS volunteers opposed the creation of an agency that distributed massive amounts of food and material relief. Volunteer Earl Martin spoke for many when he stated his aversion to the limited role of "slinging about commodities." Martin suggested, instead, a community-development program that "work[ed] closely with the people we've come here to serve."[27] VNCS administrators agreed. Atlee Beechy, VNCS's first executive director, called for a "service-centered" model that promoted self-help projects, institution building, and contact with ordinary Vietnamese. Beechy explained that close identification with the Vietnamese people "suggests a deliberate choice to be apart from military causes and associations." VNCS's operating ethos, he continued, "is to minister insofar as possible to all men in need even though they may themselves be divided ideologically, politically, and militarily."[28]

For the first year of its existence, VNCS closely followed Beechy's dictum. Though few VNCS volunteers wholeheartedly supported the U.S. war policy, they worked well with the Vietnamese government and with military advisors. Paul Leatherman, VNCS volunteer and later country director, received the Order of Merit from the South Vietnamese government.[29] VNCS volunteers spread out over the country. Recruits came from twelve different denominational backgrounds and included missionaries, doctors, agronomists, social workers, home economists, and experts in refugee resettlement and commodity distribution. Writing to his friends and family, VNCS volunteer Jonathan Newkirk found the daily tasks he faced huge and tiring and "often defying solution," but he planned to go about his work "as a positive witness in the model of Jesus" and allow the military and political tensions to play out around him.[30]

The "quiet servanthood" model began to weigh heavily on the consciences of many young VNCS volunteers and administrators, especially as they observed the course of the war. Even though VNCS made attempts to avoid an official relationship with the U.S. military, they were constantly dismayed to learn that the U.S. military felt "our work is very important in winning the war."[31] As a marine colonel told Earl Martin, "My job . . . is to kill the enemy . . . [but] we are also here with a mandate to 'win the hearts and minds' of the Vietnamese people. And that is where you come in, with your work in the refugee camps. We are glad you are part of the team."[32]

VNCS found that refusing to join "the team" was easier said than done, given the cooperation required to carry out their projects successfully. State Department figures for fiscal year 1968 show that voluntary agencies spent $13.2 million on various projects. More than half that figure, or $6.6 million, came from government contracts. The agencies also dispensed $17.4 million worth of surplus food and material aid. Of that amount, $7.9 million came from government sources and was divided among six agencies. The agencies depended on free U.S. military transport for their goods. Personnel working for voluntary agencies also received base commissary privileges, used Army postal privileges, and lived in or near military compounds. Voluntary agencies made up only a small portion of the total military and economic aid spent in Vietnam, but from the amount spent the U.S. government considered voluntary agencies to be an integral part of the war effort.[33] Paul Longacre, VNCS director from 1966 to 1967, worried about the close relations VNCS had with the U.S. military. Could VNCS, he asked the board of MCC, "maintain an identity and integrity . . . in the face of stronger military control of South Vietnam by the United States forces"?[34] Longacre did not have to wait for his answer. Secular antiwar activists and critics from within VNCS's member constituencies questioned whether a humanitarian organization should be involved in Vietnam at all.[35] The question was whether the political expectations placed on voluntary agencies negated their humanitarian and missionary impulse. Or, as Earl Martin reported after a conversation with a Vietnamese professor, "the real effect of your presence here is . . . [to obscure] the destructive nature of the total American intervention."[36] The tensions of war, the escalation of its intensity, the increasing size of U.S. forces, the corruption of Vietnamese society and government, the witness of

Vietnamese friends, and their own consciences propelled volunteers like Martin to take more critical positions regarding U.S. war policy.

WITNESSING TO THE HOME FRONT

The witness of aid workers gradually made an impact on the stateside lobbying efforts of the VNCS administrative bodies. Throughout the war, ecumenical Protestant organizations and the peace churches lobbied administration officials and Congress to alter U.S. policy in Southeast Asia. In 1965, MCC sent five letters and telegrams to President Johnson, asking for a halt to the aerial bombings and an opening of peace negotiations mediated by the United Nations.[37] Denominational executives from the National Council of Churches (NCC) personally urged Johnson to offer North Vietnam an economic carrot to enter negotiations—a massive aid package that included the development of the Mekong River Valley. During the initial stages of the war, religious leaders preferred to work with the Johnson Administration as they did on civil-rights and Great Society legislation. As one MCC executive put it, "We would reserve criticism of military policy and invest our time and energy in constructive service."[38] The possibility that VNCS volunteers might take vocal positions against the war concerned stateside administrators. They believed that public protests threatened the line of open communication established between the administration and religious leaders. When Sam Hope, a Presbyterian pastor and VNCS assistant director, suggested to stateside superiors that VNCS should "work for a de-escalation of the U.S. role as a way to alleviate suffering," he was told that it was "not in line for [VNCS] to become political and associate itself with either a hawk or dove role." Other organs of the NCC, the reply added, worked on solutions for ending the war, allowing "service workers in Vietnam to be more apolitical."[39]

An apolitical humanitarianism was not an easy thing to maintain. As the war dragged on through 1966 and into 1967, religious leaders began to wonder whether working from within the administration could lead to a change in U.S. war policy. Reinforcing this idea were reports from VNCS volunteers and Mennonite missionaries. As witnesses to the war on the ground, service workers noted the incongruities between public perceptions and what was actually taking place. Their testimony circulated widely in the antiwar circles of the religious mainstream. In one letter, for example, Longacre reported that "ulcerating conditions" and "economic hardships" made the Vietnamese express hatred for the U.S. military presence. From his perspective, military victory would "take a long time," if it came at all. Longacre wanted to balance VNCS's mission to the suffering with a credible witness against the causes of that suffering. "I think while [we] succumb[ed] to Johnson's arm twisting [in expanding VNCS programs], we should in turn knife the 'psychological warfare' mania in the back by providing our own interpretive reporting from the field."[40]

The vocal positions taken by relief workers corresponded with a more active antiwar movement on the home front. Religious critics of the war, most taking part in the ecumenical organization Clergy and Laity Concerned about Vietnam (CALCAV), began efforts to mobilize the grassroots of the U.S. religious mainstream, using "moderate tactics such as petitions, vigils, electoral politics, and rallies."[41] They did not abandon lobbying efforts but used the testimony of relief workers in Vietnam to bolster their case with policymakers. Ivan Kaufman, a representative of the NCC, told Johnson aide Bill Moyers that "VNCS reported increasing destruction of the ordinary people of Vietnam—to the point where we no longer can remain silent. We question the morality of forcing thousands of Vietnamese into refugee camps." Of his meeting with Moyers, Kaufman concluded, "Our group was received with respect because VNCS was in Vietnam—suffering alongside the Vietnamese farmer."

Religious leaders gained access to policymakers because they spoke from firsthand knowledge of the situation. The wealth of contradictory evidence gathered by aid workers, however, moved many religious critics to take more confrontational and prophetic positions. In the summer of 1967, MCC Chairman Christian Hostetter and International Voluntary Services trustee William Snyder wrote President Johnson, personally delivering the letter to the White House. Hostetter and Snyder informed Johnson that the testimony of Mennonites in the field brought them to the conclusion that "the U.S. was pursuing a self-defeating . . . and paradox[ical] policy. . . . We are trying to help the people on the one hand while at the same time our government was engaged in an escalating war that was . . . creating enormous tragic suffering for the civilian population." Snyder and Hostetter contended that "the time has come when we can no longer maintain faith with the homeless . . . and wounded to whom we minister unless we speak out as clearly as we can against the savage war in which our country is engaged." Hostetter and Snyder added that VNCS workers would continue working in Vietnam "but do not want [their] efforts to be a palliative on the conscience of a nation seeking to do good on one hand while spreading destruction on the other."[42] By late 1967, the period of quietly working with the Johnson Administration was over.

While stateside religious leaders prodded the conscience of policymakers, the letters, furlough visits, and articles of Protestant relief workers and missionaries prodded the conscience of domestic constituencies. Relief workers tried to educate the home front about Vietnamese history and nationalism; introduce to their readers the triumphs, pains, and struggles of the Vietnamese people; debunk the widely held assumption that the fight was of a free people against communism; and publish the atrocities of war.[43] Though they failed to use sophisticated theological arguments to defend their positions, their published and unpublished records present a comprehensive account of the U.S. commitment in Vietnam and a powerful moral indictment for a domestic audience often divided in its opinions about the war. It should not be surprising, claimed one letter addressed to "Christians in America," that the Vietnamese "reject" our humanitarian and missionary efforts. They cannot be blamed for linking our humanitarian efforts with the "wealthy, warring West."[44] Few relief workers were optimistic about a military solution in Vietnam. Veteran aid worker and missionary James Metzler poignantly suggested that without a vocal Christian witness against the war, "Vietnam was a tragedy not only for the Vietnamese but for American Christians as well."[45]

THE POLITICS OF CHARITY

As the war progressed into 1967, VNCS Assistant Director Sam Hope sensed a shifting attitude among VNCS's volunteers and among the staff of other voluntary agencies in Saigon. He predicted that VNCS was entering a "new stage of development" in which the ministry to suffering took a backseat to protesting the causes of that suffering.[46] A more vocal and confrontational approach fed numerous discussions and debates conducted in denominational meetings, religious magazines, and church forums.[47] What had been largely an internal debate, however, broke into the national spotlight on September 19, 1967. Forty-nine members of IVS released to *The New York Times* an open letter addressed to President Johnson. For the first time, humanitarian aid workers spoke out publicly against the war effort.

The public defections of IVS staff were front-page news. IVS was closely tied to the economic-assistance program in South Vietnam. Its work in agricultural and community development was well known among policymakers. IVS projects routinely showed up on the itineraries of visiting congressional delegations, and many IVS volunteers continued their careers with the State Department.[48] This relationship went all the way back to IVS's founding. In 1956, members of the National Security Council asked IVS to send teams of agricultural experts to Vietnam and Laos.[49]

The historically close relationship between IVS and the U.S. government began to deteriorate in 1965. At that time, IVS grew from 40 members to 175. The political views of the new recruits and IVS's public visibility caused friction between the U.S. Agency for International Development (USAID) and IVS Chief of Party Don Luce. The country director for USAID twice opposed Luce's election as chief of party—citing management problems and lack of cooperation—and asked the IVS board to remove him. The board refused and wrote to Vietnam's Ambassador Ellsworth Bunker, equating USAID's meddling in agency elections with a "serious curtailment of freedom" and a violation of IVS's contract. At Bunker's insistence, USAID withdrew its objection to Luce, but the pressure on IVS staff to integrate projects and personnel decisions with military authority intensified at the local level. As one IVS volunteer complained to Executive Director Arthur Z. Gardiner, "As IVS gets bigger . . . and with the rise in the number of American soldiers . . . [we] will experience difficulties in maintaining [our] identity. We will be mis-identified as sub-assistant provincial representatives of USAID. . . . We all would be able to accomplish much more were we not so shackled."[50]

Questions concerning agency independence and the relationship with the military confronted IVS as it did VNCS, but IVS was the most visible of the voluntary agencies and the only one operating exclusively under government contract. A series of minor skirmishes finally came to a head when a USAID education administrator refused to sanction Luce's placement of six IVS English teachers at the University of Hue. On a hot and humid July 4, 1967, Luce and seventy of IVS's staff gathered at the agency's Saigon headquarters to discuss agency problems with USAID. The assembled men and women worked as English teachers, social workers, engineers, and agronomists in the rural areas of Vietnam. Few of the faces in the room appeared to be over thirty—most were only a few years out of college. Luce started the meeting by explaining the situation in Hue. The school's dean requested IVS teachers, and Luce responded by assigning teachers from other areas. USAID rejected the placement, said Luce, because USAID denied all U.S. assistance to the university. Hue was the center of the Anti-American Struggle Movement of 1966, and it was an active hotbed of student rebellion against the South Vietnamese government.

Luce remembered the room as being charged with electricity: "We wanted to know if we were in Vietnam to meet Vietnamese needs as they defined them or to play politics with humanitarian aid."[51] The lively conversation that followed confirmed this assessment, but those gathered wanted to discuss more than their desire for administrative freedom. They wanted to discuss the future of IVS in Vietnam. One volunteer working with refugees, for example, voiced concerns that his work "eased the moral conscience of the American public and military leaders." The U.S. military caused refugees by bombings and defoliation, said another volunteer, while we "bind up the wounds and take care of the aftermath."[52]

A teacher of English voiced similar concerns. She worried that English skills gave the Vietnamese people tools to rip apart the traditional Vietnamese social order. The teachers claimed that most of their students either took jobs with the Vietnamese government or worked for the U.S. government as interpreters and spies. "We want [our students] to know that there are good Americans along with the bad . . . but are we truly helping [them] by teaching language skills?"[53] For Gene Stoltzfus, a Mennonite and six-year IVS veteran, the issue was one of basic morality. It was not unpatriotic to disassociate radically from an immoral war. He believed the war poisoned the very relationships IVS volunteers were sent to establish. Longtime Vietnamese friends expressed reservations about his work. Is it possible, he asked, to win the hearts and minds of people who did not even trust an IVS volunteer? Stoltzfus was among the group that argued for turning in PX cards, turning down Army mail privileges, refusing transport on military planes, and internationalizing IVS funding and volunteer recruitment.[54]

Stoltzfus's suggestions carried moral weight, but even these small steps spurred intense debate. Some wanted to take more concerted action against the war, while others questioned whether IVS wanted to be known for its antiwar activities. For David Gitelson, community-development specialist in the Mekong Delta region, the proper response to the war's destruction was to publicize U.S. military atrocities. Gitelson was collecting complaints from Vietnamese villagers about mistargeted bombs, crops ruined by Agent Orange, and the murder of civilians by U.S. soldiers. He planned to give these complaints to a visiting congressional delegation headed by Senator Ted Kennedy. Gitelson's activities ignited a long discussion about whether IVS should actively take part in "politics." One of Gitelson's foes shot back, "Our job is to help people. . . . [W]e are effective precisely because we are Americans in an increasingly American oriented country." Public protest was "ego-gratification" and did not take into account the long-term interests of Vietnam.[55]

At the conclusion of this exchange, a long silence ensued. It was at this point, remembered Luce, that members of IVS's Vietnamese advisory board addressed the group. "Whether U.S. policies are good or bad," one speaker concluded, "you cannot escape association with them. I advise you to tell the American people what your government is doing in Vietnam, with the hope that a change will bring a better plan than the present one." Another speaker reached a similar if not more blunt conclusion: "If you really want to help the Vietnamese people then you must help us find peace."[56]

According to Luce, the board's comments came as a shock to the young IVS volunteers. The idea that saving Vietnam meant changing American minds was the opposite of everything they were told. Protesting the war was a radical step that jeopardized IVS's funding and its mission of "people-to-people" development.[57] Yet the idea was extremely attractive to a vocal group of IVS volunteers, including Luce, Stoltzfus, and Gitelson. "It became inevitable," wrote Luce, "that our commitment to Vietnam would take on political overtones. . . . [O]ur early humanitarian motives for wishing to serve . . . were being thwarted."[58] Several days after the meeting, Luce and Gitelson were playing Ping-Pong in the Saigon headquarters. Gitelson suggested writing a letter to President Johnson to address their complaints and suggest solutions for ending the war. The two composed a letter on the Ping-Pong table that eventually made its way to Ambassador Bunker and President Johnson. Forty-six members of IVS signed the letter.[59] Five hours after telexing the letter to the White

House, Luce sent the letter to veteran Vietnam correspondent Bernard Weintraub of *The New York Times*. Luce, Stoltzfus, Willie Meyers, and Don Ronk tendered their resignations at the same time. A story summarizing the letter and announcing the resignations appeared on the front page of *The New York Times* on September 19, 1967.[60]

From all reports, after reading the *Times* article, President Johnson was livid. He understood that the letter and the resignations could not be easily dismissed. The IVS defections questioned one of the moral pillars that undergirded his Vietnam policy. Luce and his colleagues were not a group of young radicals calling for an immediate withdrawal of U.S. troops. They were from the generation of volunteers canonized in the Peace Corps, the idealistic young generation who believed that service abroad cemented ties of friendship in less-developed countries. The letter eloquently listed the failures of "the other war"—the corruption of South Vietnam's presidential elections, the inefficiencies of the Vietnamese economy, the negligence of the U.S. military, and the hatred of the Vietnamese people for the U.S. intervention. What these IVS volunteers heard and experienced contradicted the bright, shining lies of the war's military and political planners. At its most pointed, the letter read, "We are finding it difficult . . . [to help] the people in Vietnam. . . . It has become evident that our small successes only blind us to how little . . . the effect is in the face of present realities in Vietnam. Thus to stay in Vietnam and remain silent is to fail to respond to the first need of the Vietnamese people—peace."[61]

The letter and the resignations brought voluntary agencies briefly to the forefront of the antiwar movement. In testimony before Senator Kennedy's Senate subcommittee, Luce pointed to the incongruities between "winning hearts and minds" and maiming bodies and land. It was a "myth," said Luce, to assume that more money and more machines would "bring victory." U.S. technology and military might "are seen by Vietnamese peasants as the greatest threat to their well being. . . . [I]t is not difficult to understand why the NLF [National Liberation Front] finds it easier to solicit the cooperation of the villagers."[62] With generous funding from the Women's Division of the Methodist Church, Luce, along with Stoltzfus and Meyers, took this message on the road.[63] Luce appeared on the *Today* show in early October 1967 and spent the next five months touring the country, speaking to more than two hundred college, civic, and business groups, and writing articles for national magazines.[64] In May 1968, Luce joined the "Methodist Vietnam Project" and spoke to the platform committees for both the Republican and Democratic National Conventions.[65]

Luce and his colleagues argued that the United States's benevolence made little impact on the course of the war. Agricultural improvements and better livestock herds turned out to benefit the National Liberation Front, which taxed the villagers for food. An estimated 325,000 farmers had had their crops destroyed by chemical defoliation.[66] Forced reallocations of villages into "safe" districts only uprooted millions of families from their lands and the graves of their ancestors. And the infrastructure built by voluntary agencies was often destroyed later in military action.

Luce and many like-minded aid workers and missionaries openly challenged the idea that religiously based humanitarianism functioned as a complement to U.S. foreign policy. Church groups working overseas slowly realized the wide gulf between their mission and that of the state. The initial question confronting voluntary agencies in 1965 was how best to serve the suffering persons in a war zone. By 1968, the question became how best to address the root causes of suffering. The crucial idea supporting this shift was that the U.S. government was to blame for creating the misery and the refugees in Vietnam. Previously, only the regimes of communist dictators faced charges of exporting humanitarian atrocities. It was easy to support victims of Stalin, Castro, Mao, Kim Il Sung, or Ho Chin Minh, given the popular anticommunism of U.S. culture and the real human tragedy taking place. Yet in the depths of the Vietnam War, many young volunteers from IVS and VNCS believed that it was their moral duty to initiate action against U.S. government policy.

After the Tet Offensive of February 1968, this feeling intensified. Tet proved to be the turning point of the war. During a holiday cease-fire, the NLF (or Viet Cong) led attacks on all the major cities and military installations in South Vietnam. NLF guerrillas breached the walls of the U.S. embassy and fought a pitched battle on the grounds. Ironically, the Tet Offensive was both a major defeat and a victory for the NLF. Though most of the NLF's fighting force was wiped out in the battle, Tet turned the tide of public opinion in the United States. As Secretary of State Dean Rusk later described it, "When the networks broadcast footage of Vietcong sappers inside the walls of the American Embassy in Saigon, the inevitable impression was that the American effort in South Vietnam had simply gone to hell."[67] Tet also cleared away any lingering doubts among some voluntary-agency staff about their remaining mission. After 1968, the staff and new recruits of voluntary agencies, in the words of one IVS board member, "continued to be infected" by the "political awakening articulated in the [Luce] letter" and its subsequent publicity.[68]

In the summer of 1968, personnel from IVS and VNCS took the lead in organizing a monthly meeting of voluntary-agency staff to talk about common concerns and coordinate events with the domestic antiwar movement. In October 1969, at the same time as the Moratorium Movement in the United States, the group drafted a letter to President Richard Nixon and held a press conference calling for an immediate cease-fire, peace negotiations, and the phased withdrawal of U.S. troops. Later that year, they held a Christmas vigil for peace in front of Saigon's cathedral and passed out an open letter to South Vietnam's President Thieu in the form of a Christmas card. Several of those in attendance were arrested. In May 1970, seventy-five aid workers and missionaries signed a letter to President Nixon, condemning

U.S. intervention in Cambodia and the crackdown against the student movement, which, they claimed, was carried out with U.S. funds and supplies. In December 1971, a letter was sent to U.N. Secretary General U Thant, asking him to investigate potential U.S. war crimes.[69]

Once voluntary-agency personnel became critics of their own nation's foreign policy, it was not long before they sought to aid "the other side." Voluntary agencies always articulated the hope of offering humanitarian aid to war victims in North Vietnam, but the political climate was inhospitable to such charity. As one voluntary-agency director remarked, aiding North Vietnamese war victims "would be a holy and just thing to do, but it is simply impossible."[70] The American Friends Service Committee was the first to skirt the restriction on exports to North Vietnam. The Quakers sent money and medical supplies through Eastern European organizations. VNCS wanted to make a more direct approach. On September 14, 1967, VNCS Director Leatherman and several other voluntary-agency representatives asked Ambassador Bunker if they could develop programs to bring relief aid and community-development projects to areas controlled by the NLF. Bunker adamantly told Leatherman that aid to the NLF was an "act of treason" and that as "guests" of the South Vietnamese government the VNCS had no right to oppose official policy.[71]

Despite Bunker's warnings, the executive board of MCC decided to establish informal diplomatic contacts with the North Vietnamese Government (DRV). As VNCS's first director, Beechy was asked to carry out this assignment. During the summer of 1968, Beechy traveled to six DRV diplomatic missions in Paris, Algiers, Prague, Berlin, New Delhi, and Phnom Penh. According to Beechy's final report, his mission was to introduce DRV representatives to Mennonite beliefs and peace positions, review MCC's history in relief and development, and propose aid projects. Beechy was not able to convince DRV officials of the seriousness of MCC's intent, but the door was left open for sending relief supplies and medicines.[72] Two years later, Beechy and Hostetter, a former VNCS volunteer, traveled to North Vietnam on a similar mission. Beechy and Hostetter again stressed their peaceful intentions and added that they desired to work toward ending the war. Though the DRV would not accept MCC personnel, they gladly accepted relief supplies and invited Beechy and Hostetter to discuss specific development projects. Between 1970 and 1975, MCC contributed about $70,000 to relief shipments for North Vietnam and began negotiations to build hospitals and schools there once peace was restored.[73] The Beechy-Hostetter missions to the DRV did not cause the public outcry that accompanied the visits of more celebrated U.S. citizens to Hanoi, but new laws forbidding "aiding the enemy" did postpone several projects.[74] The contacts made by MCC and other voluntary agencies signaled a willingness to pursue an independent foreign policy—even if that meant making common cause with a nation at war with the United States.[75] Voluntary agencies acted on the assumption that their mission of alleviating poverty and aiding the suffering superseded national interests and boundaries.

There were limits to pursuing a critical stance against U.S. policy, however. After the IVS controversy, USAID recruited civilian administrators to oversee aid projects in every Vietnamese province. The effect of this change was the drastic reduction of voluntary-agency programs, staff, and funding. By 1971, the feeding programs of VNCS and several other agencies were unilaterally cut. In August of that same year, the South Vietnamese government terminated IVS's contract. Hugh Manke, IVS's director, issued a public letter accusing President Thieu and USAID of conspiring to oust IVS.[76] Manke believed that the South Vietnamese government was still piqued by Luce's attempts to publicize the failures of U.S. policy. The fact that IVS personnel wrote and signed letters of protest and testified before Congress about the inadequacies of the pacification and refugee programs only confirmed the image of IVS as an "overtly political organization."[77] As the war wound down, voluntary agencies that opposed the war found themselves in similar predicaments. As a result of their politicized reputations, their presence rapidly disintegrated—ending both their humanitarian missions and their roles as witness to the moral failures of U.S. foreign policy in South Vietnam.

CONCLUSION

Jim Linn, the last director of IVS, wrote an analysis of the shifting objectives and attitudes among IVS volunteers. His conclusions serve as a fitting epilogue for all religiously based humanitarian services in Vietnam. According to Linn, the "Old IVS" began with the goal of providing low-level technical development. The volunteer worked at the grassroots with Vietnamese youth groups, churches, and charitable organizations. IVS was "non-political," wrote Linn, because of the very nature of its approach. The "New IVS," however, "took on an almost opposite character." The new objectives stressed ending the war and changing the government of Vietnam. Linn, sympathetic to those who took a moral stand against the war, argued that those committed to the new IVS did so because it "provided a more relevant response to the situation in the country." IVS personnel used their language training, contacts with the media, and antiwar student groups to effect political change.[78]

As the Linn report implicitly recognized, the political stances taken by voluntary agencies provided the impetus for permanently challenging the church-state partnership abroad. The many young people who staffed IVS and VNCS were unfamiliar with the postwar partnership that had rebuilt most of Europe and parts of Asia. Without a connection to this past, many conceived their mission to be the protection of the poor and the refugees. If voluntary agencies surmised that their government caused poverty and refugee flows, it was their moral duty to call it to account.

If a prophetic stance did not change government behavior, they took it upon themselves to agitate until change occurred. To achieve their goals, they would make temporary alliances with the press, with like-minded secular groups, or with the revolutionary claims of Developing World nationals. According to one expert on postwar voluntary agencies, "in such a political climate it is not surprising that agency representatives came to see their function as compensating for government policies rather than complementing them."[79]

The new activism among voluntary agencies in Vietnam highlights the role of U.S. religion in shaping (and destroying) the post–World War II consensus on foreign policy. The U.S. government actively recruited individuals and groups willing to provide humanitarian services in Vietnam, yet many of those who participated became vocal critics of U.S. foreign policy, providing an often bitterly divided U.S. public with a compassionate and morally indignant view of the U.S. war policy. There may be no way to quantify how much influence voluntary agencies had in directly shaping the course of the Vietnam War, but they could not be ignored by those managing the war in Vietnam or in Washington, D.C., those opposing it on the home front, or the broad middle of a populace struggling to fashion a consistent and Christian position on war, peace, foreign aid, and human rights.

14 / In the Modern World, but Not of It

The "Auca Martyrs," Evangelicalism, and Postwar American Culture

Kathryn T. Long

On January 6, 1956, five young men, all evangelical missionaries from the United States, made their first face-to-face contact with members of the Huaorani, or Huao people, then called Aucas ("savages"), at a camp on a sandbar beside the Curaray River in the eastern jungles of Ecuador.[1] That Friday morning, three days after the men had established the outpost they had nicknamed Palm Beach, Jim Elliot, Nate Saint, Roger Youderian, Pete Fleming, and Ed McCully stood along the riverbank, shouting phrases in the Huao language and waving gifts toward the jungle on the other side of the river, in an attempt to encourage the Huaorani to visit their camp. Suddenly, three natives, a man and two women, did appear on the far bank. The exuberant Elliot yanked off his shirt and trousers and waded across the river to greet the visitors. After some initial hesitancy, the Huaorani spent the day on the beach, sampling lemonade and hamburgers, leafing through *Time* magazine, and watching the missionaries demonstrate such marvels of modern civilization "as rubber bands, balloons, and a yo-yo."[2] The missionaries took photographs and home movies of the encounter, the first time the Huaorani had been photographed in their own territory. Pilot Saint gave the man, nicknamed "George," three short rides over the nearby Huao village in Saint's Piper Cruiser, the small plane that had transported the missionaries and their supplies to the Palm Beach rendezvous point.[3]

The Huaorani left at nightfall and did not return the next day. The following day, Sunday, January 8, Saint's reconnaissance flight revealed a group of men heading toward the Curaray beach. In radio contact with his wife, Saint commented, "Looks like they'll be here for an early-afternoon service. Pray for us. This *is* the day!"[4] It was the last transmission from the beach. Three days later, a missionary pilot flying over the camp sighted a body, clad in khaki pants and a T-shirt, floating facedown about a quarter of a mile downriver. Friday, January 13, a ground party of Ecuadorian soldiers and missionaries reached the site and found four bodies caught in river debris; all had been speared to death. The remains of the fifth man were never recovered. In the eerie semidarkness of a tropical storm, the men were hastily buried in a common grave on the edge of the beach where they had died.[5]

Five young men, motivated by the desire to preach the Christian gospel to a hostile tribe in a remote South American jungle, lost their lives in that same isolated area. This tragic incident seemed destined to become a part of the legacy of twentieth-century Christian martyrdom that writer Susan Bergman has described as the "shadow narrative of this century's news." Eclipsed by headline coverage of wars, politics, world leaders, and celebrities, the estimated 26 million Christians throughout the world who were killed during the twentieth century at least in part because they professed the Christian faith represent, according to Bergman, "mostly unnoticed losses."[6]

Far from languishing in obscurity, however, the deaths of these five missionaries and their efforts to evangelize the Huaorani became perhaps the most highly publicized missionary story of twentieth-century American Protestantism, a narrative that quickly moved from the periphery into the spotlight of popular attention. During the week following the deaths, reports in newspapers throughout the United States focused national attention on the ideals and the fate of the slain men. Subsequent articles in *Time, Newsweek, The New York Times Sunday Magazine, Life,* and *Reader's Digest* helped sustain reader interest from the time the deaths occurred until the publication in 1957 of *Through Gates of Splendor,* Jim Elliot's wife, Elisabeth's, best-selling book-length account of the five missionaries' efforts. Coverage in the popular press, particularly influential photojournalism essays in *Life* magazine, both set the stage for Elliot's book and influenced the style and format of *Through Gates of Splendor* in ways that made it a uniquely twentieth-century version of the classic evangelical missionary martyr narrative.[7]

Through Gates of Splendor, in turn, appealed to both general and religious readers. Within the evangelical community, it accelerated the process of transforming Elliot, Saint, Fleming, Youderian, and McCully from admirable though perhaps misguided victims of hostile native peoples into icons of evangelical spirituality and missionary commitment. During the past four decades, stories of their lives, of their deaths, and of the subsequent missionary activities among the Huaorani have become an ongoing missionary saga, told in more than thirteen books, as well as via filmstrip, comic books, cassette tapes, radio drama, stage play, film, videotape, and television.[8]

What was it about these particular missionaries and their story that captured the imaginations of the American public, particularly Protestants? Why did they become such powerful religious symbols, when more than seventy other missionaries from the United States also died violent deaths in situations related to their Christian witness during the twentieth century?[9] Why was so much attention given to this particular jungle tragedy, and what might the publicity tell us about missionaries, American popular culture, and American neo-evangelicalism in the 1950s?

Clues come from three sources and their interrelationships: first, the "monuments" or records left by the men themselves, especially their photographs and diaries; second, the media coverage that initially established the public character of the event; and finally, the efforts of evangelical martyrologists to provide the didactic framework that transformed the narrative from one of tragedy to one of triumph. Together, these three elements illustrate a cooperative effort between evangelicals and the popular press. Mostly spontaneous, the collaboration indicated both an increasing evangelical sophistication during the 1950s concerning publicity, as well as a new openness on the part of the mainstream media toward neo-evangelicals, or "progressive fundamentalists."[10]

The publicity during 1956 and 1957 surrounding the story of the Ecuador missionaries both reflected and facilitated the fundamentalist reengagement with American culture characteristic of the late 1940s and the 1950s and usually symbolized by the increasing popularity of Billy Graham. Historian Joel Carpenter has emphasized two impulses that helped propel fundamentalists toward this engagement: the desire for national revival and a missionary urge to reach the world for Christ. Graham represented the push for revival; the story of the "Auca martyrs" communicated the spiritual ideals and world vision of fundamentalism to the broader American public. For evangelicals themselves, the narrative became a lodestar of ideal piety: a beacon reaffirming the missionary imperative and reminding evangelicals of their classic spiritual commitments as they faced the temptations and accommodations of cultural reengagement.[11] The story of Operation Auca, as it was called, suggested that evangelicals could indeed achieve the elusive ideal of participating *in* the modern world without becoming a part *of* that world.

PUBLICITY SURROUNDING THE MISSIONARIES' DEATHS

For the first Protestant martyrologists, such as sixteenth-century apologists John Foxe and Miles Coverdale, the "acts and monuments" of the English martyrs included "not only their beliefs and heroic actions, but the documents which recorded their achievements." These documents could be used to help rescue the martyrs from the "pit of oblivion."[12]

For those who told the story of the Ecuador missionaries, both members of the popular press and evangelical writers, visual "monuments" in the form of photographs and film likewise became a powerful element in preserving and commemorating the missionaries' lives and deaths. Saint had taken one such photograph during the men's first friendly encounter with the Huaorani on the last Friday of their lives. It is a black-and-white shot of Gimari, a young Huao woman whom the men had dubbed "Delilah." She is holding—almost dangling between her thumb and fingers—a copy of the 1956 "Man of the Year" issue of *Time* magazine, dated January 2, only four days earlier.[13]

This simple photo illustrates four key elements that contributed to the publicity surrounding the missionaries' deaths and the appeal of their story to American audiences. First, it captured the impact of the post–World War II communications revolution, a revolution that touched Protestant missions as well as all other sectors of American life. Second, it represented fundamentalist engagement in the postwar world and showed that engagement clearly as a two-way street. Third, the photo conveyed the allure technology held for Americans, and, fourth, the fascination surrounding the mysterious, and purportedly "savage," Huaorani.

The Communications Revolution

Missionaries in the 1950s might still have answered the traditional call to take the Christian message to the ends of the earth, but those geographic reaches were increasingly a part of the postwar global village. Aviation and radio technology in particular fostered rapid communication. The five missionaries had used a small plane to locate and attempt contact with the Huaorani, an isolated jungle tribe; that same plane enabled them to keep up with national and international news. As a result, they not only carried *Time* magazine with them to their jungle camp, they had the most recent issue.

In the same way, because of the communications revolution, within twenty-four hours after radio bulletins on Monday, January 9, 1956, reported the men missing, articles about them appeared in at least two U.S. newspapers, the *Chicago Daily News* and the *Milwaukee Journal.* Within forty-eight hours, many others, including *The New York Times, Chicago Tribune, Atlanta Journal,* and *Los Angeles Times,* carried the story. For approximately four days, from Wednesday, January 11, until Saturday, January 14, 1956, U.S. readers followed the daily unfolding of the missionary drama in Ecuador—from the first news of the missing men, to confirmation of their deaths at the hands of the Huaorani, to news of the burial on Palm Beach, to reports of the widows flown over the site to see their husbands' graves. This coverage reinforced the message conveyed by the copy of *Time* in Saint's photo: the sandbar on the Curaray and missionary activity there were not nearly so isolated as they might have seemed.

Neo-evangelicals and the Postwar Cultural Engagement

The presence of a news magazine on the Curaray beach also represented a second element essential to the early publicity surrounding the missionaries' deaths, the postwar cultural engagement of neo-evangelicals. Missionaries, even in the jungles of Ecuador, were reading *Time,* not to mention an occasional novel.[14] By the mid-

1950s, American evangelicals, including those conservative faith-mission groups working in Ecuador, increasingly viewed themselves as part of the broader post-war world. *Christianity Today,* destined to become the flagship publication for the emerging evangelical movement, first appeared in October of the year Elliot, Saint, McCully, Fleming, and Youderian died. Also in 1956, Billy Graham made a final break with the separatist fundamentalism of Bob Jones, Carl McIntire, and John R. Rice when he accepted an invitation from the Protestant Council of New York to hold a 1957 crusade in Madison Square Garden.[15]

Historians analyzing neo-evangelical public-relations acumen during this period have focused primarily on revivalists. However, American missionaries in Ecuador, particularly those associated with missionary radio station HCJB, based in Quito, displayed a similar sophistication as they channeled information about the missing missionaries via radio and print to the rest of the world. By Tuesday, January 10, Abe C. Van Der Puy, field director for HCJB and president of the Intermission Fellowship of Ecuador, had written the first of a series of press releases describing the mission to the Huaorani and search efforts for the men. The reports provided information for the Associated Press (AP) bulletins and other articles used in newspapers worldwide, as well as for evangelical periodicals. Coverage broadened Thursday morning, January 12, when NBC *Today* show host Dave Garroway appeared on television to conduct an interview, via two-way radio, with HCJB founder Clarence Jones about the probable deaths of at least some of the men. In their own newsletters, the missionaries later marveled that "the Auca Epic [*sic*] was world news."[16] Yet they, themselves, had played no small role in helping to make it so.

The Allure of Technology

The simple fact that photographs existed and survived from the missionaries' first contact with the Huaorani illustrated the fascination technology held for the five men, particularly for pilot Saint. Even the physical evidence remaining after the men's deaths gave mute testimony to this aspect of their lives: the "relics" of their martyrdom included Saint's Rolleiflex, a high-quality, twin-lens reflex camera, recovered from the river, as well as the skeleton of their plane, deserted on the beach, its wings stripped of fabric. Of course, a penchant for technology and a problem-solving mentality had long been characteristic of American missionaries.[17] But rarely had it been so explicitly publicized or had it dovetailed so neatly with the interests of people on the home front. The prominence of photography and of aviation transformed the story of Operation Auca and heightened popular interest in it.

For example, in addition to keeping the traditional missionary diaries and journals, the men took home movies of each phase of their efforts to contact the Huaorani, including their final days on the Curaray River. These eventually were edited as part of a thirty-six-minute inspirational film, produced in 1961 and given the same title as Elisabeth Elliot's book, *Through Gates of Splendor.* These movies, supplemented by still photographs, gave the story of what was called "Operation Auca" a sense of "you are there," new to missionary narratives yet strikingly parallel to the immediacy that drew audiences to mass-circulation photo magazines such as *Life* and *Look,* as well as to television news.[18]

The role of aviation also provided a fresh angle of interest to the efforts of the Ecuador five at a time when people in the United States had begun to travel by plane in record numbers. Early AP stories identified the men as "flying missionaries," while a *Time* magazine report described how they had prepared for their face-to-face encounter by using a plane to locate and circle isolated Huao clearings in the jungle, "shouting down greetings in Auca over a loudspeaker and dropping gifts of machetes, bright beads and clothing."[19] The description of these aerial exploits recorded in Saint's diary added an element of adventure and narrative depth to later magazine and book accounts of Operation Auca. It also reflected the men's optimism that the results of their innovative techniques would overcome the Huaorani hostility toward outsiders. Only later would a few voices wonder whether such inventive use of aviation represented an effective anthropological approach.[20]

Fascination with the "Savage Aucas"

Life magazine, which on January 30, 1956, ran a ten-page photo report of the missionaries' deaths, and which had exclusive rights to Saint's photographs, did not use the picture featuring "Delilah" and its sister publication *Time.* The editors did, however, use another of Saint's photos, one of the Huaorani man named Naenkiwi, whom the men had nicknamed "George." The caption read in part, "A Savage Auca, . . . photographed by Saint on first white contact in years with untamed Aucas."[21] Underlying both popular and evangelical interest in the missionary story and heightening its drama were a number of contrasts or tensions, including the contrast between the "stone-age" primitivism of the Huaorani and the technology and civilization of the missionaries, as well as the contrast between the savagery attributed to the native people and the "wholesome, small-college boy" image surrounding the five young men.[22]

Both newspapers and newsmagazines emphasized the latter contrast as another major angle of the story. Articles routinely demonized the Huaorani and in a somewhat more muted fashion idealized the middle-class wholesomeness of the young missionaries. The word "savage" and its derivations became the most popular descriptor for the Huaorani. The word *Auca* itself was an epithet from the Quechua language, meaning "savage" in the most derogatory sense of the word. The Huaorani were "among the world's most bloodthirsty savages," "savage, stone-age tribesmen," and "savage, head-hunting . . . Indians," who killed out of "sheer savagery" and who lived in the "green hell" of the Amazon jungles.[23]

In contrast, the popular press portrayed the missionaries as victims, "massacred" by the natives, "struck down" by their "sharp, ten-foot-long lances" in a mysterious and treacherous turn of events after their first friendly contact with the tribe.[24] However, Saint, Elliot, McCully, Youderian, and Fleming were not portrayed as hapless or helpless in meeting their deaths; rather, they were intrepid explorers of the air and the jungles, "strong young men [who] had left carpentry and law, the horrors of war and the arms of their wives to fly into a Latin-American jungle valley shadowed with death."[25]

The Huaorani were, in fact, among the most feared indigenous peoples of South America. Even so, publicity surrounding the missionaries' deaths sensationalized the Huao people and dehumanized their character. They were mistakenly identified as headhunters and described as having "the instincts of jungle beasts [combined] with human intelligence."[26] Newspapers also printed erroneous reports that the Huaorani had mutilated and decapitated the bodies. Since 1949, press coverage of both mainline Protestant and Roman Catholic missionaries had focused largely on the atrocities and suffering they had experienced at the hands of Chinese communists. Though communism played no role in the deaths of the missionaries in Ecuador, press accounts of the tragedy drew from the familiar themes of missionary courage in the face of savagery and danger.[27]

Photographs of the Ecuador five distributed by the AP, or, in a few cases, provided directly by the families, showed young men who were a far cry from the starch and formality of the Victorian missionary. They looked like "all-American boys." McCully was pictured in an open-collared shirt, rather than a suit and tie; Saint exuded the confidence of a young pilot with a grin on his face and a billed cap shoved back on his head. The AP wire service also circulated photographs of the men and their families, pictures that mirrored millions of other postwar couples doing their best to produce the "baby boom" generation. Together, the images communicated lives full of promise, lives dedicated to missionary service, lives that, according to accompanying headlines, had been tragically cut short.[28] In contrast to Huao savagery, these young men and their wives exemplified American missionary idealism, the postwar idealism that encompassed evangelicals and humanitarian workers alike and that invested other young Americans abroad, such as Roman Catholic medical doctor Tom Dooley in Laos, with a kind of celebrity status.[29]

CORNELL CAPA AND *LIFE* MAGAZINE COVERAGE

The summary and the climax to the intense publicity surrounding the men's deaths came in the form of a documentary essay in the January 30, 1956, issue of *Life* magazine entitled, "'Go Ye and Preach the Gospel': Five Do and Die." This article, produced by Cornell Capa, a photojournalist and Hungarian immigrant, picked up on earlier themes but moved beyond them to heighten the impact of the missionaries' deaths. On assignment for *Life,* Capa accompanied the search party on the Curaray River as they recovered and buried the bodies of the slain missionaries. His photographs documented the reality of what had happened: a partially submerged body, white rubber soles of tennis shoes visible and a Huao spear protruding from the right hip; the darkness and torrential storm that shrouded the quick burial service on the beach. However, Capa cared more about capturing the connection between parents and children than he did about recording scenes of death, a concern that appealed to the family-centered ethos of the United States in the 1950s. His most powerful pictures in the *Life* article were of the missionary widows, children in their arms, facing with fortitude and faith the news of their husbands' deaths.[30]

The *Life* article was the first in a popular publication explicitly to describe the men as "martyrs"; and it took full advantage of the magazine's "visually assertive" style to highlight Capa's own photographs, as well as those taken by Saint. The bold photographs were made even more powerful by Capa's decision to draw heavily from Fleming's and Saint's diaries, as well as briefly from Elliot's journal. This approach allowed the dead men to communicate their own idealism, adventurousness, and sense of mission. They had, as *Life* faithfully communicated to an America still generally in sympathy with such ideals, gone to preach the gospel to those who had never heard it, and they had trusted in God for the outcome.

The two elements of photography and first-person narrative enhanced the emotional power of the piece and provided an approach to content and format that anticipated the highly effective and similar method employed by Elisabeth Elliot in *Through Gates of Splendor.* The combination of inspiration, adventure, immediacy, and powerful images touched a chord among *Life's* readers. According to publisher Andrew Heiskell, they praised it as "the most inspiring article ever in *Life*" and "*Life's* greatest reporting feat."[31] Nearly four decades later, Capa remembered the story as his "most rewarding assignment," one that elicited "a deluge of enthusiastic letters."[32] Ironically, through this article and subsequent work, Capa, a self-described "nonobservant Hungarian Jew" and humanitarian, would come to stand second only to Elisabeth Elliot as the martyrologist who provided images and highlighted themes that would come to define for American popular culture the deaths of the five missionaries.[33]

Widespread response to newspaper coverage and the *Life* story indicated the depth of popular interest in the Ecuador martyrs. From an evangelical perspective, however, the apologetic for the men's lives was incomplete. Although most articles had been sympathetic to the missionaries and their ideals, muted criticism and questions had surfaced. A letter to the editor published in the *Milwaukee Journal* doubted the appropriateness of U.S. missionaries' trying to impose their values on "a people of a completely different life and culture from our own."[34] A Bill Vaughan column in the *Kansas City Star* satirized the dark picture of Huao savagery in the popular press by comparing it to the banalities of American civilization.[35] One writer confessed that he, "with multitudes of others—had read the news accounts of this episode and silently grumbled, 'What was the matter with 'em? Did they let some storefront sectarianism unhinge their reason to the extent that they muddled into that jungle armed only with a Bible and good intentions?'"[36]

Yet most newspapers simply focused on the drama and tragedy of the story: a missionary adventure gone dramatically awry. The pattern of news coverage, beginning with reports of the missionaries' disappearance in Huao territory and concluding with their burial, conveyed a sense of human failure. The missionaries had engaged in a heroic but ultimately futile gesture. As Elisabeth Elliot would later write, "To the world at large this was a sad waste of five young lives."[37] Even the *Life* article, with its strong overtones of valor and martyrdom, chronicled only the final months and days of five men's lives. Again, according to Elliot, "Cornell Capa wrote of death."[38]

In death, the "Auca martyrs" had become national figures. Their compatriots clearly were drawn to the story of these young men: their faith, their wholesomeness, their ingenuity, their pioneering adventures, their deaths at the hands of a jungle people. But in the news reports, the spiritual meaning of the Ecuador missionaries' deaths was still not clear, and in that sense, their transformation from victims to martyrs was not complete. As historian David Loades has pointed out, martyrologies almost always have "a didactic purpose."[39] It remained for evangelical authors, first Abe C. Van Der Puy and, most important, Elisabeth Elliot, to clarify that purpose.

The process of apotheosis that transformed five missing missionaries into the "saints of the Curaray" accelerated in August 1956 with the publication of "Through Gates of Splendor," an eighteen-page "book condensation" in *Reader's Digest,* written by Van Der Puy, who had been the missionary spokesman in Ecuador during the January tragedy. His article marked the transition from secular to evangelical narrators of the martyrs' story. The title of the piece, taken from a hymn the slain missionaries had chosen as a kind of theme for their efforts, sounded a clear note of triumph. The fourth verse proclaims, "Thine [God's] is the battle, Thine shall be the praise; When passing through the gates of pearly splendor, Victors, we rest with Thee, through endless days."[40] The dead men were no longer victims, buried in a shallow jungle grave. Rather, they were victors, and their jungle camp the gateway to heaven itself.

Although the *Reader's Digest* selection was billed as a condensation from a book by Van Der Puy soon to be published by Harper and Brothers, when the actual book appeared in May 1957, its author was Elisabeth Elliot. Even more than Van Der Puy, Elliot possessed the eyewitness perspective and literary skills to craft a powerful chronicle of Operation Auca that offered readers adventure as well as inspiration. She drew heavily from the unpublished writings of the slain men, shaped into a fast-paced narrative and given dimension through descriptions that vividly evoked the local color of missionary life in the Ecuadorian jungles. Like that of many of the most effective fundamentalist or evangelical communicators, Elliot's writing was nonsectarian but deeply evangelical.[41]

Elliot brought a sure sense of piety to the work as well as an intuitive understanding of the mood of American popular culture. The book included clear expressions of the all-out Christian commitment the men shared. Their comments represented updated versions of the call to total surrender or consecration characteristic of the Keswick piety of fundamentalism. McCully wanted to "live a life of reckless abandon to the Lord"; Saint found joy in leaving "the old life of chasing things that are of a temporal sort"; Youderian sought to "live following Him [Christ] every second of my life."[42] To Americans who in the mid-1950s had rediscovered their fascination with the frontier West, Elizabeth Elliot presented the men as "missionary pioneers—always looking . . . beyond immediate horizons." Some evangelicals at home had already made that connection. A letter to the editor of the *Sunday School Times* pointed out that the story had "especial interest to youth, with its frontier background and very modern pioneering objective," and suggested that it "might well be the base for a fine movie."[43] Finally, while the book did not dodge questions surrounding the men's death, Elliot expressed the widows' conviction that "this was not a tragedy" but, rather, "was what God had planned."[44]

With Elliot's text and a generous selection of photographs edited by Capa, *Through Gates of Splendor* was an immediate best-seller. Within eight months of its publication on May 29, 1957, more than 175,000 copies had been sold, leading one evangelical reviewer to note that "as far as circulation is concerned [it is] the leading missionary book of this generation."[45] The book was published at an ideal moment as well, in the midst of what seemed like a flurry of favorable media attention focused on neo-evangelicals. Most prominent was the extensive publicity surrounding Graham's Madison Square Garden Crusade, which opened on May 15, two weeks before the book appeared. In mid-June, a *New York Herald Tribune* photographer snapped a picture of Graham's wife, Ruth Bell Graham, reading *Through Gates of Splendor*, with the book jacket clearly visible.[46] For his part, Capa had returned to Ecuador to photograph a follow-up story on the martyrs' widows, most of whom continued in missionary service. The article appeared in *Life* a week before the book came out. Capa mentioned *Through Gates of Splendor* in the text, alerting *Life* readers to Elliot's book. In addition, on June 5, missionary Rachel Saint, older sister of pilot Saint, was featured for her Bible-translation work on Ralph Edwards's popular NBC television series *This Is Your Life*. An estimated thirty million viewers saw Saint and her language informant, a Huao woman named Dayuma, who had left the tribe before the missionaries were slain. On Sunday evening, July 7, Saint and Dayuma, described as "the first Auca Indian of Ecuador ever to visit the United States," appeared in New York at the Graham Crusade before an audience of nineteen thousand. During their few minutes at the microphone, Saint expressed her desire to translate the Bible into the Huaorani language while Dayuma told a Bible story in the Huao language. It was the first time Graham had featured missionaries on the platform of one of his U.S. crusades.[47]

A DEFINING MISSIONARY NARRATIVE

Through these appearances and the sales of *Through Gates of Splendor,* the story of the martyrs and the ongoing dream of taking the Christian gospel to the Huaorani had touched millions of people and found a place at the heart of neo-evangelicalism. It happened in part because of the kind of people the missionaries were—quintessentially "American" and self-sacrificially Christian—and the record, in journals and on film, they left of their lives. Instead of "shadow history," the story of the "Auca martyrs" had become a defining narrative: affirming the ideals of evangelical piety for believers on the home front and confirming the increasingly close ties between neo-evangelicals and mainstream America, particularly the mass media. If Graham's Los Angeles Crusade in 1949 had signaled both the "rediscovery" of neo-evangelicals by American popular culture and the evangelical commitment to engage that culture, the eighteen months between January 1956 and June 1957 demonstrated that this new cultural collaboration was well under way. In many ways, this period may have been as significant for conservative Protestants as 1949, the year Graham rose to fame, or 1976, the "year of the evangelical" in national politics.[48]

The radio, television, newspaper, and magazine attention given to the missionaries' deaths, plus the instant popularity of *Through Gates of Splendor* alongside the Graham Madison Square Garden Crusade, affirmed that neo-evangelicals had become a significant component of American public life.[49] In terms of an impact on North American history, the story of Operation Auca would leave its most enduring legacies within American evangelicalism itself. Yet during the eighteen months considered here, and to a lesser extent into the early 1960s, accounts of the deaths of the Ecuador missionaries and of subsequent efforts to contact the Huaorani continued to fascinate many outside as well as within the evangelical camp. That broader interest both revealed and reinforced the new acceptance of former fundamentalists, now neo-evangelicals.

The decision by Harper and Brothers in New York to publish *Through Gates of Splendor* provides further evidence of neo-evangelicalism's increasing cultural legitimacy. Published by the company's religious book department, *Through Gates of Splendor* had such brisk sales that it was in the same league as such 1957 Harper trade best-sellers as Jim Bishop's *The Day Christ Died* and John F. Kennedy's *Profiles in Courage*.[50] Harper had maintained a religious book division since 1926, carrying mainstream authors such as Harry Emerson Fosdick and Elton Trueblood, along with Yale church historian and missions expert Kenneth Scott Latourette.[51] *Through Gates of Splendor* reflected a tacit recognition that evangelicals had joined the mainstream. That recognition became more explicit when the book became the first of what were called the "Harper Missionary Classics," a sixteen-volume series of evangelical missionary stories—usually biographies or missionary adventure books—published between 1956 and 1966.[52] The books helped bring missionary exploits once again to the forefront of American evangelical consciousness. Volumes related to the Ecuador martyrs came to anchor the series, including *Shadow of the Almighty* (1958), *Jungle Pilot* (1959), *The Dayuma Story* (1960), and *The Savage My Kinsman* (1961). Fundamentalists themselves had published earlier classics of missionary piety and martyrdom, such as *Borden of Yale* (Moody Bible Institute, 1926) and *The Triumph of John and Betty Stam* (the China Inland Mission, 1935). From the mid-1950s to the mid-1960s, the Harper series moved evangelical missionary stories from their twentieth-century ghettoization within conservative religious publishers into the mainstream publishing world.[53]

Released under the Harper imprint and appealing to both evangelical and broader popular audiences, *Through Gates of Splendor* was widely reviewed in the popular and religious press. Comments in the popular press were generally positive. The book was portrayed as a "strangely moving" or "stirring" account that provided a spiritual answer to the question, "Why did they do it?"[54] The five men gave their lives, one reviewer summarized, because they shared the "consecration and courage" of the early Christians. "The pages flame with a faith that goes all the way back to the days of Stephen and Peter and Paul . . . a type of Christian dedication which has almost ceased to exist."[55] Themes implicit in newspaper reports of the tragedy were clearly expressed in reviews of Elliot's book: "every conceivable device in this age of science" had combined with "ageless faith" in a heroic attempt to breach what were seen to be the last frontiers of missionary expansion. One reviewer found the openness of evangelical spirituality, with its "ever-present consciousness of God and His Son" and its assurance of having "a direct mission given to each . . . by God himself," almost embarrassing. Yet in the end, she, too, found herself drawn to "this simple narrative of the gentle friendliness of five brave, young men" against the backdrop of the nuclear age, "when human life is destroyed by the thousands with one weapon of modern warfare."[56]

The reviews reflected a popular yearning for the technologically sophisticated yet theologically simple and unambiguous faith exemplified in the book's portrayal of the five young men and their wives. Americans longed for traditional values alongside technological progress: Walt Disney's California theme park, opened in 1955, celebrated both "Main Street" and "Tomorrowland."[57] Even one of the few critical reviews of *Through Gates of Splendor* ended on a poignant note, admitting that "the book succeeds in investing the tragedy with grandeur. It leaves one haunted with a feeling almost of remorse, asking oneself if the clumsiness of the approach to so delicate an operation was really inevitable. Could it in any conditions conceivably have succeeded?"[58]

Reviewers among the religious press, particularly evangelicals, entertained no such ambivalence. As might be expected, they were even more effusive than their secular counterparts. They loved the book's style—its immediacy and authenticity, its portrayal of the drama of missionary life. "And how it is written!" exclaimed Norman R. Oke in a review for the Nazarene Minister's Book Club. "You are not a spectator from afar—rather you find yourself right in that little plane over the rain-jungles of the Andes; you live . . . the dangerous, thrilling life of a missionary." Other reviewers assured readers that there were "no sticky histrionics"; instead, the narrative was a "restrained . . . story told with feeling, but not with mawkishness."[59]

Even more important than style, however, was the book's substance. Reviewers hailed it as an exemplary missionary narrative, a spiritual classic and martyrology. Published in the midst of the dramatic post–World War II conservative missionary expansion, *Through Gates of Splendor* both rode the crest of the wave of conservative missions and contributed to the spiritual energy behind it.[60] Closely tied to the book's missionary appeal, but even more celebrated, was its devotional appeal. A review in *Christianity Today* described the book as "a spiritual experience" enabling the reader "to look into the diaries—and indeed into the hearts—of these missionary heroes and see their devotion to Christ, their utter death to self, their compassionate desires to reach those who have never heard the Gospel."[61] Selections from the diaries, especially those of Elliot, were compared to the memoirs of Robert Murray McCheyne or Samuel Rutherford, and the book as a whole viewed as a spiritual classic in the tradition of David Brainerd's *Life* or Hudson Taylor's *Spiritual Secret.*[62]

Through Gates of Splendor communicated cherished evangelical values of self-denial and dedication to Christ embodied in the lives of five young men whose backgrounds and experiences resonated with those of twentieth-century readers. Although not overly emphasized, an undercurrent in several reviews celebrated the virile spirituality of the five. After sketching the men's background, reviewer Clyde Kilby concluded, "By no stretch of the imagination could any one of the five . . . be called a religious sissy." Nor, insisted another reviewer, could their Christianity be considered "sissy stuff."[63] Whether inspired by the evangelistic adventures of the men or the more self-effacing courage of their wives, readers were encouraged in the familiar terminology of Keswick holiness to view the book as "the greatest challenge to personal dedication of our generation," a book that would help "bring to fruition a deeper consecration to the will of God."[64]

For evangelicals, then, the book fulfilled the function of a classic martyrology to instruct and inspire. It provided models of self-denying piety even as evangelicals became increasingly immersed in mainstream American culture. As they risked the loss of the separatist fundamentalist identity, the book reminded them that their heritage extended beyond denominational splits and modernist controversies to include eighteenth- and nineteenth-century missionary zeal and, from even earlier, the blood of martyrs.[65] And, finally, in contrast to some later martyr stories, such as the deaths of evangelical missionaries in Vietnam during the 1968 Tet Offensive, it provided them with a clear-cut narrative of faith and "assurance of triumph in Christ," unclouded by political complications or ambiguities. *Through Gates of Splendor* set forth with understated clarity "the collision of old and new, darkness and light, and of primal fear and hatred confronted with the love of God and His cause."[66] In the narrative of their lives and deaths, the five missionaries killed by the Huaorani were captured in time as forever young, forever "all-American," forever self-sacrificing, and forever triumphant in their Christian commitment. To readers in North America, the story stood as a powerful affirmation of the ideals and goals of conservative Protestantism. In death, the five men were what American evangelicals longed to be in life: respected but spiritually radical, simultaneously embracing and rejecting the world of twentieth-century modernity.[67]

15 / Evangelists of Destruction

Missions to Native Americans in Recent Film

Jay S. F. Blossom

"I still couldn't help wondering whether these Indians would not have preferred that the sea and the wind had not brought any of us to them."
Papal representative Altamirano,
in *The Mission*

"I thought the Lord was totally on our side."
Evangelical missionary Leslie Huben,
in *At Play in the Fields of the Lord*

The interaction between "civilized" and "primitive" people has been a staple of film drama since the 1920s. Similarly, films with missionary themes have been popular throughout cinematic history. Since the 1980s and 1990s, North American studios have released four films exploring the intersection between these two popular genres. *The Mission, Black Robe, At Play in the Fields of the Lord,* and *The Mosquito Coast,* all historical dramas, have portrayed white people going into the jungle or woods to convert Native Americans.

Like literature, film is a weapon with two sharp edges. Capable of cutting deep into its subject, it also reveals the biases of its own writers and creators and their world. These four pictures address, among other topics, gender, ethnicity, and faith—issues of central importance for late-twentieth-century North Americans. Moreover, the cinematic primitivist tradition shapes all four. Through drama, passion, and stunning scenery, all show that in the interaction between white people and Native Americans, the latter always lose. Scenes of beauty inevitably give way to destruction and genocide.

SYNOPSES

The Mission (1986), directed by Roland Joffé, is set in eighteenth-century South America. The film shows Jeremy Irons as Father Gabriel, an ascetic Jesuit who establishes a mission among the Guaraní, a remote Amazonian people. The slave-trader Rodrigo Mendoza (Robert De Niro) joins Father Gabriel as an act of penance after murder, but soon their mission is disrupted by an attacking Portuguese army. Knowing that the Portuguese will enslave the Guaraní, Father Gabriel and Mendoza decide to stay at their mission and resist rather than return to civilization. Mendoza leads the Guaraní men in taking up arms against the advancing Portuguese, while Father Gabriel shuns violence and gathers the women and children for mass in the mission church. Ultimately, Gabriel, Mendoza, and virtually the whole community are gunned down by the ascendant Portuguese.

The Mosquito Coast (1986), based on a 1982 novel by Paul Theroux and directed by Peter Weir, depicts the tragedy of the charismatic but deranged inventor Allie Fox (Harrison Ford), who moves his long-suffering family from rural New England to the unspoiled Central American jungle. Once there, the Foxes establish themselves in a village, where Fox constructs his magnum opus, a mammoth ice machine powered only by ammonia. After the machine explodes, destroying the settlement and poisoning the river, the Foxes eventually seek help at the mission station of the obnoxious evangelical missionary, Spellgood (André Gregory). The Foxes had previously encountered Spellgood while on the boat bound for Central America; this time the encounter proves fatal as an irritated Spellgood shoots and mortally wounds Fox, his anti-Christian rival for the affections of the native population. *The Mosquito Coast* contains two missionary portrayals. Spellgood is a two-dimensional caricature of a fundamentalist preacher, but Fox is himself a secular missionary—zealous, Scripture-quoting, hard-working, crazed, bent on civilizing the wilderness, convinced of the righteousness of his cause. Thus, while Fox hates Spellgood and all missionaries, the object of his venom is very much like himself.

At Play in the Fields of the Lord (1991), based on a 1965 novel by Peter Matthiessen and directed by Hector Babenco, features John Lithgow and Darryl Hannah as the Huben family and Aidan Quinn and Kathy Bates as the Quarrier family, two missionary couples in 1960s-era South America who are attempting to convert the primitive Niaruna tribe. The missionaries enjoy little success, and Hazel Quarrier becomes mentally unbalanced after her small son dies of a tropical ailment. Meanwhile, an American named Moon (Tom Berenger) joins the Niaruna tribe, with whom he feels kinship because he is part American Indian himself. While Moon unwittingly exposes the Niaruna to an influenza virus to which they lack immunity, corrupt government authorities who want to open the Amazon for development simultaneously bomb the flu-ravaged village. The U.S. missionaries who do not die in the attack flee down the river toward civilization.

Black Robe (1991), directed by Bruce Beresford, is based on a 1985 novel by Brian Moore. Set in Quebec in 1634, it depicts Father Laforgue (Lothaire Bluteau) embarking on a 1,500-mile canoe journey to the Jesuits' Huron mission. He is accompanied by Daniel (Aden Young), a young Frenchman who soon abandons his thoughts of joining the priesthood when he falls in love with Annuka (Sandrine Holt), the beautiful daughter of Father Laforgue's Algonquin guide, Chomina (August Schellenberg). Various tragedies befall the party, including capture by the Algonquins' rivals, the Iroquois, who torture them. Eventually, the driven missionary Laforgue reaches the Huron settlement, where he finds the Huron smitten by disease. Although Laforgue tells them that the baptism he offers will not cure their physical illness, they nevertheless ask to be baptized.

GENDER

Despite the rise of feminism, the men's movement, and gay advocacy in the latter part of the twentieth century, traditional notions of gender pervade all four films. In these cinematic texts, women are mostly untouched by feminism—they generally occupy passive roles as objects of romantic interest or as helpers to more assertive men. Meanwhile, the men of the films assert leadership or authority not just over women but over men as well. These films confirm the conventional wisdom that men make Hollywood films with a male audience in mind and thus reinforce traditional gender roles.[1]

The normal roles for the women in these films are those of onlookers or supporters of assertive men. For example, in *The Mission,* the only woman's speaking part is that of Carlotta (Cherie Lunghi), Mendoza's mistress, whose unfaithfulness precipitates a fatal duel between Mendoza and his brother. Even this role consists of only a few lines. A stereotypic example of Latin purity—an emotional beauty with smooth skin and dark flowing hair, alluring but modest, impressed by both machismo and masculine sensitivity—Carlotta appears in the film for the sole purpose of serving as the object of desire for which Mendoza might kill his own brother.

Like Carlotta, *The Mosquito Coast's* women are weak and insignificant figures compared with the men around them. Most troubling is Fox's wife (played by Helen Mirren), who is called Mother and does not merit a name. Mother is the consummate helpmeet who neither questions her husband's increasingly irrational decisions nor complains about impossible living conditions. She cedes all responsibility for her children's health and education to her husband; Mother's principal duties are cooking, comforting, and doing what she is told. Fox's twin daughters also serve more as placeholders than as real characters. *The Mosquito Coast's* tragedy is based on the viewer's understanding of Fox's family as the victim of his idealistic schemes, and the filmmakers establish mother and daughters as the necessary family members. Their unimportance as individuals is particularly noticeable because of the active roles played by the two Fox sons. Charlie (River Phoenix) serves as the story's narrator and his father's most ardent admirer, while Jerry (Jadrien Steele) is the uncomprehending innocent whose plaintive cries amplify Fox's callousness.

The Mosquito Coast does contain one less traditional female role—the missionary Spellgood's daughter Emily, who, with Annuka in *Black Robe,* serves as a rare exception to the rule that female characters must remain passive in film. An archetypal North American teenager who acts as if she were wiling away her time at the shopping mall, Emily impudently tells Charlie near the film's beginning that she thinks of him when she is in the bathroom. She then asks him if he would like her to be his girlfriend, and he abashedly declines.[2] At the end of the film, Emily plays a pivotal role. Just before Spellgood shoots Fox, Charlie and Jerry seek out Emily and ask her for help in escaping from their mad father. She provides the boys with keys to the mission's car.

Emily's parallel in self-assertion is Annuka, the daughter of the Algonquin guide Chomina in *Black Robe.* Although appearing at first as a demure maiden, Annuka hatches a plan of escape from the barbaric Iroquois that involves acquiescing to her guard's sexual advances and then bludgeoning him. This exercise of her will strengthens Annuka, for afterward she challenges Laforgue directly for the first time, telling him to leave her ailing father alone to die in the Algonquin way. Taking on his role as guide, Annuka interprets her father's prophetic dream, saying that Father Laforgue must continue on to the Huron settlement by himself. Not even Emily Spellgood is so bold.

Even so, taken together, these active women appear notable precisely because they serve as exceptions to the prevalent depiction of women in the films. In three of the four, women are more passive objects than active subjects. *The Mission*'s Carlotta, *The Mosquito Coast*'s Mother, and *At Play*'s Hazel Quarrier and Andy Huben are only supporters of men or the focus of men's lustful attentions. They are sometimes stable (Mother and Andy) and sometimes emotional (Carlotta and Hazel), but not major actors.

As important as male-female relations are, gender conventions define all-male environments as well. Critics have noted that men can be "degendered, regendered, or a-gendered" by writers or filmmakers and that men in groups continually renegotiate their masculinity.[3] In *The Mission, The Mosquito Coast, At Play in the Fields of the Lord,* and *Black Robe,* the renegotiation of masculinity usually results in the depiction of clergymen as feminized. Gendering is, of course, based in part on factors other than reproductive organs. These filmmakers define their regendered masculinity in terms of musical ability, emotional sensitivity, aggressiveness, and sexual virility.

Significantly, the three principal characters in these films who play musical instruments are priests. Father Xantes, the Catholic priest in *At Play in the Fields of the Lord,* plays the organ, sings, and comforts Andy when she seeks refuge in his modest church from both a rainstorm and her own doubts. Xantes serves as a strong contrast to almost all the other men in the film, but especially Andy's own husband—

confident, brash, insensitive Leslie. *The Mission*'s Father Gabriel is also a musician. After the martyrdom of his predecessor, Gabriel wins over the Guaraní with his oboe rather than with force. He is sensitive, kind, and soft-spoken; however, the portrait is complex. As the superior of an order and a mission, Gabriel has responsibilities that require him to be firm, and for a time he is even able to hold sway over the murderer and slave-trader Mendoza. At the film's close, however, Mendoza turns the tables, choosing to resign from the order rather than comply with Gabriel's demand to resist the Portuguese invaders nonviolently. Predictably, Mendoza plays the aggressive role, leading the armed defense of the mission, while Gabriel retreats to the church with the women and children.[4]

Black Robe's Father Laforgue presents yet another feminized musical priest, albeit more ambiguously than in the other films. Although his playing of the recorder occupies only a few seconds of film, Laforgue exhibits many other stereotypically feminine qualities—he gets lost after only a few minutes in the woods alone, cannot hunt, carries no weapon, relieves himself like a woman, and chokes when he puffs on the Algonquins' pipe. He shuns sexual activity, even discouraging it in others. When stripped, humiliated, and forced to sing in front of the Iroquois, Laforgue sings "Ave Maria," a hymn to the great feminine icon of Christianity, while his fellow captive, Chomina, chants an Algonquin war cry. In spite of this feminization, Laforgue is not passive. Indisputably the driving force behind the film, he proves himself unswerving, absolutely unafraid of death, and determined to reach the Huron mission at any cost. Surrounded by hunters and warriors, Laforgue appears feminized, but his fortitude serves as an odd counterexample to this image.

Feminization always exists as a comparison to a more masculine figure. Father Xantes, Andy Huben's understanding confessor, in *At Play in the Fields of the Lord*, is compared to her extremely masculine husband, Leslie. The alter ego of *The Mission*'s Father Gabriel is the brash, violent Mendoza. In *Black Robe*, Father Laforgue's feminization emerges in contrast to the Native Americans all around him and in contrast to his assistant, Daniel, who rejects the celibate life in favor of the pleasures of sexuality. In addition, the campy buffoonery of the missionary Spellgood in *The Mosquito Coast* contrasts with Fox's autocratic egocentricity.

Viewed together, then, these films portray a noticeable correlation between ministerial status and feminization. Except for Leslie Huben, virtually all clerical figures in the films display characteristics of feminization. All are contrasted with the more aggressive, violent, or self-confident men around them.

ETHNICITY

Another issue that has captured the North American consciousness since the 1960s is ethnicity. The civil-rights movement, originally organized to promote equality for

African Americans, has spread to Hispanics, Native Americans, and others. Viewers might expect that films made in the 1980s and 1990s would be cognizant of these issues, portraying Native Americans in a way that emphasizes their self-identity and their cohesiveness as distinct cultures. *The Mission, The Mosquito Coast, At Play in the Fields of the Lord,* and *Black Robe* all address ethnicity directly—indeed, the most obvious similarity of the films is their portrayal of the interaction between whites and nonwhites. However, the maxim that film is a conservative medium seems appropriate here. All depict Native Americans in extremely problematic ways. Perhaps because screenwriters tend to construct films so that the protagonist will be a person with whom an ideal viewer will be able to identify, nonwhites in most films are portrayed as "other"—sometimes innocent, sometimes noble, sometimes vicious, sometimes mild, but always separated from white Americans and Europeans by an unbridgeable chasm.

In these particular films, the Native Americans are not only "other," they are largely also stupid and weak pawns and victims. One Canadian critic has described this phenomenon in an analysis of *Under Fire,* another film about North Americans in Central America: "Its portraits of Nicaraguans are at best two-dimensional. . . . [T]he viewer never has access to the thoughts, feelings, hopes, and fears of the Nicaraguans at a level of depth or complexity comparable to that of the three American journalists. . . . It is through these outsiders that the film's moral and political issues are played out."[5] The critic's appraisal of *Under Fire* pinpoints the problematic treatment of nonwhite people in the missionary films as well: (1) their portraits are two-dimensional, (2) their interior lives are closed to the audience, and (3) their culture serves as the battleground for white men's conflicts.

The Guaraní of *The Mission* fit the cinematic paradigm of ethnicity perfectly, serving uniformly as pawns in the European power struggle. Musical, happy, playful, and pious, they fall under the authority of the Europeans. Not only are the Guaraní completely dominated by the Spanish and Portuguese, but the filmmakers symbolically strip them of their ability to communicate. The Guaraní speak to one another in their own language, but their speech is never subtitled. For the film audience, they remain completely inscrutable and, therefore, completely other—flat characters unable to express a full range of emotions, victims in a power struggle over which they have little understanding or control. Consequently, the audience is forced to identify with the Europeans.

Indigenous life in *The Mosquito Coast* also corresponds to this depiction. Like the Guaraní, *The Mosquito Coast*'s Central Americans are simple people who have no ambition of their own. Fox and Spellgood alternately dominate them, for the villagers give their loyalty to Fox when he arrives but shift back to the charismatic Spellgood while Fox and his sons are making an ill-fated trip to deliver ice to a remote village. When the Foxes finally see Spellgood's mission at the end of the film, the camera focuses on a small chapel in which mesmerized natives sit, staring blankly at a videotaped Spellgood sermon. Curiously, the Central Americans in *The Mosquito Coast* can all speak English, but they do not speak much. Instead, they are victims of Fox's and Spellgood's imperialistic ambitions.

The Native Americans in *At Play in the Fields of the Lord* are also, ultimately, the victims of imperialism, but they are objectified in a manner somewhat different from the objectification of *The Mission* and *The Mosquito Coast*. The Niaruna of *At Play* are first of all fierce, and the missionaries themselves are extremely wary of them. Near the end of the picture, Leslie Huben erects a barbed-wire fence around the mission compound, but his action is an admission of defeat: instead of taming the "wild" natives, the missionaries acknowledge their weakness by jailing themselves. Not only are the Niaruna people warlike, but they are also verbal. *At Play* includes several scenes in which subtitles open their language—and, therefore, their minds—to the movie viewer. Here also Moon, the missionary who "goes native" by joining the Niaruna village, is seen struggling with the language, looking foolish and confused, while the native people have the upper hand. Moon's hosts appear to have a real culture, with a religion and established family life. They are self-sufficient and decide, albeit on Moon's suggestion, to refuse the missionaries' gifts, which might enslave them. Nonetheless, despite the more balanced treatment *At Play* gives its Native Americans, the film partly follows the paradigm of ethnicity established in the two earlier pictures. Once again, the natives' thoughts are mysterious, and although subtitles reveal some of the Niaruna language, the subtitles are not used consistently. *At Play* also places responsibility for the people in the hands of Moon, who tries unsuccessfully to save them from the outside aggressors they do not understand. And finally, once again the Native Americans end up as innocent victims of civilization, as disease and technology destroy a society that had existed in perfect harmony with nature.

The portrayal of Native Americans in *Black Robe* is fundamentally different from their depiction in any of the other films. First, the events take place early in the history of European settlement of the Western Hemisphere, and the natives are still a powerful and threatening force. Unlike Laforgue and Daniel, the Algonquins and Iroquois fight, hunt, hike, and canoe with ease; the woods are their home. Second, the Native Americans are members of separate and competing nations, and they hate one another even more than they despise the French. Third, the natives are savage and uncouth by bourgeois standards. They torture and kill their captives and break wind and copulate unselfconsciously. Fourth, the Algonquins, Hurons, and Iroquois have their own languages, which are interpreted for the film audience by subtitles. These subtitles allow the audience to understand their motives even better than the audience can understand the taciturn priest Laforgue. Fifth, Laforgue himself—a conservative Roman Catholic who believes that Native Americans are "savages [who] live in outer darkness"—is so foreign to most late-twentieth-century film audiences that the natives themselves appear almost normal by comparison. Unlike the priest, the Algonquins, Hurons, and Iroquois marry, enjoy sex, have families, provide for themselves, dance and smoke, love their friends, and hate their enemies. More than the other films, *Black Robe* enables audiences to empathize with the indigenous people.

The chief difference between *Black Robe*'s natives and those of the other missionary films is power. The Algonquins, Hurons, and Iroquois of *Black Robe* are not the property of Europeans. Although the native peoples do make alliances with the European newcomers, neither the French nor the Dutch can control them. Father Laforgue does not wield control over his Algonquin guides but, rather, remains at their mercy. Not only is the film world's paternalism toward nonwhites breathtakingly absent in *Black Robe,* but the picture breaks the typical ethnicity paradigm of two-dimensional natives whose thoughts are mysterious and whose society becomes a battleground for European conflicts.

FAITH

Audiences might expect the missionaries of *The Mission, The Mosquito Coast, At Play in the Fields of the Lord,* and *Black Robe* to be people of unshakable conviction and supreme self-confidence. In fact, while the films do show missionaries with this kind of strong conviction, this self-confident faith becomes equivalent to arrogance. The appealing characters are those who must address their own doubts as they enter foreign cultures; paradoxically, the admirable figures are those who struggle for their *own* salvation rather than for the salvation of others.

Throughout *The Mosquito Coast,* commitment equals ideology, if not fanaticism. Fox and Spellgood are repugnant characters—self-confident to the point of arrogance. Although mortal enemies, the two are alike in their domineering temperament, their work ethic, and their determination. Yet these qualities alone do not make a film character hateful. Instead, their lack of concern for others and their lack of self-doubt or self-criticism mark them as offensive and despicable. On the other hand, audiences can identify with Fox's son Charlie. While he cannot help admiring his father's ingenuity and vision, Charlie also recognizes Fox's fatal hubris. In his ambivalence, Charlie captures the essence of the dramatic film hero—the figure who learns about himself, grows up, and works out his salvation with fear and trembling.

At Play in the Fields of the Lord offers similar examples of arrogant antiheroes interacting with doubting heroes. Hazel Quarrier and Leslie Huben are culturally insensitive, paternalistic, and narrow-minded. They constantly spout evangelical platitudes and readily condemn their opponents. Just as Spellgood hates Fox for offering technology to the natives as an alternate source of meaning, Hazel and

Leslie fear and distrust Xantes, a Catholic priest and thus the natural enemy of Protestant fundamentalism. At the same time, the humility that Hazel's husband, Martin, and Leslie's, wife, Andy, show about the mission to the Niaruna and even about their own belief in God serves as an appealing alternative to their spouses' self-assurance. Andy never musters the confidence of her husband and, instead, seeks out the mistrusted priest for reassurance, while Martin suffers a crisis of faith as a result of his son's death from a tropical disease. "God did not take my son; death took my son," he says. "But if God did take my son, God is not welcome to my son!" When his fellow missionary reprimands Martin for this outcry, he replies, "I'll try to make my own peace with the Lord. . . . But if I cannot—well, then I cannot."

Martin's anguish over his child's death and his doubt about divine sovereignty strike the audience as human and appealing. In contrast, audiences of *Black Robe* have difficulty in understanding Father Laforgue's motivations, and this contributes to a profound ambivalence about his mission. In one sense, the priest seems a classic religious imperialist who thinks *his* way is the only right way. Yet Laforgue readily admits his own limitations, and his austerity and honesty provide handholds for audiences who seek positive traits in their protagonist. Because *Black Robe* imbues both self-confidence and self-doubt in one character, audiences feel unsure whether Laforgue deserves praise or condemnation.

By definition, missionaries are people who share their religious faith with others, yet most film missionaries are not bent on conversions. Paradoxically, Father Gabriel and Rodrigo Mendoza, Martin Quarrier, and even Father Laforgue appear to struggle more with their own questions and misgivings than with those of the Native Americans whom they try to convert. Self-confident missionaries like Spellgood and Leslie Huben look ugly and even preposterous on film, while filmmakers idealize doubt.

HISTORICITY

Of the four missionary films, only *The Mission* claims to be a true story, while the others are based on popular novels. Nevertheless, even works of fiction are built around kernels of truth. Brian Moore's *Black Robe* is steeped in historical research, while Peter Matthiessen clearly intended his novel *At Play in the Fields of the Lord* to be a fairly realistic portrayal of the threats to Amazonia during the 1960s. Director Peter Weir of *The Mosquito Coast* has claimed that even his film, with its improbable central character, has real parallels in the contemporary world: "Central America is full of Allie Foxes," Weir told a journalist during the 1986 filming. "I've heard of four of them since I've been here in Belize. Many of them came down here in the late sixties."[6] Thus, all the films make either direct or indirect claims to historical accuracy.

The Mission claims to be historical, but some scholars have condemned it for serious lapses. While some of the liberties the filmmakers took may be excusable—such as placing the fledgling Guaraní mission above the majestic Iguaçu Falls rather than in less scenic locales in Paraguay—other historical mistakes seem less defensible. The film portrays the Jesuits as protectors of a naturally musical hunter-gatherer people who embraced Christianity because the missionaries' musical abilities impressed them, but the historical record shows a different scenario. By the middle of the eighteenth century, when the film is set, the Guaraní—an agricultural rather than hunter-gatherer people—had already been living in Jesuit communities for a century, having originally settled there to secure a more predictable source of food. The Jesuits had trained the men to be a well-organized militia, and the Guaraní were competent in the use of European arms. Some were literate and protested the destruction of their missions by writing letters to the king of Spain. When their towns were destroyed, they did not return to the jungle but sought larger cities where they could sell their labor. The filmmakers might have credited the Guaraní with more initiative, since they and not the Jesuits led the armed rebellion against the armies that sought to implement the Treaty of Madrid of 1750.[7]

Although a work of historical fiction, *Black Robe* seems truer than *The Mission* in its treatment of Native Americans. In an "author's note," novelist and screenwriter Moore reveals that the details of the story—including the Native Americans' and Jesuits' names for each other ("Blackrobes" and "Savages")—are based on primary sources and consultations with academic historians. The writer's research reveals itself in countless details, and a reviewer in *American Historical Review* pronounced the picture accurate with two exceptions: a true Huron village would have been surrounded by cornfields rather than forest, and the Native Americans were more fun-loving and quick to laugh than the serious natives depicted in the film. On the other hand, the film's implication that the Jesuits ultimately failed to convert the Canadian natives is clearly false—more than sixteen thousand baptisms before 1672 led to a native church that French priests admired for its zeal and devotion.[8]

The other two films, *At Play in the Fields of the Lord* and *The Mosquito Coast*, seem plagued less by outright inaccuracies than by exaggeration. In *At Play*, Hazel Quarrier is too xenophobic and protective to be true; Leslie Huben, too arrogant; his wife, Andy, too naïve. The Niarunas' acceptance of Moon into their community and his ability to learn their language and way of life is extraordinary. Nearly all the film's dramatis personæ are painted with an extremely broad stroke, as if each character has been allowed only a single underscored personality trait.[9] The exaggeration in *The Mosquito Coast* is also implausible and even absurd, but here it seems to serve a purpose. The picture is really the portrait of a madman, a kind of *Moby-Dick* in which Captain Allie untiringly pursues the ice machine, his own white whale. Because the story is narrated through the eyes of Fox's admiring son Charlie, the other characters only exist for chemical reactions with Fox or Charlie.

The contemporary settings of these two films may explain the filmmakers' tendency to caricature their principals. By overstating the flaws they see in contemporary society, they confront those issues. Thus, by portraying a corrupt local official who bombs the Niaruna village, *At Play* reprimands developers who destroy rain forests for economic motives. With Fox's gigantic ice machine, *The Mosquito Coast* mocks inappropriate technology and secular idealism. Moon reminds audiences that no one can retreat to a pristine world. And the evangelical missionaries serve as symbols of the vanity and arrogance of the North American missionary enterprise as a whole. *At Play in the Fields of the Lord* and *The Mosquito Coast* mock missionaries partly because they were convenient objects of derision. But these films also attempt to make a more general criticism about the audacity of Europeans and white North Americans who try to mold the world in their own likeness.

Although *The Mission* and *Black Robe* have proved more historical than the other two films, these, too, bear messages for contemporary audiences. Both close with captions that neatly convey some of the filmmakers' own values. *The Mission,* a work of liberation theology–style religious idealism, announces: "The Indians of South America are still engaged in a struggle to defend their land and their culture. Many of the priests who, inspired by faith and love, continue to support the rights of Indians for justice, do so with their lives." Desiring to connect the Roman Catholic clergy with the preservation of indigenous peoples, the film simplifies the complex motivations that brought missionaries to South America in the first place. Criticisms of liberation theology that have called the movement "too white" or "too clergy-oriented" seem warranted here, since the film sees Native Americans only as victims in need of liberal Roman Catholic leadership.

If *The Mission* praises the Jesuits as defenders of Native Americans, *Black Robe* sends the opposite message. "Fifteen years later," the closing caption reads, "the Hurons, having accepted Christianity, were routed and killed by their enemies, the Iroquois. The Jesuit mission to the Hurons was abandoned, and the Jesuits returned to Quebec." This note of finality seals the message manifest throughout the film— that European Christianity was inherently incompatible with Native American culture. Both Chomina, the Native American, and Laforgue, the French priest, understand this message clearly; each knows that the other is unknowable. *Black Robe* serves not so much as an elegy to a lost Native American civilization as a lesson that oil and water cannot mix.

DESTRUCTION

Film as a medium thrives on dramatic images, and the most memorable and spectacular images in the four missionary films are those of nature. The mighty Iguaçu Falls that almost cost Jeremy Irons his life during the filming of *The Mission,*[10] the endless jungle canopy that Moon poetically labels "the fields of the Lord," and *Black Robe*'s majestic Canadian wilderness are not merely backdrops for the films, but they put the characters into perspective, preparing audiences to recognize the destruction that missionaries brought and still bring to Native American life. The glorification of nature that pervades these missionary films became possible only in the two decades before the films were made. Previously, many movies set in remote lands were actually filmed on Hollywood back lots, with low-quality stock footage of rain forests and tropical animals spliced into the higher-quality domestic film at awkward intervals. In contrast, *The Mission, The Mosquito Coast, At Play in the Fields of the Lord*, and *Black Robe* were all filmed on location. Such filming allowed directors to take advantage of the most impressive local color. *The Mission* was actually shot in three locations: the city scenes in the historic town of Cartagena, Colombia; the mission scenes in remote jungle outside of Santa Marta, Colombia; and the waterfall scenes in Argentina. The filming of *The Mosquito Coast* took 150 crewmembers and actors to Belize, in Central America. *At Play in the Fields of the Lord* was shot near Belém, Brazil, and *Black Robe* at Canadian national parks.

The releases of *The Mission, The Mosquito Coast*, and several other pictures during the 1980s—among them, *Out of Africa, The Color Purple, The Clan of the Cave Bear*, and *The Emerald Forest*—prompted a 1986 article about primitivism in *American Film* magazine. Critic Dave Kehr traces some of the common themes of these films: They usually highlight sensuous images of scantily dressed natives, lush foliage, and secluded swimming holes, all of which indicate fertility and sexuality. They celebrate the supposed innate spirituality of native people, and they tend to paint these natives as innocent children, living in equilibrium with nature. Indeed, primitive societies are so idyllic in the movies that they often inspire Europeans to join them. In all the films, scenes of natural beauty fulfill the desires of writers and filmmakers to declare the purity and glory of nature in contrast with the sordidness and hypocrisy of Western civilization.[11]

Lurking behind the primitivist mythology that pervades the missionary films is a universal assumption about life in the Western Hemisphere before the arrival of whites. *The Mission, The Mosquito Coast, At Play in the Fields of the Lord*, and *Black Robe* drink deeply of this presupposition: they all imply that Native Americans lived in stable and even static societies that experienced their first or most damaging disruption from Europeans. Domesticity always accompanies Christianity in the movies, and domesticity inevitably destroys the unique and happy lives of simple people, stripping them of their independence and forcing them to obey and rely on Europeans. Once the natives are domesticated, destruction is unavoidable. In *Black Robe* and *At Play in the Fields of the Lord*, disease strikes first but does not bring about genocide. Instead, *Black Robe* tells its audience that the Hurons, by becoming pacifists upon their conversion to Christianity, allowed the Iroquois to destroy them. In *At Play in the Fields of the Lord* and in *The Mission,* armed aggression by non-native governors—secular powers rather than religious authorities—kills many natives and scatters the rest. In *The Mosquito Coast,* Fox's exploding ice machine symbolizes Western technology gone awry. The machine contaminates the river, and this represents the destruction of all natural resources by the inappropriate technology North Americans introduce to developing nations around the world.

The missionary movies, then, despite their differences, agree on fundamental principles: (1) Before the arrival of Europeans, Native American societies were stable and healthy. (2) Europeans have an insatiable desire to domesticate Native Americans and to force their religion (or belief in technology, in the case of Fox) on them. (3) Domestication and Christianization lead inexorably to destruction—not only the devastation of traditional ways of life but, ultimately, the annihilation of Native American people themselves. It is possible to challenge the historical accuracy of some of these principles—for example, pretechnological societies were never static and seldom edenic; instead, populations were stable because of lack of food, inadequate medical care, disease, and other deprivations[12]—yet virulent diseases did indeed accompany Europeans to the Americas, Christians did enslave and murder Native Americans, and missionaries did drastically alter the cultures of indigenous peoples.

It is, perhaps, more helpful to understand these missionary movies as reflections of the society that produced them—the Western world in the late twentieth century. On the one hand, filmmakers and viewers look at the history of Western civilization's interaction with Native Americans and condemn the violence and destruction. And yet the same filmmakers and viewers also find inspiration in various kinds of heroism: the determination of *Black Robe's* Father Laforgue, who unswervingly pursues his goals and explores uncharted territory; the courage of Moon in *At Play in the Fields of the Lord,* who abandons his meaningless life to join a harmonious preindustrial paradise; the generosity and strength of *The Mission's* Father Gabriel and Rodrigo Mendoza, who follow their consciences and nobly attempt to save innocent people from naked aggression.

Set in their cinematic contexts, these protagonists fill viewers with ambivalence, and that helps explain why these movies are satisfying and why they illumine the modern religious imagination so well. They allow viewers to envision the possibility of understanding, coexisting with, and even rising above the evil in their own traditions. Like the remorseful papal legate in *The Mission,* white North American Christians can look at the destruction caused by religious imperialism and say, "Thus have we *made* the world. Thus have *I* made it." And yet, these same viewers can appreciate Charlie in *The Mosquito Coast,* who both recognizes his father's grave shortcomings and admires him for all his strengths.

These films serve better as primary sources revealing late-twentieth-century culture than as secondary sources about the missionaries they portray. North Americans hold high expectations for themselves as a people, and so they wring their hands over their shortcomings. Yet they also hold an inflated sense of the importance of their history and believe that they have a mandate to spread their technology, government, and ideals around the world, and so they glory in their successes. Feelings of both superiority and self-doubt percolate through these cinematic texts, and thus, they illumine a fundamental ambivalence about history and North American cultural ideals.

Notes

INTRODUCTION

We use *America* to refer to a broad cultural region embracing the United States and Anglophone Canada that exhibited similar expansionist impulses. We use *United States* and *Canada* when more geographic specificity seems warranted. These uses are not always precise; they often overlap. We trust that the context will make the meaning clear.

1. J. K. Fairbank, "Assignment for the '70s," *American Historical Review* (February 1969): 877. Dana L. Robert, "From Missions to Mission to Beyond Missions: The Historiography of American Protestant Foreign Missions since World War II," in *New Directions in American Religious History*, ed. Harry S. Stout and D. G. Hart (New York: Oxford University Press, 1997), 362–93, and "Shifting Southward: Global Christianity Since 1945," *International Bulletin of Missionary Research* (April 2000): 50–58. For concise, well-crafted surveys of the history of U.S. missions (which have informed our thinking), see Patricia R. Hill, "The Missionary Enterprise," in *Encyclopedia of the American Religious Experience*, ed. Charles H. Lippy and Peter W. Williams (New York: Charles Scribner's Sons, 1988), 3: 1,683–96, and the entries for "Missions, Evangelical Foreign" and "Missions, Mainline Protestant Foreign," in *Dictionary of Christianity in America*, ed. Daniel G. Reid et al. (Downers Grove, Ill.: InterVarsity Press, 1990). The title and introduction to the present book are adapted from the title and introduction to John K. Fairbank, ed., *The Missionary Enterprise in China and America* (Cambridge, Mass.: Harvard University Press, 1974). The epigraph comes from Arnold Rose's response to a fellow academic, at a conference in India, when the latter identified himself as a former missionary. William R. Hutchison, *Errand to the World: American Protestant Thought and Foreign Missions* (Chicago: University of Chicago Press, 1987), 1.

2. Important recent studies of the foreign missionary enterprise in U.S. society and culture include selected chapters in Fairbank, *Missionary Enterprise;* Wayne Flynt and Gerald W. Berkley, *Taking Christianity to China: Alabama Missionaries in the Middle Kingdom, 1850–1950* (Tuscaloosa: University of Alabama Press, 1997); Patricia R. Hill, *The World Their Household:*

The American Woman's Foreign Mission Movement and Cultural Transformation, 1870–1920 (Ann Arbor: University of Michigan Press, 1985); Hutchison, *Errand to the World;* Amanda Porterfield, *Mary Lyon and the Mount Holyoke Missionaries* (New York: Oxford University Press, 1997); and selected essays in Andrew F. Walls, ed., *The Missionary Movement in Christian History: Studies in the Transmission of Faith* (Maryknoll, N.Y.: Orbis, 1996).

3. See, for example, Melville's early stories "Typee" and "Omoo"; Mark Twain's scathing 1901 essay "To the Person Sitting in Darkness" in *The North American Review* and several follow-up exchanges with missionary defenders; Dunne's unforgettable turn-of-the-century Mr. Dooley and his Irish wisdom brought to bear, for example, on the "haythen" Chinese in "The Chinese Situation," in *Mr. Dooley: Now and Forever* (Stanford: Academic Reprints, 1954), 134–39; Cronin's *The Keys of the Kingdom* (1937); Michener's deft portrayal of pioneer Hawaii missionary Abner Hale in his bestseller *Hawaii* (1959); and Hersey's fictional portrayal of a figure based loosely on his father, a YMCA secretary in China, in *The Call* (1985).

4. Robert D. Kaplan, *The Arabists: The Romance of an American Elite* (New York: Free Press, 1993), 8. Richard Madsen, *China and the American Dream: A Moral Inquiry* (Berkeley: University of California Press, 1995), 137–40.

5. S. Wells Williams, *The Middle Kingdom,* 2 vols. (New York: John Wiley, 1847).

6. Anecdotal evidence of the connection between returned missionaries and the shaping of history, religion, language, and area-studies programs in colleges and universities abounds. The impact of the missionary on the academy at home is actually better documented for England and Scotland than it is for the United States, where the field remains open for detailed investigation. For the phenomenon in the United Kingdom, see Andrew Walls, "The Nineteenth-Century Missionary as Scholar," in *The Missionary Movement in Christian History,* ed. Walls, 187–98, and Norman J. Girardot, *The Victorian Translation of China: James Legge's Oriental Pilgrimage* (Berkeley: University of California Press, 2002).

7. For a short but incisive portrait of Fryer, see Jonathan Spence, *To Change China: Western Advisors in China 1620–1960* (New York: Penguin, 1980), 140–60.

8. For the institute's founding and early development, see Philip West, *Yenching University and Sino-Western Relations 1916–1952* (Cambridge, Mass.: Harvard University Press, 1978), 187–94.

9. The influence of returned missionaries on theological trends is discussed with focus on China in a stimulating if tentative way in Lian Xi, *The Conversion of Missionaries: Liberalism in American Protestant Missions in China, 1907–1932* (University Park: Pennsylvania State University Press, 1997), chap. 7.

10. T. Christopher Jesperson, *American Images of China 1931–1949* (Stanford: Stanford University Press, 1996); W. A. Swanberg, *Luce and his Empire* (New York: Scribner, 1972).

11. See the analysis of these complex relationships in James A. Field Jr., "Near East Notes and Far East Queries," in *The Missionary Enterprise in China and America,* ed. John K. Fairbank (Cambridge, Mass.: Harvard University Press, 1974), 23–55. Dodge's own children carried on the tradition; one later was president of the American University of Beirut, another was first president of the Near East Foundation, and another married a Robert College professor. Today, there is still a distinguished Cleveland Dodge Chair in Middle Eastern Studies at Princeton University.

12. Though all of these aspects of the impact of the foreign missionary movement on religious life in the United States are important, few have received sustained attention by scholars. Hill, "The Missionary Enterprise," offers an important start. Joel Carpenter, in his ground-breaking *Revive Us Again: The Reawakening of American Fundamentalism* (New York: Oxford University Press, 1997), stresses several times the importance of foreign missions for the conservative forces and institutions he describes but does not delve deeply into the problem. Andrew Walls provides perceptive insights and a guide to future queries in "The American Dimension of the Missionary Movement," in *The Missionary Movement in Christian History*, 221–40. For a case study of the growth of bureaucratic, corporate-like missionary management structures and fund-raising techniques around the turn of the century, see Valentin H. Rabe, *The Home Base of American China Missions, 1880–1920* (Cambridge, Mass.: Harvard University Press, 1978). The important research of Dana Robert shows that missionary women and women's missions organizations exercised a major influence on gender roles in North American Protestant culture in the nineteenth and early twentieth centuries. Indeed, Robert argues that the foreign missionary movement proved the largest factor in women's creation of a visible role in public life. See her *American Women in Mission: A Social History of Their Thought and Practice* (Macon, Ga.: Mercer University Press, 1996) and "The Influence of American Missionary Women on the World Back Home," *Religion and American Culture: A Journal of Interpretation* 12 (Winter 2002): 59–90.

13. In Honolulu, for example, there still exists among the old Caucasian families an elite social organization called "The Missionaries' Children," limited to those who can trace their lineage back to those first missionaries.

14. Some of this story, for the late 1940s, is told in Jesperson, *American Images of China 1931–1949.*

CHAPTER 1

1. Rev. Alex. Crummell, *The Future of Africa: Being Addresses, Sermons, etc., etc., Delivered in the Republic of Liberia* (1862; reprint, New York: Negro Universities Press, 1969), 133–48.

2. The leading scholarship on Crummell—for example, Wilson Jeremiah Moses, *Alexander Crummell: A Study of Civilization and Discontent* (New York: Oxford University Press, 1989); idem, *The Golden Age of Black Nationalism: The History of an Idea in America from Alexander Crummell to Marcus Garvey* (Rumford, R.I.: Black Smith Shop, 1978)—treats him as a "civilizationist." My goal here is not to disagree with this treatment but to situate civilizationism in a different context than Moses has drawn. Similarly, I try to place thought about the "precedence of civilization or Christianization" (William R. Hutchison, *Errand to the World: American Protestant Thought and Foreign Missions* [Chicago: University of Chicago Press, 1987], 63) in the context of U.S. race relations.

3. For instance, Deborah E. McDowell, "In the First Place: Making Frederick Douglass and the Afro-American Narrative Tradition," in *Critical Essays on Frederick Douglass,* ed. William L. Andrews (Boston: G. K. Hall, 1991), 195–208; James Oliver Horton, *Free People of Color: Inside the African American Community* (Washington, D.C.: Smithsonian Institution

Press, 1993), 80–96 (with Lois Horton), 98–120. In a classic article, William H. Becker asserts that "every human community defines and authenticates those models of manhood that serve to guide its members in their growth toward mature humanity" and that nineteenth-century African Americans accepted a call to African missions because of "black manhood: African mission provided a dramatic symbol of the Afro-American as man, as leader, as authoritative carrier of God's word to those racial brothers who do not possess it." Becker, "The Black Church: Manhood and Mission," *Journal of the American Academy of Religion* 40 (1972): 316–33; quotations on 317, 325.

4. Frederick Douglass, *Life and Times of Frederick Douglass, Written by Himself: His Early Life as a Slave, His Escape from Bondage, and His Complete History*, rev. ed. (1881; reprint, New York: Collier, 1962), 143–44.

5. Moses, *Crummell*, 95, 110, 114–115.

6. "—Honour to Whom Honour Is Due," *African Repository and Colonial Journal* 1 (1825): 87.

7. J. Gus Liebenow, *Liberia: Quest for Democracy* (Bloomington: Indiana University Press, 1987), 19.

8. David E. Swift, *Black Prophets of Justice: Activist Clergy before the Civil War* (Baton Rouge: Louisiana State University Press, 1989), 34–39.

9. Contemporary accounts mentioned high mortality among the settler population. A recent study arguing that this mortality was the highest ever recorded is Antonio McDaniel, *Swing Low, Sweet Chariot: The Mortality Cost of Colonizing Liberia in the Nineteenth Century* (Chicago: University of Chicago Press, 1995), esp. 83–106. Jefferson seems to have been the first to propose the expatriation of black infants. The argument was made again in Jesse Burton Harrison, *Review of the Slave Question* (Richmond, 1833).

10. For Clay's comments, see his speech reported in *A View of Exertions Lately Made for the Purpose of Colonizing the Free People of Color, in the United States, in Africa, or Elsewhere* (Washington, D.C.: U.S. Congress, 1817), 3; and Charles S. Johnson, "Bitter Canaan: The Story of the Negro Republic," in *Black Classics of Social Science,* ed. Wilbur H. Watson (New Brunswick, N.J.: Transaction, 1987), 19. I examine colonization and the settlement of Liberia in greater detail and with a fuller bibliography than here in "The American Enlightenment in Africa: Jefferson's Colonization and Black Virginians' Migration to Liberia, 1776–1840," *Eighteenth-Century Studies* 31 (1998): 261–82; and "'Circular addressed to the Colored Brethren and friends': An Unpublished Essay by Lott Cary, Sent from Liberia to Virginia, 1827," edited with an explanatory introduction and epilogue by John Saillant, *Virginia Magazine of History and Biography* 104 (1996): 481–504.

11. John Saillant, "Lemuel Haynes's Black Republicanism and the American Republican Tradition, 1775–1820," *Journal of the Early Republic* 14 (1994): 317.

12. Colonization was in the "English tradition of encouraging troublesome populations to migrate and then expecting them to be a commercial, political and spiritual credit to the nation which had desired their departure." Marie Tyler-McGraw, "Richmond Free Blacks and African Colonization, 1816–1832," *Journal of American Studies* 21 (1987): 208.

13. "For the African Repository," *African Repository and Colonial Journal* 1 (1825): 109.

14. "American Colonization Society," *African Repository and Colonial Journal* 8 (1832): 236. The black colonizationist narratives of the 1850s collected by Wilson Jeremiah Moses all agree on this point. See *Liberian Dreams: Back-to-Africa Narratives from the 1850s,* ed. Moses (University Park: Pennsylvania State University Press, 1998).

15. George W. Williams, *History of the Negro Race in America from 1619 to 1800* (New York: Putnam's, 1883), 98.

16. The *African Repository and Colonial Journal* would continue for decades to be a major channel of news about missionary efforts in West Africa. Missionary reports in such periodicals were important sources of U.S. citizens' impressions of Africa. Hutchison, *Errand,* 1.

17. "Considerations in Reference to a Mission in Africa," *African Repository and Colonial Journal* 1 (1825): 118.

18. "Missions to Africa," *African Repository and Colonial Journal* 3 (1827): 264–65.

19. "Methodist Mission to Liberia," *African Repository and Colonial Journal* 6 (1831): 335–36.

20. Henry Litchfield West, *The Liberian Crisis* (Washington, D.C.: American Colonization Society, 1933), 11.

21. Sylvia M. Jacobs, "The Historical Role of Afro-Americans in American Missionary Efforts in Africa," in *Black Missionaries and the Missionary Movement in Africa,* ed. Sylvia M. Jacobs (Westport, Conn.: Greenwood, 1982), 7–11.

22. "Review," *African Repository and Colonial Journal* 4 (1828): 198. Similar reasoning led British missionaries to transport Christian black West Indians to Ghana to serve as evangelists. F. L. Bartels, *The Roots of Ghana Methodism* (Cambridge: Cambridge University Press, 1965), 29.

23. Joseph A. Conforti, *Samuel Hopkins and the New Divinity Movement: Calvinism, the Congregational Ministry, and Reform in New England between the Great Awakenings* (Grand Rapids: Eerdmans, 1981), 143–56.

24. "Circular addressed to the Coloured Brethren and friends." The text examined here appears in the *Eleventh Annual Report of the American Colonization Society* (1828): 88–94. It is reprinted in "Documents—Letters, Addresses, and the Like Throwing Light on the Career of Lott Cary," ed. Miles Mark Fisher, *Journal of Negro History* 7 (1922): 427–48.

25. For example, Joseph Tracy, *Natural Equality* (Windsor, Vt., 1833); Robert Walsh, *African Colonization* (Fredericksburg, Va.: Arena Office, 1829), 14–21.

26. Rev. William B. Hoyt, *Reminiscences of Liberia and Cape Palmas, with Incidents of the Voyage* (Hartford: Henry J. Fox and Wm. B. Hoyt, 1852), 22, 68.

27. *Slaves No More: Letters from Liberia, 1833–1869,* ed. Bell I. Wiley (Lexington: University Press of Kentucky, 1980), 15–17.

28. Moses, *Crummell,* 90.

29. "Letter from Zion Harris, Caldwell [Liberia], May 26, 1851," appendix in *Liberia; Or, Mr. Peyton's Experiments,* Sarah J. Hale (1853; reprint, Upper Saddle River, N.J.: Gregg, 1968), 253–54.

30. "[Letter from Jasper Bouch,] Clay–Ashland, Liberia, May 10, 1852," in Hale, *Liberia,* 257–58.

31. J. M. Wainwright, *A Discourse, on the Occasion of Forming the African Mission School Society, Delivered in Christ Church, in Hartford, Connecticut* (Hartford: H. F. J. Huntington, 1828), 20–21.

32. Wainwright, *Discourse*, 5–20.

33. J. B. Taylor, *Biography of Elder Lott Cary, Late Missionary to Africa* (Baltimore: Armstrong and Berry, 1837), 13.

34. "African Intellect," *African Repository and Colonial Journal* 1 (1825): 253.

35. Saillant, "American Enlightenment in Africa"; John Lewis, "First Impressions of a Liberian Colonist," *African Repository and Colonial Journal* 25 (1849): 116; Charles Henry Huberich, *The Political and Legislative History of Liberia* (New York: Central Book Company, 1947), 1: 827–44.

36. "Liberia—Fifty Years Hence: A Tale," *African Repository and Colonial Journal* 2 (1826): 245.

37. Moses, *Crummell*, 131.

38. Christopher Fyfe, *A History of Sierra Leone* (London: Oxford University Press, 1962), 14–31.

39. For a view of British missions, see Rev. Samuel Abraham Walker, *Missions in Western Africa, among the Soosoos, Bulloms, &c. Being the First Undertaken by the Church Missionary Society for Africa and the East* (Dublin: William Curry, Jun. and Company, 1845), 174–77 (on U.S. missions); 181–87 (on instruction and texts in native languages and on men's willingness to risk disease and death); and passim (on "superstitions"). For missions and U.S. nationalism, see Hutchison, *Errand*, 44.

40. A twentieth-century judgment that the settlers had no interest in missionary work and, in fact, opposed it appears in J. Du Plessis, *The Evangelisation of Pagan Africa: A History of Christian Missions to the Pagan Tribes of Central Africa* (Cape Town: J. C. Juta, 1929), 101–7.

41. "Colonization Society," *African Repository and Colonial Journal* 1 (1825): 290.

42. "The Late Rev. Jacob Oson," *African Repository and Colonial Journal* 4 (1828): 283–84. Oson's life was recounted also in Mrs. E. F. Hening, *History of the African Mission of the Protestant Episcopal Church in the United States, with Memoirs of Deceased Missionaries, and Notices of Native Customs* (New York: Stanford and Swords, 1850), 17.

43. "Important Intelligence from Liberia," *African Repository and Colonial Journal* 2 (1826): 262–63.

44. Harriette G. Brittan, *Scenes and Incidents of Every-Day Life in Africa* (New York: Pudney and Russell, 1860), 28–29.

45. Ibid., 32–33.

46. Ibid., 130.

47. Hening, *History*, 55, 188–89.

48. Anna M. Scott, *Day Dawn in Africa: Or, the Progress of the Prot. Epis. Mission at Cape Palmas, West Africa* (1898; reprint, New York: Negro Universities Press, 1969), 30–31.

49. George S. Brown, *Brown's Abridged Journal, Containing a Brief Account of the Life, Trials and Travels of Geo. S. Brown, Six Years a Missionary in Liberia, West Africa: A Miracle of God's Grace* (Troy, N.Y.: Press of Prescott and Wilson, 1849), 85.

50. Taylor, *Biography of Elder Lott Cary*, 43–44.

51. "Circular addressed to the Coloured Brethren and friends." Archibald Alexander, *A History of Colonization on the Western Coast of Africa* (1846; reprint, New York: Negro Universities Press, 1969), esp. chap. 23, "Wars with the Natives," 581–95.

52. Sir Harry Johnston, *Liberia* (1906; reprint, New York: Negro Universities Press, 1969), 1: 131.

53. Alexander Hance to J. H. B. Latrobe, Cape Palmas, April 7, 1838, in Wiley, *Slaves No More*, 218.

54. Peyton Skipworth to John H. Cocke, Monrovia, April 22, 1840; and Sion Harris to Samuel Wilkeson, Caldwell [Liberia], April 16, 1840, both in Wiley, *Slaves No More*, 52–54. Tom W. Shick, *Behold the Promised Land: A History of Afro-American Settler Society in Nineteenth-Century Liberia* (Baltimore: Johns Hopkins University Press, 1977), 39–41.

55. Brown, *Journal*, 135, 308, 310.

56. My argument here rests on Jane Jackson Martin, "The Dual Legacy: Government Authority and Mission Influence among the Glebo of Eastern Liberia, 1834–1910" (Ph.D. diss., Boston University, 1968).

57. Ibid., 15.

58. Scott, *Day Dawn*, 48–69.

59. Martin, "Dual Legacy," 80–81.

60. Ibid., 81–82.

61. Ibid., 120.

62. Ibid., 130.

63. Missionaries' reactions to federal and state efforts to remove the southeastern Native Americans are discussed in Henry Warner Bowden, *American Indians and Christian Missions: Studies in Cultural Conflict* (Chicago: University of Chicago Press, 1981), 164–78; and William G. McLoughlin, *The Cherokees and Christianity: Essays on Acculturation and Cultural Persistence,* ed. Walter H. Conser Jr. (Athens: University of Georgia Press, 1994).

64. Martin, "Dual Legacy," 150.

65. Ibid., 143.

66. Dr. C. Abayomi Cassell, *Liberia: History of the First African Republic* (New York: Fountainhead, 1970), 222. A similar settling of differences between the settlers and the missionaries, both of whom feared the natives, is described in Brown, *Journal,* 165–66. Brown took the side of the settlers against the other missionaries, whom he considered too factious.

67. Martin, "Dual Legacy," 203.

68. Brittan, *Scenes,* 221.

69. Martin Robinson Delany, *The Condition, Elevation, Emigration, and Destiny of the Colored People of the United States, Politically Considered* (Philadelphia: by the author, 1852), 10, 169.

70. Martin Robinson Delany, "Official Report of the Niger Valley Exploring Party," in *Search for a Place: Black Separatism and Africa, 1860,* ed. Howard H. Bell (Ann Arbor: University of Michigan Press, 1969), 102–11. Delany's African policies are sharply criticized in Tunde Adeleke, *UnAfrican Americans: Nineteenth-Century Black Nationalism and the Civilizing Mission* (Lexington: University Press of Kentucky, 1998), 43–69.

71. Crummell, "Our National Mistakes and the Remedy for Them," in Crummell, *Des-*

tiny and Race: Selected Writings, 1840–1898, ed. Wilson Jeremiah Moses (Amherst: University of Massachusetts Press, 1992), 188–89.

72. Ibid., 185–86.

73. Hutchison, *Errand,* 67–69.

74. Tom W. Shick, "Rhetoric and Reality: Colonization and Afro-American Missionaries in Early Nineteenth-Century Liberia," in Jacobs, *Black Americans and the Missionary Movement,* 56.

75. Payne, "The Colonists and the Natives," *African Repository and Colonial Journal* 25 (1849): 139.

76. Brittan, *Scenes,* 297.

77. J. W. Lungenbeel, "Education of Colored Persons for the Missionary Work," *African Repository and Colonial Journal* 26 (1850): 260.

78. Douglass's opposition to colonization is discussed in David W. Blight, *Frederick Douglass' Civil War: Keeping Faith in Jubilee* (Baton Rouge: Louisiana State University Press, 1989), 122–47.

79. "Conversations of Lafayette," *African Repository and Colonial Journal* 1 (1825): 39.

80. See Brown, *Journal,* for an example.

81. The attraction of many early-twentieth-century African-American missionaries and pro-mission African Americans to Garveyism indicates one way the idea of black manhood exercised in Liberia merged into U.S. popular culture. See Randall K. Burkett, *Garveyism as a Religious Movement: The Institutionalization of a Black Civil Religion,* ATLA Monograph Series, No. 13 (Metuchen, N.J.: Scarecrow, and the American Theological Library Association, 1978), 184; Randall K. Burkett, ed., *Black Redemption: Churchmen Speak for the Garvey Movement* (Philadelphia: Temple University Press, 1978), 3–18. The idea appeared in highbrow literary culture in Melvin B. Tolson, *Libretto for the Republic of Liberia* (New York: Twayne, 1953), in which Liberia is introduced in stanza 1 as "No micro-footnote in a bunioned book / Homed by a pedant / With a gelded look: / You are / The ladder of survival dawn men saw / In the quicksilver sparrow that slips / The eagle's claw!"

CHAPTER 2

1. Amanda Berry Smith, *An Autobiography: The Story of the Lord's Dealings with Mrs. Amanda Smith the Colored Evangelist* (1893; reprint, N.Y.: Oxford University Press, 1988), 505.

2. There is a growing body of literature documenting the comparative study of religion in the United States in the late nineteenth century. One might do well to start with Richard Hughes Seager, *The World's Parliament of Religions: The East/West Encounter, Chicago, 1893* (Bloomington: Indiana University Press, 1995).

3. On the genre of Victorian travel writing, see Mary Louise Pratt, *Imperial Eyes: Travel Writing and Transculturation* (New York: Routledge, 1992).

4. For more on this theme and the emergence of racial and religious identity among African Americans in the early nineteenth century, see my forthcoming *African-American Communal Narratives: Religion, Race, and Memory in Nineteenth-Century America.*

5. On the dramatic effects of the Haitian Revolution on people in the United States, see

David B. Davis, *Revolutions: Reflections on American Equality and Foreign Liberations* (Cambridge, Mass.: Harvard University Press, 1990), 49–54; and Alfred N. Hunt, *Haiti's Influence on Antebellum America: Slumbering Volcano in the Caribbean* (Baton Rouge: Louisiana State University Press, 1988).

6. Floyd J. Miller, *The Search for a Black Nationality: Black Emigration and Colonization, 1787–1863* (Urbana: University of Illinois Press, 1975), viii.

7. The Protestant Episcopal Church was the first white church to turn over its African mission work to blacks in 1835. It was followed by the Presbyterian Church in 1843, which established Lincoln University as a training ground for black African missionaries. See Walter L. Williams, *Black Americans and the Evangelization of Africa, 1877–1900* (Madison: University of Wisconsin Press, 1982), 10, 12. On African-American missions to Africa, see Sylvia M. Jacobs, ed., *Black Americans and the Missionary Movement in Africa* (Westport, Conn.: Greenwood, 1982); Sandy D. Martin, *Black Baptists and African Missions: The Origins of a Movement, 1880–1915* (Macon, Ga.: Mercer University Press, 1989); and P. J. Staudenraus, *The African Colonization Movement, 1816–1865* (New York: Farrar, Straus and Giroux, 1980).

8. Julie Winch, "American Free Blacks and Emigration to Haiti," CISCLA Working Papers Series, Eleventh Caribbean Congress, Universidad Interamericana de Puerto Rico, 1988, 1, 8, 12–15, 17, 21.

9. Howard H. Bell, ed., *Black Separatism and the Caribbean, 1860* (Ann Arbor: University of Michigan Press, 1970); David M. Dean, *Defender of the Race: James Theodore Holly, Black Nationalist Bishop* (Boston: Lambeth, 1979); Miller, *Search,* 237; C. W. Mossell, *Toussaint L'Ouverture, The Hero of Saint Domingo, Soldier, Statesman, Martyr; or Hayti's Struggle, Triumph, Independence, and Achievements* (Lockport, N.Y.: Ward and Cobb, 1896).

10. *Pine and the Palm* (May 11, 1861).

11. In seeking to link the nationalist or racial themes of these works with the explicitly Christian narratives, I intend to counter the more common tendency of contemporary scholarship to divorce black nationalist ideology from its Protestant context. Scholars like Floyd Miller have labeled much of the antebellum ideology of emigration as "proto-Pan-Africanism," anticipating the growth of a more secular movement in the late nineteenth century. Yet this kind of description excises these nationalist narratives from the more encompassing religious cosmologies within which they are contained; many blacks had specific plans for the future of the race, to be sure, but their views of the future were most often encapsulated, more or less explicitly, within broader religious assertions about the destinies of all peoples of the world. See Miller, *Search.*

12. M. B. Bird, *The Black Man; Or, Haytian Independence* (1869; reprint, New York: Books for Libraries, 1971), vi, 48, 50.

13. Sir Spenser St. John, *Hayti; or the Black Republic,* 2d ed. (New York: Scribner and Welford, 1889), vii, ix, 289.

14. By his own account, St. John had a rough time in Haiti. There, during a period of intense civil strife in the late 1860s during the brief presidency of Salnave, St. John and other members of the British government were caught up in conflict. As he described it, "the diplomatic corps was continually forced to interfere to check the arbitrary conduct of the authorities, who seized our ships, arrested our subjects, insulted us in the streets, and to awe the

disaffected employed bands of villainous negroes and negresses to parade the town, who murdered those selected by their enemies" (ibid., 118).

15. Dean, *Defender*, 82. Those standard interpretations included the oft-cited epic of the Revolutionary era by Moreau de Saint-Mery, *Description topographique, physique, civile, politique et historique de la partie francaise de l'isle Saint Domingue*, 3 vols., the first of which appeared in 1797; a two-volume description of the country by Charles Mackenzie, a British consul-general who resided there in 1826–1827 and published his *Notes on Haiti* in 1830; and James Anthony Froude, *The English in the West Indies; or, The Bow of Ulysses* (1888).

16. Holly, "Thoughts on Hayti," *Anglo-African Magazine* (July 1859): 219.

17. Background information on Saunders is contained in a biographical note by Maxwell Whiteman, *Haytian Papers: A Collection of the very interesting proclamations and other official documents, together with some accounts of the rise, progress, and present state of the kingdom of Hayti* (Boston: Caleb Bingham, 1818), n.p.

18. "Memoir presented to the American Convention for Promoting the Abolition of Slavery, and Improving the Condition of the African Race," delivered in Philadelphia on Dec. 11, 1818, in Saunders, *Haytian Papers*.

19. J. Dennis Harris, "A Summer on the Borders of the Caribbean Sea" (1860), in Bell, *Black Separatism*, 167.

20. Mossell, *Toussaint*, xix.

21. Saunders, *Haytian Papers*, 153.

22. Holly, "Thoughts," *Anglo-African Magazine* (June 1859): 185–86.

23. Brown, *"St. Domingo: Its Revolutions and Its Patriots," delivered before the Metropolitan Athenaeum, London, and St. Thomas' Church, Philadelphia, 1854* (Boston, 1855), 12, 22.

24. Holly, "Thoughts," *Anglo-African Magazine* (June 1859): 186. On white anthropological theories in the United States and Britain in the nineteenth century, see Mia Elisabeth Bay, "The White Image in the Black Mind: African American Ideas about White People, 1830–1925" (Ph.D. diss., Yale University, 1993); George M. Fredrickson, *The Black Image in the White Mind: The Debate on Afro-American Character and Destiny, 1817–1914* (New York: Harper and Row, 1971); George Stocking Jr., *Victorian Anthropology* (New York: Free Press, 1987).

25. Dean, *Defender*, 20. Lydia Maria Child also referred to L'Ouverture's royal background several times in her biographical sketch in *The Freedmen's Book* (Boston: Ticknor and Fields, 1865), 34.

26. Holly, "A Vindication of the Capacity of the Negro for Self-Government and Civilized Progress" (1857), in Bell, *Black Separatism*, 60.

27. On African-American renderings of U.S. history, see Maffly-Kipp, *Communal Narratives*, chap. 4.

28. Lewis, letter of April 6, 1861, *Pine and the Palm* (June 8, 1861). Miller, *Search*, 242.

29. *Colored American* (Aug. 5, 1837).

30. Letter from the Reverend A. A. Phelps, *National Era* (Jan. 7, 1847): 3. See also Solomon P. Hood, "The A.M.E. Church in the West Indies," *AME Christian Recorder* (Nov. 20, 1890): 1.

31. Holly, "The Church at Hayti," *Churchman* (Nov. 1, 1855): 288.

32. "Domestic Life in Hayti," *AME Church Review* (April 1887): 400.

33. *Pine and the Palm* (June 8, 1861).

34. Mossell, *Toussaint,* 378, 382.

35. Holly, "The Church at Hayti," 288.

36. *Pine and the Palm* (May 18, 1861); Hunt, *Haiti's Influence,* 179; Holly, "The Church at Hayti," 288.

37. Mossell, *Toussaint,* 385, 459.

38. Ibid., 461–62, 465.

39. *National Era* (Nov. 4, 1847): 2.

40. Dean, *Defender,* 2, 20, 23; Holly, *Vindication,* 64.

41. Holly, *Vindication,* 65; idem, "Thoughts" (June 1859): 187.

42. Miller, *Search,* 80–86. Samuel E. Cornish, later the editor of the first black newspaper, *Freedom's Journal,* initially had supported the Haitian emigration movement. By the late 1820s, his paper ran an active anti-emigration campaign.

43. Miller, *Search,* 248; Solomon P. Hood, "The AME Church in the West Indies," *AME Christian Recorder* (Nov. 20, 1890): 2.

44. Winch, "Free Blacks," 16; Bruce Dain, "Haiti and Egypt in Early Black Racial Discourse in the United States," *Slavery and Abolition* 14 (1993): 142; Chris Dixon, "An Ambivalent Black Nationalism: Haiti, Africa, and Antebellum African-American Emigrationism," *Australasian Journal of American Studies* 10 (1991): 22 n. 11.

45. It should be noted, however, that southern blacks also emigrated. In 1859, several hundred Louisiana blacks left New Orleans (Miller, *Search,* 236).

CHAPTER 3

1. Joel Hawes, *The Help of the Lord, the Seal of the Missionary Work. A Sermon Preached at New Haven, Ct., Sept. 8, 1846 before the American Board of Commissioners for Foreign Missions* (Boston: n.p., 1846), 16.

2. On ABCFM history, see especially Rufus Anderson, *Memorial Volume of the First Fifty Years of the American Board of Commissioners for Foreign Missions* (Boston: n.p., 1862); Fred Field Goodsell, *You Shall Be My Witnesses: An Interpretation of the History of the American Board, 1810–1960* (Boston: American Board of Commissioners for Foreign Missions, 1959); William Ellsworth Strong, *The Story of the American Board: An Account of the First Hundred Years of the American Board of Commissioners for Foreign Missions* (Boston: Pilgrim, 1910); John A. Andrew III, *Rebuilding the Christian Commonwealth: New England Congregationalists and Foreign Missions, 1800–1830* (Lexington: University of Kentucky Press, 1976); Donald Philip Corr, "'The Field Is the World': Proclaiming, Translating, and Serving by the American Board of Commissioners for Foreign Missions" (Ph.D. diss., Fuller Theological Seminary, 1993); and Charles L. Chaney, *The Birth of Missions in America* (South Pasadena, Calif.: William Carey Library, 1976).

3. For perspectives on annual sermons, particularly their early incarnations, see Corr, "'The Field Is the World,'" 13–55; Charles I. Foster, *An Errand of Mercy: The Evangelical United Front, 1790–1837* (Chapel Hill: University of North Carolina Press, 1960); Alan Frederick Perry, "The American Board of Commissioners for Foreign Missions and the London Missionary Society in the Nineteenth Century: A Study of Ideas" (Ph.D. diss., Washington University, 1974).

4. The literature on Protestant millennial thought is vast. While this essay examines its radical, transcendent, and global implications within the context of mission theology, most recent studies focus on millennialism as it spurred Protestant commitments to nationalism, social reform, social control, and a special U.S. covenant with God. For the nineteenth century, see especially Martin Marty, *Protestantism in the United States: Righteous Empire,* 2d ed. (New York: Charles Scribner's Sons, 1986); Paul E. Johnson, *A Shopkeeper's Millennium: Society and Revivals in Rochester, New York, 1815–1837* (New York: Hill and Wang, 1978); Ruth H. Bloch, *Visionary Republic: Millennial Themes in American Thought, 1756–1800* (Cambridge, Mass.: Harvard University Press, 1985); Robert H. Abzug, *Cosmos Crumbling: American Reform and the Religious Imagination* (New York: Oxford University Press, 1994); James Turner, *Without God, Without Creed: The Origins of Unbelief in America* (Baltimore: Johns Hopkins University Press, 1985); Curtis D. Johnson, *Redeeming America: Evangelicals and the Road to Civil War* (Chicago: Ivan R. Dee, 1993); and Michael Barkun, *Crucible of the Millennium: The Burned-Over District of New York in the 1840s* (Syracuse: Syracuse University Press, 1986).

5. Millennialism is commonly linked to a Protestant conviction that the United States and its people represented a "new Israel," specially chosen as God's earthly agent. The idea of chosenness can serve a host of religious and political agendas. It is precisely this capacity for wide cultural application beyond theological constraints, however, that counsels caution when the analytical focus narrows to the Protestant religious community itself. For a thoughtful recent consideration of the United States and its elected status in the late nineteenth century, see James H. Moorhead, "The American Israel: Protestant Tribalism and Universal Mission," and Knud Krakau, "Response," in *Many Are Chosen: Divine Election and Western Nationalism,* ed. William Hutchison and Hartmut Lehmann (Minneapolis: Fortress, 1994), 145–201. See also Conrad Cherry, ed., *God's New Israel* (Englewood Cliffs, N.J.: Prentice-Hall, 1971); Charles G. Sellers, *The Market Revolution: Jacksonian America, 1815–1846* (New York: Oxford University Press, 1991); Richard T. Hughes and C. Leonard Allen, *Illusions of Innocence: Protestant Primitivism in America, 1630–1875* (Chicago: University of Chicago Press, 1988); Keith W. F. Stavely, *Puritan Legacies: Paradise Lost and the New England Tradition, 1630–1890* (Ithaca: Cornell University Press, 1987); Ernest Tuveson, *Redeemer Nation* (Chicago: University of Chicago Press, 1968).

6. On secular visions of national progress, see Frederick Merk, *Manifest Destiny and Mission in American History* (New York: Vintage, 1966); Robert Johannsen, *To the Halls of the Montezumas: The Mexican War in the American Imagination* (New York: Oxford University Press, 1985); Reginald Horsman, *Race and Manifest Destiny: The Origins of American Anglo-Saxonism* (Cambridge, Mass.: Harvard University Press, 1981); Sellers, *Market Revolution;* George M. Fredrickson, *The Inner Civil War* (New York: Harper and Row, 1965); and Eric Foner, *Politics and Ideology in the Age of the Civil War* (New York: Oxford University Press, 1980).

7. Hutchison also points out the chastening impulse of self-critique and broadly humanitarian aims, particularly as evidenced in the work of the ABCFM's "senior secretary" Rufus Anderson. Significantly, the ABCFM's annual sermons reveal a much broader base of concern. See Hutchison, "New England's Further Errand: Millennial Belief and the Beginnings of Foreign Missions," *Proceedings of the Massachusetts Historical Society* 94 (1982): 57–58,

63; and idem, *Errand to the World* (Chicago: University of Chicago Press, 1987). Recent studies have given more attention to the critical, less accommodating component of Protestant thought. See, for example, John G. West, *The Politics of Revelation and Reason: Religion and Civic Life in the New Nation* (Lawrence: University Press of Kansas, 1996); James Rohrer, *Keepers of the Covenant: Frontier Missions and the Decline of Congregationalism, 1774–1818* (New York: Oxford University Press, 1995); Ian H. Murray, *Revival and Revivalism: The Making and Marring of American Evangelicalism, 1750–1858* (Carlisle, Penn.: Banner of Truth Trust, 1994); Jonathan Sassi, "To Envision a Godly Society: The Public Christianity of the Southern New England Clergy, 1783–1833" (Ph.D. diss., University of California–Los Angeles, 1996); Mark S. Schantz, "Religious Tracts, Evangelical Reform, and the Market Revolution in Antebellum America," *Journal of the Early Republic* 17 (1997): 425–66; and Mark Y. Hanley, *Beyond a Christian Commonwealth: The Protestant Quarrel with the American Republic, 1830–1860* (Chapel Hill: University of North Carolina Press, 1994). For the period 1880–1920, James H. Moorhead notes the potential of Protestant universalism to provide a basis for self-criticism and a mitigation of cultural chauvinism. See Moorhead, "The American Israel," 153–54.

8. Rufus Anderson powerfully undermined U.S. claims to a natural cultural superiority in his detailed summation of ABCFM mission philosophy in 1869. See Anderson, *Foreign Missions: Their Relations and Claims* (New York: n.p., 1869), esp. 91–119.

9. Recent works on evangelical Protestantism's particular cultural confrontations include Abzug, *Cosmos Crumbling;* Richard Carwardine, *Evangelicals and Politics in Antebellum America* (New Haven: Yale University Press, 1993); Mark A. Noll, *One Nation Under God? Christian Faith and Political Action in America* (San Francisco: Harper and Row, 1988); West, *Politics of Revelation and Reason;* William G. McLoughlin, *Cherokees and Missionaries, 1789–1839* (New Haven: Yale University Press, 1984); Francis Paul Prucha, ed., *Cherokee Removal: The William Penn Essays and Other Writings* (Knoxville: University of Tennessee Press, 1981); and Ronald G. Walters, *American Reformers* (New York: Hill and Wang, 1978).

10. Abzug, *Cosmos Crumbling,* viii.

11. Mark Hopkins, "Sermon, Before the American Board of Commissioners for Foreign Missions," in *Miscellaneous Essays and Discourses* (Boston: n.p., 1847), 441–42.

12. Henry Smith, *The True Missionary Spirit in the Church the Measure of Her Christian Principle. A Sermon, Before the American Board of Commissioners for Foreign Missions at Their Meeting in Springfield, Mass.* (Boston: n.p., 1862), 6.

13. William Hutchison notes the centrality of the church in the early-nineteenth-century missionary vision, as well as how "the missions of church and nation converged and blended." I find in ABCFM sermons a sustained effort to distinguish between the U.S. "church" and the U.S. "nation" and subordinate the domestic church to the gospel's global mission. See Hutchison, *Errand,* 50–53.

14. Archibald Alexander, "Objections Obviated and God Glorified, by the Success of the Gospel Among the Heathen," *National Preacher* (Oct. 1829): 254–55.

15. John Codman, *The Duty of American Christians to Send the Gospel to the Heathen. A Sermon Preached at Hartford, Sept. 14, 1836, Before the American Board of Commissioners for Foreign Missions* (Boston: n.p., 1836), 9, 19.

16. Leonard Bacon, *The Relation of Faith to Missions. A Sermon Preached at Troy, New York, September 7, 1852, Before the American Board of Commissioners for Foreign Missions* (Boston: n.p., 1852), 14.

17. John Rice, "The Power of Truth and Love," *National Preacher* (Oct. 1828): 66, 74–76, 77.

18. M. L. P. Thompson, *The Great Promise. A Sermon Preached at Providence, R.I., September 8, 1857, Before the American Board of Commissioners for Foreign Missions* (Boston: n.p., 1857), 15; Joseph Thompson, *The Word of Life the Law of Missions. A Sermon Preached Before the American Board of Commissioners for Foreign Missions* (Boston: n.p., 1867), 23.

19. Smith, *True Missionary Spirit*, 7, 13, 17, 23, 25.

20. Andrew F. Walls, *The Missionary Movement in Christian History* (Maryknoll, N.Y.: Orbis, 1996), 237.

21. Samuel Hanson Cox, *The Bright and the Blessed Destination of the World. A Discourse Delivered at Pittsfield, Mass. on the Evening of Tuesday, Sept. 11, 1849* (New York: n.p., 1849), 29.

22. Nathan Beman, *The Gospel Adapted to the Wants of the World. A Sermon Preached in Providence, R.I., Sept. 9. 1840, Before the American Board of Commissioners for Foreign Missions* (Boston: n.p., 1840), 7–8.

23. Ibid., 5, 7, 10, 18.

24. Isaac Ferris, *Thy Kingdom Come. A Discourse Delivered at Boston, September 12, 1848, Before the American Board of Commissioners for Foreign Missions* (Boston: n.p., 1848), 13.

25. Cox, *Bright and the Blessed*, 27–28.

26. William Adams, *Christianity Designed for the World and the World Designed for Christianity. A Sermon Preached at Cincinnati, Ohio, October 4, 1853, Before the American Board of Commissioners for Foreign Missions* (Boston: n.p., 1854), 5.

27. Ibid.

28. Robert W. Patterson, *Elements of Christianity that Tend to Secure its Diffusion and Universal Prevalence. A Sermon, Before the American Board of Commissioners for Foreign Missions, at the Meeting in Philadelphia, Pa., October 2, 1859* (Boston: n.p., 1859), 14, 17.

29. Charles White, *Power Belongeth Unto God. A Sermon Preached at Hartford, Connecticut, September 12, 1854, Before the American Board of Commissioners for Foreign Missions* (Boston: n.p., 1854), 8, 32, 50–51.

30. The Prudential Committee, including four authors of annual sermons, issued a sweeping injunction against confounding either physical means or improvements with the singular mission of preaching the gospel and "saving men." Board Secretary Rufus Anderson and Mark Hopkins (Prudential Committee member, president of Williams College, and board president in 1857) prominently advocated this Christocentric approach. See *Report of the American Board of Commissioners for Foreign Missions, Presented at the Forty-Seventh Annual Meeting* (Boston: n.p., 1856), 51–67. See also Hutchison, *Errand*, 62–90; and Hanley, *Beyond a Christian Commonwealth*, 81–83. Firm pronouncements called missionaries to account, however, precisely because the struggle was particularly intense in the field. As Andrew F. Walls has recently observed, "Among the words *American evangelical missions* the word most people will hear first and loudest is the word *American*." Yet cultural exchange and

adaptation, Walls has also noted, is inescapably a component of any missionary outreach. See Walls, *Missionary Movement in Christian History*, 226–27. While board sermons have limited value as gauges of specific missionary behavior, they reveal much about the principles that leaders accepted as a basis for evaluating practice. For some recent considerations of missionaries in the field, see, for example, William G. McLoughlin, "The Missionary Dilemma," *Canadian Review of American Studies* 16 (1985): 395–409; McLoughlin, *Cherokees and Missionaries;* Keith R. Widder, "The Missionaries of the Mackinaw Mission, 1823–1837: Presbyterians and Congregationalists on the American Frontier," *American Presbyterian* 67 (1989): 273–81; Briton C. Busch, "Whalemen, Missionaries, and the Practice of Christianity in the Nineteenth-Century Pacific," *Hawaiian Journal of History* 27 (1993): 19–113; and Amanda Porterfield, "The Impact of Early New England Missionaries on Women's Roles in Zulu Culture," *Church History* 66 (March 1997): 67–80.

31. Edward Kirk, *Christian Missions—A Work of Faith. A Sermon, Before the American Board of Commissioners for Foreign Missions, at Their Meeting in Chicago, Illinois, October 3, 1865* (Boston: n.p., 1865), 12, 16.

32. Thomas De Witt, "The Gospel Harvest, and Christian's Duty," *National Preacher* (Dec. 1830): 100–101.

33. George W. Bethune, *Paul, the Missionary. A Sermon Preached at Newark, New Jersey, October 29, 1856, Before the American Board of Commissioners for Foreign Missions* (Boston: n.p., 1856), 16–17.

34. Adams, *Christianity Designed*, 34, 37, 38.

35. Ibid., 36–37.

36. William Allen, "Freedom Conferred Only by the Gospel," *National Preacher* (Oct. 1832): 70, 74, 76–77.

37. See, for example, Thomas R. Hietala, *Manifest Design* (Ithaca: Cornell University Press, 1985); and James H. Moorhead, *American Apocalypse* (New Haven: Yale University Press, 1978).

38. William McMurray, *The Spiritual Conquest of the Church. A Sermon Preached in Philadelphia, Sept. 18, 1833, Before the American Board of Commissioners for Foreign Missions* (Boston: n.p., 1833), 4–5, 14–17.

39. Ibid., 17–22.

40. Ibid., 20–22, 29–30.

41. Thomas H. Skinner, *Progress, the Law of the Missionary Work. A Sermon Preached in Rochester, N.Y., Sept. 1843 Before the American Board of Commissioners for Foreign Missions* (Boston: n.p., 1843), 12–14, 27.

42. Ibid., 45.

43. David H. Riddle, *Ground of Confidence in Foreign Missions. A Sermon, Preached at Portland, Maine, September 9, 1851, Before the American Board of Commissioners for Foreign Missions* (Boston: n.p., 1851), 8, 20, 23.

44. Bethune, *Paul, the Missionary*, 30–31.

45. Richard Storrs, *The "Things which are not:" God's chosen instruments for advancing His Kingdom. A Sermon, Preached at Cleveland, Ohio, October 1, 1861, Before the American Board of Commissioners for Foreign Missions* (New York: n.p., 1861), 38.

46. Ibid., 32–33, 38–39.

47. Ibid., 41, 44.

48. Ibid., 45.

49. Presbyterian divine Jonathan F. Stearns's annual sermon marked the formal end of his denomination's cooperation with the ABCFM. His final charge—"The Great Commission"—reaffirmed core themes that had guided the annual deliveries for decades: the agency of Christ acting through the Church universal; the primary mission of individual spiritual transformation; and the certainty of a global, millennial revolution. He also reflected on the years of cooperative effort. See Stearns, *The Great Commission. A Sermon Before the American Board of Commissioners for Foreign Missions, at Their Meeting in Brooklyn, N.Y., October 4, 1870* (Cambridge, Mass.: n.p., 1870).

50. Elisha L. Cleaveland, *Motives to the Missionary Work. A Sermon, Before the American Board of Commissioners for Foreign Missions, at Their Meeting in Rochester, N.Y., October 6, 1863* (Boston: n.p., 1863), 3–4, 17.

51. Jonathan Condit, *The Missionary Enterprise a True Development of the Life of the Church. A Sermon, Before the American Board of Commissioners for Foreign Missions, at Their Meeting in Worcester, Mass., October 4, 1864* (Boston: n.p., 1864), 6, 27.

52. Ibid., 7, 20, 28.

53. Lauren P. Hickok, *The Complete Idea of the World's Conversion to Jesus Christ. A Sermon Before the American Board of Commissioners for Foreign Missions, at Their Meeting in Pittsfield, Mass., September 25, 1866* (Boston: n.p., 1866), 5, 9, 17. See also Jonathan Edwards, *The Nature of True Virtue* (1755; reprint, Ann Arbor: University of Michigan Press, 1971). On the significance of the Edwardsean legacy for the ABCFM, see J. A. De Jong, *As the Waters Cover the Sea: Millennial Expectations in the Rise of American Missions* (Kampen, Netherlands: J. H. Kok, 1970).

54. Hickok, *Complete Idea*, 9.

55. Ibid., 6, 16.

56. Gordon Wood, *The Radicalism of the American Revolution* (New York: Knopf, 1992).

57. Christopher Lasch, *Revolt of the Elites and the Betrayal of Democracy* (New York: W. W. Norton, 1995), 15–16.

CHAPTER 4

1. *Baptist Missionary Magazine* (Aug. 1867): 234–35, 240–41, 258–62, 323–26.

2. *Macedonian and Home Mission Record* (July 1867): 26, 28.

3. See, for example, *Baptist Missionary Magazine* (July 1862): 209, (Aug. 1862): 315, (Sept. 1863): 333–34, (July 1864): 215–17, (Aug. 1864): 339–41.

4. English Baptist missionaries also argued that the meager number of European missionaries and their high cost precluded any chance that they alone could reach the vast numbers of Native Americans with the gospel. Under this plan, the European missionary did not evangelize or serve as pastor of a local church but planted churches and resolved issues of discipline and doctrine. Brian Stanley, *The History of the Baptist Missionary Society, 1792–1992* (Edinburgh: T and T Clark, 1992), 47–52.

5. Roger G. Torbet, *A History of the Baptists,* 3d ed. (Valley Forge: Judson, 1963), 247–49; *American Baptist Magazine and Missionary Intelligencer* (Jan. 1821): 36; *American Baptist Magazine* (June 1828): 167. See also *American Baptist Magazine and Missionary Intelligencer* (Jan. 1822): 254 and (May 1822): 346; *American Baptist Magazine* (March 1827): 77 and (Jan. 1828): 14. For similar arguments in later years, see *American Baptist Magazine* (Aug. 1848): 306; *Baptist Missionary Magazine* (April 1853): 110–11 and (July 1873): 223.

6. *American Baptist Magazine* (July 1835): 288; ibid. (July 1845): 154. See also (Oct. 1835): 404, (July 1838): 155, (Jan. 1839): 15, and (April 1842): 93.

7. C. H. Carpenter, *Self-Support, Illustrated in the History of the Bassein Karen Mission from 1840–1880* (Boston: Rand, Avery, 1883), 32–44; *American Baptist Magazine* (April 1842): 87–90 and (July 1844): 203.

8. Adoniram Judson, the lionized patriarch of U.S. Baptist missions, had ordained Ko Thah-a, a Burmese preacher, in 1829, but this action had been considered an exception. After Abbott's actions, missionaries ordained eight more Karen or Burmese over the next eight years, and the numbers climbed steadily after that. Carpenter, *Self-Support,* 147–64; *American Baptist Magazine* (Dec. 1829): 414.

9. Although a few attempts had been made to establish some sort of seminary, individual missionaries had conducted most of the education of indigenous pastors on a tutorial or mentoring basis. By 1846, the ABMU reported more than four thousand baptized Karen church members and nearly fifteen hundred more requesting baptism, led by two ordained Karen pastors and thirty-four "native assistants" in thirty-two churches. At that time, the ABMU had forty missionaries in Burma, about half of whom worked primarily among people other than the Karen. Robert. G. Torbet, *Venture of Faith: The Story of the American Baptist Foreign Mission Society and the Woman's American Baptist Foreign Mission Society, 1814–1954* (Philadelphia: Judson, 1955), 236.

10. The 1843 annual report underscored this concern: "The men whom we send out to preach must themselves be taught, or else a most imperfect type of Christianity must be propagated among the nations, and they would, in the end, in all probability, relapse into heathenism" (*American Baptist Magazine* [June 1843]: 125–26, 154–55).

11. Dana L. Robert, *American Women in Mission: A Social History of Their Thought and Practice, Modern Mission Era, 1792–1992: An Appraisal* (Macon, Ga.: Mercer University Press, 1996); Patricia R. Hill, *The World Their Household: The American Woman's Foreign Mission Movement and Cultural Transformation, 1870–1920* (Ann Arbor: University of Michigan Press, 1985).

12. *Baptist Missionary Magazine* (Dec. 1848): 444–52; Mrs. J. G. Binney, *Twenty-Six Years in Burmah: Records of the Life and Work of Joseph G. Binney, D.D.* (Philadelphia: American Baptist Publication Society, 1880), 7, 192–207.

13. *Baptist Missionary Magazine* (Nov. 1857): 386–87. See also (July 1858): 204; *Watchman & Reflector* (May 22, 1851): 81.

14. *Macedonian and Home Mission Record* (July 1867): 28. See also the appeal of the black Baptist preacher Leonard Grimes in James Melvin Washington, *Frustrated Fellowship: The Black Baptist Quest for Social Power* (Macon, Ga.: Mercer University Press, 1986), 62.

15. For representative articles, see *Home Evangelist* (July 1863): 26 and (Jan. 1866): 2; *Macedonian and Record* (June 1869): 21 and (Oct. 1871): 39; *Home Mission Monthly* (Jan. 1878): 18–19.

16. A list of officers and board members of the ABHMS, as well as their terms of service, is found in *Baptist Home Missions in North America: Including a Full Report of the Proceedings and Addresses of the Jubilee Meeting, and a Historical Sketch of The American Baptist Home Mission Society, Historical Tables, etc., 1832–1882* (New York: American Baptist Home Mission Society, 1883), 547–49. These have been compared to the list of officers of the ABMU between 1850 and 1890, published annually in the *Baptist Missionary Magazine.* In addition to the officers of each organization, many delegates served on annual committees for each of the organizations, so the linkage ran even deeper.

17. Baptist officials regularly noted the essential similarity and interconnected relationship between the two agencies. For example, see *Home Mission Record* (Sept. 1859): 34; *Home Mission Monthly* (Aug. 1882): 213–15.

18. When a Baptist minister suggested that Baptists form a separate organization to train black ministers, Simmons not only employed the terminology of native ministry but consciously upheld the foreign missionary model to defend the current system in the South. "If it is desirable to have a separate *national* organization to educate a native ministry in the South," he argued, "why should there not be another still to relieve the Missionary Union from the work of educating the native ministry on the foreign field?" *Macedonian and Record* (July 1868): 25; see also *Home Mission Monthly* (Dec. 1881): 254.

19. "The converts and the workers going out from such schools in Burmah, in Assam, among the Telugus, and among the colored people of this country, are the men and women who today are lifting their people with a courage equaled by no other instrumentality." *Home Mission Monthly* (Aug. 1881): 170. See also *Home Evangelist* (July 1863): 26 and (March 1866): 9; *Macedonian and Home Mission Record* (July 1868): 27 and (Feb. 1872): 7; *Home Mission Monthly* (Jan. 1879): 100, (June 1879): 190, and (Aug. 1880): 149.

20. Although many Baptist women traveled south under the secular common-school model of the "Yankee schoolm'arm," evangelical missionary work drove the women's work. In 1867, an ABHMS leader reported that women comprised the majority of those categorized as "assistant missionaries" and credited them for sparking "the most remarkable revivals on our mission field." A decade later, women formed their own organization, the Woman's American Baptist Home Mission Society (WABHMS), which they modeled after an auxiliary to the ABMU, the Woman's Baptist Foreign Missionary Society. The first annual report of the WABHMS declared its purpose to be "the evangelization of the women among the freedpeople and Indians, the heathen immigrants and the new settlements of the West." *Macedonian and Record* (March 1867): 9; *Home Mission Monthly* (Dec. 1878): 90.

21. *Baptist Missionary Magazine* (Oct. 1853): 419. See also *Baptist Missionary Magazine* (Nov. 1852): 430 and (July 1865): 206–7. Eventually, this type of female evangelism became known as "Zenana Work." Hill, *The World Their Household*, 5, 58.

22. Evelyn Brooks Higginbotham, *Righteous Discontent: The Women's Movement in the Black Baptist Church, 1880–1920* (Cambridge, Mass: Harvard University Press, 1993), 94.

23. Evelyn Brooks Higginbotham, "En-Gendering Leadership in the Home Mission

Schools," *American Baptist Quarterly* 12 (1993): 15. Eight years earlier, the WABHMS had presented this same reasoning in its first annual report; *Home Mission Monthly* (Dec. 1878): 90.

24. *Home Mission Monthly* (Aug. 1880): 148–49.

25. Like ABHMS officials, Jones believed that the health of the black community depended upon black seminaries and emphasized that blacks wanted "academic and theological training" equal to that of the "best trained men of other denominations." Walter Brooks made a similar appeal: "We do not want an education that 'is good enough for colored people,' but that degree and kind of mental training and culture . . . which is deemed necessary to the best interests, comfort and general usefulness of white youth" (*Home Mission Monthly* [Aug. 1880]: 148–49; [Jan. 1881]: 8).

26. In 1869, the ABHMS convened a meeting of its leading teachers from its various schools in the South to discuss educational policy. The following were among the four main questions considered: "Should we aim to teach the higher English and classical studies in each of our schools, or should we establish a central High School or Collegiate Institutes for the more advanced, or would it be better for those prepared for college to enter our Universities or Colleges at the North where they would have the elevating and social influence of cultivated white students?" The group concluded that although a few exceptional students should be educated in the North, most should be educated in the South, "lest the preacher be separated from the people he is to serve." *Macedonian and Record* (Oct. 1869): 37.

27. Northern Baptist conflicts over racial equality emerged in several ways. In 1864, a debate broke out over the reelection of Ira Harris as president of the ABMU because his voting record as a U.S. senator was seen as a limitation on the expansion of rights for blacks. Harris, however, regained the presidency. At the same time, ABHMS officials found it necessary to publish a policy stating that they would not send funds to educate blacks unless the donor specifically indicated that desire. On the other hand, other Baptists used the mission among blacks to try to overcome prejudice among fellow white Baptists. Facing a congregation opposed to the ABHMS's work among freedpeople, a Baptist preacher reported that he "lovingly and patiently and faithfully ploughed them and harrowed them, and cross-ploughed them again, in my preaching and teaching, until they *stopped* saying 'nigger,' and began to give and pray for the salvation of the souls of all for whom Jesus Christ died, without distinction of race or color." *Christian Recorder* (July 15, 1865): 109–10; *Macedonian and Home Mission Record* (June 1870): 22 and (Jan. 1872): 4.

28. *Baptist Missionary Magazine* (Dec. 1853): 476 and (Feb. 1867): 39. Hamilton Literary and Theological Institution evolved into Colgate University; the University of Lewisburg eventually became Bucknell University.

29. Morehouse regularly published statements about the capabilities of blacks. Referring to a special meeting of the ABHMS held in Nashville in 1888, Morehouse wrote, "The large number of very black men, some of them among the ablest in the gatherings, is conclusive proof that the genuine negro is as capable of as high attainments as his brother of lighter color, even his brother of the white cuticle" (*Home Mission Monthly* [Nov. 1888]: 279; see also [July 1886]: 166).

30. *Home Mission Monthly* (Nov. 1888): 304 and (Aug. 1896): 277.

31. *Home Mission Monthly* (June 1889): 144–45. A committee on black education had

made this same point seven years earlier at the jubilee meeting of the ABHMS. See *50th Anniversary of ABHMS,* 72, 93; also *Home Mission Monthly* (March 1884): 61.

32. Ann Judson had effectively established female conversion and education as primary goals for Baptist missionary women in the 1820s. Female educational efforts, however, were not seen as a central priority of missionary work until after the Civil War. *American Baptist Magazine and Missionary Intelligencer* (Jan. 1823): 18–20; Joan Jacobs Brumberg, *Mission for Life* (New York: Free Press, 1980), 13–19, 79–105; Hill, *The World Their Household.*

33. Ultimately, this thinking evolved into what Higginbotham, *Righteous Discontent,* 20–21, has termed the "Female Talented Tenth," which, she argues, provided the basis for interracial cooperation among women. *Home Mission Monthly* (Aug. 1881): 170.

34. James McPherson, "White Liberals and Black Power in Negro Education, 1865–1915," in *African Americans and Education in the South, 1865–1900,* ed. Donald G. Nieman (New York: Garland, 1994), 250.

35. *Macedonian and Record* (May 1870): 17.

36. Charles H. Corey, *A History of the Richmond Theological Seminary, with Reminiscences of Thirty Years' Work among the Colored People of the South* (Richmond: J. W. Randolph, 1895), 55–57, 64.

37. Quoted in Sandy Dwayne Martin, "The American Baptist Home Mission Society and Black Higher Education in the South, 1865–1920," in *African Americans and Education,* ed. Nieman, 234.

38. Washington, *Frustrated Fellowship,* 70–81, 95–105.

39. *Macedonian and Record* (July 1868): 25.

40. Most fully articulated by Rufus Anderson, the corresponding secretary of the American Board of Commissioners for Foreign Missions, the theory argued that missionaries should try to establish churches that were self-governing, self-propagating, and self-supporting. William R. Hutchison, *Errand to the World: American Protestant Thought and Foreign Missions* (Chicago: University of Chicago Press, 1987); Charles Forman, "A History of Foreign Mission Theory" in *American Missions in Bicentennial Perspective,* ed. R. Pierce Beaver (South Pasadena, Calif.: William Carey Library, 1976); Wilbert R. Shenk, "The Origins of the Three-Selfs in Relation to China," *International Bulletin of Missionary Research* 14 (1990): 29–30.

41. *Missionary Magazine* (July 1854): 218–26.

42. Wayland argued that preachers would enjoy the most success whose "habits of thought are not greatly elevated above those of his hearers." He criticized U.S. ministers who sought "to build up a good society" while collecting around them "the rich and the well-conditioned" instead of laboring to save souls. Arguing that "in the church of Christ there is no ministerial caste," Wayland declared that success among the Karen came from "rude" and unlettered men who worked with only a few books, some tracts, and the New Testament translated into their language. The prosperity of Baptist churches in western New York and the successful establishment of Rochester University grew from the efforts of earlier generations of "plain men, generally of ordinary education" who "preached repentance towards God, and faith in our Lord Jesus Christ." Francis Wayland, *The Apostolic Ministry: A Discourse Delivered in Rochester, N.Y, before the New York Baptist Union for Ministerial Education, July 12, 1853* (Rochester: Sage and Brother, 1853), 19–20, 51–57.

43. *Baptist Missionary Magazine* (July 1866): 220–25 and (July 1873): 223–24.

44. Nathan Hatch, *The Democratization of American Christianity* (New Haven: Yale University Press, 1989).

45. In 1853, Wayland sparked a widespread debate among Baptists of the Northeast by criticizing elitist pastors. Barnas Sears responded by arguing that since spiritual truth must be presented to the intellect, congregations needed educated ministers to open channels of thought. "Rhapsodical and ranting preaching may produce high excitement with an ignorant people," Sears declared, "but it will not elevate them, nor fit them for well-directed activity and influence." Thirty or forty years previously, Sears claimed, hardly a person could be found in Burma who believed in the existence of an eternal God, but now two-thirds to three-fourths of the people believed in one, thanks to missionaries who had elevated the people "not so much by oral preaching, as by books and schools." Barnas Sears, *An Educated Ministry: An Address Delivered Before the N.Y. Baptist Union for Ministerial Education, at its Anniversary, Held in Rochester, July 12, 1853* (New York: Lewis Colby, 1853), 9–12.

46. Darlene Clark Hine, "The Anatomy of Failure: Medical Education Reform and the Leonard Medical School of Shaw University, 1882–1920," in *African Americans and Education*, ed. Nieman, 130–43.

47. McPherson, "White Liberals and Black Power," 250; Adolph H. Grundman, "Northern Baptists and the Founding of Virginia Union University: The Perils of Paternalism," *Journal of Negro History* (1978): 26–41.

48. *Baptist Missionary Magazine* (July 1854).

49. "The gifts which are available for the awakening and conversion of men are not always adequate to their organization into an intelligent and effective force," the missionaries concluded. *Baptist Missionary Magazine* (July 1873): 223–24.

50. *Home Evangelist* (March 1863): 10; *Macedonian and Home Mission Record* (July 1870): 26, (Dec. 1869): 46, and (Dec. 1867): 50.

51. *Home Evangelist* (Jan. 1866): 2; *Macedonian and Home Mission Record* (Feb. 1869): 6, (Nov. 1869): 41, (June 1870): 22, and (Oct. 1871): 39.

52. Washington, *Frustrated Fellowship*, 124–31.

53. Kevin K. Gaines, *Uplifting the Race: Black Leadership, Politics, and Culture in the Twentieth Century* (Chapel Hill: University of North Carolina Press, 1996); McPherson, "White Liberals and Black Power," 247–69; Grundman, "Northern Baptists," 26–41.

54. James McPherson, *The Abolitionist Legacy: From Reconstruction to the NAACP* (Princeton: Princeton University Press, 1975), 184; Grundman, "Northern Baptists," 30.

55. Eventually, in 1906, the ABHMS made John Hope the first black president of Atlanta Baptist College (later Morehouse College). Addie Louise Joyner Butler, *The Distinctive Black College: Talladega, Tuskegee and Morehouse* (Metuchen, N.J.: Scarecrow, 1977), 107–11; McPherson, "White Liberals and Black Power"; Grundman, "Northern Baptists," 35–37.

56. Higginbotham, *Righteous Discontent*, 25–26, makes the point about the implicit support for social equality in the Talented Tenth model.

57. One variation of black action came from African Americans in distinctively black denominations like the African Methodist Episcopal Church and the African Methodist Episcopal Zion Church, who built educational institutions without the help of whites. James D.

Anderson, *The Education of Blacks in the South, 1860–1935* (Chapel Hill: University of North Carolina Press, 1988), 238–51; Nieman, *African Americans and Education,* viii.

58. John K. Fairbank, "Introduction: The Many Faces of Protestant Missions in China and the United States," in *The Missionary Enterprise in China and America,* ed. John K. Fairbank (Cambridge, Mass.: Harvard University Press, 1974), 13–14; Philip West, "Christianity and Nationalism: The Career of Wu Lei-ch'uan at Yenching University," in *Missionary Enterprise,* ed. Fairbank, 226–48; Higginbotham, *Righteous Discontent,* 21; W. E. B. DuBois, "The Talented Tenth," in *The Negro Problem* (1903; reprint, Miami, Fla.: Mnemosyne, 1969), 75.

59. Howard University would be the institutional exception to this statement, since it was created by an act of the federal government. But even here, missionary-minded evangelicals proved to be the driving force behind the congressional action that produced Howard. Atlanta University and Leland University, technically independent of any missionary agency, still had strong ties to evangelical agencies, Atlanta to the American Missionary Association (AMA) and Leland to northern Baptists. McPherson, *Abolitionist Legacy,* 143–54 and appendix B; Joe M. Richardson, *Christian Reconstruction: The American Missionary Association and Southern Blacks, 1861–1890* (Athens: University of Georgia Press, 1986), 75–78, 123.

60. Technically, the Congregationalists did not operate a denominational agency for either foreign or home missions. Nevertheless, they dominated the interdenominational American Board of Commissioners for Foreign Missions and its home missionary counterpart, the American Missionary Agency.

61. Richardson, *Christian Reconstruction,* 146–51, 189–91; McPherson, *Abolitionist Legacy,* appendix B.

62. Accusing evangelicals of placing proselytizing above education, Octavius Frothingham declared that the "sectarian" spirit of evangelical theology mixed secular with religious principles, threatening to compromise both. Robert C. Morris, *Reading, 'Riting, and Reconstruction: The Education of the Freedmen in the South, 1861–1870* (Chicago: University of Chicago Press, 1981), 61; Richardson, *Christian Reconstruction,* 74.

63. The decline in financial support played a key part in the demise of the AFUC. Ronald Butchart claims that donors switched from the AFUC to the denominational societies for "ideological" reasons, as wealthy northerners sought agencies that could control a threatening black population. This analysis has its flaws, though. Apart from an absence of evidence to support this transfer of support, Butchart leads one to the peculiar conclusion that refined Unitarians from Boston decided that their money would be better spent by the revivalistic Methodists after all. Ronald E. Butchart, *Northern Schools, Southern Blacks, and Reconstruction: Freedmen's Education, 1862–1875* (Westport, Conn.: Greenwood, 1980), 205.

64. Unlike the Garrisonians and the evangelicals, most Republicans had tied their conceptions of black citizenship and education to a free-labor ideology. When this ideology disintegrated during the Depression of 1873, the Republican Party dropped its commitment to black "uplift," contributing to the official abandonment of Reconstruction in 1877. Eric Foner, *Reconstruction: America's Unfinished Revolution, 1863–1877* (New York: Harper and Row, 1988). For claims that missionaries lost interest in freedpeople, see the following articles

in *African Americans and Education,* ed. Nieman: Nieman's introduction (ix–x); Roy E. Finkenbine, "'Our Little Circle': Benevolent Reformers, the Slater Fund, and the Argument for Black Industrial Education, 1882–1908," 70–86; J. M. Stephen Peeps, "Northern Philanthropy and the Emergence of Black Higher Education—Do-Gooders, Compromisers, or Co-conspirators?" 293–311.

65. McPherson, *Abolitionist Legacy,* 144–45.

66. The additional activities in black higher education by the AMA, the Presbyterian Board of Freedmen's Missions, and the Freedmen's Aid Society of the Methodist Episcopal Church suggest that up to 1895, evangelical missionaries played a more significant role in black education than the philanthropic efforts of the Slater and Peabody Funds. After Booker T. Washington captured the attention of northern philanthropists, however, northern philanthropic support for industrial education overwhelmed evangelical giving to liberal-arts colleges. *Home Mission Monthly* (Nov. 1888): 301; Anderson, *Education of Blacks,* 132–37, 252–55.

67. *Baptist Home Missions in North America,* 80, 84. *Home Mission Monthly* (Nov. 1888): 302 and (Aug. 1893): 253.

68. Industrial education drew increasing support toward the end of the century from northern businesspersons, politicians, and philanthropists who tended to favor it as a means to shape southern blacks into a passive working class. Anderson, *Education of Blacks,* 38–39; Finkenbine, "'Our Little Circle,'" 70–86; McPherson, *Abolitionist Legacy,* 212–18.

69. The arguments for industrial education often reinforced ideas that denigrated the intellectual capabilities of blacks by proclaiming manual labor as their proper position in society. Northern Baptist officials continued to push for the academic education of black leaders well after Reconstruction had ended, and northern Baptist racial views consistently appeared in ABHMS publications as points of tension with southern Baptists. Writing during an 1889 tour of the South, Morehouse bemoaned the "inherited prejudices" of the mass of southern whites, their opposition to northern educational policies, and the failure of Democrats to grant blacks legitimate opportunities. "The average white man and white woman of the South," he wrote, "have no sort of an understanding of the capacities, the attainments and the possibilities of the colored people." *Home Mission Monthly* (April 1889): 87–89; see also (April 1881): 81–83, (Nov. 1884): 276–77, (Sept. 1885): 226–27, (Feb. 1890): 44–45.

70. Most evangelical missionaries added industrial education to their schools in the 1880s and 1890s but maintained a strong theological and classical education component to their schools. The need for some blacks to receive the best academic education available served as the overriding point of Morehouse's Talented Tenth speech. At the 1890 Mohonk Conference on black education, home missionary leaders rejected pleas from philanthropists to embrace the industrial-education model. A decade later, as they labored to increase the endowment for black colleges, ABHMS officials attempted to win support from that great fount of Baptist philanthropy, John Rockefeller, but were refused by his philanthropic advisor. The educational philosophy of the ABHMS's schools did not match the industrialist's belief that black professional education should be scaled back and the denominational schools "Hamptonized." ABHMS officials still refused to abandon their ideal of classical education. Anderson, *Education of Blacks,* 70–72, 132–35, 251–55.

71. For instance, Butchart, *Northern Schools,* 35, insists that the evangelical push for black schooling stemmed from an ideology built upon racist fear of unregulated freedpeople, the desire to manipulate and control, and a search for order in the republic. Higginbotham, *Righteous Discontent,* 26–27, argues that northern whites worked for black education partly out of humanitarian concerns and partly because they feared black rebellion; an educated black leadership would preserve national security by mitigating the impact of black demagogues.

72. *Home Evangelist* (Jan. 1866): 1; *Baptist Home Missions in North America,* 72; Corey, *History of the Richmond Theological Seminary; Home Mission Monthly* (Dec. 1890): 347.

73. *Home Mission Monthly* (May 1885): 73, (Nov. 1888): 305, (Sept. 1890): 273.

74. For examples of anti–Roman Catholicism, see *Home Mission Monthly* (July 1880): 143 and (Sept. 1883): 188. Hopes for African-American missionaries in Africa can be found in *Macedonian and Home Mission Record* (Feb. 1871): 8 and (Nov. 1872): 44. Also in *Home Mission Monthly* (Jan. 1879): 100, (Aug. 1881): 161, (Jan. 1884): 11, (Dec. 1888): 343–45, and (Feb. 1890): 51. Also, Thomas Jefferson Morgan, *Africans in America* (New York: American Baptist Home Mission Society, 1898), 22–23.

75. Butchart, *Northern Schools,* 205; *Home Mission Monthly* (June 1889): 145.

CHAPTER 5

1. Abel Stevens, *The Centenary of American Methodism: A Sketch of its History, Theology, Practical System, and Success.* With a statement of the plan of the Centenary Celebration of 1866 by John M'Clintock, D.D. (New York: Carlton & Porter, 1865), 180, 185–87. Stevens prefaced his statement about Methodist missions with the insistence that Methodism was, from the beginning, intrinsically missionary: "Methodism was essentially a missionary movement, domestic and foreign. It initiated not only the spirit, but the practical plans of modern English missions." Stevens—indeed, the whole church—then endeavored to make and keep missions central. For a similar succinct estimate today, pertaining to Protestant missions generally, see Alvyn Austin, "Loved Ones in The Homelands: The Missionary Influence on North America," *Evangelical Studies Bulletin* 14 (Spring 1997): 1–5.

2. Compare the judgment of George G. Cookman, *Speeches Delivered on Various Occasions, by George G. Cookman, of the Baltimore Annual Conference, and Chaplain to the Senate of the United States* (New York: George Lane, 1840), 127–37:

What is Methodism? Methodism, sir, is a *revival of primitive New Testament religion,* such as glowed in the bosom and was seen in the lives of the apostles and martyrs.

It is a *revival of the vital, fundamental doctrines of the Christian faith.*

It is a *revival of the original New Testament organization,* particularly in restoring the itinerancy and brotherhood of the ministry, and the *right* administration of church discipline.

It is a *revival of the social spirit,* the free and ancient manner of social worship.

It is, above all, a *revival of the missionary spirit,* which, not content with a mere *defensive* warfare upon Zion's walls, goes forth *aggressively,* under the eternal promise, to the conquest of the world.

3. *History of the Methodist Episcopal Church in The United States of America*, 4 vols. (New York: Carlton & Porter, 1864–1867); *The History of the Religious Movement of the Eighteenth Century Called Methodism* (New York: Carlton & Porter, 1858–1861); *A Compendious History of American Methodism* (New York: Eaton & Mains; Cincinnati: Curts & Jennings, n.d. but 1867/1868); *Supplementary History of American Methodism* (New York: Eaton & Mains, 1899); *Memorials of the Introduction of Methodism into the Eastern States* (Boston: Charles H. Pierce, 1848); *Memorials of the Early Progress of Methodism in the Eastern States* (Boston: C. H. Pierce, 1852, c. 1851); *An Essay on Church Polity* (New York: Carlton & Porter, 1847); *The Women of Methodism* (New York: Carlton & Porter, 1866). Many of these publications went through several editions. And he produced a variety of other works.

4. See especially J. M. Reid, *Missions and Missionary Society of the Methodist Episcopal Church*, 2 vols. (New York: Phillips & Hunt, 1879). See also the revised and extended edition with J. T. Gracey, 3 vols. (New York: Eaton & Mains, 1895, 1896). Wade Crawford Barclay, *Early American Methodism, 1769–1844*, *The Methodist Episcopal Church, 1845–1939*, *Widening Horizons, 1845–95*, vols. 1–3 of *History of Methodist Missions*, 5 vols. (New York: Board of Missions of the Methodist Church, 1949–), vols. 1–3 by Barclay, vol. 4 by J. Tremayne Copplestone. Dana L. Robert, *American Women in Mission: A Social History of Their Thought and Practice* (Macon, Ga.: Mercer University Press, 1996).

5. No one captured the machine aspect of U.S. Methodism better than George Cookman. He conceived of the entire movement as a set of "wheels within wheels." Cookman, *Speeches Delivered on Various Occasions*, 134–37.

6. What, even today, constitutes the basic structure of the church? To non-Methodists, that might seem to be the congregation. Not so. In Methodism, the annual conference is "the basic body in the Church" or "the fundamental" body of the church. *The Book of Discipline of the United Methodist Church 1996* (Nashville: The United Methodist Publishing House, 1996), 31, 679, 23. The annual conference enjoys that distinction constitutionally, operationally, theologically, and historically. It was and is prior to ministries, members, lay officers, congregations. Prior to conference, of course, was Mr. Wesley, but then by Stevens's day he was with Methodists only in spirit. Conference carried on his role.

7. *Minutes of the Methodist Conferences, Annually Held in America: from 1773 to 1813, Inclusive* (New York: Daniel Hitt and Thomas Ware for the Methodist Connexion, 1813), 5–6.

8. This is a point that I cover in *The Methodist Conference in America. A History* (Nashville: Kingswood Books/Abingdon, 1996). See especially chapters 6 and 8.

9. "Circular address, and Constitution of the Missionary and Bible Society, of the Methodist Episcopal Church in America," *The Methodist Magazine* (June 1819): 277–79. [Note: The name was subsequently simplified to Missionary Society.]

10. See *Consecrated Talents: Or, The Life of Mrs. Mary W. Mason* (New York: Carlton & Lanahan, 1870), 82–85.

11. On the development and role of auxiliaries, see Barclay, *Early American Methodism*, 1, 291–303.

12. Barclay, *Early American Methodism*, 1, 280. Nathan Bangs, one of the architects of the new society, its principal head in early years, the drafter of its reports through 1837, and thereafter "Resident Corresponding Secretary" until 1844, in his retrospective on its creation,

quotes an endorsement made by the Reverend Thomas L. Douglass, of the Tennessee Conference, who reassured his readers, "The men to be aided and sanctioned as missionaries are to be approved by our annual conferences, and to act under the direction of our bishops." *A History of the Methodist Episcopal Church,* 8th ed., 4 vols. (New York: Carlton & Porter, 1860; originally published 1838–1841), 3: 179. On the role of Bangs, see Reid, *Missions and Missionary Society of the Methodist Episcopal Church,* 1: 28–30.

13. Reid, *Missions and Missionary Society of the Methodist Episcopal Church,* 1: 19–24.

14. *The Doctrines and Discipline of the Methodist Episcopal Church* (1832): 22, 24.

15. The 1836 General Conference dedicated in that year's *Discipline* a section to "Support of Missions," which delegated the preponderance of the agency for missions to the annual conferences, both through the directives it gave about the establishment and use of conference auxiliaries and the guidance it offered concerning launching of new conference missions. *The Doctrines and Discipline of the Methodist Episcopal Church* (1836): 174–78.

16. *Annual Report of the Missionary Society of the Methodist Episcopal Church* (1837): 17, 22. At this point, the society divided its missions into three categories: "Foreign and Aboriginal," "Domestic Missions Among the Destitute White Settlements," and "Missions for People of Colour." The Philadelphia Conference missions fell among the middle category. Among the few foreign efforts then drawing support were those in Liberia and South America.

17. Francis H. Tees et al., *Pioneering in Penn's Woods. Philadelphia Methodist Episcopal Annual Conference Through One Hundred Fifty Years* (n.p.: The Philadelphia Conference Tract Society of the Methodist Episcopal Church, 1937), 98.

18. *Minutes of the Annual Conferences of the Methodist Episcopal Church* (1829–1839): 194, 254, 318, 378, 450, 534, 622. The conference would also report that item, by individual collections or receipts, and initially it did not aggregate the amounts. See for 1834, Quest. 17 "What has been contributed for the support of Missions, and what for the publication of Bibles, Tracts, and Sunday school books?" rendered in simple summary table. *Minutes of the Philadelphia Conference of the Methodist Episcopal Church* (1834): 10, 34 (typescript version of apparently printed minutes at Duke University). Note: the titles of the minutes or proceedings of this and other conferences vary over time and are standardized in the above manner.

19. *Minutes of the Annual Conferences of the Methodist Episcopal Church* (1839–1845): 42, 135, 229, 333, 440, 568. Items marked * were identified as "very imperfect." Their imperfection can be confirmed at the receiving end. The *Annual Report of the Missionary Society of the Methodist Episcopal Church* (1844) listed 1843 receipts from Philadelphia as $1,985.35 in contrast to the $4,403.23 reported by the conference in the *Minutes.*

20. *Minutes of the Annual Conferences of the Methodist Episcopal Church* (1846–1851): 12, 102, 200, 312, 421, 556. The *Annual Report of the Missionary Society of the Methodist Episcopal Church* (1849) listed receipts from Philadelphia as partially from 1848 and from 1849 and the amount as $4,373.85.

21. *Minutes of the Annual Conferences of the Methodist Episcopal Church* (1852–1856): 16, 166, 339, 505. The *Annual Report of the Missionary Society of the Methodist Episcopal Church* (1854) listed 1852–1853 Philadelphia receipts as $11,783.89.

22. *Minutes of the Annual Conferences of the Methodist Episcopal Church* (1856–1857): 19,

227. Beginning in 1857, the *Minutes* rendered the accounts from the conferences in elaborate tables that specified the receipts from the various benevolences by charge, that is, by each circuit or station.

23. *The Methodist Centennial Year-Book for 1884,* ed. W. H. De Puy (New York: Phillips & Hunt; Cincinnati: Walden & Stowe, 1883), 129, 124. *The Methodist Centennial Year-Book* tracks the total receipts from 1820 through 1882. Philadelphia's percentage of the whole does not vary that dramatically, but its steadiness as the major supporter was achieved despite the dramatic growth in the number of conferences and of the population of the whole Methodist Episcopal Church (MEC). There were, for instance, only twenty-two conferences from 1832 to 1836, as opposed to ninety-nine in 1882.

24. *Minutes of the Philadelphia Conference of the Methodist Episcopal Church* (1839): 13.

25. Ibid., 14–15. By 1841, the conference added lines for Elders, Deacons, Col. Preachers, Schools, and Scholars. Ibid., (1841): 10–11.

26. Ibid., (1842): 14. The conference passed two other resolutions pertaining to Bible societies and one stipulating days for fasting and prayer—first Friday in October and Good Friday.

27. "Report of the Committee on an Uniform Plan of Finance," *Minutes of the Philadelphia Conference of the Methodist Episcopal Church* (1842): 18–19.

28. *Minutes of the Philadelphia Conference of the Methodist Episcopal Church* (1846): 13.

29. Ibid., (1848): 10. The *Discipline* specified that such dates be set, mandating with regard to missions, "It shall be the duty of each annual conference to appoint some month within the conference year, in which missionary collections shall be taken up within their respective bounds, and also to make such arrangements concerning branch societies as may be deemed expedient." *The Doctrines and Discipline of the Methodist Episcopal Church* (1848): 179.

30. In 1839, the denomination reorganized the Missionary Society, incorporating it through an act of the New York Senate and Assembly. Its affairs were vested in a Board of Managers "of not less than thirty-two lay members, and of so many clerical members, not exceeding that number" "to be annually elected at a meeting of the Society to be called for that purpose, and held in the city of New York." *Annual Report of the Missionary Society of the Methodist Episcopal Church* (1854): 5–6.

31. "The resident corresponding secretary shall, by virtue of his office, be a member of the New-York conference, to which, in the interval of the General Conference, he shall be held responsible for his conduct, and the New-York conference shall have power by and with the advice of the managers of the Missionary Society of the Methodist Episcopal Church and consent of the bishop presiding, to remove him from office: and in case of removal, death or resignation, the New-York conference with the concurrence of the presiding bishops, shall fill the vacancy until the next ensuing General Conference." *The Doctrines and Discipline of the Methodist Episcopal Church* (1836): 177–78.

32. *Minutes of the Philadelphia Conference of the Methodist Episcopal Church* (1847): 6.

33. Ibid., 5.

34. Ibid., (1848): 5–6.

35. *The Doctrines and Discipline of the Methodist Episcopal Church* (1848): 177–85. General Conference expanded the largely passive, permissive eight-point program of the 1836 *Disci-*

pline into a seventeen-paragraph venture that assigned major responsibilities for conferences, both in themselves and as overseers of the circuits and stations. The major points in this program are elaborated in the discussion of Durbin's work.

36. Reid, *Missions and Missionary Society of the Methodist Episcopal Church,* I: 32–39.

37. For further information on Durbin, see the entry in *The Methodists* by James E. Kirby, Russell E. Richey, and Kenneth E. Rowe (Westport, Conn.: Greenwood Press, 1996), 291–92; also the estimates of him by John A. Roche, *The Life of John Price Durbin* (New York: n.p., 1889) and "John Price Durbin," *Methodist Quarterly Review* 69 (May 1887): 329–54.

38. *Minutes of the Philadelphia Conference of the Methodist Episcopal Church* (1835): (typescript version of apparently printed minutes), n.p. but 10.

39. J. P. Durbin was, for instance, listed first as delegate to the 1844 General Conference. *Minutes of the Philadelphia Conference of the Methodist Episcopal Church* (1844): 10.

40. Ibid., (1845): 12.

41. Ibid., (1846): 14.

42. Ibid., (1849): 5. This office is now known as the district superintendent. By that time, the *Minutes* listed a North German Mission in N. Phila. District and South German Mission in S. Phila. District; *Minutes of the Philadelphia Conference of the Methodist Episcopal Church* (1849): 5–6.

43. Tees, *Pioneering,* 117–19.

44. *Minutes of the Philadelphia Conference of the Methodist Episcopal Church* (1850): 6.

45. *Minutes of the Troy Conference* (1851): 21–22. Troy outlined the program, derived from a communiqué from Durbin, in a set of eight resolutions that specified agency, action, calendar, and follow-up procedures.

46. "Minutes Erie Conference for the Year 1850," *Minutes of the First Twenty Sessions of the Erie Annual Conference* (Published by Order of the Conference, 1907), 257.

47. For Erie, see ibid. Compare *Minutes of the Maine Annual Conference* (1850): 10–11 and *Minutes of the New England Annual Conference* (1851): 30–31.

48. *Minutes of the Philadelphia Conference of the Methodist Episcopal Church* (1851): 12.

49. Ibid., 8.

50. *Annual Report of the Missionary Society of the Methodist Episcopal Church* (1854): 9. As an interim step, the General Conference of 1844 had empowered the bishops to take such action. *The General Conferences of the Methodist Episcopal Church From 1792 to 1896,* ed. Lewis Curts (Cincinnati: Curts & Jennings; New York: Eaton & Mains, 1900), 367–68.

51. *Annual Report of the Missionary Society of the Methodist Episcopal Church* (1854): 33.

52. *Minutes of the Philadelphia Conference of the Methodist Episcopal Church* (1856): 14, 1. Philadelphia, at this point, created thirteen standing committees. Missions was third on the list, being preceded by Public Worship and Necessitous Cases. To the latter, incidentally, the conference stewards were appropriately appointed.

53. *Minutes of the Annual Conferences of the Methodist Episcopal Church* (1859): 1. The preceding year, it had begun to include tables, one of "Appointments of Preachers, With Their Post Office Address," another listing names of all preachers by year of admission to the conference, 1806 being the first. *Minutes of the Philadelphia Conference of the Methodist Episcopal*

Church (1858): 9–12, 19–20. By 1859, to those two items, Philadelphia added a very interesting "Plan of Statistics for Annual Minutes."

54. See the *Minutes* for various actions, including memorials on the New Chapter on Slavery, which were referred to "Committee on the State of the Church." For instance, "A memorial from a Convention of laymen, held at Cambridge, Md., March 5th, 1861, also the action of the male members of the Cambridge Station, upon the subject of the New Chapter on Slavery, were presented and referred to the same Committee." The report proposed and conference passed a resolution calling for repeal of New Chapter. Then "the Conference directed the printing in tract form of 5,000 copies of the report of the Committee on the State of the Church; also, its publication in the Christian Advocate and Journal, Methodist, and Baltimore Christian Advocate." *Minutes of the Philadelphia Conference of the Methodist Episcopal Church* (1861): 8–12.

55. *Minutes of the Philadelphia Conference of the Methodist Episcopal Church* (1864): 15, 44–45.

56. Ibid., 47–48.

57. *Journal of General Conference/MEC/1864*, 485–86.

58. Tees, *Pioneering*, 102.

59. *Minutes of the Philadelphia Conference of the Methodist Episcopal Church* (1862): 13.

60. *Minutes of the Eightieth Session of the Philadelphia Conference of the Methodist Episcopal Church* (1867). The minutes also include "Forty-Sixth Annual Report of the Missionary Society of the Methodist Episcopal Church, within the Bounds of the Philadelphia Conference, for Promoting Domestic and Foreign Missions," 65–116.

61. Ibid., 6–7.

62. Ibid., 65.

63. Ibid., 10, 47.

64. Ibid., 10.

65. *Minutes of the Philadelphia Conference of the Methodist Episcopal Church* (1868): 12.

INTRODUCTION TO PART II

1. Patricia R. Hill, "The Missionary Enterprise," in *Encyclopedia of the American Religious Experience,* ed. Charles H. Lippy and Peter W. Williams (New York: Charles Scribner's Sons, 1988), 3: 1,687, and Patricia R. Hill, *The World Their Household: The American Woman's Foreign Mission Movement and Cultural Transformation, 1870–1920* (Ann Arbor: University of Michigan Press, 1985), esp. chap. 6. Hill's pathbreaking book remains crucial to understanding women's role at home as well as abroad.

2. Michael Parker, *The Kingdom of Character: The Student Volunteer Movement for Foreign Missions (1886–1926)* (Lanham, Md.: American Society of Missiology and University Press of America, 1998).

3. Oscar E. Brown, quoted without original citation in Emily S. Rosenberg, *Spreading the American Dream: American Economic and Cultural Expansion, 1890–1945* (New York: Hill and Wang, 1982), 28.

4. William R. Hutchison, *Errand to the World: American Protestant Thought and Foreign Missions* (Chicago: University of Chicago Press, 1987), 111.

CHAPTER 6

1. See Robert T. Handy, "The Christian Conquest of the World (1890–1920)," chap. 5 in *A Christian America: Protestant Hopes and Historical Realities,* 2d ed. (New York: Oxford University Press, 1984), for a vigorous description of this expansionist era.

2. "Our Roll of Subscribers," *The Church at Home and Abroad* (April 1888): 330 (hereafter *CHA*); the author here reported that there had been 10,000 subscribers to the new combined publication by the end of January 1887, and that number had since then more than doubled to more than 26,000. The author anticipated subscriptions of 30,000 by the end of 1888. See also Marvin R. Vincent et al., "Introduction," *CHA* (Jan. 1887): 1–2.

"Introducing Our Readers to the Board of Foreign Missions," *CHA* (Jan. 1887): 69, reported that the new magazine would take over from the *Foreign Missionary,* the Board of Foreign Missions' magazine; this "introduction" indicated that the circulation of its counterpart, *Home Missionary,* had been the larger of the two. *The Church at Home and Abroad* took over the *Assembly Herald* in 1894 and began to publish under that name in 1898. I am grateful to Gina Overcash, E. H. Little Library, Davidson College, Davidson, N.C., for help in tracing this history.

3. The aim of the magazine's editors to appeal to a large cohort of Presbyterian laity was clearly stated by Marvin R. Vincent, " 'The Church at Home and Abroad,' " *CHA* (Jan. 1887): 3–6; recognizing the immense circulation of secular monthlies and their popular character— "addressing . . . the masses rather than . . . the scholarly minority" (4)—he set out several policies for the magazine's content. These included the focus on "living topics" or current issues, "new topics" simplified for consumption by untrained readers, and "lessons [in] the form of stories" (4–5).

Donald A. Luidens, "Numbering the Presbyterian Branches: Membership Trends Since Colonial Times," in *The Mainstream Protestant Decline: The Presbyterian Pattern,* ed. Milton J. Coalter, John M. Mulder, and Louis B. Weeks (Louisville: Westminster John Knox Press, 1990), 39, sets PCUSA membership in 1890 at around 875,000. This number rose to around one million members by 1900.

4. The quotations come from "Negro Philosophy," *CHA* (March 1890): 199.

5. Although the pattern structuring this essay came to my attention while reading through other northern mission magazines of the period (mainly the Presbyterian *Woman's Work for Woman and Our Mission Field,* the Methodist *Heathen Woman's Friend, Aggressive Methodism,* and the *Methodist Review*), *The Church at Home and Abroad* provided a particular wealth of detail and carefully tracked work with the three groups under consideration. Each issue included a section treating "Freedmen," and one issue per year focused on missions to the Mormons, and to Roman Catholics in both the United States and "Papal Europe" (May and August, respectively).

6. Rev. D. S. Kennedy, "Our Denominational Policy in the Development of the Negro," *CHA* (July 1894): 59.

7. The phrase comes from Myra Jehlen, *American Incarnation: The Individual, the Nation, and the Continent* (Cambridge, Mass.: Harvard University Press, 1986).

8. R. H. Allen, D.D., "Cheering Words for the Freedmen from the West," *CHA* (April 1890): 321. Allen here quoted a report of the Synod of Indiana.

9. "Our Nation's Work for the Colored People," *CHA* (Aug. 1890): 141: "We need to be guarded against a tendency to think of their weaknesses and vices as peculiar to Negro nature and not, as they really are, characteristic of all human nature under similar conditions."

10. H. N. Payne, D.D., "Are the Negroes an Exceptional Class?" *CHA* (Nov. 1891): 428: "The position of the Presbyterian Church is unmistakable. We stand by these three declarations, 'God hath made of one blood all nations of men for to dwell on all the face of the earth' (Acts 17:26). 'One is your Master, even Christ, and all ye are brethren.' (Matt. 23:8) 'In as much as ye have done it unto one of the least of these my brethren, ye have done it unto me.' (Matt. 25:40) This is our confession of faith on this subject, and we desire no revision. In the eyes of God all men are equal, and Jefferson's immortal declaration includes the Blacks with the Whites."

I thank Julie Byrne for pointing out that racism based on assumptions about the essential nature of the "other," the very kind of racism that writers in *The Church at Home and Abroad* opposed and answered, became common currency in the broader culture during Reconstruction, helped along by the theories of biological determinism coming into vogue at the time; see, for instance, George Fredrickson, *The Black Image in the White Mind: The Debate on Afro-American Character and Destiny, 1817–1914* (Middletown, Conn.: Wesleyan University Press, 1971); Stephen Jay Gould, *The Mismeasure of Man* (New York: W. W. Norton, 1981); and William Stanton, *The Leopard's Spots: Scientific Attitudes toward Race in America* (Chicago: University of Chicago Press, 1960).

11. See, for instance, "Samples From Our Letter File: No. 6," *CHA* (March 1894): 236: "Some look up the Presbyterian Church as a great curiosity. They come to our Sunday school to see how we teach the Bible. We pack the shorter Catechism into them every time they come."

12. For a concise explanation of the historic Presbyterian confidence in learning and the necessity of a trained ministry, see James H. Smylie, *A Brief History of the Presbyterians* (Louisville: Geneva Press, 1996), 25, 74–75. Smylie also notes that the PCUSA did separate its black members from the larger membership; in 1894, the denomination formed the Afro-American Presbyterian Council, led by black ministers and aimed at overseeing the church's evangelism in the black South. Separate black synods existed until the 1950s (105).

On educational missions, see also the more meditative but still historical Gayraud S. Wilmore, *Black and Presbyterian: The Heritage and the Hope* (Philadelphia: Geneva Press, 1983), 63.

Accounts of educational work among freedpeople include: Rev. I. B. Crowe, "Our Work among the Freedmen," *CHA* (March 1892): 257–58; "Among the Colored People of the South," *CHA* (Dec. 1897): 475–77; "Thirty Years," *CHA* (June 1895): 508–10; and "Affiliated Schools," *CHA* (Aug. 1897): 105. Articles often focused on particular schools. For only two examples, see "Mary Allen Seminary," *CHA* (Oct. 1891): 336, and "Ingleside Seminary," *CHA* (Sept. 1897): 186.

13. Rev. J. E. Rawlins, "The Board's Work in Richmond, Va.," *CHA* (April 1897): 280–82,

describes the author's work as pastor of the First Colored Presbyterian Church in Richmond. This black pastor himself believed that Presbyterians brought something unique to the blacks they ministered to: "Our church, with its intelligent and orderly worship . . . has an important work to accomplish, which it is doing quietly but effectively. Other systems to a large extent appeal to the emotional—ours to the intellectual and spiritual natures" (282).

Contrast this attitude, however, with that described in Eric Foner, *Reconstruction: America's Unfinished Revolution: 1863–1877* (New York: Harper and Row, 1988), 92, regarding the introduction of a more sedate style of worship: " 'The old [black] people were not anxious to see innovations introduced in religious worship,' an AME leader later wrote, recalling how one black minister from the North with an undemonstrative preaching style was mocked as a 'Presbyterian' by his Southern flock."

14. Rev. R. H. Allen, "A Quarter-Century's Work Among the Freedmen," *CHA* (June 1890): 531.

15. See, for example, R. D. J., "Voices from the Southland," *CHA* (Sept. 1890): 243–45; Mrs. M. G. P. Rice, "Light in the 'Black Belt' of Virginia," *CHA* (Nov. 1890): 430; and Mrs. R. A. Cottingham, "Life Among the Lowly in the Southland," *CHA* (May 1897): 322.

16. "Samples From Our Letter File: No. 10," *CHA* (March 1894): 237.

17. See, for example, Crowe, "Our Work among the Freedmen," 257, who tried in this article to steer the focus of potential donors to the cause away from race and toward the cause of an informed freed citizenship.

Foner, *Reconstruction,* 145, notes that even some missionaries indulged in racist slurs against their charges. He cites the example of the predominantly Congregational American Missionary Association's (AMA) dismissing one teacher for such insensitivity. The AMA "urged teachers to 'dispossess [their] thoughts of the vulgar prejudice against color' and treat blacks in every respect 'as we would if they were white.' "

One gathers from the continuous appeals in *The Church at Home and Abroad* for money, and from the plaintive tone of exhortations to give, that the PCUSA's work among freedpeople was not widely supported by its members. According to "Young People's Societies," *CHA* (Feb. 1898): 109, only a fraction of the denomination's congregations contributed to the Board of Missions for Freedmen. See also Mrs. Franklina Gray Bartlett, "Southern Negro Education," *CHA* (March 1897): 199–200; E. P. C., "Fighting Against Growth," *CHA* (Nov. 1895): 415–16; Edward P. Cowan, "Important: Do Not Forget the Freedmen," *CHA* (Dec. 1894): 514; and "As Much as Last Year," *CHA* (March 1898): 229.

18. "Negro Philosophy," 199 (emphasis added).

19. R. H. Allen, "Concerned for the Freedmen," *CHA* (Oct. 1891): 335.

20. S. F. Wentz, "Helps and Hindrances," *CHA* (June 1896): 507.

21. Rev. D. S. Kennedy, "Work with the Colored Race," *CHA* (Jan. 1895): 54.

22. Allen, "Concerned for the Freedmen," 335.

23. "Facts for Christian Workers," *CHA* (Nov. 1890): 427.

24. The quoted phrase comes from an unsigned editorial note in the May 1896 issue of *CHA,* page 420.

25. "The Negro at the Atlanta Exposition," *CHA* (Oct. 1895): 269; Rev. H. N. Payne, "The Negro at the Exposition," *CHA* (Dec. 1895): 495–97.

26. Allen (quoting a report from the Synod of Columbia), "Cheering Words," 321–22. Cf. "Address of Booker T. Washington," *CHA* (April 1896): 307. Speaking at a home missions rally at Carnegie Hall in New York City, Washington said, "My friends, there is no escape; you must help us raise our civilization or yours will be lowered. When the South is poor, you are poor; when the South is ignorant, you are ignorant; when the South commits crime, you commit crime. When you help the South, you help yourselves."

27. Allen, "Cheering Words," 321–22.

28. "Our Routine of Work," *CHA* (May 1896): 422.

29. Foner, *Reconstruction,* 91–92, 146; he calls efforts to educate freedpeople by northern missionary and educational societies "a typical nineteenth-century amalgam of benevolent uplift and social control" (146).

See also Henry Lee Swint, *The Northern Teacher in the South, 1862–1870* (Nashville: Vanderbilt University Press, 1941), 80–83.

30. The phrase quoted in this section's title comes from "Roman Catholicism," *CHA* (July 1890): 48; the unnamed author quoted one cardinal's response—that "we must be Catholics first, and citizens afterward"—to Leo XIII's January 1890 declaration that civil laws took second place to divine ones.

The scope of missions to Roman Catholics is more difficult to determine from the reports in *The Church at Home and Abroad* than from those about freedpeople or even Mormons in the West. The work took place as part of both home and foreign missions. From around 1850, Roman Catholics constituted the largest formal religious community in the United States (R. Laurence Moore, *Religious Outsiders and the Making of Americans* [New York: Oxford University Press, 1986], 50). Compared, therefore, to the work among freedpeople and Mormons, missions to Roman Catholics, foreign and domestic, were larger but more diffuse geographically.

A sampling of articles on specific Catholic work includes: Rev. Dr. Mathews, "Missions to Papal Europe," *CHA* (Aug. 1890): 117; "Romanists and Mexicans," *CHA* (Nov. 1897): 363–64; "Missions in Guatemala," *CHA* (March 1894): 205, and related notes on 206; Rev. Francesco Pesaturo, "Italians in the United States," *CHA* (April 1895): 332–34; and Rev. Alexander Robertson, "A Visit to the Reformed Spanish Church," *CHA* (May 1893): 347–49.

Another element contributing, perhaps, to the difficulty in quantifying missions to Roman Catholics, especially in contrast with the work with freedpeople, may be that the work in the South focused largely on establishing schools—that is, on developing an institutional solution to the problems of superstition and ignorance—while the idea driving the work with Roman Catholics—opposition to foreign control of the U.S. way of life—can, in one sense, be understood as anti-institutional. Catholics missionized by Protestants, as will be seen, were to read their Bibles and develop, as individuals, dreams and desires separate from those of Rome. Of course, U.S. public schools became major sites of conflict during this era. But Protestants understood schools as institutions for developing individuals, not, as for Catholics opposed to Americanization, as institutions for reproducing an institution. On the schools conflict, see Jay P. Dolan, *The American Catholic Experience: A History from Colonial Times to the Present* (Notre Dame: University of Notre Dame Press, 1985), 263–93; and Handy, *Christian America,* 87–90.

31. Rev. J. H. Barton, "Romanism in the West," *CHA* (Feb. 1895): 142, recounted how Jesuits in his Idaho mission territory "make a specialty of winning persons without seeming to do so." Similarly, John Gillespie, D.D., "Roman Catholic Missions in China," *CHA* (March 1890): 218–21, wrote that the Jesuits gained entry to China by "recourse to that unscrupulous cunning and artifice for which Jesuitism has since become the synonym" (219).

32. "The Mexicans in the United States," *CHA* (Nov. 1893): 388.

33. "Roman Catholicism," 47, quoting Pope Pius IX; see also "Romanism at Its Worst," *CHA* (Nov. 1893): 376.

34. "New England, Roman Catholic," *CHA* (March 1893): 202–3. This article reports that the one million members of the "Romish Church" in the region outnumbered the Congregationalists, Methodists, Baptists, and Episcopalians put together. "This is truly alarming! The enemy is getting literally behind our Home Mission forces as Sherman got behind the Confederates by his memorable march to the sea" (202).

35. "Leaven vs. Legislation," *CHA* (Sept. 1890): 248. See also an unsigned, untitled note in *CHA* (March 1894): 206: "A prominent resident of Mexico is reported recently to have stated that 'Roman Catholic influence is less in Mexico to-day than in the United States, where there is hardly a statesman who dares open his lips against the Pope.'"

36. "Leaven vs. Legislation," 248, 249. See also an accompanying article, "Realistic," *CHA* (Sept. 1890): 249, which refers to "preaching places" established in a Wisconsin town as "forts."

37. "Realistic," 249.

38. Note, for instance, the title of one article on Roman Catholic opposition to Protestant Bible distribution: "Some Nineteenth Century Medievalism" (Rev. J. B. Kolb, *CHA* [Nov. 1895]: 388–89).

39. For example, "Leaven vs. Legislation," 245. Roman Catholics apparently did not distinguish Presbyterians from other Protestant missionary groups either. See Rev. Isaac Boyce, "The Story of a Brave Life," *CHA* (March 1894): 210–12, whose Mexican protagonist suffered ostracism for becoming a "Protestant"; and Alexander Robertson, "An Italian Village Embracing Protestantism—'A Peaceful Revolution,'" *CHA* (May 1894): 370. At a gathering of "Reformed Christians," the pastor declared to them, "Yes . . . we are protestants [*sic*], with this difference, that we protest against error, whilst they protest against the truth."

Handy, *Christian America*, 82–100, describes the Protestant rage for interdenominational cooperation in the years following the Civil War.

40. Rev. Jesse F. Forbes, "The Roman Catholic Church as Seen by a City Pastor," *CHA* (Feb. 1894): 132–34.

41. "Romanists and Foreigners," *CHA* (Aug. 1893): 133, 134.

42. Forbes, "City Pastor," 132–34. He wrote that the Bible "had previously been a sealed book" to his formerly Catholic converts (133), and the absence of the Bible's liberating influence on the United States "would blot out the light from the heaven of civil as well as religious liberty. It would make the United States like Spain and other countries dominated for centuries by Papal power. It should not, it must not be true in the United States" (134).

43. Kolb, "Nineteenth Century Medievalism," 388. "Nevertheless," Kolb wrote, "Bible

distribution goes on. A colporteur in [the same town] has sold upwards of ninety Bibles this month" (389).

44. Robertson, "Peaceful Revolution"; he wrote that Bibles "were eagerly read and studied, and passed from hand to hand and from house to house." One convert "begged for books for himself and his companions. The eagerness displayed by all to obtain a book was very remarkable" (369, 370).

See also Rev. W. H. Lester Jr., "Three Reasons for Missions to Catholic Countries," *CHA* (Nov. 1895): 387–88. Explaining the second of his reasons, Lester wrote, "The Bible is not circulated [in Catholic countries]; not even the Catholic version, much less the Protestant" (387).

45. Rev. John Menaul, "Mission Work in New Mexico," *CHA* (Nov. 1891): 414–15. This convert-evangelist "is careful to leave a selected supply of tracts if they will be accepted" (415).

46. "Home Missions: Notes," *CHA* (Aug. 1893): 116.

47. "Mexicans in the U.S.," 388. These Roman Catholic conquerors, the writer continued, "built a few temples, but they established no factories. They built a few inferior cities, but they developed no industries. They subdued the savage, but the silence of the valleys was not disturbed by a single lathe or spindle."

Similar indictments of Roman Catholic indolence and wasted resources and opportunities can be found in "Romanists and Mexicans," 364; "Romanists and Foreigners," 133; and an unsigned, untitled note in *CHA* (April 1895) quoting a "Catholic gentleman": " 'You look for education [in Catholic Mexico] and you do not find it, you look for intelligence and you do not find it, you look for industry and you do not find it, you look for morality and you do not find it, [*sic*] This Church has had the sole chance to make the Mexican people and they have failed' " (285).

48. "New Mexico," *CHA* (Nov. 1891): 412.

49. "Romanists and Foreigners: Romanists," *CHA* (Aug. 1895): 112.

Cf. Rev. J. Milton Greene, D.D., "Christian Heroism in Mexico," *CHA* (March 1894): 207–210, in which he argued that the climate of Roman Catholic countries encouraged a sensualism that distracted from industriousness. The "perpetual summer" in those countries seemed "to chant a lullaby and discourage effort in any direction. To be an active, self-resisting consistent Christian in such a climatic environment, is far more difficult than it is amidst more favorable surroundings" (208).

50. Glenn Porter, *The Rise of Big Business, 1860–1910* (Arlington Heights, Ill.: Harlan Davidson, 1973), especially 71–84, in which Porter covers "The Great Merger Wave" that occurred in the United States for a decade, starting in 1895 (78).

51. Rev. J. Milton Greene, D.D., "The Morals of Mexico," *CHA* (March 1892): 234.

52. Greene, "Christian Heroism," 209.

53. Alexander Robertson, "The Observance of the Lord's Day in Venice," *CHA* (Dec. 1894): 470.

54. See, for instance, Greene, "Morals of Mexico," 234: "Given a nation without a Bible, without a Sabbath, without the knowledge of the law of God, without a pure, Christian literature, without even a leaven of right moral sentiment as to the relations of man to man,

and much less of man to God, a nation where all moral distinctions are confused and vague, and all religious thinking is crooked and perverse, where not even the protest of a godly ministry is heard against sin . . . all its evils aggravated by an abundance of money, how can we expect anything but a constant decline in morals?"

Pageantry was not in itself offensive to the missionaries, who objected to the wasteful-ness and frivolity of Roman Catholic parades and festivals (see, for example, Robertson, "Mariolatry in the Church of Rome," *CHA* [Jan. 1894]: 8–9; and Rev. D. Y. Iddings, "Holy Week in Guatemala," *CHA* [Sept. 1890]: 233–35). In the eyes of Protestant missionaries, pag-eantry needed to be directed at the proper object of reverence. See, for example, Dudycha, "Home Mission Letters: Minnesota," 126: "As Decoration [Day] is not observed in this place, I thought it well to take our Sabbath-school out for a May walk on that day. With each child bearing an American flag we will proceed to the grove."

55. "Romanists and Foreigners: Romanists," 112.

56. The phrase comes from Gillespie, "Roman Catholic Missions in China," 221.

57. The quoted phrase in this section's title comes from a description of polygamy found in "The Mormons," *CHA* (May 1896): 388.

58. See, for instance, Rev. R. G. McNiece, D.D., "Home Mission Letters: Utah," *CHA* (Sept. 1890): 266; "Utah," *CHA* (Jan. 1893): 39; and Rev. Josiah McClain, "Home Mission Letters: Utah," *CHA* (May 1893): 376.

At least some Mormons also felt that one had to choose between Mormonism and U.S. citizenship and statehood (see "The Mormons," *CHA* [May 1894]: 402).

59. "The Evangelization of the Great West," *CHA* (Jan. 1888): 30. While Presbyterians, and other Protestant groups, conducted missions to Mormons throughout the West, I focus here on the case of Utah because Mormon population concentrated there, and because the question of Utah's statehood presented itself with such urgency to the editors of *The Church at Home and Abroad* during the years under consideration in this essay.

In "The Mormons" (May 1894), 388, the author detailed the extent of Presbyterian work in Utah: "We have now twenty-six churches; one dozen mission stations; twenty-five minis-ters, six of whom are installed pastors; forty-four elders; sixteen deacons, and about twelve hundred church members. The average enrollment in our mission schools during the past twenty years has been about 2500; the Sabbath-schools have averaged more than 3000. The present enrollment [in 1896] is 3984. And yet a large part of Utah remains untouched."

60. Note, for example, the title of one anti-Mormon editorial: "Theocracy vs. Republi-canism," *CHA* (May 1897): 328.

See also "The Mormons," *CHA* (May 1894): 399–402, which praised the exclusion of Mormons from the World Parliament of Religions. "It is a political institution in its outward form—and in its inner life it is a secret order with exceedingly worldly ends in view" (399).

61. "President Harrison in Utah," *CHA* (Aug. 1891): 130, quoting from the *Salt Lake Trib-une,* revealed part of the political basis for the anti-polygamy passion of the missionaries: that multiple wives jumbled the smooth functioning of the home, understood as the seat of re-publican virtue. President Harrison said, "That which characterizes and separates us from nations whose political experience and history has been full of strife and discord, is the Ameri-can home, where one mother sits in single, uncrowned honor, the queen." This reverence for

U.S. motherhood grew out of the nineteenth-century ideal of women's particular fitness for things spiritual (see, for example, Colleen McDannell, *The Christian Home in Victorian America, 1840–1900,* Religion in North America [Bloomington: Indiana University Press, 1994], 1–19, 127–49). Yet Harrison's comment, as quoted here, emphasized the political, rather than the eternal, payoff of motherhood. Paradoxically, the mother of republicanism has here become a "queen," a word suggestive of the same kind of decadence decried in polygamy.

62. Leonard J. Arrington and Davis Bitton, *The Mormon Experience: A History of the Latter-day Saints* (New York: Knopf, 1979), 244. Arrington and Bitton write that some Mormons ignored the official declaration and continued to contract plural marriages (184). Articles in *The Church at Home and Abroad* may bear this assertion out. When statehood became official, missionary worries shifted—after a brief moment of hope for Utah's redemption—to suspicion that the renunciation of polygamy was a calculated ploy, a limited-time offer about to be rescinded on states' rights grounds. See, for example, Rev. S. E. Wishard, "Letters: Utah," *CHA* (Aug. 1897): 137; and Rev. O. S. Wilson, "Home Mission Letters: Utah," *CHA* (Nov. 1897): 373, for expressions of such fears.

Cf. Rev. Newton E. Clemenson, "Home Mission Letters: Utah," *CHA* (March 1897): 211; "Utah's Statehood," *CHA* (May 1897): 328; and "The Mormon Priesthood," *CHA* (July 1897): 49. All three accounts reported that practices did return to those of prestatehood days.

63. Rev. F. W. Blohm, "Utah," *CHA* (April 1897): 292.

64. See, for instance, "Home Missions: Notes," *CHA* ([Feb.] 1894): 126–27, in which the author expressed worry over the Mormons' missions to western Native Americans.

65. S. E. Wishard, D.D., "The Utah Situation," *CHA* (Aug. 1891): 131.

66. "The Mormons" (May 1894), 401, quoting from the Mormon text *Key to Theology:* "The United States of America was the favored nation, raised up with institutions adapted to the protection and free development of the necessary truths and their practical results." Yet the editorial writer in *The Church at Home and Abroad* noted that Mormon culture held no respect for "American" institutions, writing that "it was never their custom to regard Independence Day as worthy of notice. The birthday of these great facts in national life: freedom of religious opinion, liberty of thought and speech and worship, and a government 'of the people, by the people and for the people' stirs no emotion of pleasure in a Mormon heart" (401–2).

67. Arrington and Bitton, *Mormon Experience:* The federal government increased its antipolygamy pressure during the 1880s, beginning with the Edmunds Act in 1882—which made polygamy a felony, disfranchised polygamists and barred them from office, and placed elections under presidential oversight (180–81), and—culminating in the Edmunds-Tucker Act in 1887—which dissolved the church incorporation and allowed for the confiscation of church property by federal authorities (183). When the Supreme Court upheld the law in May 1890, the church leadership considered its options through the summer, and in September, President Wilford Woodruff officially suspended the practice of polygamy, declaring in his "Manifesto," "Inasmuch as laws have been enacted by Congress forbidding plural marriages, which laws have been pronounced constitutional by the court of last resort, I hereby declare my intention to submit to those laws, and to use my influence with the members of the Church over which I preside to have them do likewise" (183).

68. "The Mormons," *CHA* (May 1895): 389.

69. Ibid. (May 1893): 372.

70. Ibid. This commentator called the church's hostility to personal liberty "the great evil of Mormonism."

71. "Home Missions," *CHA* (May 1895): 380. Cf. "Gleanings from Home Mission Letters: Utah," *CHA* (July 1897): 62, complete with editorial emendation in brackets: "Mormon *people* growing more tolerant of other faiths—not so the priesthood. [Always so.]"

72. "The Mormons," *CHA* (May 1893): 372. Guarantees of religious freedom to Mormons were discussed as well in "Sheldon Jackson College, Salt Lake City, Utah," *CHA* (May 1898): 383.

73. Rev. S. L. Gillespie, "Home Mission Letters: Utah," *CHA* (May 1890): 463.

74. Arrington and Bitton, *Mormon Experience,* 247. The church leadership officially disbanded the Mormon "People's party" in 1891. The resulting diversity of affiliation did have its limits, however: church leaders "encouraged" at least some members to join the Republican Party, for fear that the federal government would misinterpret a "mass migration" of Mormons to the more sympathetic Democrats.

See Wishard, "Utah Situation," 132. Wishard worried that this shift in party affiliations would prove temporary. Citing his "past experience with Mormon duplicity," he predicted that Mormons would transform themselves for the sake of obtaining statehood, then "backslide into the old doctrine of the supremacy of the priesthood, and . . . proceed to fashion all legislation in the interests of polygamy and the supremacy of the priesthood" (132).

75. Rev. William Wallace, "Foreign Mission Letters: Mexico," *CHA* (Aug. 1891): 173.

76. Rev. Theodore Lee, "Letters: Utah," *CHA* (Feb. 1893): 128. Cf. Rev. J. A. Livingston Smith, "The Utah Situation," *CHA* (Nov. 1894): 411. Smith, unlike other missionaries writing in *The Church at Home and Abroad,* advocated statehood for Utah, comparing it to God's grace, always coming before one was fully prepared for it: "coming as grace and not as our desert, it has all the demonstration and power of a Gospel lesson to saint and sinner, to Mormon and missionary, if only we had faith to believe and eyes to see and hearts to receive" (411).

77. Rev. J. McClain, "From Ordained Ministers: Utah," *CHA* (Jan. 1890): 76.

78. Smith, "Utah Situation," 411.

79. "The Mormons," *CHA* (May 1895), 391.

80. S. E. Wishard, D.D., "Mormonism and Utah," *CHA* (May 1890): 432.

81. Wishard, "Utah Situation," 133.

82. 1 Cor. 2:4–6.

CHAPTER 7

1. Helen Barrett Montgomery, *The Preaching Value of Missions* (Philadelphia: Judson, 1931), 17.

2. Mrs. Gracey served as editor until 1901. Miss Elizabeth C. Northup was editor 1902–1906, followed by Mrs. George W. Isham. Louise McCoy North, *The Story of the New York Branch of the Woman's Foreign Missionary Society of the Methodist Episcopal Church* (New York: New York Branch, 1926), 171–72.

3. R. Pierce Beaver, *American Protestant Women in World Mission,* 2nd ed. (Grand Rapids: Eerdmans, 1980), 145. The original 1968 edition was titled *All Loves Excelling.*

4. Ibid., 155.

5. Caroline Atwater Mason, *Lux Christi: An Outline Study of India* (New York: Macmillan, 1902), ix.

6. See Louise A. Cattan, *Lamps Are for Lighting: The Story of Helen Barrett Montgomery and Lucy Waterbury Peabody* (Grand Rapids: Eerdmans, 1972).

7. Other women on the tour included Dr. Mary Riggs Noble, M.D., India; Miss Jennie V. Hughes, a school principal from China; Mrs. Etta D. Marden, head of the Congregational mission in Istanbul [?]; Miss Florence Miller, field secretary of the Christian Women's Board of Missions; Miss Kate Boggs Schaffer, secretary of the Missions Home and Foreign in the Lutheran Church; and Miss Ella D. MacLaurin, secretary of the American Baptist Board. See Helen Barrett Montgomery, *Helen Barrett Montgomery: From Campus to World Citizenship* (New York: Fleming H. Revell, 1940), 122. Abby Gunn Baker chaired the Washington, D.C., celebration; see *The Story of the Washington Celebration of the Woman's National Foreign Missionary Jubilee* (n.p.: [Jubilee Committee], 1911).

8. See Beaver, *American Protestant Women,* 152–53; and Patricia R. Hill, *The World Their Household: The American Woman's Foreign Mission Movement and Cultural Transformation, 1870–1920* (Ann Arbor: University of Michigan Press, 1985), 161–65.

9. Montgomery, *Helen Barrett Montgomery,* 133, in a tribute by Lucy Peabody.

10. One of the confusing elements in compiling a list of textbooks is that the "year" corresponded somewhat to our "school year." Some volumes indicate that they were published in April. Apparently, the goal was to bring the book out in April so that summer schools could prepare teachers to teach it during the "school year," fall through spring. Thus, a book would be published in April for the fall, and that year would be the designated year of the book. But some books are actually copyrighted in the year prior to the one for which they are the designated textbook. Usually, the dating can be clarified by reading the committee's preface to the book.

11. Beaver, *American Protestant Women,* 156–57.

12. The Interdenominational Conference of Women's Boards of Foreign Missions became the Federation of WBFM in 1916. See Beaver, *American Protestant Women,* 157 n. 5.

13. Beaver, *American Protestant Women,* 157–62.

14. Mason, *Lux Christi,* v.

15. Dana Robert, *American Women in Mission* (Macon, Ga.: Mercer University Press, 1996), 271.

16. See Beaver, *American Protestant Women,* 164–66. Sue Weddell, *More Than Paper and Ink* (New York: Committee on Christian Literature for Women and Children, [1962]).

17. Hill, *The World Their Household,* 3.

18. Ibid., 1, quoting Charles Forman, who says there were 934 missionaries in 1890, nearly 5,000 in 1900, and more than 9,000 in 1915.

19. William Elliot Griffis, *Dux Christus: An Outline Study of Japan* (New York: Macmillan, 1904), 103.

20. Ibid., 156.

21. Mason, *Lux Christi,* 106, 107, 113.

22. Ibid., 10, 12.

23. Griffis, *Dux Christi*, vii.

24. Mason, *Lux Christi*, 7, 7–8.

25. Montgomery, *Western Women in Eastern Lands*, 159.

26. Ibid., 170–71, 173.

27. J. Gregory Mantle, *Bible-Women in Eastern Lands* (London: Unwin, 1904).

28. Beaver, *American Protestant Women*, 156.

29. Hill, *The World Their Household*, 141.

30. Ibid., 148.

31. Montgomery, *Western Women in Eastern Lands*, 136, 114.

32. Robert, *American Women in Mission*, 279 ff.; see esp. 313–14.

33. Mary Ninde Gamewell, *Ming-Kwong: "City of Light"* (West Medford, Mass.: CCUSFM, 1924), 204.

34. See Robert, *American Women in Mission*, 302. Other denominations were undergoing the same process. The United Brethren Church's women's board was merged into a general board in 1909. Women of the Methodist Episcopal Church, South, were stripped of their power in 1910. Disciples of Christ women lost their forty-five-year separate identity in 1919.

35. Beaver, *American Protestant Women*, 184–86, 194–96. The Committee on Christian Literature for Women and Children was the only agency that continued to exist through the DOM's Committee on Christian Literature and World Literacy.

36. Hill, *The World Their Household*, 54.

37. Ibid., 53.

38. Frederick J. Heuser Jr., "Culture, Feminism, and the Gospel: American Presbyterian Women and Foreign Missions, 1870–1923" (Ph.D. diss., Temple University, 1991), 21.

39. Margaret L. Bendroth, "Women and Missions; Conflict and Changing Roles in the Presbyterian Church in the USA, 1870–1935," *American Presbyterians* 65 (1987): 49.

40. Ibid., 50, 55. To prove his "manhood and . . . masculine power," Macartney kept two loaded, pearl-handled pistols in his desk drawer.

41. Robert, *American Women in Mission*, 189–254.

42. Beaver, *American Protestant Women*, 198. Applegarth authored *Lamp-Lighters across the Sea* in 1920, *Honorable Japanese Fan* in 1923, *Please Stand By* in 1927, and *Going to Jerusalem* in 1929, all for juniors.

43. Kawai authored the 1934 volume, *Japanese Women Speak*. Other contributors to *Women and the Way* were Mrs. A. K. Matthews (South Africa), Tseng Pao-swen (China), Helen Kim (Korea), Baroness W. E. Van Boetzelaer (Netherlands), Una Saunders (England), Gnanambal Gnanadickam (India), Mrs. Flora Amoranto Ylagan (Philippines), Mrs. Frederic M. Paist (United States), Jorgelina Lozada White (Argentina), and Muriel Lester (England). See Robert, *American Women in Mission*, 291.

44. Robert, *American Women in Mission*, 291. From the beginning of foreign missions, women sought to cooperate with men. While the CCUSFM was more successful, the Student Volunteer Movement was first to publish study textbooks. They turned that ministry over to the Young People's Missionary Movement, which eventually became the Missionary Education Movement, under the Foreign Missions Conference of North America. The CCUSFM came to cooperate closely with the Missionary Education Movement (MEM).

CHAPTER 8

1. *Christian Guardian* (hereafter *CG*) (Jan. 29, 1908): 17.

2. The Woman's Missionary Society of the Methodist Episcopal Church in Canada was organized in 1876. In 1880, women of the larger Methodist Church of Canada (which had been formed in a union of three branches of Canadian Methodism in 1874) organized a missionary society in Hamilton, Ontario, and a few other local groups were formed. The next year, the national Woman's Missionary Society was organized. The Methodist Episcopal Church and the Methodist Church of Canada united in 1884 to form the Methodist Church (Canada, Newfoundland, Bermuda), and following this the two women's societies joined. This group traditionally dated its history from the founding of the larger group, which, by the time of the union, had placed its own missionaries in the field. See Marilyn Färdig Whiteley, "Canadian Methodist Women and Missions: The Transformation of 'Pious, Plodding' Females," *Methodist History* 34 (1996): 104–18.

3. See Neil Semple, *The Lord's Dominion: The History of Canadian Methodism* (Montreal: McGill Queen's University Press, 1996). The 1911 census, for example, recorded slightly more than one million for each group, Presbyterian, Methodist, and Anglican.

4. Patricia Hill, *The World Their Household: The American Woman's Foreign Mission Movement and Cultural Transformation, 1870–1920* (Ann Arbor: University of Michigan Press, 1985), 83–84.

5. *CG* (April 9, 1890): 229.

6. Ibid. (Oct. 9, 1889): 650.

7. United Church/Victoria University Archives (Toronto) (hereafter UCA), Picton Methodist Church records, 77.409L/1–3, WMS minute book 1882–1887, Oct. 2, 1882.

8. *CG* (Sept. 30, 1896): 627.

9. UCA, Cataraqui Methodist Church records, 77.354L/1–4, WMS minute book 1902–1912, Aug. 19, 1909.

10. Alberta Conference Archives (Edmonton) (hereafter ACA), Alberta Branch WMS letter book, 75.387/334, Ada Magrath to Mrs. Miles, Nov. 25, 1912.

11. *CG* (Nov. 4, 1891): 693.

12. Ibid. (Feb. 13, 1889): 101.

13. *Seventh Annual Report of the Woman's Missionary Society of the Methodist Church, Canada, for the Year 1887–1888* (Toronto: William Briggs, 1888), 23.

14. *CG* (Oct. 9, 1889): 650.

15. UCA, Gorrie Methodist Church records, 93.089L 1–2, WMS minute book 1885–1907, Nov. 24, 1885; Feb. 8, 1886; June 11, 1888; July 20, 1892.

16. UCA, Hamilton, Centenary Methodist Church records, 96.074L 6–4, WMS minute book 1887–1890, Sept. 13, 1887.

17. UCA, London, Queen's Avenue Methodist Church records, 77.522L (reel 6), WMS minute book 1893–1902, Feb. 5, 1894.

18. ACA, Alberta Conference Branch WMS, 75.387/326, minute book 1909–1922, annual meeting June 1913, 104.

19. *CG* (Dec. 14, 1892): 789.

20. The first mention of this is found in the minutes of the original Hamilton group for

October 1, 1881 (UCA, Hamilton, Centenary Methodist Church records, 78.080C/10, minute book 1880–1883).

21. *Missionary Outlook* (hereafter *MO*) (Oct. 1889): 153, address by Janet Jackson to the annual meeting of the Niagara Conference.

22. For one particularly strong statement of this argument, see *CG* (Nov. 10, 1909): 9.

23. Fifty-nine remained after the elimination of groups that lacked consistent data because of such factors as the division of congregations during this period. My thanks go to my husband, Hugh Whiteley, for graphing and analyzing my spreadsheet data.

24. Coincident with union was an apparent change in the missionary collections of about half of the congregations. Changes were both positive and negative, but there were twice as many positive changes as negative.

25. Montreal and Ottawa Conference Archives (Montreal), Montreal, St. James Methodist Church records, WMS minute book 1912–1922, Oct. 1912.

26. UCA, WMS General Board of Managers records, 78.080C 002–2, minute book 1887–1891, April 4, 1888.

27. UCA, London Branch WMS records, 78.080C/10, minute book 1894–1914, 31.

28. *CG* (Oct. 20, 1897): 659.

29. Saskatchewan Conference Archives (Saskatoon) (hereafter SCA), Alexander Methodist Church records, A381 XV. A. 3867, WMS minute book 1903–1912, Jan. 1905; Manitoba Conference Archives (Winnipeg) (hereafter MCA), Dominion City Methodist Church records, WMS minute book 1910–1917, Sept. 1910; ACA, Edmonton, McDougall Methodist Church records, 75.387/3220, WMS minute book 1909–1911, March 30, 1910.

30. British Columbia Conference Archives (Vancouver) (hereafter BCCA), New Westminster Methodist Church, WMS letter book 1890–1907, April 15, 1901.

31. BCCA, Victoria, Centennial Methodist Church Records, WMS minute book 1891–1901, Nov. 1895 and Feb. 1898.

32. John D. Thomas, "'The Christian Law of Living': The Institutionalization of Christian Stewardship in The Methodist Church (Canada, Newfoundland, Bermuda), 1884–1925," *Canadian Methodist Historical Society Papers* 9 (1991–1992): 109–28.

33. *CG* (June 19, 1895): 389.

34. Ibid. (Sept. 17, 1902): 600.

35. This was supplied, and in the 1902 edition of the Methodist *Doctrine and Discipline,* the presidents of both groups were listed as ex officio members of the official board.

36. *MO* (Nov. 1888): 17.

37. *CG* (Jan. 2, 1889): 5; *MO* (Sept. 1887): 132.

38. For a further development of this subject, see Marilyn Färdig Whiteley, "The Methodist Woman's Missionary Society and Social Christianity: Towards 'A Broader Culture, A Wider Experience'" (paper presented at the Canadian Historical Association, Ottawa, Ontario, May 30, 1998). For the relationship of Helen Barrett Montgomery to the Social Gospel in the United States, see Hill, *The World Their Household,* 183–84.

39. UCA, London, Wellington Street Methodist Church records, 77.022L 3–6, WMS minute book 1901–1904, Dec. 4, 1902.

40. UCA, Toronto, Trinity Methodist Church records, 94.026L 5–5, WMS minute book

1905–1910, Dec. 3, 1908; ACA, Edmonton, McDougall Methodist Church records, 75.387/3226, WMS minute book 1920–1922, executive meeting, Sept. 8, 1920.

41. The work was among eastern European immigrants, most of whom would now be classified as Ukrainian but were referred to in contemporary reports as Galician, Ruthenian, or Austrian.

42. MCA, Winnipeg, Greenwood Methodist Church records, WMS minute book 1917–1921, Dec. 1922 and subsequent entries.

43. ACA, Norwood Methodist Church records, 79.15.114, WMS minute book 1909–1915, March 1910 and June 1915.

44. ACA, Edmonton, McDougall Methodist Church records, 75.387/3220, WMS minute book 1909–1911, April 1910; 75.387/3223, WMS minute book 1914–1916, Dec. 1915. At the 1915 meeting, held at the home, the auxiliary heard "five Ruthenian girls [sing], 'Jesus is born' and 'We'll hang up Grandma's Stocking'"!

45. SCA, Regina, Wesley Methodist Church records, 381 XV. A. 3060, WMS minute book 1913–1917, June 1915, May 1916, Jan. 1920.

46. MCA, Dominion City Methodist Church, WMS minute book 1910–1917, May 1911, Aug. 1911, Sept. 1911.

47. SCA, Wolseley Methodist Church, A381 XV. A. 4459, WMS minute book 1905–1910, Sept., Oct., and Nov. 1908; MCA, Dauphin Methodist Church records, WMS minute book 1905–1910, July, Sept., and Oct. 1909.

48. ACA, Edmonton, McDougall Methodist Church records, 75.387/3224, WMS minute book 1916–1919, Nov. 20, 1917.

49. ACA, Alberta Branch WMS records, 75.387/327, minute book 1922–1933, 38.

50. ACA, Alberta Branch WMS records, minute book 1922–1933, 41.

51. *CG* (May 15, 1889): 309. This research is based on the Canadian Methodist periodicals the *Christian Guardian* and the *Missionary Outlook* and on records of the Woman's Missionary Society. Minutes of congregations within the five Ontario conferences of the United Church of Canada are located in the United Church/Victoria University Archives in Toronto. The conferences outside Ontario have archives in locations specified in the notes. I have visited all the conference archives and have examined the manuscript minutes of fifty WMS auxiliaries, and also the surviving manuscript records of WMS district and branch organizations.

CHAPTER 9

1. "Prospectus of the Toronto Bible Training School," Sept. 5, 1894, Tyndale Seminary Archives. See also Ronald Sawatsky, "Elmore Harris: Canadian Baptist Extraordinaire," unpublished paper, University of Toronto, 1980, copy in Tyndale Seminary Archives.

2. TBTS Executive Council minutes, May 14, 1894, Tyndale Seminary Archives. The five hundred applicants may be exaggerated: the CIM Register of Applications (copy in CIM/OMF Archives, Toronto) lists 327 *formal* applications between 1888 and the end of 1893. Nevertheless, they are an astounding cross-section of continental evangelicalism. One-half (161) were Canadians, the majority from Ontario (138), particularly Toronto (59) and Hamilton (27). The rest came from nineteen states, from as far as California and Missouri, led by

Nebraska (29), New York (24), and Illinois (19). The CIM had sent sixty-six missionaries to China, making it one of the largest North American missions in China, and the largest Canadian one.

3. Two studies firmly situate the Bible school in the U.S. landscape: Virginia Leeson Brereton, *Training God's Army: The American Bible School, 1880–1940* (Bloomington: Indiana University Press, 1990); and William Vance Trollinger Jr., *God's Empire: William Bell Riley and Midwestern Fundamentalism* (Madison: University of Wisconsin Press, 1990). What is missing from both books is the international dimension. For example, they exclude both Canada and China.

4. The material on the CIM is voluminous: CIM authors published some 350 titles before World War II. Critical secondary material, however, is limited. The recent authoritative history is A. J. Broomhall, *Hudson Taylor and China's Open Century*, 7 vols. (Sevenoaks, U.K.: OMF, 1881–1889), hereafter cited as Broomhall, *HTCOC*. Daniel W. Bacon, *From Faith to Faith: The Influence of Hudson Taylor on the Faith Missions Movement* (Philadelphia: OMF, 1984), lists more than thirty faith missions that were created, inspired, or modeled on the CIM. The classic history of the North American CIM is Dr. and Mrs. Howard Taylor, *"By Faith": Henry W. Frost and the China Inland Mission* (Philadelphia: CIM, 1938). See also Alvyn J. Austin, "Blessed Adversity: Henry W. Frost and the China Inland Mission," in *Earthen Vessels: American Evangelicals and Foreign Missions 1880–1980,* ed. Joel Carpenter and Wilbert Shenk (Grand Rapids: Eerdmans, 1990).

5. Quoted in *Christian Week* (April 28, 1992).

6. Joel A. Carpenter, "Propagating the Faith Once Delivered: The Fundamentalist Missionary Enterprise, 1920–1945," in Carpenter and Shenk, *Earthen Vessels,* 106.

7. Joel A. Carpenter, "Fundamentalist Institutions and the Rise of Evangelical Protestantism, 1929–1942," *Church History* 49 (1980): 67.

8. Brereton, *Training God's Army,* 128.

9. Carpenter, *Revive Us Again: The Reawakening of American Fundamentalism* (New York: Oxford University Press, 1997), 83.

10. Carpenter, "Propagating the Faith," 105. MBI's records indicate that more than 160 former students and/or alumni went to China between 1895 and 1950. This figure does not include those before 1894.

11. *TBC Recorder* (Dec. 1946): 5.

12. Dana L. Robert, *American Women in Mission: A Social History of Their Thought and Practice* (Macon, Ga.: Mercer University Press, 1996), chap. 5, "Women and Independent Evangelical Missions," discusses the role of women in faith missions, using the Africa Inland Mission as a case study.

13. Brian A. McKenzie, "A History of the Toronto Bible College" (diss. proposal, typescript in Tyndale Archives), 37.

14. Marshall Broomhall, *The Jubilee Story of the China Inland Mission* (1915; reprint, London: CIM, 1929), 30.

15. Broomhall, *HTCOC,* 4: 106.

16. Ibid., 7: 43.

17. Christof Sauer, "The Importance of Henry Grattan Guinness for the Opening of the

Sudan-belt to Protestant Missions: His Vision and the Resulting Attempts and Missionary Organizations," paper prepared for North Atlantic Missiology Project conference, Fuller Theological Seminary, March 1998. See also Michelle Guinness, *The Guinness Legend* (London: Hodder and Stoughton, 1989), 100.

18. Letter from Emma Dreyer to Charles Blanchard (president of Wheaton College), Jan. 1916, Moody Bible Institute library, 6.

19. Alvyn J. Austin, *Saving China: Canadian Missionaries in the Middle Kingdom, 1888–1959* (Toronto: University of Toronto Press, 1986), 3–8.

20. Edith L. Blumhofer, *The Assemblies of God: A Chapter in the Story of American Pentecostalism,* vol. 1, *To 1941* (Springfield, Mo.: Gospel Publishing House, 1989), 29–30.

21. Henry Weston Frost, "The Days that are Past," typescript memoirs in OMF Archives, Toronto, 310–11 (hereafter cited as Frost, "Memoirs").

22. This was actually the second Bible school in Canada. The first, a temporary effort in 1885 by Mrs. Lucy Osborne, relocated to Brooklyn Union Missionary Training Institute. TMTI lasted at least until 1894, for it was still in operation when TBTS was founded as a more respectable alternative. Lindsay Reynolds, *Footprints: The Beginnings of the Christian and Missionary Alliance in Canada* (Willowdale, Ontario: Christian and Missionary Alliance in Canada, 1982), 193–95.

23. Frost, "Memoirs," 397.

24. Ibid., 431–32.

25. Among the first students were three young women from Iowa who arrived penniless at the CIM home. During their five-month stay in Toronto, spent praying for funds, they were occasional students at TBTS. One was Anna Wood (Mrs. W. E. Tyler), mother of W. W. Tyler, Canadian director of the CIM (1947–1965), and four generations of TBC graduates.

26. J. H. Hunter, *A Flame of Fire: The Life and Work of R. V. Bingham, D.D.* (Toronto: SIM, 1961), 255–56, 139, 264.

27. Gary R. Corwin, "Rowland Victor Bingham," in *Biographical Dictionary of Christian Missions,* ed. Gerald H. Anderson (New York: Macmillan Reference, 1998), 64.

28. McKenzie, "History of the Toronto Bible College," 24, 29.

29. Charles M. Johnston, *McMaster University,* vol. 1, *The Toronto Years,* 102.

30. G. A. Rawlyk, "McMaster University," in *Canadian Baptists and Christian Higher Education* (Kingston, Ontario: McGill-Queen's University Press, 1988), 38.

31. McKenzie, "History of the Toronto Bible College," 39.

32. *TBC Recorder* (June 1924): 5.

33. Hunter, *Flame of Fire,* 237.

34. Ibid., 258.

35. John McNicol, "The Perils of Ultra-Fundamentalism," *TBC Recorder* (March 1949): 1–2.

36. Robert K. Burkinshaw, *Pilgrims in Lotus Land: Conservative Protestants in British Columbia, 1917–1981* (Montreal: McGill-Queen's University Press, 1995).

37. Taylor, *"By Faith,"* 308–12.

38. Carpenter, "Propagating the Faith," discusses the Wheaton-MBI-CIM connection; quotation from 117.

39. Carpenter, *Revive Us Again,* 67–68.

40. Frank Houghton, *The Two Hundred: Why They Were Needed; How They Responded; Who They Are; Where They Are* (Philadelphia: CIM, 1932). See also Carpenter, "Propagating the Faith."

41. Michael Griffiths to the author via e-mail, Oct. 1998.

CHAPTER 10

1. Minutes of the Fourteenth Annual WCTU Convention (hereafter cited as WCTU Minutes), 1887, 16, WCTU Archive, Evanston, Ill.

2. F. Max Müller, *Auld Lang Syne* (New York: Charles Scribner's Sons, 1899), 134.

3. Shamsundar Manohar Adhav, *Pandita Ramabai* (Madras: Christian Literature Society, 1979), ix–xi; Uma Chakravarti, *Rewriting History: The Life and Times of Pandita Ramabai* (Kali: n.p., 1998).

4. Mary Lucia Bierce Fuller, *The Triumph of an Indian Widow* (New York: American Auxiliary of the Ramabai Mukti Mission, 1928), 17.

5. Emily J. Bryant, "Pundita Ramabai Sarasvati," *Century Illustrated Monthly Magazine* (Sept. 1887): 797–98.

6. Fuller, *Triumph,* 19.

7. Frances Willard, *Glimpses of Fifty Years: The Autobiography of an American Woman* (Chicago: Women's Temperance Publications, 1889), 559.

8. Printed in the *Union Signal* (Jan. 10, 1884): 15.

9. F. Max Müller, *Autobiography* (New York: Longmans, Green, 1902), 2: 155–56, 228; idem, *Auld Lang Syne,* 133–42; "Marriage Reform in India," *Our Day* (1890), 258.

10. Clementina Butler, *Pandita Ramabai Sarasvati* (New York: Fleming H. Revell, 1922), 26.

11. Ramabai left Wantage for a lengthy stay with the Max Müller family at Oxford, where she recovered from nervous prostration. Muller, *Auld Lang Syne,* 140.

12. For religious, nationalist, feminist, and political aspects of Ramabai's conversion, see Gauri Viswanathan, *Outside the Fold: Conversion, Modernity and Belief* (Princeton: Princeton University Press, 1998).

13. Ramabai's complex relationship with the Sisters of St. Mary is chronicled in A. B. Shah, ed., *The Letters and Correspondence of Pandita Ramabai, compiled by Sister Geraldine* (Bombay: Maharashtra State Board for Literature and Culture, 1977).

14. A. K. Clare, *A History of the Cheltenham Ladies' College, 1853–1953* (London: Faber and Faber, 1954).

15. F. Cecily Steadman, *In the Days of Miss Beale: A Study of Her Work and Influence* (London: Ed. J. Burrow and Co., 1931); Elizabeth Shillito, *Dorothea Beale, Principal of the Cheltenham Ladies' College, 1858–1906* (London: Society for Promoting Christian Knowledge, 1920); Elizabeth Raikes, *Dorothea Beale of Cheltenham* (London: Archibald Constable and Co., 1908).

16. Caroline Healey Dall, *The Life of Dr. Anandibai Joshee* (Boston: Roberts Brothers, 1888).

17. Tragically, Joshee never realized her potential. She was seriously ill at her graduation and, after a few months of residency in Boston, returned to India where she died, barely twenty-two years old. In addition to Dall's biography, see a contemporary account by F. Max Müller in his *Auld Lang Syne,* 142–48.

18. Pandita Ramabai, *The High-Caste Hindu Woman* (Philadelphia: J. B. Rodgers Printing Co., 1888).

19. Willard, *Glimpses,* 557, 561.

20. WCTU Minutes, 83.

21. Ibid., 46.

22. Ibid., 100; Mary A. Livermore, *The Story of My Life* (Hartford: A.D. Worthington and Co., 1899).

23. "President's Address," WCTU Minutes, 84.

24. Mary Allen West, "Joseph Cook," *Union Signal* (July 21, 1887): 10.

25. "Maine WCTU," *Union Signal* (Oct. 6, 1887): 1.

26. "Rhode Island," *Union Signal* (Oct. 27, 1887): 11.

27. M. H. Gerow, "Connecticut Annual WCTU Convention," *Union Signal* (Nov. 14, 1887): 10.

28. *Union Signal* (July 21, 1887): 14.

29. "Illinois," *Union Signal* (Dec. 15, 1887): 10.

30. *Union Signal* (July 21, 1887): 9.

31. Frances Willard, "The High-Caste Hindu Woman," *Union Signal* (Aug. 4, 1887): 12.

32. "The Ramabai Association," *Boston Morning Journal* (Dec. 14, 1887).

33. J. Holloway, *Edward Everett Hale: A Biography* (Austin: University of Texas Press, 1956).

34. *Our Day* (March–April 1894): 185.

35. "Hindoo Society," *Boston Morning Journal* (April 6, 1888): 1.

36. "Visiting Teachers . . . The Pundita Ramabai to Arrive To-Day," *San Francisco Chronicle* (July 14, 1888): 8.

37. "The Pundita Speaks," *San Francisco Chronicle* (July 16, 1888).

38. "The Pundita," *San Francisco Chronicle* (July 21, 1888).

39. N. G. Clark, "Questions to Specialists," *Our Day* (1888): 170–71; see also "Editorial Note," *Our Day* (1888): 445–48.

40. Pandita Ramabai to A. T. Pierson, in "Ramabai's Institution for Child-Widows," *Missionary Review of the World* (Jan. 1889): 85.

41. "The Pandita Ramabai," *Missionary Review of the World* (July 1889): 523.

42. Adhav, *Pandita Ramabai,* 183–85.

43. Fannie M. English, "Notes from the India Central Conference," *Woman's Missionary Friend* (June 1896): 344.

44. "Uniform Study for May: The King's Daughters in Heathen Lands," *Heathen Woman's Friend* (April 1892): supp. no. 4, 1,2.

45. "Miss Soonderbai Powar," *Missionary Review of the World* (March 1892): 240.

46. WCTU Minutes, 1892, 63.

47. See, for example, the report from the *Harvest Field* printed in "India: A Hindu Lady Reformer," *Missionary Review of the World* (Feb. 1890): 130.

48. See, for example, "The Child Widow," *Baptist Missionary Magazine* (March 1888): 63–65; *Baptist Missionary Magazine* (Oct. 1900): 588.

49. William Haslam, *From Death Into Life* (London: Morgan and Scott, ca. 1880).

50. Helen S. Dyer, *Pandita Ramabai* (New York: Fleming H. Revell, 1911), 35.

51. C. C. Starbuck, "Extracts and Translations from Foreign Periodicals"; H. B. Hartzler, "Dr. Pentecost at Northfield" (Jan. 1893): 26–29; "Questions to Specialists," *Our Day* 11 (1893): 68–75.

52. Mrs. J. T. Gracey, "Pundita Ramabai Once More," *Heathen Woman's Friend* (Sept. 1892): 56.

53. Dyer, *Ramabai,* 61.

54. Müller, *Auld Lang Syne,* 142.

55. "India," *Christian Alliance* (June 12, 1896): 572.

56. F. Max Müller, "Child Widows in India," *Our Day* (March–April 1894): 563.

57. "Keswick Convention Mission Report," *Keswick Week* (1896): 217.

58. Walter B. Sloan, "The Influence of the Keswick Convention on Missionary Work," *International Review of Missions* (Oct. 1914): 719; W. B. Boggs, "India," *Missionary Review of the World* (Jan. 1895): 5.

59. Albert Norton, "Pandita Ramabai's Camp-Meeting," *Earnest Christian* (April 1899): 131.

60. "The Famine in India as a Missionary Opportunity," *Missionary Review of the World* (May 1897): 481.

61. Pandita Ramabai, "Famine Widows," *Missionary Review of the World* (April 1898): 279.

62. Dyer, *Ramabai,* 102–3.

63. "Personal Mention," *Woman's Missionary Friend* (March 1898): 267.

64. "Our Post Office Box," *Woman's Missionary Friend* (March 1897): 256; *The Gospel in All Lands* (April 1889): 189.

65. "Personal Notes," *Woman's Missionary Friend* (April 1897): 280.

66. *The Annual Catalogue of the A.M. Chesbrough Seminary 1897–1898* (North Chili, N.Y.: A. M. Chesbrough Seminary), 6–7. Emma Sellew Roberts, "The High-Caste Widows of India at the A. M. Chesbrough Seminary," *Missionary Tidings* 2 (1898): 7–8.

67. Emma Sellew Roberts, "Pandita Ramabai and Her Work," *Missionary Tidings* (June 1898): 5.

68. Fuller, *Triumph of an Indian Widow,* 41; Elizabeth Baker, *Chronicles of a Faith Life* (Rochester, N.Y.: n.p., ca. 1916), 98 ff.; "Ramabai's Famine Widows," *Missionary Review of the World* (April 1898): 281.

69. "General Missionary Intelligence," *Missionary Review of the World* (March 1899): 234.

70. *Keswick Week* (1898): 188.

71. Pierson, "Ramabai," 487.

72. Minnie F. Abrams, "A Bible Training School," Woman's Missionary Friend (Feb. 1901): 56.

73. *Women's Missionary Friend* (1908).

74. "A Hindu Paper on Pundita Ramabai," *Missionary Review of the World* (July 1903): 553.

75. Minnie Abrams, "How the Recent Revival Was Brought About in India," *Latter Rain Evangel* (July 1909): 8.

76. "Growth and Revival in Ramabai's Work," *Record of Christian Work* (Oct. 1905): 857.

77. William Ellis, "Have Gift of Tongues: Girl Widows of Christian Church in India Develop Wonderful Phenomena," *(Chicago) Daily News* (Jan. 14, 1908).

78. Abrams, "Revival," 5.

79. Minnie Abrams, *The Baptism of the Holy Ghost and Fire* (Kedgaon: Mukti Mission Press, 1906); the *(Calcutta) Indian Witness* and the *Bombay Guardian* carried many reports of tongues speech in India and documented the progress of Pentecostal teaching, 1906–1908.

80. Adhav, *Ramabai*, 44.

CHAPTER 11

1. Townsend to "Friends," August 5, 1939. Townsend Archives (hereafter TA), Waxhaw, N.C., #2450. The terms *fundamentalism* and *fundamentalist* as used in this chapter refer to that revivalistic segment of Protestantism in the first decades of the twentieth century that could be described as conservative or evangelical.

2. The Summer Institute of Linguistics (SIL), along with its sister organization the Wycliffe Bible Translators (WBT), is now the largest independent Protestant missionary organization in the world.

3. Traditionally, missionaries incorporated Native Americans into Spanish work. Townsend felt that the language barrier, as well as the racism of the Spanish-speakers, kept Native Americans perpetually second-class citizens. Consequently, he hoped to found a new work in Mexico that would focus on their needs.

4. President Wilson sent in troops in 1914. During World War I, both the United States and Germany meddled in Mexico's internal affairs, trying to gain the upper hand. Pancho Villa's raids across the U.S.-Mexican border in 1916 did not help Mexico's image in the United States.

5. Arthur J. Drossaerts (archbishop of San Antonio), foreword to *No God Next Door: Red Rule in Mexico and Our Responsibility*, by Michael Kenny (New York: William J. Hirten, 1935), iv.

6. Josephus Daniels, *Shirt-Sleeve Diplomat* (Chapel Hill: University of North Carolina Press, 1947), 66.

7. John A. Britton, *Revolution and Ideology: Images of the Mexican Revolution in the United States* (Lexington: University Press of Kentucky, 1995), 96. The essays in Leslie Bethell, ed., *Mexico since Independence* (Cambridge: Cambridge University Press, 1991), and Alan Knight, *U.S.-Mexican Relations, 1910–1940: An Interpretation* (San Diego: Center for U.S.-Mexican Studies, 1987), are useful in this context.

8. Britton, *Revolution and Ideology*, provides an excellent introduction to this community and its impact in both Mexico and the United States. See also Helen Delpar, *The Enormous Vogue of Things Mexican: Cultural Relations between the United States and Mexico, 1920–1935* (Tuscaloosa: University of Alabama Press, 1992).

9. Charles A. Hale, "Frank Tannenbaum and the Mexican Revolution," *Hispanic American Historical Review* 75 (1995): 215.

10. George Marsden, *Fundamentalism and American Culture: The Shaping of Twentieth-Century Evangelicalism: 1870–1925* (New York: Oxford University Press, 1980), 209, demonstrated how in the 1920s socialism/communism/Bolshevism were lumped in with modernism and evolutionism as cobelligerents against Bible belief.

11. Elvira Townsend to Karl Hummel, Dec. 28, 1933, TA.

12. Townsend to Elvira, Dec. 13, 1933, TA #01717; Townsend to Elvira, Dec. 20, 1933, TA #01716; Townsend's journal, Dec. 28, 1933, 986, TA #01791. See also James and Marti Hefley, *Uncle Cam: The Story of William Cameron Townsend, Founder of the Wycliffe Bible Translators and the Summer Institute of Linguistics* (1974; reprint, Huntington Beach, Calif.: Wycliffe Bible Translators, 1995), 79–80. Townsend was traveling a path already well worn by the U.S. Left and the Mexican government. Mexico, knowing its image in the United States needed help, used "techniques of hospitality" (interviews, tours, favors, friendships) to "reinforce the favorable predispositions of the leftist visitors." A tour of rural schools was a familiar "technique," as education was frequently of great interest to the Left. John Dewey had been personally escorted on such a tour in 1926 by Vice-Minister of Education Moisés Sáenz. The visitors, in turn, shared their insights with the U.S. public through their publications. Dewey wrote three articles for *The New Republic* after his trip. See Britton, *Revolution and Ideology,* 66–71, 94. The use and acceptance of "techniques," of course, in no way precludes genuine feeling on either side.

13. TA #01716.

14. Townsend to Elvira, Jan. 23, 1934, TA #01897. See also Townsend's travel inventory, TA #01892.

15. Townsend to Nymans, April 8, 1934, TA #01882; Ramírez to Townsend, March 15, 1934, TA #01886. (Translations from Spanish originals are the responsibility of the author.)

16. W. Cameron Townsend, "Is Religion Doomed in the Land of Cuauhtemoc?" TA #42599. See also Townsend, "The Big Fight in Mexico: Church vs. State," TA #42598. Those familiar with SIL's history will recognize that Townsend was presenting here the germ of his vision for SIL, especially its two foundational principles—"nonsectarianism" and "service to all"—two tenets that many, if not most, of his recruits never fully understood, and that repeatedly landed him in trouble both within his own organization and with supporters at home.

17. Townsend to Karl, Oct. 8, 1935, TA #01922. See also Hefley, *Uncle Cam,* 90. When the novelist and somewhat jaundiced adventurer Max Miller visited Tetelcingo in 1936 after hearing in a bar that there he would "have a sight of the true primitive," he was disappointed to discover that he could drive right to the spot and that a U.S. citizen had already been living there for a year. Although "William Thompson" was not there, Miller decided it was obvious the people "loved" the "Professor of Languages" because of the "hallowed way they spoke of him." He figured his own pleasant reception was "probably due to the fact I was coasting on the crest of his wave." Max Miller, *Mexico around Me* (New York: Reynal and Hitchcock, 1937), 287–94.

18. Townsend to Legters, Nov. 14, 1935, TA #01917; Hefley, *Uncle Cam,* 92.

19. Elvira Townsend, untitled article, *Moody Church News* (June 1936), TA #01983.

20. Townsend to Ken and Gene, Feb. 20, 1937, TA #02157.

21. Townsend to Cárdenas, Jan. 29, 1936, Archivo General de la Nación (hereafter AGN), Mexico City, Fondo Lázaro Cárdenas (hereafter FLC), 710.1/1598.

22. Telegram, Cárdenas to Uranga, March 1, 1938, AGN.

23. E. Townsend, *Moody Church News.* What Townsend accomplished in just the next six months, with the considerable help of several government agencies, is quite remarkable. His

report to Cárdenas in June 1936 listed forty-three completed and ongoing projects, including a better road to the town (the residents did not want the president to suffer so many "bumps" the next time he visited), a "siphon" irrigation system for the new park, literacy campaigns, new crops introduced to the region via a model farm, the school repaired and resupplied, several dairy cows and pigs purchased, a barber shop constructed and supplied, new uniforms for the town basketball team, a truck donated (when Max Miller visited, Townsend had been gone for several weeks, and the truck was out of gas), a large clock placed on the square (so that the school could have regular hours and doctors' prescriptions could be more regularly followed), and so on. Townsend to Cárdenas, AGN. Within a year, better drinking water had been secured, a laundry built, and two small houses for a community center donated by U.S. Ambassador Josephus Daniels. Townsend to Cárdenas, Dec. 26, 1936, AGN.

24. Cárdenas to Townsend, March 28, 1936, AGN.

25. Townsend to Karl, Sept. 19, 1936, TA #01976. Ken Pike, SIL's Nobel Prize–nominated linguist, provides an entertaining account of the first such nine-course dinner at the palace. One item discussed at the table was a recent *Collier's* article in which ex-President Calles accused Cárdenas of being a communist. Calling the article "dirty," Pike wrote that he took pictures that evening to illustrate newspaper articles in which "some of us may try a few digs in the other direction." Pike to Folks, Oct. 5, 1936, TA #02068. Pike recorded that after that first dinner, "we went home to walk on air for a while."

26. Marjorie Becker, *Setting the Virgin on Fire: Lázaro Cárdenas, Michoacán Peasants, and the Redemption of the Mexican Revolution* (Berkeley: University of California Press, 1995). In addition, Townsend and SIL provided an antidote for the argument that Mexico was against religion. In 1948, when Manuel Gamio, the prominent Mexican anthropologist, attended a reunion at Columbia University, he found himself forced to defend Mexico's stand on religion. While agreeing that Calles had fallen into "certain unnecessary exaggerations," he mentioned the work of SIL as the kind of religious effort the Mexican government could embrace. He told Townsend that he was pleasantly surprised to find that "many people knew something of what you do and those that were unacquainted with your work expressed their approval when I explained to them the religious but nonsectarian nature of your work, the scientific and at the same time practical and constructive program of the Institute." His audience was also impressed to hear of how Cárdenas had embraced the SIL. Gamio to Townsend, May 27, 1948, TA #05521.

27. At one point, Cárdenas sent them 2,500 pesos to build a nice house in Tetelcingo, a significant gift in a village where 200 pesos could build a decent home. The Townsends used the money to build ten small houses for the caretakers of the five-thousand-tree orange grove recently planted, at Townsend's request, along the federal highway. Elvira to Cárdenas, Feb. 1938, TA #2311.

28. Townsend to Cárdenas, April 7, 1936, AGN, FLC, 710.1/1598; Vásquez to Sanchez, April 15, 1936, TA #02075; Townsend to Vásquez, June 25, 1936, AGN; "Cárdenas es Proletarista no Comunista," AGN (published as "Commoner, Not Communist, Is Cardenas," in the *Tulsa Daily World* [June 21, 1936]).

29. Townsend to Cárdenas, Oct. 30, 1937, AGN. The emphasis is Townsend's.

30. Previously, Cárdenas had nationalized the railways and turned them over to the

unions, but this action did not cause much international fuss because the railways were a losing financial proposition. The oil companies, however, made large profits in Mexico and had been interfering in Mexico's internal affairs for years. Now they refused to accept decisions by arbitrators and the Mexican Supreme Court that they must raise wages and increase safety standards for their workers. As the conflict escalated, it became an issue of Mexican nationalism. Good discussions can be found in Alan Knight, "The Rise and Fall of Cardenismo, c.1930–c.1946," in Bethell, *Mexico since Independence,* and in Knight, *U.S.-Mexican Relations.* See also Daniels, *Shirt-Sleeve Diplomat.*

31. Townsend to Father, March 6, 1938, TA #02309; Hefley, *Uncle Cam,* 105; W. C. Townsend, *The Truth about Mexico's Oil* ([Los Angeles]: published by members and friends of the SIL, 1940), 15. After Cárdenas left, Townsend used the pen to write him a letter of appreciation. His second act with the historic pen was to write to President Franklin Roosevelt to plead Mexico's cause.

32. Cárdenas's expropriation marked the "first major act of its kind," the first time foreign oil companies had been expelled from an underdeveloped country in the name of national sovereignty. The oil companies, who had been trying to make an example of Mexico, found Mexico making an example of them. With this act, Cárdenas, more than any other individual, may have destroyed the hegemony of big oil throughout the world. George Philip, *Oil and Politics in Latin America: Nationalist Movements and State Companies* (Cambridge: Cambridge University Press, 1982), 224.

33. W. C. Townsend, "Mexico Confiscates the Oil Industry," TA #42593; Daniels, *Shirt-Sleeve Diplomat,* 227, 258. Burt McConnell, in his collection of editorial opinion from around the country, professed to find "almost unanimous editorial objection to the fundamental principles advanced by Mexico in support of her program of confiscation." One supposes that it reflects well on McConnell that he admitted in his preface that his work was financed by Standard Oil. Burt M. McConnell, *Mexico at the Bar of Public Opinion: A Survey of Editorial Opinion in Newspapers of the Western Hemisphere* (New York: Mail and Express, 1939), iv. Not every U.S. editor bought the oil party line, of course. Liberal journals, including the *Christian Century,* held a more balanced opinion.

34. Sáenz to Cárdenas, March 21, 1938, AGN, FLC, 577/10. Sáenz was a good friend of Townsend. His invitation to visit Mexico got Townsend across the border in 1933. Townsend named one of SIL's first airplanes the *Amauta Moisés Sáenz.*

35. Elvira to Guelph and Karl, March 31, 1938, TA #02308; Daniels to McIntyre, April 4, 1938, TA #02415.

36. "Flyer," TA #02271; Elvira to Marroquín, May 1, 1938, TA #02302; Elvira to Mrs. Cárdenas, May 3, 1938, TA #2301; Amalia Cárdenas to Elvira, May 17, 1938, TA #02350.

37. Townsend to Cordell Hull, Sept. 10, 1938, TA #02287; Hefley, *Uncle Cam,* 107.

38. "Report of Mr. and Mrs. W. C. Townsend For the Year Sept. 1937–Sept. 1938," TA #02283; "Justice to Mexico," TA #42594. The annual report was sent to the Pioneer Mission Agency.

39. Townsend to Marroquín, Sept. 15, 1938, TA #0228?; Townsend to Cárdenas, Sept. 1938, TA #902284; Townsend, *Truth about Mexico's Oil,* ii, 1, copy in author's possession.

40. Townsend to Kelly, March 28, 1940, TA #02614; Townsend to Beteta, Dec. 27, 1939, TA #02425; Townsend to Kelly, Dec. 13, 1942, TA #02703. The Kelly-Mencken relationship

is described in Carl Bode, *Mencken* (Carbondale: Southern Illinois University Press, 1969), 149–51.

41. Townsend to Rodríguez, Sept. 27, 1936, AGN, FLC, 710.1/1598; Townsend to Beteta, Sept. 7, 1937, TA #02104.

42. Daniels to Townsend, Nov. 20, 1947, TA #04795; "Report of General Director—Board of Directors' Meeting—August, 1948," TA #05248; Townsend to Bentley, Oct. 22, 1948, TA #05234; Townsend to Applequist, Nov. 11, 1949, TA #05847.

43. Townsend to Kenneth and Evelyn, Oct. 23, 1948, TA #05232; Townsend to Bermudes, July 9, 1951, TA #06922; Wells to Dean, Aug. 29, 1951, TA #907213; Townsend to Beteta, Jan. 1, 1952, TA #07791; Kruckman to Townsend, Jan. 13, 1952, TA #07175; Kruckman to Townsend, Feb. 11, 1952, TA #08141. Kruckman, who also wrangled Townsend an invitation to speak at the Press Club, was completely convinced of Cárdenas's greatness, writing, "I have never known of another ruler so utterly selfless." He compared Cárdenas's qualities to those of Jesus, the Duke of Windsor, and Whittaker Chambers!

44. Townsend to Will and Etta, Dec. 26, 1951, TA #6790; Townsend to Friends, TA #06841; Townsend to Dale, Jan. 29, 1954, TA #10344. Some of Townsend's constituency were concerned that the book did not present a strong "testimony." One writer bemoaned the fact that something that had taken so much effort would not "come through the fires which are to 'try every man's work.'" He went on to accuse Townsend of becoming "ashamed of Jesus" in his effort to "be popular among atheistic intelligentsia." Fischer to Townsend, Feb. 4, 1952. Some in SIL, concerned about just this sort of reaction, urged Townsend to publish the book on his own with no public SIL connection. Townsend would not hear of it, writing, "I think that you realize how much I've tried during the years our Institute has been operating in Latin America to defend these countries against misunderstandings and the avarice of monied interests in the U.S.A. I can't think of our Institute going back on that stand now." TA #10294.

45. Sample copies of responses from congressmembers on file with the author. Townsend to George McGhee, Dec. 12, 1961, TA #19729.

46. Numerous documents including Kenneth T. Weathers, "Some Intimate Observations Relating to the Short-Lived Inter-American Service Brigade," draft copy in author's possession; "Proyecto de Trabajo," AGN, FLC, 710.1/1598; Townsend to Cárdenas, April 25, 1939, AGN, FLC, 463.1/18.

47. Beteta to Townsend, Oct. 19, 1939, TA #2504; Townsend to Cárdenas, TA #02272; "Ante-Proyecto Para La Organizacion de Una Asociacion Internacional de Amigos de Mexico," TA #02076.

48. Townsend to Cárdenas, Sept. 13, 1937, TA.

49. Vásquez to Townsend, Jan. 8, 1937, TA #02212.

50. TA #02381.

51. Townsend to Karl, June 13, 1939, TA #02459; Townsend to Mildred, July 15, 1939, TA #02455; Townsend to Friends, Aug. 5, 1939, TA #02450.

52. Joel A. Carpenter, *Revive Us Again: The Reawakening of American Fundamentalism* (New York: Oxford University Press, 1997).

53. Ibid., 46, 112; Ironside to "my dear sister," Jan. 11, 1938, TA #02367; Ironside to Elvira, March 7, 1938, TA #02359.

54. Cárdenas eventually decided not to accept LeTourneau's help for political reasons.

55. Townsend, "Memorandum for Ambassador Cooper," Oct. 24, 1946, TA #04261; Townsend to Sam Rayburn, Aug. 5, 1957, TA #12761; William T. Cormack, "How Communistic Is Guatemala?" TA #942716. Townsend used his mother's surname to avoid involving SIL.

56. TA #06488, 06675. It is ironic that the man who once wrote to Cárdenas that he could not sleep at night thinking "of the crimes against humanity being committed by the oil companies" is often accused of being in league with them and/or the CIA in meddling in Latin American affairs and promoting the "genocide" of Native Americans. See Gerard Colby and Charlotte Dennett, *Thy Will Be Done: The Conquest of the Amazon: Nelson Rockefeller and Evangelism in the Age of Oil* (New York: HarperCollins, 1995). As it turns out, Colby and Dennett chose precisely the wrong man against whom to level such charges.

57. Richard Pierard, "*Pax Americana* and the Evangelical Missionary Advance," in *Earthen Vessels: American Evangelicals and Foreign Missions, 1880–1980,* ed. Joel Carpenter and Wilbert Shenk (Grand Rapids: Eerdmans, 1990), 179.

INTRODUCTION TO PART III

1. For the extraordinary hoopla stirred up by the "Laymen's Report," as it was called, see John R. Fitzmier and Randall Balmer, "A Poultice for the Bite of the Cobra: The Hocking Report and Presbyterian Missions in the Middle Decades of the Twentieth Century," in *The Presbyterian Presence: The Twentieth-Century Experience,* ed. Milton J. Coalter et al. (Louisville: Westminster John Knox Press, 1991).

2. Patricia R. Hill, "The Missionary Enterprise," in *Encyclopedia of the American Religious Experience,* ed. Charles H. Lippy and Peter W. Williams (New York: Charles Scribner's Sons, 1988), 3: 1,695.

3. Ibid.

4. For a survey, see Angelyn Dries, O.S.F., *The Missionary Movement in American Catholic History* (Maryknoll, N.Y.: Orbis Books, 1998).

CHAPTER 12

I presented an abbreviated version of this chapter to the American Historical Association, San Francisco, Dec. 1993. I wish to thank Gerald Anderson, L. Gregory Jones, Van Harvey, David Hollinger, William R. Hutchison, Richard Madsen, Susan McArver, Thomas A. Tweed, and, especially, my research assistant, Seth Dowland, for helpful critiques. Frances Webb and Elizabeth Lipscomb of Randolph-Macon Woman's College graciously helped to check my citations.

1. For the weakening—or, perhaps, redefining—of the missionary impulse, see Lian Xi, *The Conversion of Missionaries: Liberalism in American Protestant Missions in China, 1907–1932* (University Park: Pennsylvania State University Press, 1997), esp. 4–6; Paul A. Varg, *Missionaries, Chinese, and Diplomats: The American Protestant Missionary Movement in China, 1890–1952* (Princeton: Princeton University Press, 1958), chaps. 7–10; William R. Hutchison, *Errand to the World: American Protestant Thought and Foreign Missions* (Chicago: University of Chi-

cago Press, 1987), chaps. 5–6; and Grant Wacker, "Second Thoughts on the Great Commission: Liberal Protestants and Foreign Missions, 1890–1940," in *Earthen Vessels: American Evangelicals and Foreign Missions, 1880–1980,* ed. Joel Carpenter and Wilbert Shenk (Grand Rapids: Eerdmans, 1990), 281–300. Epigraph quoted in Xi, *Conversion of Missionaries,* 207. For details about Adams, see Thomas A. Tweed, "An American Pioneer in the Study of Religion," *Journal of the American Academy of Religion* 60 (1992): 437–64, quotation by Tweed on 437.

2. The Presbyterian Board of Foreign Missions hosted the luncheon on Wednesday, Nov. 2, 1932. For details, see "Better Missionaries Urged by Mrs. Buck," *The New York Times* (Nov. 3, 1932): 19; "'The Best or Nothing,'" *The New York Times* (Nov. 6, 1932): sec. 2, 1; "Mrs. Buck: Lauds Chinese; Faces Missionaries' Charges," *Newsweek* (April 22, 1933): 26. Different accounts give different specifics. I have followed *The New York Times* (Nov. 3). Many years later, Buck said that she had expected a small, private meeting with a delegation from the missions board. Her authorized biographer, Theodore Harris, added that the Women's Committee of the board had arranged the meeting. The Reverend Henry Sloane Coffin, a liberal theologian at New York's Union Theological Seminary, offered the invocation, which suggests that the luncheon may have been staged by liberal forces on the missions board. However the luncheon came about, Buck chose not to mention the event in her autobiography, and her sister quietly overlooked it in her hagiographic study of Buck. See Buck's remarks in Theodore F. Harris (in consultation with Pearl S. Buck), *Pearl S. Buck: A Biography* (New York: John Day, 1969), 1: 307–9, and Harris's own discussion of the event in vol. 2, subtitled *Her Philosophy as Expressed in Her Letters* (New York: John Day, 1971), 2: 279. (Though the first Harris volume was not designated vol. 1 by the publisher, for the sake of clarity I have so designated it throughout.) See also *My Several Worlds: A Personal Record* (New York: John Day, 1954); Cornelia Spencer [Grace Sydenstricker Yaukey], *The Exile's Daughter: A Biography of Pearl S. Buck* (New York: Coward-McCann, 1944); Nora Stirling, *Pearl Buck: A Woman in Conflict* (Piscataway, N.J.: New Century, 1983), 125–27. Peter Conn's definitive scholarly biography of Buck, *Pearl S. Buck: A Cultural Biography* (Cambridge: Cambridge University Press, 1996), briefly mentions the event on 148–49.

A word about Peter Conn's long, erudite, and often brilliant biography of Buck, published in 1996, is in order. Conn argues that Buck was a "secular, feminist missionary, who inherited a need for vocation from her father and a yearning for female emancipation from the example of her mother's sad defeats." Though this hypothesis represents a good start, Conn underplays the special religious intensity of Buck's early commitments and later disillusion with the evangelical tradition. My essay aims in part to fill that gap. Conn, *Buck,* 381.

3. *Is There a Case for Foreign Missions?* (New York: John Day, 1932); "Is There a Case for Foreign Missions?" *Harper's* (Jan. 1933): 143–55 (I use the *Harper's* text for subsequent references); *(Shanghai) Evening Post* (April 14–15, 1933), described in *China Weekly Review,* 282. See also E. Stanley Jones: "Is There a Place for the Unusual Missionary?" *Christian Century* (April 26, 1933): 548. Needs of the time: "Mrs. Buck Resigns," *Christian Century* (May 10, 1933): 611–12. Fine and sound: "Mrs. Buck Resigns Her Mission Post," *The New York Times* (May 2, 1933): 15. Hartford and Seattle papers noted in "Mrs. Buck Under Fire as a 'Heretic,'" *Literary Digest* (May 6, 1933): 15, 18.

4. Free attachments: "A Protestant among the Presbyterians," *America* (April 29, 1933):

77. Etherealized animalism: the Reverend J. McIntire, *The New York Times* (June 22, 1936): 8, quoted in Charles Silver, "Pearl Buck, Evangelism and Works of Love: Images of the Missionary in Fiction," *Journal of Presbyterian History* 51 (1973): 220. Cynicism: Wisconsin Presbyterian pastor Marvin M. Walters to Robert E. Speer, Nov. 26, 1932, quoted in Xi, *Conversion of Missionaries*, 221. Hurricane of the times: "Mrs. Buck Resigns; Board Accepts 'With Deep Regret,'" *Christianity Today* (May 1933): 35. Charles Erdman to Robert E. Speer, March 25, 1933, quoted in James Alan Patterson, "Robert E. Speer and the Crisis of the American Protestant Missionary Movement, 1920–1937" (Ph.D. diss., Princeton Theological Seminary, 1980), 153; *China Weekly Review* (April 22, 1933): 282–83.

5. Robert E. Speer to William Miller, April 1, 1933, quoted in Patterson, "Robert E. Speer," 153; "Pearl Buck, Heretic," *The Nation* (May 17, 1933): 546. Buck officially resigned on May 1, 1933. Conn, *Buck*, 154. The controversy won extensive coverage in *The New York Times* (April 12, 13, 14, 1933) and a full-page story in *Newsweek*, as noted above. The Presbyterian Board of Foreign Missions accepted Buck's resignation "with regret"—prompting another round of controversy about the meaning of the words "with regret." Did they mean that the missions board was sorry she had fallen into doctrinal error? Or sorry she quit? Additional controversy stemmed from confusion about Buck's relationship with the board. What, exactly, had she resigned from? By April 1933, she was no longer receiving a salary from the board, but her husband did, and she worked under board appointment. "Mrs. Buck Resigns Her Mission Post," 15; "Mrs. Buck Resigns," 35.

6. Streets of Nanking: *My Several Worlds*, 191. For Buck's influence, see below.

7. Michael H. Hunt, "Pearl Buck—Popular Expert on China, 1931–1949," *Modern China* 3 (1977): 33–34, 45–47. Subject of China: James C. Thomson, "Pearl S. Buck and the American Quest for China," in *The Several Worlds of Pearl S. Buck: Essays Presented at a Centennial Symposium*, ed. Elizabeth J. Lipscomb et al. (Westport, Conn.: Greenwood, 1994), 14. For the quotation, see Conn, *Buck*, xiv.

8. Horrible sin: Buck to Mother and Father and Clifford, Feb. 2, 1918, Pearl S. Buck Collections, Lipscomb Library, Randolph-Macon Woman's College (RMWC). All references are to Pearl S. Buck unless otherwise indicated.

9. Beauty-loving people: Buck to Home-people, Sept. 17, 1917. Servant class: Buck to Home-people, probably Oct. 14, 1917. Official class: Buck to Home-people, Sept. 17, 1917. Opium and drunkenness: Buck to Mrs. Coffin, Dec. 12, 1918. Slave in the family: Buck to Mother [in-law], April 11, 1919. Foot binding: Buck to Home-people, Sept. 17, 1917. Infanticide: Buck to Mrs. Coffin, Dec. 12, 1918. All of the foregoing at RMWC. Given to the devil: quoted without citation in Stirling, *Buck*, 52. Superstition: Buck to Grace and Vincent Buck, March 15, 1919, RMWC, quoted in Conn, *Buck*, 65. Stirling's well-researched but unfootnoted work is filled with details drawn from interviews, Buck family papers, and archival materials. Stirling's working papers are deposited at RMWC. My own spot-checks of Stirling's quotations against the original sources persuade me of her reliability.

10. Others to Christ: Buck to Mrs. Coffin, Dec. 12, 1918, RMWC. Weighs terribly: Buck to Emma Edmunds White (dated by White Aug. 29, 1918), RMWC. Buck's sister, Grace Yaukey, who also served as a Presbyterian missionary in China, said virtually nothing about religion in her biography of Buck. Yaukey did acknowledge, however, that after Pearl married,

she avidly involved herself in her husband's missionary work, setting up Sunday schools, running a day school, and talking with Chinese women. Spencer, *Daughter,* 137–38.

11. Buck to [B]rother, April 8, 1918, RMWC.

12. "China the Eternal," *International Review of Missions* (Oct. 1924): 581. For a survey of the tenets of liberal Protestant missionary thought, see William R. Hutchison, "Modernism and Missions: The Liberal Search for an Exportable Christianity, 1875–1935," in *The Missionary Enterprise in China and America,* ed. John K. Fairbank (Cambridge, Mass.: Harvard University Press, 1974).

13. Personal unworthiness: "China and the Foreign Chinese," *Yale Review* 21 (1932): 541–47.

14. Marked the times: "What Religion Means to Me," *Forum and Century* (Oct. 1933): 195–200. Oppression in Asia: "God Becomes a Convenience," *Forum* (Sept. 1936): 99, 104–5.

15. Supernaturalism: "Easter 1933," *Cosmopolitan* (May 1933): 169; "What Religion Means to Me," 195; *My Several Worlds,* 66. Miracles: "Case for Foreign Missions," 143–44. Superstitious missionaries: "Case for Foreign Missions," 145; "God Becomes a Convenience," 103.

16. Existence of Jesus: "Easter 1933," 169–70; "Case for Foreign Missions," 150–51. Existence of God: "What Religion Means to Me," 197, 199; "God Becomes a Convenience," 103. Figure of Jesus: "Case for Foreign Missions," 151. Universal: "Easter 1933," 16.

17. Come to hate: "And Yet—Jesus Christ," *Far Horizons* (Jan. 1932): 10; missionary pot: "God Becomes a Convenience," 102.

18. Only work they could find: "Case for Foreign Missions," 146. See also "Laymen's Mission Report," *Christian Century* (Nov. 23, 1932): 1,435. Buck said that people in the United States did not want to waste their best on foreign lands, hence faulting the senders as well. Two years for four thousand: "Laymen's Mission Report," 1,435; see also "Case for Foreign Missions," 146; *The Spirit and the Flesh* (1936; reprint, New York: John Day, 1957), 44, 94.

19. Chinese thought: "Give China the *Whole* Christ," *Chinese Recorder* (July 1932): 451; see also "Case for Foreign Missions," 144; "Advice to Unborn Novelists," *Saturday Review of Literature* (March 2, 1935): 513; "God Becomes a Convenience," 103–4. Eye to eye: "Give China the *Whole* Christ," 451.

20. "God Becomes a Convenience," 103; see also "And Yet—Jesus Christ," 8; "Case for Foreign Missions," 144.

21. Chinese ears: "Case for Foreign Missions," 145. Wang Lung: *The Good Earth* (1931; reprint, New York: Washington Square Press/Simon and Schuster, 1973), 88–89. Words not understood: "Laymen's Mission Report," 1,436; first-rate minds: Xi, *Conversion of Missionaries,* 113 n. 51.

22. "Laymen's Mission Report," 1,436. See also "Give China the *Whole* Christ," 452; *Spirit and the Flesh,* 113; *My Several Worlds,* 199. Whether Buck's indictment of missionaries was fair is, of course, an entirely different matter. For a vigorous rejoinder, see Andrew Porter, "'Cultural Imperialism' and Protestant Missionary Enterprise, 1780–1914," *Journal of Imperial and Commonwealth History* 25 (1997): 367–91.

23. Bind the wounded: "And Yet—Jesus Christ," 10; "Laymen's Mission Report," 1,437. Dwelt among them: "Laymen's Mission Report," 1,437. See a difference: "Laymen's Mission Report," 1,435. Human race: "Case for Foreign Missions," 152. Buck sometimes said that mis-

sionaries should address spiritual needs, but she remained vague about what that might entail. See, for example, "Give China the *Whole* Christ," 452.

24. Missionary personalities sometimes turned up in Buck's later works, but I am not aware that she devoted sustained attention to the question of this essay, the morality of the missionary impulse. See Silver, "Pearl Buck," esp. 217. Family values: *My Several Worlds,* 326; *The Child Who Never Grew* (New York: John Day, 1950), 10, 34. Buck hoped to accompany President Nixon on his visit to the PRC in 1972, but the PRC denied her a visa, claiming that her novels had vilified the Chinese people. Stirling, *Buck,* 317. *East Wind, West Wind: Pearl Buck: The Woman Who Embraced the World,* prod. Craig Davidson and Donn Rogosin, 85 min., Refocus Films, 1993, videocassette, suggests that the PRC refused a visa for a less grandiose reason: Mao's wife disliked her.

25. Religious organizations: Buck to Florence Lurty, Aug. 10, 1938, Pearl S. Buck Family Trust archives, quoted in Conn, *Buck,* 202. Organization's sake: "Can the Church Be Religious?" *Christian Century* (Dec. 22, 1943): 1,499. This essay intimates a measure of lingering attachment to Christianity, if not the church, but other evidence suggests that this attachment was rapidly evaporating. Atheism denied: Letter July 31, 1955, to "Father —," in Harris, *Buck,* 2: 254. Faith in human beings: "This I Believe," *New York Herald Tribune* (Feb. 18, 1952), quoted in Harris, *Buck,* 2: 255; see also the letter on the same page. Immortality: *A Bridge for Passing* (New York: John Day, 1961, 1962), 255–56; see also 182–83. Cope with it: Buck to Marjorie Ashbrook Temple, May 2, 1967, Pearl S. Buck Foundation archives, quoted in Conn, *Buck,* 375. Buck was buried according to her instructions, without ceremony or officiating minister. "Pearl Buck Buried on Her Farm Home," *The New York Times* (March 10, 1973): 34. Stirling argued that Buck remained purely agnostic, refusing to embrace the principled atheism of her husband, Richard J. Walsh. Stirling, *Buck,* 260–62.

26. *My Several Worlds,* 96–97, 371, 49.

27. Social reform efforts: Paul A. Doyle, *Pearl S. Buck* (New York: Twayne Publishers, Inc., 1965), chap. 7; Stirling, *Buck,* chaps. 15–21. Noninfluence in Washington, D.C.: Hunt, "Pearl Buck," 43, 55–58. Conn's biography offers rich documentation for the breadth of her social concerns and the impressiveness of her charitable accomplishments, especially regarding the treatment of women at home and abroad. Conn rightly calls her a "secular missionary." See Conn, *Buck,* 4, and chaps. 6–7. One could argue that Buck transferred the idealism she had once vested in the church to the American nation itself. See, for example, *My Several Worlds,* 406–7. I owe this point to Sean Burt, "'What America Means to Me': Pearl S. Buck's Religious Evaluation of America," MTS seminar paper, Duke Divinity School, 2000.

28. T. S. Eliot, "The Hollow Men," in *The Complete Poems and Plays, 1909–1950* (1930; New York: Harcourt, Brace and Company, 1952), 58.

29. William Ernest Hocking et al., *Re-Thinking Missions: A Laymen's Inquiry After One Hundred Years* (New York: Harper and Brothers, 1932), esp. chaps. 1–3, and its ancillary reports, provoked a storm of controversy. The skirmish is contextualized in Hutchison, *Errand to the World,* chap. 6, and in John R. Fitzmier and Randall Balmer, "A Poultice for the Bite of the Cobra: The Hocking Report and Presbyterian Missions in the Middle Decades of the Twentieth Century," in *The Presbyterian Presence: The Twentieth-Century Experience,* ed. Milton J. Coalter et al. (Louisville: Westminster John Knox Press, 1991).

30. To be sure, in the late nineteenth century, independent faith missionaries scornful of theological relativism and all but the most superficial forms of cultural accommodation were clambering off the ships in growing numbers every year. But Buck seemed oblivious to their existence—which said something about her own economic and social location.

31. Thomson, "American Quest," 10; Xi, *Conversion of Missionaries*, 10–21, 29, 143, 158, and throughout; Paul A. Varg, "Motives in Protestant Missions, 1890–1917," *Church History* 23 (1954), reprinted in *Modern American Protestantism and Its World*, ed. Martin E. Marty (Munich: K. G. Saur, 1993), 13: 6–15, quotation on 12; Charles W. Forman, "Evangelization and Civilization: Protestant Missionary Motivation in the Imperialist Era II: The Americans," *International Bulletin of Missionary Research* (April 1982), reprinted in Marty, *Modern American Protestantism*, 13: 41–44; Irwin T. Hyatt, "Protestant Missions in China, 1877–1890," in *American Missionaries in China: Papers from Harvard Seminars*, ed. Kwang-Ching Liu (Cambridge, Mass.: Harvard University Press, 1966), 93–126; M. Searle Bates, "The Theology of American Missionaries in China, 1900–1950," in Fairbank, *Missionary Enterprise*.

32. See, for example, John Lofland and Rodney Stark, "Becoming a World-Saver: A Theory of Conversion to a Deviant Perspective," *American Sociological Review* 30 (1965): 862–75; and John Lofland, "'Becoming a World-Saver' Revisited," *American Behavioral Scientist* 20 (1977): 805–18, for classic discussions of the stages religious converts typically traverse. Sociologists of religion who have studied deconversion—the process of self-consciously moving from a positive religious tradition to none at all—note that such movement often involves both pain and disparagement of the tradition abandoned. William Sims Bainbridge, "The Sociology of Conversion," in *Handbook of Religious Conversion*, ed. H. Newton Malony and Samuel Southard (Birmingham, Ala.: Religious Education Press, 1992), 187; and Lewis R. Rambo, *Understanding Religious Conversion* (New Haven: Yale University Press, 1993), 27, 39–40, 53–54.

33. *Several Worlds*, 51. Home here: Interview notes with Ross Terrill, Dec. 26–27, 1971, quoted in Conn, *Buck*, 372. See the summaries of clinical research on missionary children in Jeanne Stevenson-Moessner, "Cultural Dissolution: 'I Lost Africa,'" *Missiology: An International Review* 14 (1986): 314–24; and "Missionary Motivation," *Sociological Analysis* 53 (1992): 189–201. For autobiographical and fictional ruminations on these tensions, see John Espey, *Minor Heresies, Major Departures: A China Mission Boyhood* (Berkeley: University of California Press, 1994), esp. 78; and John Hersey, *The Call: An American Missionary in China* (New York: Knopf, 1985).

34. Financial resentments: *Spirit and the Flesh*, 98; see also Stirling, *Buck*, 20; Kyle Crichton, "Preacher's Daughter," *Collier's* (Feb. 7, 1942): 37. Photographs of the rambling, multi-floored missionary compound in Nanking (see Stirling, *Buck*, 118 ff.), and the family's extensive travels through Russia, Europe, and North America, suggest that Buck suffered more in her imagination as an adult than she ever did as a child (*My Several Worlds*, 139, 291). Conn argued that sexual incompatibility created some of the distance between Pearl and Lossing Buck. Conn, *Buck*, 59, 62–63, 88, 158, 171. More broadly, for Buck's thinking about conventional norms, see Buck to Emma Edmunds White, May 29, 1931, RMWC; Stirling, *Buck*, 86–88, 143–46; Conn, *Buck*, 103, 117, 128. Stirling, *Buck*, 143. Womanhood: *The Exile* (1936),

283, quoted in Conn, *Buck,* 20. Conn argued that Buck's anger about Christian misogyny constituted the deepest root of her alienation from Christianity.

35. Told a friend: Buck to Emma Edmunds White, Jan. 4, 1929, RMWC. Flesh from flesh: Buck to Mrs. Clarence H. Hamilton, Jan. 9, 1930, Boston University archives, quoted in Conn, *Buck,* 111. Giving up Carol: *Child Who Never Grew,* 21, 29, 31. No one listening: Stirling, *Buck,* 76. Church music: *Child Who Never Grew,* 26. Christians' insensitivity: "God Becomes a Convenience," 104. Marian G. Craighill, a missionary and Buck's close friend in China in the 1920s, also felt that Carol's situation undermined Buck's faith. Craighill to Nora Stirling, Feb. 14, 1976, RMWC.

36. At least one member of the Nobel Prize Committee voted to give the award to Buck primarily because of *Fighting Angel.* Doyle, *Buck,* 67; see also 71–76. In his detailed biography of Buck, Conn acknowledged Absalom's influence on Pearl but presented it principally as a foil against which Pearl defined her own adult life. For example, Conn wrote: "When she was a child, Pearl tended to see her father in heroic terms. As she grew older, she decided that he was a simple fanatic, touched with an apocalyptic fever." My argument is that Absalom was less a foil than a beloved ideal that Pearl could neither wholly embrace nor wholly abandon. Conn, *Buck,* 3, 135. See also 4, 39, 101, 134, 150–51, 188, 197, 204, 225, 238, 375.

37. *Spirit and the Flesh,* 21, 36–37.

38. Love for Absalom: *My Several Worlds,* 6, 257; "Advice to Unborn Novelists," 513; Harris, *Buck,* 1: 81; Conn, *Buck,* 151 (though Conn, remarkably, claims that Buck did not mean what she said). Buck eviscerated one clerical reviewer of *Fighting Angel* who had the temerity to call her father "bigoted" and "dogmatic." Buck to Mr. Billings, Jan. 13, 1947, in Harris, *Buck,* 2: 252. Foreign domination: this and the preceding three sentences drawn from Jost O. Zetzsche, "Absalom Sydenstricker [repeated in Chinese characters] (1852–1931): A Ruling Minority of One" (paper presented to the North Atlantic Missions Project conference, Fuller Theological Seminary, March 1998). Zetzsche's work, based on Sydenstricker's own writings in the *Chinese Recorder* and elsewhere, leaves an image of a man intellectually rigorous and personally admirable.

39. Relations with Chinese and whites: *Spirit and the Flesh,* 81, 85, 93, 152–53. Other religions: *My Several Worlds,* 66–68.

40. Buck to "Father —," July 31, 1955, in Harris, *Buck,* 2: 254. Buck's sister confirmed that she shielded her father from unsettling religious discussions. Spencer, *Exile's Daughter,* 171. Complete in anyone: Buck to Emma Edmunds White, Nov. 13, 1931, RMWC.

41. *Spirit and the Flesh,* 49, 102, 50.

42. On my work: Buck to Emma Edmunds White, Jan. 25, 1938, RMWC. What people say: Buck to Emma Edmunds White, Feb. 15, 1937, RMWC.

43. Enveloped, assimilated: "China the Eternal," 575, 583. Chinese stock: *My Several Worlds,* 255, quotation on 248. Historians James C. Thomson, Michael Hunt, Charles W. Hayford, and Lian Xi have made similar observations, but to somewhat different ends. Thomson, "American Quest," 15; Hunt, "Pearl Buck," 52, 56; Hayford, "From 'Farmer' to 'Peasant': Orientalism, Rhetoric, and Representation in Modern China" (paper presented at the Rhetoric of Social History Scholars Workshop, University of Iowa, summer 1992), 22–24; Xi, *Conversion of Missionaries,* 111.

44. Fencing and evasion: *Child Who Never Grew,* 14. The quotation referred to the physician who forthrightly apprised Buck of Carol's malady, but it applied to Buck's outlook in general. Quotations from "Tribute to Dr. Machen," *The New Republic* (Jan. 20, 1937): 355.

45. Utmost cruelty: Buck quoted in Irvin Block, *The Lives of Pearl Buck: A Tale of China and America* (New York: Thomas Y. Crowell, 1973), 159–60.

CHAPTER 13

1. Willard Krabill, "Report of MCC Representative on the Vietnam Voluntary Agency Refugee Team, October 16–28, 1965," 2–3. Personal files of Willard Krabill in author's possession.

2. Willard and Grace Krabill, interview by the author, Goshen, Ind., Feb. 8, 1998.

3. Krabill, "Report of MCC Representative," 4.

4. Hubert H. Humphrey to Eugene Sheffield (director, American Council of Voluntary Agencies [ACVA]), Oct. 9, 1965. Letter found in "Final Report on Vietnamese Refugees and Displaced Persons of ACVA Delegation" (henceforth ACVA Final Report), Oct. 1965, 15.

5. This argument is made most persuasively by J. Bruce Nichols, *The Uneasy Alliance: Religion, Refugee Work, and U.S. Foreign Policy* (New York: Oxford University Press, 1988). Nichols's analysis is the foundation for many of my comments here. I am fleshing out the historical record. One nonreligious agency was active in Saigon in 1954–1975, the International Rescue Committee. In 1965, several other nonreligious organizations appeared in Vietnam, but their presence was small. The International Rescue Committee had a fairly substantial program after 1965, and representatives from the committee attended the fact-finding trip mentioned at the beginning of this chapter.

6. Frances Fitzgerald, *Fire in the Lake: The Vietnamese and the Americans in Vietnam* (Little, Brown, 1972), 269.

7. Richard H. Hunt, *Pacification: The American Struggle for Vietnam's Hearts and Minds* (n.p.: Westview, 1995), 31. Hunt's book is the latest study in a growing literature about the "other war." All this literature mentions the presence of missionary and voluntary agencies in the context of pacification and refugee relief but does not attempt to assess the role played by these organizations or attempt to contextualize the relationship between these agencies and the federal government or with the Vietnamese people.

8. MCC News Service, "Krabill Sees Role for MCC in Vietnam," Nov. 5, 1965, IX-12–4, folder 1963–75, Mennonite Historical Archives, Goshen, Ind. (henceforth MHA).

9. Krabill interview.

10. ACVA Final Report, 18.

11. Ibid., 1.

12. Ibid., 11.

13. Hans J. Morgenthau, "Human Rights and Foreign Policy," in *Moral Dimensions of American Foreign Policy,* ed. Kenneth Thompson (n.p.: Transaction, 1984), 345.

14. William McGuire King, "The Reform Establishment and the Ambiguities of Influence," in *Between the Times: The Travail of the Protestant Establishment in America, 1900–1960,* ed. William Hutchison (Cambridge: Cambridge University Press, 1989).

15. "The History of IVS, 1953–1988," typescript, history file, IVS Archives.

16. In 1951, the MCC Executive Committee agreed to start a project in Vietnam, but a French colonial government suspicious of U.S. intentions rejected the plans. MCC invitation from the U.S. government is found in minutes, MCC Executive Committee, no. 21, Oct. 6, 1950; and minutes, MCC Executive Committee, no. 2, April 28, 1951.

17. William T. Snyder to Orie O. Miller, June 23, 1954; and Snyder to Joan Kain (assistant director, Advisory Committee on Voluntary Foreign Aid, Department of State), Sept. 6, 1954. Both letters quoted in Luke Martin, "An Evaluation of a Generation of Mennonite Mission, Service and Peacemaking in Vietnam, 1954–1976," July 1977, 7–8, Mennonite Historical Library, Goshen College, Goshen, Ind.

18. William T. Snyder to Orie O. Miller, July 21, 1954. Martin, "Evaluation of Mennonite Mission," 8.

19. John Osborne, "The Tough Miracle Man of Vietnam," *Life* (May 13, 1957): 156–57.

20. Gordon Smith, *The Blood Hunters* (n.p.: Worldwide Prayer and Missionary Union, 1943). Laura Smith, *Gongs in the Night* (n.p.: Zondervan, 1943); idem, *Farther into the Night* (n.p.: Zondervan, 1954); and idem, *Victory in Vietnam* (n.p.: Good News Publishers, 1966). The Christian and Missionary Alliance (CMA) published several magazines devoted to work in Vietnam. The *French Indo-China & East Siam Mission* magazine was published quarterly in Vietnam and distributed beginning in 1921. Eventually, the magazine became the *Call of Vietnam*. Work among the hill tribes had its own magazine, beginning in 1954, called *Jungle Frontiers*. In similar ways, Vietnam was introduced to a broad audience of U.S. Roman Catholics by the best-selling books of "medical missionary" Thomas Dooley. Thomas Dooley, *Deliver Us from Evil: The Story of Vietnam's Flight to Freedom* (New York: Farrar, Straus and Cudahy, 1956); *The Edge of Tomorrow* (1958); and *The Night They Burned the Mountain* (1960).

21. In 1962, two CMA missionary doctors and an MCC corpsman were kidnapped by the National Liberation Front (NLF) from Banmenthuot in the Central Highlands. The next year, two Wycliffe team members were ambushed and executed. IVS lost a volunteer in an NLF ambush in 1965.

22. Johnson quotation in L. Gardner, *Pay Any Price: LBJ and the Wars for Vietnam* (n.p.: Ivan Dee, 1991), 271.

23. Hunt, *Pacification*, 1.

24. "Krabill Sees Need for Continued MCC Presence in Vietnam," MCC News Service, VN-MCC file 5, folder 1958–65, IX-12–5, MHA.

25. MCC Annual Reports 1965, A-23–4, IX-5–2, folder 1963–67, MHA.

26. Row's remarks found in Jill K. Gill, "Peace Is Not the Absence of War but the Presence of Justice: The NCC's Reaction and Response to the Vietnam War" (Ph.D. diss., University of Pennsylvania, 1996), 152.

27. Earl Martin to MCC, Akron, Pa., Oct. 1967, MCC Vietnam correspondence. Quoted in Paul Toews, *Mennonites in American Society, 1930–70: Modernity and the Persistence of Religious Community* (n.p.: Herald, 1996), 316.

28. "VNCS Objectives and Philosophy"; and Atlee Beechy, "Report of VNCS, 20 August 1966," box 5, folder VNCS 1965–66, Beachy Papers, MHA.

29. MCC News Service, VN-MCC file 5, folder 1967–71, IX-12–5, MHA.

30. Newkirk quotation found in David E. Leaman, "Politicized Service and Teamwork Tensions—The MCC in Vietnam, 1966–69" (Goshen College, 1987, typescript), 39.

31. Doug Hostetter, "Vietnam Journal," Nov. 17, 1966, Doug Hostetter Papers, box 1, file 1, MHA.

32. Earl Martin, *Reaching the Other Side: The Journal of an American Who Stayed to Witness Vietnam's Postwar Transition* (n.p.: Crown, 1978), 39.

33. Senate Committee on the Judiciary, *War-Related Civilian Problems in Indochina, Part 1: Vietnam Hearings before the Subcommittee of the Committee on the Judiciary*, 92d Cong., 1st sess., 1971, 59–60.

34. Longacre's report to MCC administrators is found in Longacre to Robert Miller, Dec. 14, 1965, and Dec. 29, 1965. Letters referenced in Hope Renae Nisly, "Witness to a Way of Peace: Renewal and Revision in Mennonite Peace Theology, 1950–71" (master's thesis, University of Maryland, 1992), 89.

35. John Howard Yoder, Mennonite theologian and peace activist, likened sending humanitarian organizations into Vietnam to placing Christian social workers in the concentration camps of World War II Germany. Yoder to Paul Peachy, Nov. 29, 1965, quoted in Cornelius Dyck, ed., *The Story of Mennonite Central Committee: Documents* (n.p.: Herald, 1980), 88.

36. Quoted in Earl Martin, "Reflections on the Mennonite Role in Vietnam" (typescript, MCC-Vietnam Study Project, Doug Hostetter Papers, MHA).

37. Minutes and attachments of MCC Peace Section, Sept. 1, 1966, folder 2, box 4, IX-7–8, MHA.

38. Wilbert Shenk to Paul Longacre, April 23, 1965. Quoted in Martin, "Evaluation of Mennonite Mission," 86.

39. Sam Hope, "Personal Reflections on Our Experience in Vietnam," May 22, 1969, IX-12, folder Vietnam 1969. James McCraken (CWS stateside director) to Hope, Sept. 6, 1967, IX-6–3, folder Vietnam Office June 1967, MHA.

40. Paul Longacre to Robert Miller, May 7, 1966, MCC-VN correspondence, MHA. Quoted in Toews, *Mennonites in American Society*, 316.

41. See Mitchell K. Hall, *Because of Their Faith: CALCAV and Religious Opposition to the Vietnam War* (New York: Columbia University Press, 1990). Hall's is the only book on "moderate" or mainstream religious opposition to the war.

42. Doug Hostetter and William Snyder to President Johnson, July 11, 1966, quoted in Dyck, *Story of MCC*, 111.

43. See, for example, Sam Hope, "Letters from Vietnam," *Journal of Presbyterian History* 47 (1969): 3; Gene Stoltzfus, "Vietnam: Everyone's Tragedy," *Gospel Herald* (Oct. 17, 1967): 937–38; idem, "What the War Is Doing to the Vietnamese People," *Gospel Herald* (Feb. 20, 1968): 153; Donald Sensenig, "The Missionary in Vietnam," *Gospel Herald* (June 8, 1965): 190–91; James Metzler, "Vietnam, American Tragedy," *Gospel Herald* (May 2, 1967): 393; Doug Hostetter, "The Politics of Charity," *Christian Century* (Sept. 18, 1974); Willard Krabill, "Vietnam: Soul-Sick and War-Weary," *Gospel Herald* (Jan. 25, 1966): 66–69; David Neismith, "The Costs of War," *Saturday Evening Post* (April 22, 1967); Midge Austin Meinertz, ed., *Witness in Anguish* (Church World Service, 1975).

44. "Letter to American Christians," written by Mennonite missionaries and aid workers in Vietnam, Nov. 1967, MCC-VN correspondence, MHA.

45. James Metzler to President Lyndon Johnson, Oct. 21, 1967, MCC-VN correspondence, MHA.

46. Sam Hope, "The Challenge to Christian Missions in Southeast Asia Today" (address to the World Missions Conference, Montreat, N.C., July 30, 1968), IX-6–3, folder VNCS 1968, MHA.

47. Marie Regier, "Focus on Denominations," *Mennonite* (Oct. 5, 1965): 50–52; Ronald Woelk, "Credibility in Vietnam," *Mennonite* (Oct. 12, 1965): 640; "Congregations Begin to Look at Vietnam: Concerns Expressed Through Prayer and Acts," *Mennonite* (Feb. 22, 1966): 128; "Alternatives in Vietnam," *Christian Century* (March 10, 1965): 931–32; "Christian Consensus on Vietnam," *Christian Century* (Sept. 8, 1965): 1,083–84.

48. John Lewallen, "The Reluctant Counterinsurgents: IVS in Laos," in *Laos: War and Revolution,* ed. Nina Adams and Alfred McCoy (New York: Harper and Row, 1981).

49. This is suggested in an interoffice NSC memorandum. Box 3, folder IVS, White House Office files, National Security Affairs, OCB series, Dwight D. Eisenhower Presidential Library, Abilene, Kans.

50. Quotations from Winburn Thomas, "The Vietnam Story of IVS" (typescript, 1971), IVS archives, Washington, D.C., 166–67, 196.

51. Don Luce and John Sommers, *Vietnam: The Unheard Voices* (Ithaca: Cornell University Press, 1968), 11.

52. Ibid., 15.

53. Ibid., 16.

54. Richard Beaird, "Minutes of IVS Team Meeting," *IVS Reporter* (Aug. 1967): 6–7, IVS Archives. See also Stoltzfus, "Everyone's Tragedy," 937–38.

55. Luce and Sommers, *Unheard Voices,* 16.

56. Ibid., 17–18.

57. Beaird, "Minutes," 7.

58. Luce and Sommers, *Unheard Voices,* xi–xii.

59. The large size of IVS made it impossible to predict uniformity in opinion. See Peter Donovan to "Dear Friends," June 10, 1967. Seven similar letters found in folder Letters 1968, IVS archives.

60. Lynn Kamm, "Targeted for Death in the Mekong Delta," *National Catholic Reporter* (Oct. 9, 1992). Kamm's source for this information was Tom Fox, IVS volunteer, friend of Gitelson and Luce, and the *National Catholic Reporter*'s editor.

61. Luce et al. to President Johnson, Sept. 19, 1967. Board minutes, 1966–67, IVS Archives.

62. "Hearts and Minds in Vietnam," *Congressional Record,* 90th Congress, 1st sess., 1967, 285–793–10688.

63. Gill, "Peace Is Not the Absence of War," 261.

64. Don Luce, "The Luce Newsletter" (Jan. 9, 1968), Luce file, IVS Archives. See also idem, "The Making of a Dove," *Progressive* (1968); idem, "Vietnam: Life in a Sad Land," *Saturday Review* (June 1, 1968); idem, "The National Liberation Front: Why Do South Vietnamese Join?" *War/Peace Report* (April 1968).

65. William MacKaye, "Methodists Push Viet Peace," *The Washington Post* (Dec. 29, 1968): C4. Luce file, IVS Archives.

66. This figure found in Patrick Hatcher, *Suicide of an Elite: American Internationalists and Vietnam* (Stanford: Stanford University Press, 1990), 107.

67. Dean Rusk, *As I Saw It* (New York: W. W. Norton, 1990), 477.

68. Thomas, "Vietnam Story of IVS," 204.

69. Various letters found in Protest Letter file, IVS Archives.

70. Quotation from CRS Director Bishop Edward Swanstrom by James Douglass, "Catholicism, Power, and Vietnamese Suffering," in *American Catholics and Vietnam,* ed. Thomas Quigley (Grand Rapids: Eerdmans, 1968), 102.

71. Minutes, Inter-Office Peace Section memorandum, Oct. 1967, IX-12, folder Vietnam, 1967, MHA. Meeting mentioned in Martin, "Evaluation of Mennonite Mission," 102, and in "Volunteer Aides in Saigon Dispute," *The New York Times* (Sept. 15, 1967): 1–2.

72. Beechy, "Summer Assignment, 1968," box 3, folder DRVN #2, Beechy Papers, MHA.

73. Beechy, "Hanoi: The Wounds of War," box 3, folder DRVN #5, Beechy Papers, MHA.

74. Gill, "Peace Is Not the Absence of War," 242–44, 285–86.

75. Martin, "Evaluation of Mennonite Mission," 110–11.

76. Peter Osnos, "South Vietnam Accused of Ousting U.S. Team," *The Washington Post* (Aug. 2, 1971).

77. Hugh Manke, "The Expulsion of IVS—Another Casualty of the War," *War/Peace Report* (Sept. 1971): 7–8.

78. Jim Linn, "International Voluntary Services—An Analysis of the Termination of IVS in Vietnam" (unpublished report to IVS/DC, Oct. 1971), 3–4. File Board Minutes 1971–72, IVS Archives.

79. Nichols, *Uneasy Alliance,* 105.

CHAPTER 14

1. In 1956, this group of indigenous people were known as "Aucas," a pejorative Quechua word meaning "savages" or "wild ones." The group later identified themselves as "Huaorani," sometimes spelled "Waorani" or "Waodani" (the first is based on Spanish pronunciation, the latter two reflect Anglicized spellings), meaning "the people." "Huao" or "Wao" is the singular and the adjective form. "Auca" occasionally appears in this chapter in quoted material or in the context of phrases used by the missionaries, such as "Operation Auca," but I have preferred "Huaorani" or "Huao." See James A. Yost, "Waorani," in *Encyclopedia of World Cultures,* vol. 7 (1994).

2. Abe C. Van Der Puy, "Through Gates of Splendor," *Reader's Digest* (Aug. 1956): 71.

3. My narrative is based on Van Der Puy, "Gates of Splendor," 70–72; and Elisabeth Elliot, *Through Gates of Splendor* (New York: Harper and Brothers, 1957), 189–91.

4. Elliot, *Gates of Splendor,* 194.

5. See photographer Cornell Capa's description of the light and atmosphere quoted in Elliot, *Gates of Splendor,* 238. A helicopter from the U.S. Air Rescue Service, based in Panama, helped the ground party locate the bodies.

6. Susan Bergman, ed., *Martyrs: Contemporary Writers on Modern Lives of Faith* (New York: HarperCollins, HarperSanFrancisco, 1996), 3. Bergman, 15, cites David Barrett and Todd M. Johnson, *Our World and How to Reach It,* for an estimated total of 26,625,000 Christians who have been martyred in the twentieth century.

7. Accounts of David Brainerd (1718–1747) and Harriet Newell (1793–1812) provided nineteenth-century U.S. evangelicals with prototypical missionary martyr stories, though death came through disease rather than violence; Jonathan Edwards, *The Life of David Brainerd,* ed. Norman Pettit, vol. 7 of *Works of Jonathan Edwards* (New Haven: Yale University Press, 1985); Leonard Woods, *A Sermon Preached at Haverhill, Mass., in Remembrance of Mrs. Harriet Newell, Wife of the Rev. Samuel Newell, Missionary to India Who Died at the Isle of France, Nov. 30, 1812, Aged 19 years; To Which Are Added Memoirs of Her Life* (Boston: printed by Samuel T. Armstrong, 1814).

8. At least two biographical sketches of Jim Elliot, who in death became the best known of the five, have been posted on the Internet, and Christian vocalists Scott Wesley Brown and Twila Paris have written songs based on excerpts from Elliot's published journals.

9. The number is an estimate based on accounts by evangelical martyrologists James and Marti Hefley in *By Their Blood: Christian Martyrs of the Twentieth Century,* 2d ed. (Grand Rapids: Baker Book House, 1996), and includes thirty-two U.S. missionaries killed in 1900 during the Boxer Rebellion and nineteen killed during the 1960s in Vietnam, as well as others who were killed in Africa and South America. The Hefleys did not always identify the nationality of missionaries who were killed.

10. I am using "neo-evangelical," "evangelical," and Joel Carpenter's term "progressive fundamentalist" interchangeably in this chapter to refer to representatives and heirs of a separatist U.S. "fundamentalist remnant" in the 1930s who, in turn, rejected fundamentalism's separatist stance and began to reengage U.S. culture during the late 1940s and the 1950s. Joel A. Carpenter, *Revive Us Again: The Reawakening of American Fundamentalism* (New York: Oxford University Press, 1998), 8, 176, 196; also Carpenter's definition of U.S. fundamentalism, 6–9. For Carpenter's discussion of this group's growing media savvy, see 228.

11. Carpenter, *Revive Us Again,* 177, 186.

12. Susan Wabuda, "Henry Bull, Miles Coverdale, and the Making of Foxe's Book of Martyrs," in *Martyrs and Martyrologies,* ed. Diana Wood (Oxford: Blackwell, 1993), 245, 258.

13. Elliot, *Gates of Splendor,* 119; *Time* (Jan. 2, 1956) featured General Motors president Harlow Herbert Curtis as Man of the Year.

14. Elliot, *Gates of Splendor,* 186.

15. William Martin, *A Prophet with Honor: The Billy Graham Story* (New York: William Morrow, 1991), 221, 224, 239; Billy Graham, *Just As I Am: The Autobiography of Billy Graham* (New York: HarperCollins Worldwide, 1997), 298–303.

16. "The Auca Epic," *The Echo,* bulletin of the World Missionary Radio Fellowship (Feb. 1, 1956): 3. Clarence Wesley Jones Papers, OS1, Archives of the Billy Graham Center, Wheaton College, Wheaton, Ill.

17. Andrew F. Walls, "The American Dimension of the Missionary Movement," in Andrew F. Walls, *The Missionary Movement in Christian History: Studies in the Transmission of Faith* (Maryknoll, N.Y.: Orbis, 1996), 222, 223; also Richard V. Pierard, "Pax Americana

and the Evangelical Missionary Advance," in *Earthen Vessels: American Evangelicals and Foreign Missions, 1880–1980*, ed. Joel A. Carpenter and Wilbert R. Shenk (Grand Rapids: Eerdmans, 1990), 163.

18. Elisabeth Elliot and Cornell Capa, narrators, *Through Gates of Splendor* (Chester Springs, Penn.: Good News Productions, 1961). That the immediacy of film, photography, and television fascinated people of the 1950s is indicated by the popularity of Edward R. Murrow's *See It Now* television programs and the philosophy behind the mass-circulation weekly photo magazines. James T. Patterson, *Grand Expectations: The United States, 1945–1974* (New York: Oxford University Press, 1996), 349; James Guimond, *American Photography and the American Dream* (Chapel Hill: University of North Carolina Press, 1991), 155.

19. "Ecuador: Mission to the Aucas," *Time* (Jan. 23, 1956): 30. By 1957, domestic airlines would surpass trains in the number of passengers carried (Patterson, *Grand Expectations,* 314); "5 Flying Missionaries Lost in Jungle," *Chicago Sun-Times* (Jan. 11, 1956): 2; "Killed by Aucas: One of Five Flying Missionaries from U.S. Is Victim in Amazon Jungle," *Kansas City Times* (Jan. 11, 1956): 1.

20. "'Go Ye and Preach the Gospel': Five Do and Die," *Life* (Jan. 30, 1956): 12, quoting Nathaniel Saint's diary. In "Reflections on the Auca Tragedy," *Practical Anthropology* 3 (1956): 1, Robert B. Taylor wondered whether "different methods" might be more successful in "future efforts," particularly a greater emphasis on language learning. See also the response to Taylor's comments and a defense of the men's approach in "Letters to the Editor," *Practical Anthropology* 3 (1956): 37–41. For further analysis of the limitations of the aerial approach, see James O. Buswell III, "Cultural Ethos of Primitive Tribes: Yir Yiront, Kaingang, and Auca," *Practical Anthropology* 15 (1968): 177–88.

21. "'Go Ye and Preach the Gospel,'" 11. Later books and articles identified the natives by their Huaorani names. For Naenkiwi and Gimari ("Delilah"), see Rosemary Kingsland, *A Saint Among Savages* (London: Collins, 1980), 80.

22. "Ecuador: Mission to the Aucas," 30.

23. "Missionaries Feared Slain by Savage Tribe," *Los Angeles Times* (Jan. 12, 1956): 1; "Bury Bodies of 5 Missionaries Savages Killed," *Chicago Daily Tribune* (Jan. 14, 1956): 3; "Go Ye . . . and Preach," *Portland Oregonian* (Jan. 15, 1956): M3; Dewey Linze, "The Unsubdued Aucas: Behind the Murder of Five Missionaries," *Los Angeles Times* (Jan. 17, 1956): section 2, 4; "4 Missionaries Found Slain: Only a Remote Chance That Fifth Escaped Indians in 'Green Hell,'" *Chicago Daily News* (Jan. 13, 1956): 5.

24. "Bodies of 5 Missionaries Slain in Jungle Located," *Los Angeles Times* (Jan. 14, 1956, final edition): 1; "Slain Missionaries' Widows Planning to Continue Work," *Oregonian* (Jan. 16, 1956): 2.

25. Joseph P. Marshall, "Five Short-Lived Missionaries Reach Ecuador's Auca Region after Varied Backgrounds," *Oregonian* (Jan. 22, 1956): 16.

26. Quoted from a U.S. government report that formed the basis of a widely circulated Associated Press story, taken here from "Auca Tribe Murderous," *Oregonian* (Jan. 14, 1956): 2; cf. Hal Hendrix, "Auca Indians Live in Trees and Chatter Like Animals," *Kansas City Times* (Jan. 13, 1958): 2. In Linze, "The Unsubdued Aucas," and elsewhere, Huaorani were characterized as headhunters, confused with a neighboring tribe, the Shuar.

27. Christian missionaries were expelled from China after the founding of the People's Republic in October 1949. Some of the 9,500 Protestants and Catholics were killed, others imprisoned. Their stories dominated press coverage of missions during the first half of the 1950s. See, for example, "Sufferers in China: Faith of U.S. Missionaries Stood Up to Red Tyranny," *Life* (Dec. 26, 1955): 125, 126; "Communism's Mark on a Holy Man's Face: Emaciated Italian Bishop Gains Freedom from Red China as Some Captive Americans Are Also Released," *Life* (Oct. 3, 1955): 43–44; "Four Years in a Red Hell: Father Rigney's Own Story of His Trial by Torture," advertisement in the *Chicago Sun-Times* (Jan. 11, 1956): 43, for a series of articles to begin January 15. "Go Ye . . . and Preach," editorial in the *Portland Oregonian* (Jan. 15, 1956) connected the "Auca expedition" and the "barbarous treatment missionaries have received at the hands of Asian Communists."

28. *Chicago Daily News* (Jan. 12, 1956): 2; *Chicago American* (Jan. 12, 1956): 2; *Milwaukee Journal* (Jan. 10, 1956): 1; *Seattle Post Intelligencer* (Jan. 11, 1956): 1; *Portland Oregonian* (Jan. 14, 1956): 1.

29. *Deliver Us from Evil: The Story of Vietnam's Flight to Freedom* (New York: Farrar, Straus and Cudahy, 1956), Tom Dooley's dramatic (and embellished) first-person account of efforts to evacuate Roman Catholic refugees from North Vietnam, first appeared as a condensed book in the April 1956 *Reader's Digest*. See James T. Fisher, *Dr. America: The Lives of Thomas A. Dooley, 1927–1961* (Amherst: University of Massachusetts Press, 1997), 71–76; also the review of Fisher's book by Scott Flipse, "Deconstructing Dr. America," *American Catholic Studies Newsletter* 24 (1997): 14, 15.

30. Cornell Capa and Richard Whelan, eds., *Cornell Capa: Photographs* (Boston: Little, Brown, Bulfinch, 1992), 22. " 'Go Ye and Preach the Gospel,' " 18, 19.

31. Andrew Heiskell, "Danger and Dedication," *Life* (May 13, 1957): 187.

32. Capa and Whelan, *Capa*, 152.

33. Ibid., 11, 152. Capa's follow-up articles for *Life* were "The Martyrs Widows Return to Teach in Jungle" (May 20, 1957): 24–33; also "Child among Her Father's Killers: Missionaries Live with Aucas" (Nov. 24, 1958): 23–29. He also served as photo editor for *Through Gates of Splendor* and collaborated with Elisabeth Elliot in producing the film with the same name. He encouraged Elisabeth Elliot's efforts to portray the humanity of the Huaorani through her own photographs, later published along with some of his in Elliot, *The Savage My Kinsman* (New York: Harper and Brothers, 1961), with Capa as picture editor and author of the foreword for that book. Subsequently, he served as photo editor for a number of other books dealing with evangelical missionaries in South America.

34. "Dominant Culture," letter to the editor from Holly S., *Milwaukee Journal* (Jan. 22, 1956): section 5, 2. For a similar response, see the Alverto Curruth letter in letters to the editors, *Life* (Feb. 20, 1956): 15.

35. Bill Vaughan, "This Man's Mind Is Full of Aucas," *Kansas City Star* (Jan. 15, 1956): D14.

36. Murray L. Wagner, review of *Through Gates of Splendor* by Elisabeth Elliot, *Staunton (Va.) News Leader*, n.d. In "Newspaper Clippings—1957–1965," box 1, folder 6, Elisabeth Howard Elliot Papers, Archives of the Billy Graham Center, Wheaton College, Wheaton, Ill.

37. Elliot, *Gates of Splendor*, 252.

38. Elisabeth Elliot, introductory narration of the film *Through Gates of Splendor.*

39. David Loades, "Introduction," in *Martyrs and Martyrologies,* xvii.

40. Van Der Puy, "Gates," 74. See also Edith G. Cherry, "We Rest on Thee, Our Shield and Our Defender," in *Hymns: The Hymnal of Inter-Varsity Christian Fellowship,* comp. and ed. Paul Beckwith (Downers Grove, Ill.: InterVarsity, 1952), 9. The phrase "Saints on the Curaray" is from J. C. Macaulay, "The Five Valiant Saints on the Curaray," review of *Through Gates of Splendor* by Elisabeth Elliot, *Sunday School Times* (June 8, 1957): 453 (1).

41. Elliot identified the men as "representing three different 'faith-missions'" and sharing a "common belief in the Bible as the literal and supernatural and perfect word from God to man." Elliot, *Gates of Splendor,* 121. Carpenter, *Revive Us Again,* 140, points to the evangelical but nonsectarian character of Charles Fuller's "Old Fashioned Revival Hour" as one key to its popularity.

42. Elliot, *Gates of Splendor,* 51, 68, 75. For Keswick piety "at the very heart of the fundamentalists' missionary impulse," see Carpenter, *Revive Us Again,* 82.

43. Elliot, *Gates of Splendor,* 95; cf., 127, 145 for references to "five pioneering missionary families" and to Saint, McCully, and Jim Elliot as "the three pioneers." See also the letter from "an Alabama reader" in notes on "Open Letters," *Sunday School Times* (Aug. 11, 1956): 630 (2). Beginning with the "[Davy] Crockett Craze" in 1955, Westerns rose to new popularity on television and on film, according to James L. Baughman, *The Republic of Mass Culture: Journalism, Filmmaking, and Broadcasting in America since 1941* (Baltimore: Johns Hopkins University Press, 1992), 87. The widows were approached with offers to make a commercial film about the story, which they rejected.

44. Elliot, *Gates of Splendor,* 252.

45. Review of *Through Gates of Splendor* by Elisabeth Elliot, *The Evangelical Christian* (Feb. 1958): n.p. By Feb. 1958, *Gates* had sold 105,000 copies exclusive of sales in connection with seven book clubs; see "Tips for the Bookseller," *Publishers' Weekly* (Feb. 17, 1958): 90, 92. For other sales figures, see "News and Trends of the Week," 21; and the advertisement in *Christianity Today* (July 8, 1957): 19. The book would remain in print almost continuously for twenty-five years; in 1996, two fortieth-anniversary editions were issued.

46. While the early publicity for Graham's crusades came primarily from the print media, television became a major publicity factor in New York City. During the days immediately prior to the opening meeting, Graham appeared on *The Steve Allen Show* and was interviewed by Walter Cronkite, John Cameron Swayze, and Dave Garroway, among others. He was on the cover of *Newsweek* and subsequently featured in *Life* and *Look.* Martin, *Prophet with Honor,* 231; Graham, *Just As I Am,* 306–9. The photograph of Ruth Graham was reprinted in *Billy Graham New York Crusade News* (June 21, 1957): 1.

47. "Auca Spoken in New York," *Translation* (Fall 1957): 15. For a sympathetic account of Rachel Saint's role in missionary work to the Huaorani, see Kingsland, *Saint among Savages.* Graham had become a world figure and had increased his own international awareness with his London crusade in 1954, a European tour in 1955, and a tour of India and the Far East in 1956. In 1966, Kimo Yaeti and Komi Gikita, two of the Huaorani who had participated in the killing of the Ecuador missionaries and who subsequently had converted to Christianity, were highly visible participants in Graham's brainchild, the Berlin Congress on Evange-

lism. Martin, *Prophet with Honor,* 185, 327, 328; "Bible-Whackers in Berlin," *Time* (Nov. 14, 1966): 62.

48. For 1949, see Carpenter, *Revive Us Again,* chap. 12; for *Newsweek's* designation of 1976, see George M. Marsden, *Religion and American Culture* (San Diego: Harcourt Brace Jovanovich, 1990), 262.

49. For example, Henry R. Luce, publisher of *Time* and *Life* and the son of missionaries, as well as DeWitt Wallace, publisher of *Reader's Digest* and the son of a Presbyterian minister, channeled their own sense of mission into affirming the U.S. way of life. But both created publications that provided a platform for a more explicit evangelical message in broad support of their "Americanism." See Martin, *Prophet with Honor,* 129; and John Heidenry, *Theirs Was the Kingdom: Lila and DeWitt Wallace and the Story of the Reader's Digest* (New York: W. W. Norton, 1993), 209, 253.

50. "What America Reads," the best-seller list compiled by the *New York Herald Tribune* for September 22, 1957, listed *The Day Christ Died* as fifth; *Profiles in Courage* as eighth; and *Through Gates of Splendor* as fifteenth; cf. Charles A. Madison, *Book Publishing in America* (New York: McGraw-Hill, 1966), 407. See also "News and Trends of the Week," 22, where Eugene Exman of Harpers complained that the popularity of *Through Gates of Splendor* had been underreported on best-seller lists.

51. Eugene Exman, *The House of Harper: One Hundred and Fifty Years of Publishing* (New York: Harper and Row, 1967), 235–37.

52. For a list of the books in the series, see the frontispiece of Jean Dye Johnson, *God Planted Five Seeds* (New York: Harper & Row, 1966). Listed alphabetically by author, the books included: Lois Carlson, *Monganga Paul* (1966) [Congo]; Homer E. Dowdy, *The Bamboo Cross* (1964) [Vietnam], *Christ's Witchdoctor* (1963) [Guyana], and *Out of the Jaws of the Lion* (1965) [Zaire]; Frank and Marie Drown, *Mission to the Headhunters* (1961) [Ecuador]; Elisabeth Elliot, *The Savage My Kinsman* (1961) [Ecuador], *Shadow of the Almighty* (1958) [Ecuador], and *Through Gates of Splendor* (1957) [Ecuador]; Russell T. Hitt, *Cannibal Valley* (1962) [New Guinea], *Jungle Pilot* (1959) [Ecuador], and *Sensei* (1965) [Japan]; Jean Dye Johnson, *God Planted Five Seeds* (1966) [Bolivia]; Bruce E. Porterfield, *Commandos for Christ* (1963) [Bolivia]; Ethel Emily Wallis, *The Dayuma Story* (1960) [Ecuador] and *Tariri* (1965) [Peru]; Kenneth L. Wilson, *Angel at Her Shoulder* (1964) [Taiwan]. Country or regional listings are my own; eleven of the sixteen books relate to South American missions, six of those to Ecuador. Harper and Row also published one final book related to the Auca story: Ethel Emily Wallis, *Aucas Downriver* (1973). The book was not identified as part of the Missionary Classics series, which apparently had gone out of print.

53. See Mary Geraldine Guinness (Mrs. Howard) Taylor, *Borden of Yale, '09: The Life That Counts* (Chicago: Moody Press, 1926); and Mrs. Howard Taylor, *The Triumph of John and Betty Stam* (Philadelphia: China Inland Mission, 1935). Carpenter, *Revive Us Again,* 25, notes the paucity of outlets for fundamentalist books during the 1930s and 1940s.

54. Lucy B. McIntire, "Exalting Story of Dedicated, Betrayed Lives," review of *Through Gates of Splendor* by Elisabeth Elliot, *Savannah Morning News* (June 2, 1957): n.p.; Frederic G. Hyde, "Missionaries Keep Faith," review of *Through Gates of Splendor* by Elisabeth Elliot, *Philadelphia Inquirer* (June 2, 1957): n.p.; Will Stevens, "Martyrdom in the Jungle," review

of *Through Gates of Splendor* by Elisabeth Elliot, *San Francisco Examiner* (Aug. 5, 1957): n.p. Copies of newspaper reviews cited here and following can be found in the Elisabeth Howard Elliot Papers, box 1, folder 6.

55. Stevens, "Martyrdom in the Jungle."

56. Charles L. Allen, "5 Christian Heroes Accepted Challenge," review of *Through Gates of Splendor* by Elisabeth Elliot, *Atlanta Constitution* (June 21, 1957): n.p.; McIntire, "Exalting Story."

57. Patterson, *Grand Expectations*, 342.

58. Review of *Through Gates of Splendor* by Elisabeth Elliot, *Geographical Magazine* (March 1958): n.p.

59. Norman R. Oke, "Book of the Month Review" of *Through Gates of Splendor* by Elisabeth Elliot, *Nazarene Minister's Book Club* (Aug. 1957): n.p., copy in Elliot Papers, "Magazine Clippings, 1957," box 1, folder 4; Lucy Barajikian, "Five Transient Flames," review of *Through Gates of Splendor* by Elisabeth Elliot, *The King's Business* (July 1957): 37; "Through Gates of Splendor" by Elisabeth Elliot, *Christian Youth* (Sept. 29, 1957): 50.

60. The number of "conservative evangelicals" serving as career missionaries increased from 9,216 in 1953 to 13,255 in 1956, an increase of 4,039 or 44 percent during the three-year period, about the same as the growth rate during the four-year period from 1956 to 1960, when the numbers grew from 13,255 to 18,724, an increase of 5,469 or 41 percent. Based on table 2 in Robert T. Coote, "The Uneven Growth of Conservative Evangelical Missions," *International Bulletin of Missionary Research* 6 (1982): 120.

61. Larry Ward, "Five Martyrs of Auca," review of *Through Gates of Splendor* by Elisabeth Elliot, *Christianity Today* (April 29, 1957): 35.

62. Macaulay, "The Five Valiant Saints on the Curaray," 2 [454], reprinted in the *Christian Reader's Review* (Sept.–Oct. 1957): 4; cf. Barajikian, "Five Transient Flames," 37; Edman, "Do Read Biographies," 34; Herbert C. Jackson, review of *Through Gates of Splendor* by Elisabeth Elliot, *Review and Expositor* (July 1958): 322.

63. Clyde S. Kilby, review of *Through Gates of Splendor* by Elisabeth Elliot, *Eternity* (June 1957): 36; review of *Through Gates of Splendor* by Elisabeth Elliot, *Power* (Sept. 1957): 4.

64. "Fifteen Books for Christmas Giving," *Moody Monthly* (Nov. 1957): 28; *Church Library Bulletin* (Sept. 1957): n.p., Elliot Papers, box 1, folder 4.

65. For a recent example of such a connection made explicit, see Donald T. Williams, "John Foxe," *Historians of the Christian Tradition: Their Methodology and Influence on Western Thought*, ed. Michael Bauman and Martin I. Klauber (Nashville: Broadman and Holman, 1995), 132. Dana Robert, "From Missions to Mission to Beyond Missions: The Historiography of American Protestant Foreign Missions Since World War II," in *New Directions in American Religious History*, ed. Harry S. Stout and D. G. Hart (New York: Oxford University Press, 1997), 378, notes the ongoing inspirational role of missionary biography among U.S. evangelicals.

66. Christian Family Bookshelf promotional advertisement, *Eternity* (Oct. 1957): 1.

67. George Marsden, Joel Carpenter, and others have discussed the ambivalence at the heart of conservative evangelicals' attitude toward U.S. culture. Marsden's fundamentalists "seemed undecided as to whether they were living in Babylon or Israel." Carpenter's subjects

wrestled with indecision "as to whether they were alienated outsiders or quintessential Americans." Marsden, *Fundamentalism and American Culture: The Shaping of American Evangelicalism, 1870–1925* (New York: Oxford University Press, 1980), 228; Carpenter, *Revive Us Again*, xii, cf. 242.

CHAPTER 15

1. See Linda Williams's own introduction to her edited volume *Viewing Positions: Ways of Seeing Film* (New Brunswick, N.J.: Rutgers University Press, 1995), 1–2.

2. The film version of Charlie's relationship with Emily differs considerably from that of Theroux's novel. The Emily of the novel is less precocious and more pious, acting more as Charlie's tagalong than as sexual aggressor. Charlie assents to her proposal as long as she promises to keep everything secret. Paul Theroux, *The Mosquito Coast* (Boston: Houghton Mifflin, 1982), 98.

3. See, for example, William Burgwinkle, "Negotiating Masculinity: Gendering within Sex," in *Translations/Transformations: Gender and Culture in Film and Literature East and West: Selected Conference Papers,* ed. Valerie Wayne and Cornelia Moore (Honolulu: College of Languages, Linguistics and Literature, University of Hawaii, and the East-West Center, 1993).

4. Although Gabriel's celebration of the Mass appears a feminized act in comparison with Mendoza's armed defense of the mission, Jesuit priest and activist Daniel Berrigan, who served as an adviser on Jesuit matters during the filming and later wrote a journal about his experiences, disagrees. He strenuously objected to the screenplay's original ending, in which Gabriel was to die at prayer with the people in the church, but approved of the way the film eventually was shot: Gabriel leading the peaceful Guaraní out of the church in a solemn eucharistic procession. "In the style of Martin Luther King and Gandhi, Gabriel is extricated from a passive fate. He takes in hand his life and the lives of his people and leaves the mission church in procession bearing the Blessed Sacrament (as in a plague or other catastrophe in nature). So doing, he confronts the worst and evokes the best in the massed adversaries, renegade Indians, and mercenaries." Daniel Berrigan, *The Mission: A Film Journal* (San Francisco: Harper and Row, 1986), 129. See also 96, 124.

Although Berrigan insists that the film's ending depicts Father Gabriel in an aggressive posture—facing the world with sacrament in hand—I maintain that Gabriel's pacifist position is a feminization in comparison with Mendoza's active resistance to the invaders. Unlike Berrigan, most film audiences are not likely to associate the Mass with engagement with the world.

5. Paul S. Cowen, "A Social-Cognitive Approach to Ethnicity in Films," in *Unspeakable Images: Ethnicity and the American Cinema,* ed. Lester D. Friedman (Urbana: University of Illinois Press, 1991), 360.

6. Digby Diehl, "The Iceman Cometh," *American Film* (Dec. 1986): 49.

7. See Barbara Ganson, "'Like Children under Wise Parental Sway': Passive Portrayals of the Guaraní Indians in European Literature and *The Mission*," in *Colonial Latin American Historical Review* 3 (1994): 399–422; and James Schofield Saeger, "*The Mission* and Historical Missions: Film and the Writing of History," *Americas* 51 (1995): 393–416. I am grateful to Kathryn Long for bringing these articles to my attention.

8. Olive Patricia Dickason, review of *Black Robe, American Historical Review* 97 (1992): 1,169. For more information on the ultimate success of the Jesuits in Canada, see James Axtell, *The Invasion Within: The Contest of Cultures in Colonial North America* (New York: Oxford University Press, 1985), 117–25.

9. Two other minor mistakes manifest an unfamiliarity with the evangelical subculture: Martin Quarrier baptizes converts "in the name of our Lord Jesus Christ" rather than in the name of the Father, the Son, and the Holy Spirit, and the missionaries' slow-dance to Big Band music—almost unthinkable among evangelical Protestants during the 1960s, when the novel and film are set.

10. At one point during the shooting, Irons slipped on the wet rock of the falls and dangled by his hands above the void (Berrigan, *The Mission,* 138).

11. Dave Kehr, "Call of the Wild," *American Film* (Dec. 1986): 43–47, 53–54. *Black Robe* and *The Mosquito Coast* call the primitivist ideal into question. As critic Kehr notes, *The Mosquito Coast* is an exaggeration and a parody of the traditional genre. *Black Robe,* on the other hand, incorporates certain elements of primitivism while displaying its dark, unappealing side as well.

12. Russell Thornton, *American Indian Holocaust and Survival: A Population History since 1492* (Norman: University of Oklahoma Press, 1987), 37–41. Three of the four films were based on novels, which serve as helpful comparisons to the films: Peter Matthiessen's *At Play in the Fields of the Lord* (New York: Random House, 1965); Brian Moore's *Black Robe* (New York: E. P. Dutton, 1985); and Paul Theroux's *The Mosquito Coast.* In addition, Daniel Berrigan published his thoughts about serving as a consultant to Roland Joffé as *The Mission.* Valuable helps in the examination of any major film are two film yearbooks, *Magill's Cinema Annual,* edited by Frank N. Magill (Pasadena, Calif.: Salem Press, annual), and *The Motion Picture Guide,* published annually in Chicago or New York with various editors. A selective list of the film reviews on which I have relied includes Terrence Rafferty's review of *At Play in the Fields of the Lord* in *The New Yorker* 67:43 (Dec. 16, 1991), 117–19; reviews of *Black Robe* by Richard Alleva (*Commonweal* 119:1, 17–18), Richard A. Blake (*America* 166:2, 38–39), and Terry Eagleton (*TLS, The Times Literary Supplement* 4635: 20); reviews of *The Mission* by David Neff (*Christianity Today* 30:18, 63–64), Tom O'Brien (*Commonweal* 113:20, 631–32), and James M. Wall (*Christian Century* 103:40, 1,181–82); and reviews of *The Mosquito Coast* by Stanley Kauffmann (*The New Republic* 195:25, 26), Terrence Rafferty (*The Nation* 243:20, 683–84), and Judith Williamson (*New Statesman* 113:2,916, 24). Two theoretical works that have informed my thinking are Linda Williams's edited volume *Viewing Positions* and Lester D. Friedman's edited volume *Unspeakable Images: Ethnicity and the American Cinema.*

Contributors

Alvyn Austin teaches Asian Studies at University of Toronto schools. His research interests include missions in China.

Daniel H. Bays is Professor of History and Director of Asian Studies at Calvin College in Grand Rapids, Michigan. His research area is modern China.

Jay S. F. Blossom is a doctoral candidate in American religious history at Duke University.

Edith L. Blumhofer is Professor of History and Director of the Institute for the Study of American Evangelicals at Wheaton College. She has written several books on post–Civil War American religious history.

Jay Riley Case is Assistant Professor of History at Malone College in Canton, Ohio. His primary area of research is nineteenth-century American evangelicalism and the missionary movement.

Scott Flipse is Associate Director of the University of Notre Dame's Washington D.C. Semester and a Pew *Civitas* Fellow at the Brookings Institution.

Mark Y. Hanley is Associate Professor of History at Truman State University in Kirksville, Missouri. He works in nineteenth-century American religious history.

Nancy A. Hardesty is Professor of Religion at Clemson University in Clemson, South Carolina. She is the author of several works on women and American Christianity.

Kathryn T. Long is Associate Professor and Chair of the History Department at Wheaton College. She has broad research interests in the history of American Christianity.

Laurie F. Maffly-Kipp is Associate Professor of Religious Studies and Adjunct Associate Professor of American Studies at the University of North Carolina at Chapel Hill. She has written widely on African-American Protestant culture and religion in the American West.

Russell E. Richey is Dean and Professor of Church History at Candler School of Theology, Emory University. He has published on many aspects of the history of the Methodist experience in America.

John Saillant is Associate Professor of English and History at Western Michigan University. His research and writing focus on race and culture in nineteenth-century America.

William L. Svelmoe is Assistant Professor of History at Saint Mary's College in Notre Dame, Indiana. His research area is the history of North American Protestantism, particularly missions.

Grant Wacker is Professor of Church History at Duke University, where he focuses on American religious history.

Marilyn Färdig Whiteley is an independent scholar who lives in Guelph, Ontario, where she works on Canadian religious history.

Anne Blue Wills completed her doctorate at Duke University in 2001. She is visiting assistant professor at Queen's College and adjunct assistant professor at Davidson College, North Carolina. Her research focuses on religion and culture in the United States.

Index